Jet Age Aesthetic

Jet Age Aesthetic

The Glamour of Media in Motion

Vanessa R. Schwartz

Yale University Press
New Haven and London

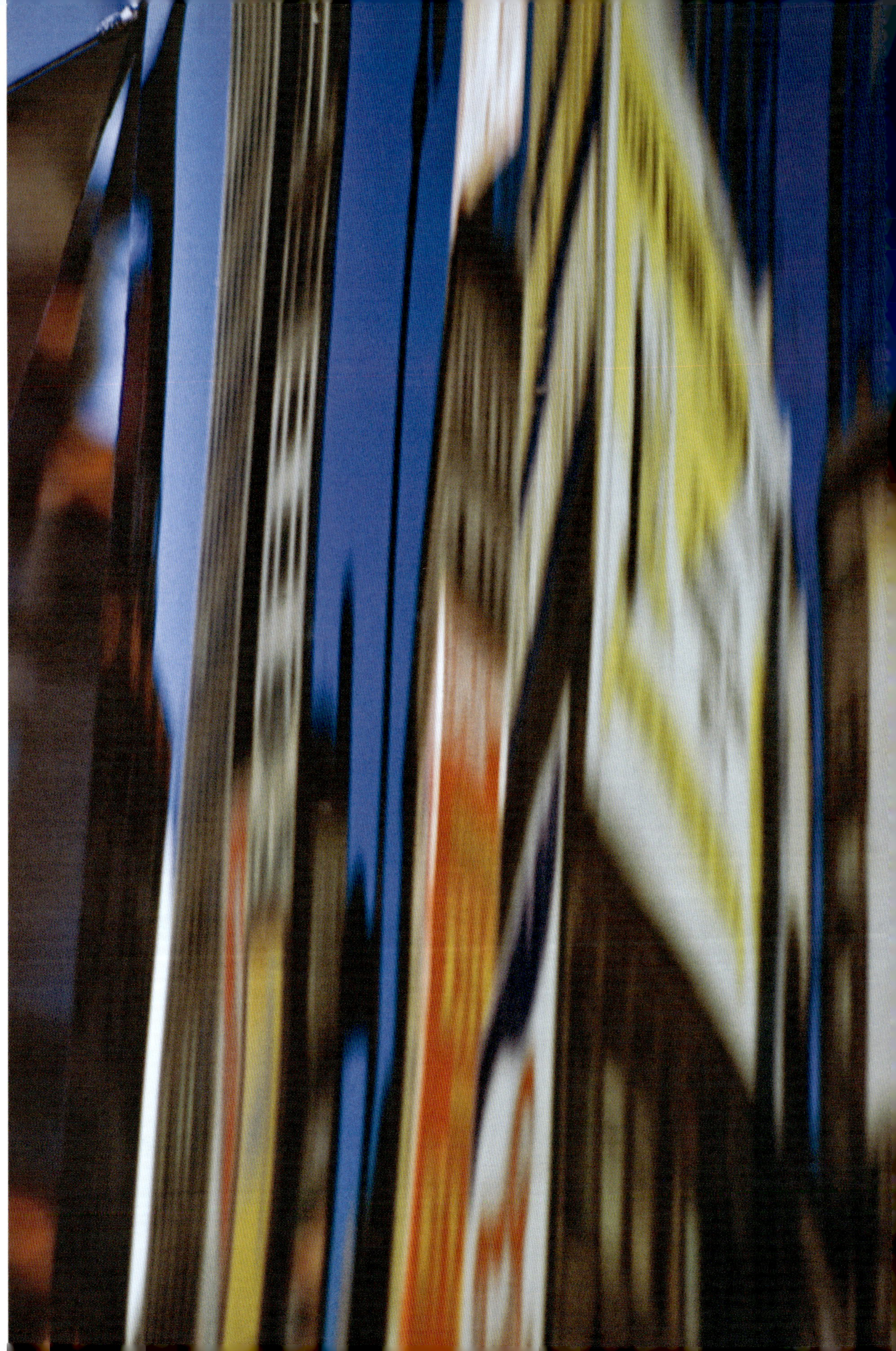

Contents

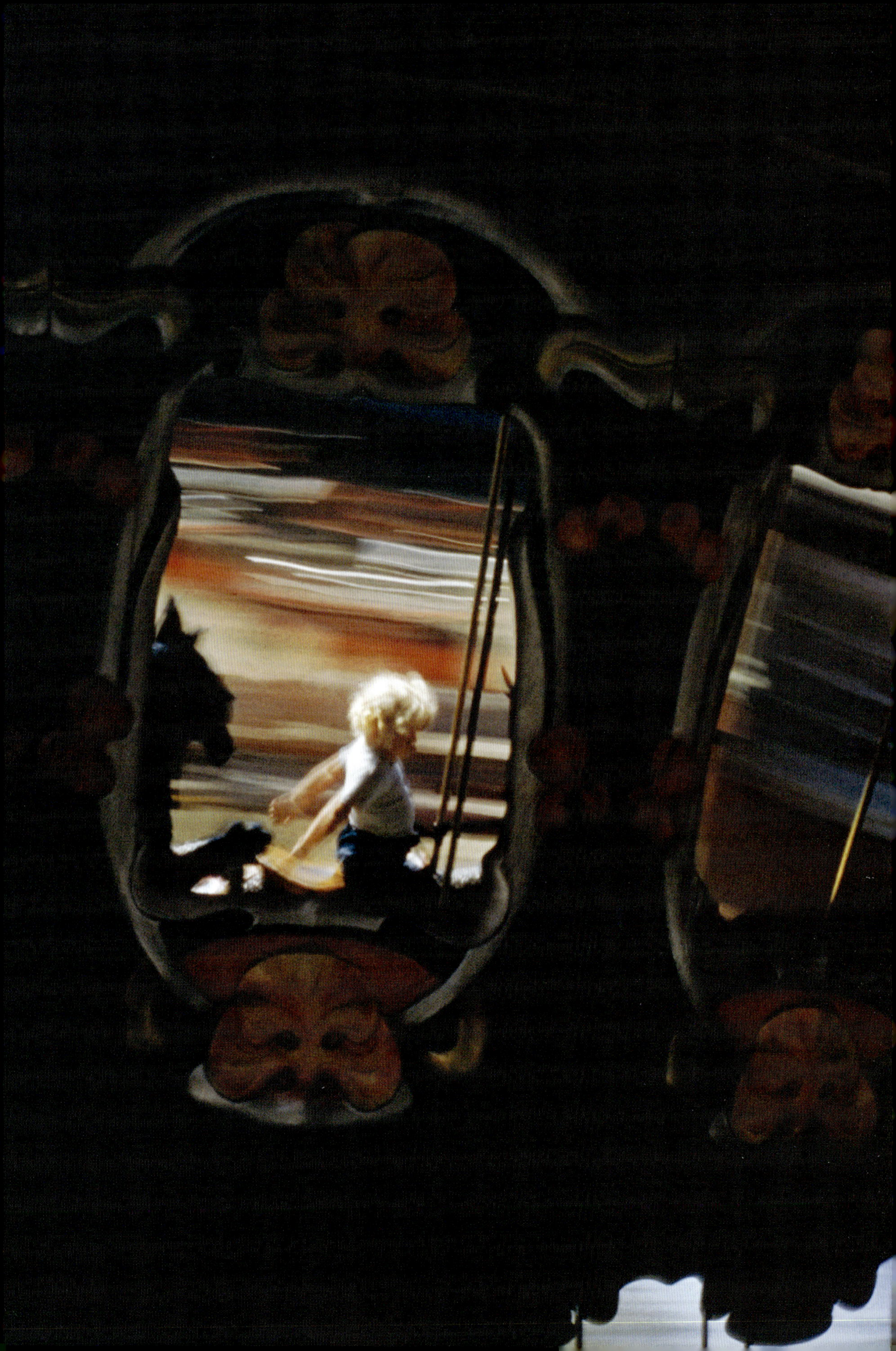

Acknowledgments

The longer a book takes to write, the longer the list of people and institutions one accumulates to gratefully acknowledge, which I do here. Yet every one of my scholarly projects has also been rooted in a moment from my always colorful childhood spent with a mother whose patron saint was Auntie Mame, and who thus never modified her sharp-tongued wit because she was speaking to a child. When I was eleven and seeking to assert my own aesthetic, I asked my mother if I could redecorate my room, having outgrown the fun-house orange and red shag rug, yellow dressers, and Barnum & Bailey posters that hung on my walls. (Never once did it dawn on me this was a crazy decorative scheme!) I proposed to paint the room sky blue, replace the shag with a deep blue wall-to-wall carpet, purchase a silver desk with metal swivel chair, and place a mirrored and silver coffee table in the center of the room, on which I would put a television. She looked me straight in the eye and said, "Why don't you go live in an airplane?" Finally, I took her advice. I'm sorry she is not here to see the result.

Driven by the will to understand my mother's dismissal of my seemingly bad taste, I reached out to legitimate authorities and am grateful they answered my call. This book has been generously supported and underwritten by research fellowships and associated institutions that have provided funds and time for me to work on it, as well as access to research collections. I want to thank the John Randolph Haynes Foundation, the Getty Scholars Program and Getty Research Institute, the Cullman Center at the New York Public Library, the Smithsonian Institution, the John Simon Guggenheim Foundation, the Andrew W. Mellon Foundation, and the Terra Foundation for American Art. I am grateful for the Provost's Advancing Scholarship in the Humanities and Social Sciences Fellowship at the University of Southern California, and I thank Beth Meyerowitz, the USC Dornsife College of Arts and Sciences, and Dean Peter Mancall.

With those funds and that time, I traveled to many archives and collections. I want to thank the staffs of the San Francisco Airport Museum; the Flight Path Learning Center at Los Angeles International Airport (LAX), especially the indomitable Trojan Ethel Pattison; Special Collections, Yale University; the Library of Congress; the archives of the Aéroports de Paris; the Air France Archives; Special Collections, University of Miami; the Transportation Library, Northwestern University; Special Collections, the University of Chicago; Special Collections, New York Public Library; Getty Images, London, especially Justyna Zarnowska; the International Center for Photography; the Center for Creative Photography; the Fondation Yves Saint Laurent; the Walt Disney Company Archives, especially Kevin Kern and Becky

Cline, and Jenny Cohen of the Disney Corporation; the Heritage Center at the Anaheim Public Library; and the New-York Historical Society. Studying the work of Ernst Haas also brought me into contact with people who knew him. Inge Bondi met with me twice and shared her research, teaching me a great deal about the history of photography as scholar and witness. Philip Gittelman also shared his archive of materials regarding Magnum Films. Alex Haas and Victoria Haas, the children of Cynthia Seneque and Ernst Haas, have enlivened what is usually dusty research for me. I have also benefited from the research assistance of Laura Kalba, Luci Marzola, Kelsey Chung, and Marc Castellini. Sammy Goldenberg was a model undergraduate research assistant and wrote a prizewinning senior thesis at USC about LAX under my direction. Ellen MacFarlane, Myles Little, Aaron Rich, Isabel Wade, and Ben Gaylord were the remarkable Oompa-Loompas who helped get this manuscript out the door. They have my thanks and their freedom. My thanks also to Yale University Press, especially Katherine Boller and Sarah Henry. Heidi Downey made my prose better. Jason Weems provided a generous and helpful manuscript review.

Like any project that has taken shape over this many years, I also shared my unpublished work in many scholarly settings at the invitation of generous colleagues. They have left their indelible marks on its pages. I extend my appreciation to Will Straw, Joanne Sloane, Peter Geimer, Romy Golan, Chris Wood, Jan Von Brevern, Willa Silverman, David Bell, Phil Nord, Seth Koven, Dominique Kalifa, Kim Timby, Christian Delage, Thierry Gervais, Britt Salvesen, Paul Roth, Gaëlle Morel, Laura Wexler, Anne Higonnet, André Gunthert, Marie Thébaud Sorger, and most especially Nathalie Roseau. I want to especially acknowledge several colleagues with whom I developed long-term and ongoing intellectual ties. In Paris, I would like to express my warm appreciation to Antoine de Baecque and Emmanuelle Loyer: hosts, interlocutors, and *compagnons de route*. I have been privileged to work with the team at the Terra Foundation, especially Veerle Thielemans and Francesca Rose. In Geneva, Jean-François Staszak and Estelle Sohier made my visits especially productive, memorable, and fun. In Israel, Ruth Iskin, Moshe Sluhovsky, and Gal Ventura welcomed me in the Negev and in Jerusalem. I have never been happier as an historian than to watch the sun rise in a crater in the Negev while pondering the antiquity of the trails there, engrossed in writing a book about modern mobility, while feeling as if I had also gone home.

For the duration of this project, USC has been my academic home and Santa Monica my residence. At USC, I have had the good fortune to have Richard Fox, Elinor Accampo, and Nathan Perl-Rosenthal as friends and interlocutors. The Department of Art History has become my home despite my being a wandering and undisciplined thinker; I thank my Chairs, Kate Flint and Amy Ogata. My intellectual energies on campus have been most fulfilled by the Visual Studies Research Institute, a volunteer fire department from across the campus. When Jennifer Miller got her PhD in art history, I told her if the VSRI ever became a more legitimate operation, I would ask her to come back. She is more than our associate director. She is a colleague and friend who loves hard work as much as she loves going to the happiest place on earth. VSRI faculty Kate Flint, Amy Ogata, Laura Serna, Ann Marie Yasin, Sherry Velasco, Akira Lippit, Pani Norindr, Henry Jenkins, Michael Renov, Vittoria Di Palma, Julian Gutierrez-Albilla, and especially Nancy Lutkehaus and Daniela Bleichmar, made me happy to come to campus. These colleagues and the Art History VSRI squad—Susanna Berger, Jennifer Greenhill, Suzanne Hudson, and the irrepressibly intellectual Megan Luke—sustain me beyond my personal work. The VSRI's "special guest star," WJT (Tom) Mitchell has modeled intellectual generosity and openness. Participants in the Mellon Sawyer Seminar, especially those not already mentioned: David Henkin, Martin Jay, Michael Leja, Billie Melman, Sumathi Ramaswamy, the late François Brunet, and my sister from another mother, Jennifer Tucker, have improved my thinking on so many subjects. Debby Silverman and I had to return to New York as Cullman Center Fellows during the same year to figure out we could talk more in L.A. A silver lining to that otherwise cold, gray year.

I have been fortunate to work with a number of talented postdoctoral fellows as I wrote this book. Ellen MacFarlane, Justin Underhill, Allan Doyle, Estelle Blaschke, Aaron Wile, Jason Nguyen, and John Blakinger helped the VSRI and my schemes, never questioning why I was taking them to Disneyland while saying it was work.

The friends and family who lived through this book while refraining from asking "When are you finally going to finish it?" are owed a special debt for that and much more. Elinor Accampo, Peter Mancall, Diane Winston and Chris Bugbee, Jennifer Tucker, Heidi Tinsman, Jon Weiner and Judy Fiskin, Steve Byrnes and Jamie Mandelbaum, Karen Kornbluh and Jim, Daniel and Sam Halpert, Aurie Hall, Marcy, Ellis and Graham Wilder, all embraced the spirit of travel—oh, the places we've been! Stephanie Friedman and Leo Charney have journeyed with me through both time and space; I hope they will remember my past if there comes a time I can't because they were almost always there. Marie-Karine Schaub and Jean-François, Melchior and Eliane Staszak have proved that you are never too old to make new friends who feel like family. The Posels, en gros, have been my dream family to have married into. David Houts helped make my family, and then together with Leo and Isaac Houts and Becky Berman, we all became a twenty-first-century bicoastal Brady Bunch, proving you need jets to raise our village. My father, Ron Schwartz, has been the greatest influence in my life. I hope we will meet up in the Good Place and that it really is good.

This book is my professional mid-century modern. Certain friends and mentors continue to show me the ropes in so many ways. Lynn Hunt remains a model of clear thought, practical advice, and essential intelligence. At vital junctures she has always said the key thing. Nancy Troy and

Wim deWit know that work friends are real friends. Nancy loves her phone almost as much as I do and generously problem-solves, whether the dilemma is archival, historiographic, or familial. Three people I first met in Berkeley continue to be fellow-travelers. Ed Dimendberg made my career when I was a grad student and saved this book from being thrown into the Seine. My respect and admiration for his intellectual eclecticism and commitment to ideas are boundless. I speak to Sarah Farmer almost every day. She is country mouse to my city mouse. Our friendship proves that opposites attract, and I still thank her for driving to Disneyland with me after my exams in 1990. Deborah Cohen arrived a few years after I did in Berkeley like a whirlwind—all brilliance, humor, and generosity. Her advice on this book made it both smarter and more user-friendly; her interventions at key moments in my life and in this book changed both immeasurably. When I picked Daniela Bleichmar as a post-doc fifteen years ago, I had no idea that I was going to get both a valued friend and respected colleague out of that pile. Our collaboration in graduate teaching and in writing has been an important part of this project.

This book is about the future arriving in the present and is dedicated to those people who gave my present a future. It is dedicated to my doctoral advisees (and a few honorary ones), also known as "the minions," in reference to the irrepressible yellow creatures who speak their own nonsense language and create mayhem in the lab of Gru, the crazed but lovable villain of the *Despicable Me* movies. Enough said. Our antics together may have slowed its production, but their many gifts are apparent on every page, and their presence made my devotion to scholarship and research feel worthwhile. Laura Kalba, Jason Hill, Brian Jacobson, Ryan Linkof, Anca Lasc, Matthew Fox-Amato, Catherine Clark, Mark Braude, and Nadya Bair have completed their theses and published books. Kelly McCormick, Jonathan Dentler, Aaron Rich, and Natalia Lauricella will soon. Your work is cited in the endnotes, but beyond that, our conversations gave this book lift. It has been a joy to be taught by you in these years.

The other person to whom this book is dedicated is my daughter, Rachel Sophie Isaacs Schwartz. This book was written between the time of her Bat Mitzvah and her college graduation. As in the dream ballet in the musical *Billy Elliot,* it has felt like watching the little dancer take flight next to the grown one. Rachel's intellectual, creative, and artistic talents impelled this project forward in ways she probably cannot name, while she was also the only person who could get me to not work on my book, and happily so. We took vacations in many places. I watched her rehearsals and performances. We talked about school, politics, and love. She attended my conferences and cocktail parties (with the graduate students!). And we took so many trips to Disneyland, Disneyland Paris, and Tokyo Disneyland. It has also been my joy to be taught by *you* in these years, even if saying so makes you think I am comparing you to my students. More important, and definitely incomparably, you have been the love of my life since the day you were born.

I earned million-miler status on United Airlines while writing this book, giving me Gold Status for life. There is only one person with whom I share that status: my wife, Rebecca Isaacs, with whom I have been the same number of years that I have been a United flyer: twenty-nine. Her patience, generosity, kindness, and sense of adventure have guided us through sometimes stormy skies, allowed us to often fly in comfort in the front of the plane, and always to cross the globe, together. Whether ensconced in European splendor or sitting on a recommissioned prop plane in the jungles of Latin America, she has enriched every book and made living a form of learning. Although I anticipate a future life on the move together, especially chasing our runaway bunny, the sun always sets in the west. Standing beside her on our balcony watching the orange-pink skies of Santa Monica at the close of day may not exactly match the colors of my childhood bedroom in Manhattan, but I know I am home. And it *is* better than living in an airplane.

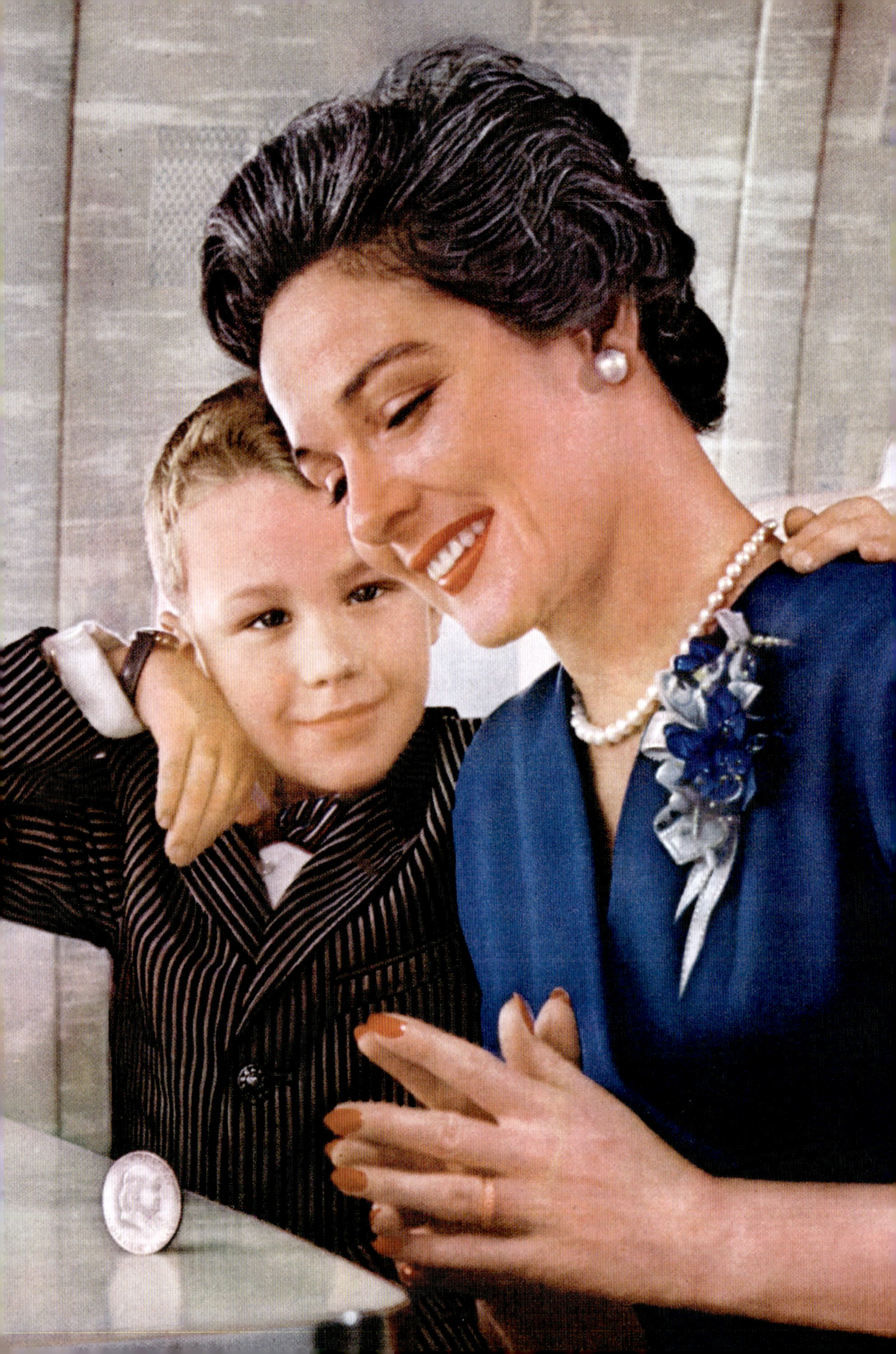

Introduction

In May 1957, architect William Pereira addressed attendees at the Jet-Age Airport Conference in New York. He and his partner, Charles Luckman, had recently accepted the invitation to plan the renovation of Los Angeles International Airport. On this occasion, a gathering of leading civil engineers and urban planners, Pereira insisted that attendees were more than members of an industry going about their usual business. They were witnesses to the dawn of a new era: "At this very moment, history is classifying mankind in an age—the Jet Air Age. . . . Where, before it took hundreds, even thousands of years to progress on a universal basis with a device invented by man to move himself, today it takes a few months or years. In effect, we are realizing our future now almost as fast as we can visualize it. . . . We are moving people."[1] The jet plane would speed people across the world, Pereira said, thereby accelerating time as well as the pace of progress itself. It was the kind of language that permeated forward-thinking views in the western world at mid-century.

Metaphors of speed, motion, and "going places" also were used to describe social change. Historian David Potter in his classic work *People of Plenty* noted that "the American measures his worth by the distance he has progressed from his point of departure rather than the position he occupies. . . . Mobility and change are natural by-products of his quest for success; departure from the patterns of the past is a matter of course."[2] Pereira extended this vision beyond the nation to the entire planet, pointing to the role jets would play as agents of global change while "moving people as fast as could be visualized." Speed and its visualization, Pereira said, would define an era—one named for the new transport vehicle that would simultaneously represent and convey it: the jet age.

This book defines the jet age and asks what it meant for the jet to have defined a period. Was it no more than indicating that objects had aerodynamic style? Was it just shorthand for the era of mass travel and the rise of tourism and leisure? Was it used to denote the arrival of the fastest form of commercial transport?

Pereira's use of the term "jet age," just as regular transatlantic commercial service by jet was to commence, suggested that the planes were so

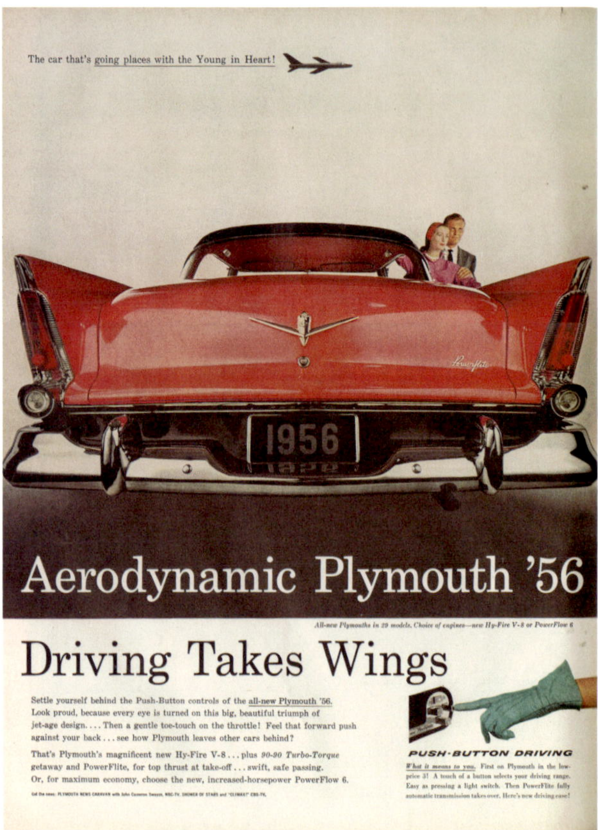

Fig. 0.1 Plymouth advertisement. *Life*, December 26, 1956

significant that they not only could represent an era but also alter the very nature of time. Rather than focus on what would change if and when people could travel more quickly, Pereira pointed to something more complex. The speed of the jet promised to make time itself seem to move faster—or at least subjective experience of the passage of time would be fundamentally altered in an age when people would move as fast as "could be visualized." Although by the mid-twentieth century it was becoming commonplace to understand the impact of technology and transportation as influencing social organization more generally—after all, a masterful synthesis of this point of view (Lewis Mumford's *Technics and Civilization*) had been published in 1934—never had a means of transport named an age before the changes it promised were realized. The jet age seemed to change time by suggesting that the future had arrived in the present.

In the 1950s, the jet age could have been defined as a style, especially one associated with aerodynamic motion.[3] But when used as an adjective, "jet age" described objects seen as on the technological cutting edge. Advertisers, for example, sold the 1956 Plymouth by promoting it as the "triumph of jet-age design." Its fins deliberately evoked the wings of a jet (fig. 0.1). In a different mode, a 1955 advertisement for a General Electric transistor radio declared that the device "belongs in the jet age." By using

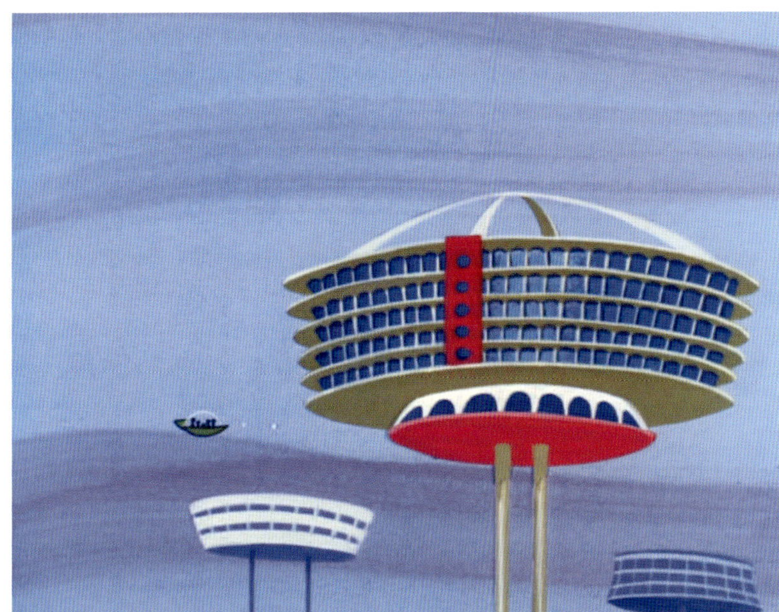

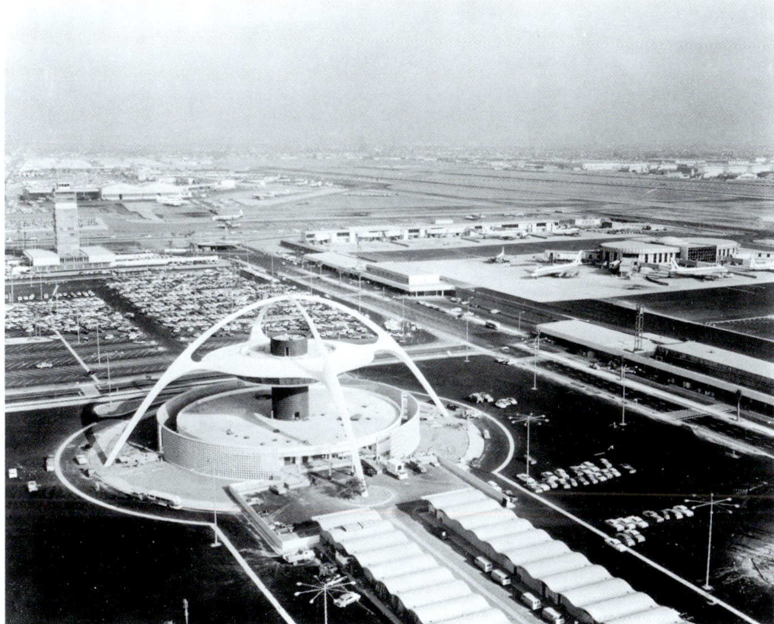

Fig. 0.2 Scene from *The Jetsons* television program, 1962. Warner Brothers. DVD screen capture

Fig. 0.3 Pereira & Luckman, Theme Building, Los Angeles International Airport, 1962

the term "in" rather than "to," the ad also emphasized the immanence of the moment—that the jet age, like the new radio, stood as the culmination of a future that had already arrived.[4] This futuristic moment is evident in many aspects of the popular cartoon television series *The Jetsons,* which debuted in 1962. The Jetsons, a family of four, lived in a future in which homes were sky-high apartments that resembled the Theme Building, which had just opened at Los Angeles International Airport (figs. 0.2, 0.3). They and their neighbors traveled in flying vehicles that resembled the cars the show's viewers already drove. Thanks to the jet, people now lived in a world moving so fast that the future had caught up to the present, and such transitions, eased by technology, had become smoothly effortless.

The phrase "jet age" first appeared in the United States and England to refer to military aircraft that had entered service during World War II.[5] The development of the jet engine had been heralded as the greatest technological advance in the history of aviation, especially if it could be applied to civil aviation. What difference did the jet's speed make in ordinary travel time? Flying had already sped things along compared to other forms of travel, and it certainly defined long-distance voyages, especially those between continents. In 1946 it had taken twenty-four hours to fly from New York to Paris, and four and a half days crossing the sea by ocean liner. The Lockheed Starliner, a new passenger plane powered by four turbo-compound radial engines introduced in 1956, made the transatlantic journey in only fourteen hours. But in 1958 the Boeing 707, traveling 500 to 600 miles an hour, cut that journey in half, taking the seven or so hours it still more or less takes to get from New York to Paris. In its inaugural trip it refueled in Gander, Newfoundland, and thus it took eight hours and fourteen minutes to reach Le Bourget, where it received the sort of fanfare that recalled Charles Lindbergh's New York–to–Paris flight in 1927.[6] To imagine that only thirty-one years before, one man's flight across the Atlantic had seemed like a heroic act.

The jet also increased load capacity, which made ticket prices drop, thereby expanding its passenger market. Its speed also appealed to time-conscious business users and tourists, who became part of a growing market of flyers. This led those in the burgeoning airline industry and expanding travel business to anticipate that transatlantic flight would become the preferred method of travel between the old and new worlds. They were right. By 1958, more people flew across the Atlantic than took the boat, contributing to the belief that the jet would have a major social impact.

Only a decade earlier this growth would have seemed unlikely. Fuel costs were prohibitive, and the jet had a limited flying range. Journalists questioned the viability of the jet age and, sensitive to the dangers of the new technology, asked whether such a moment had arrived prematurely. The remarkable technological promise heralded by advocates of civilian jet service had been dampened by several spectacular crashes of the first jet plane used in commercial flight: the De Havilland Comet, a British jet operated by BOAC and launched in 1952. In fact, five Comets out of the twenty-one flown had technical difficulties that challenged their status as safe for passenger flight. Journalists asked why anyone might use what still seemed an experimental technology, given that other fast-enough airplanes flew without unnecessary risk.[7] Still, engineers insisted it was only a matter of time before these problems were sorted out.[8]

The jet's disastrous start made the successful and steady debut of Pan Am's Jet Clipper America, a Boeing 707, all the more cause for celebration

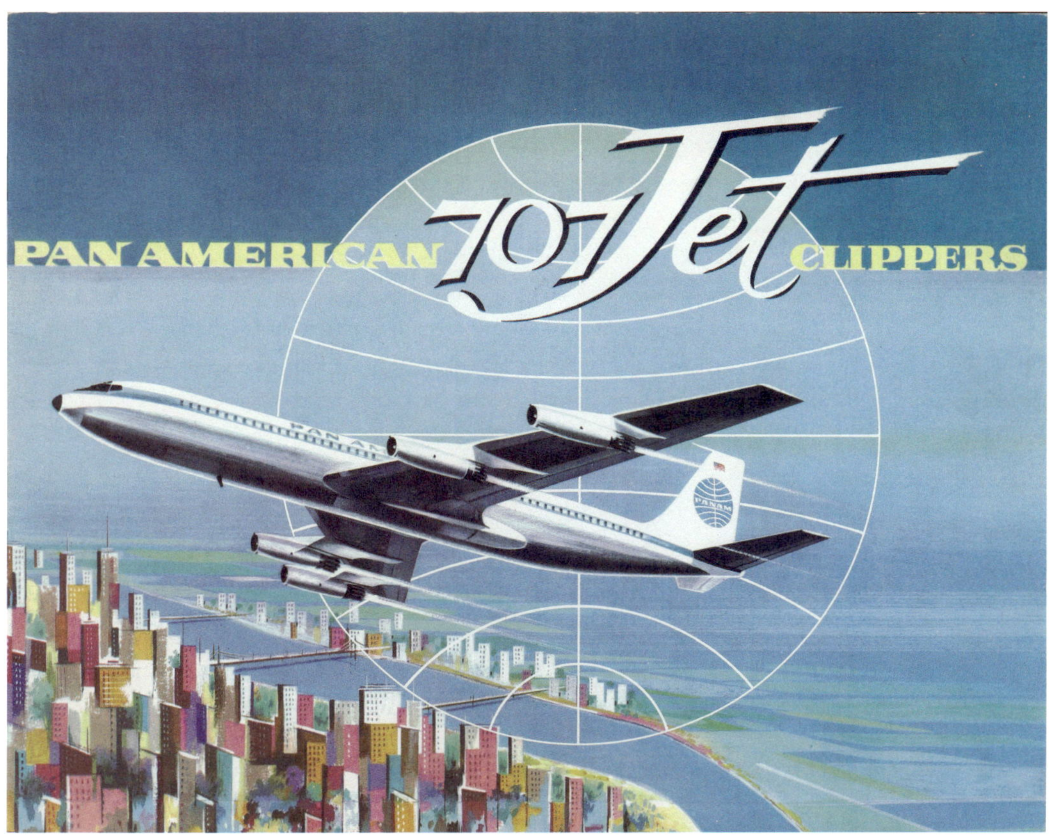

Fig. 0.4 Pan Am brochure, 1958. Image featuring Boeing 707

in 1958 (fig. 0.4). The promised dawn of the jet age finally seemed to have arrived. Although the boosters of the airline industry were prepared to convince people to do the unthinkable—hurtle through the atmosphere in a metal tube at more than 500 miles an hour—it turns out that people did not need all that much convincing. By the end of the 1960s, what had once been imagined as an activity reserved for a class of travel elites had become part of the lives of ordinary people.

At the start, jets moved people, mostly from Europe and the United States, to all parts of the world. The jet age was producing the anticipated expansion of air travel and inaugurating the era of mass tourism.[9] Jets also moved some people from all parts of the world to other places, once and for all. Decolonization of the French, British, and Dutch Empires in particular coincided with the advent of the jet, and such emigration was served by the new planes.[10] In short, people the world over flew for the first time in the 1960s. In 1959 in the United States, 56 million air passengers flew; by 1965, 92 million; and by 1970, 153 million. By the early 1970s, more than half of all Americans had flown. In fact, flying became so common that by the end of the jet's first decade of service, magazine articles, novels, and poems describing the experience of flight itself had all but disappeared, even though that experience once had been the decade's defining quality.[11]

And yet the story of the jet covering those distances was not just about its speed. As a special issue of *Le Monde Economique* dedicated to air travel suggested, "Every aspect of our time is marked by movement . . . [and] the aircraft is the most eloquent symbol of this transformation."[12] The jet alone did not cause the movement but embodied it, the periodical reported in 1959. It was not that the movement was fast (although it was); rather, it was the quality of the movement that struck people most. In one of the Boeing Company's best-known ads of the period, we are presented with a mother and little boy in what amounts to a scene of domestic comfort in the new Boeing 707 (rather than glamorous, cutting-edge, high-tech luxury). Thanks to the jet's ride, described as serene and vibrationless, passengers would be able to hear their watches tick and see a coin balance on a table. The altitude is "weatherless" (and seemingly viewless, from the peek of empty sky one can spy over the boy's shoulder).[13] A flower (a metaphor for Mom herself, no doubt) would remain fresh through the entire flight (fig. 0.5). This ad points to the aspect of traveling in a jet that observers often identified as most significant at the time, and entirely different from other forms of flight: that of going far and fast while seeming to go nowhere at all—fluid motion and sensationless travel.

The deprivation of experience became the jet's characteristic quality, as important as its speed. As a 1954 *Newsweek* article noted, jet travel "will seem like slipping through space. No vibrations, no lurches, and no sense of speed."[14] Without the piston-operated engine, the ride inside the plane was quieter and the plane transmitted little of its characteristic vibration. In short, the ride itself made the trip less of a physical experience, and "less" experience became the value of jet travel. As a 1959 American Airlines brochure placed at every seat on their jet service explained, "There is no sensation of speed whatsoever in jet cruising. The flight is smooth beyond anything you have ever experienced. Vibration, the major cause of travel fatigue, is gone. Engine noise is so reduced you hear only the air flow passing the fuselage. It is a hard thing to describe the cushioned, insulated sense of comfort you will know in jet flight."[15] Even before passengers were instructed regarding the novelty of what they were about to experience, guidebooks such as *Fodor's* had already made similar promises. After emphasizing the unprecedented 500- to 600-mile-per-hour pace that would allow the vehicle to speed from one place to another, the doxa of speed was replaced by an emphasis on smoothness: "You'll find the jet takes off smoothly and climbs with a feeling of steadiness and certainty that piston engine and even turbo-prop planes don't have. . . . You'll be free from the fatiguing elements of vibration and noise."[16] There was, of course, noise emitted by the engines, and this noise became the basis for complaints about noise pollution in residential areas near airports, but the relative experience inside the jet plane, especially among those who had flown on piston-planes, was that the new planes were remarkably better because they were so quiet. As Milton Roberts of San Diego, California, explained,

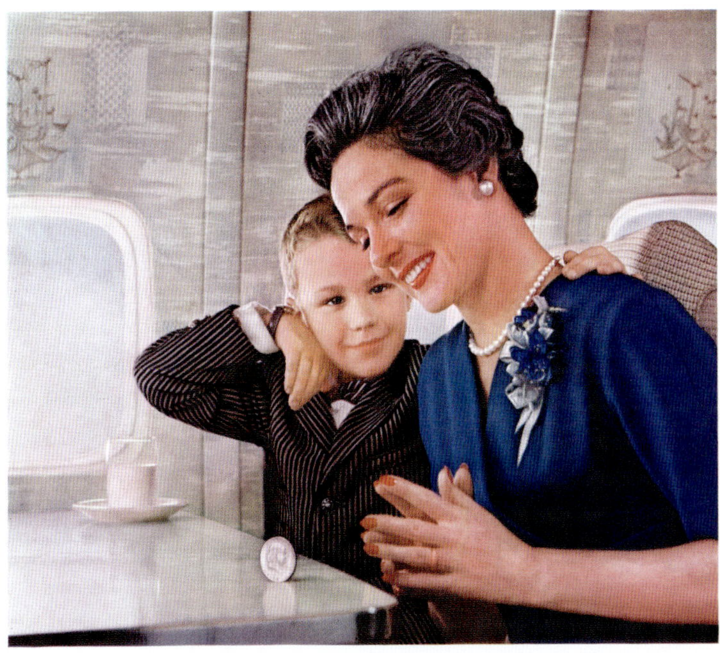

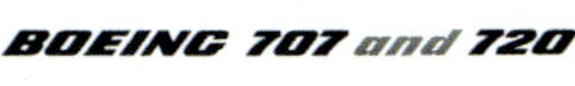

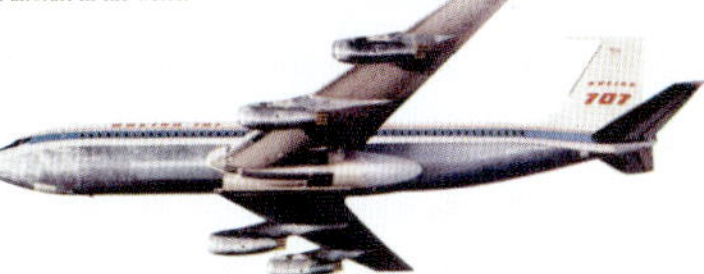

Fig. 0.5 "The coin, the watch and the flower." Boeing advertisement, 1958

"This is just like sitting in an armchair; it's wonderful. I really had no idea that the 707 tourist section was so comfortable." Florence Vita of Los Angeles went further, saying, "This flight is fabulous. I just cannot get over the feeling that we're standing still. Why, there doesn't seem to be any motion at all in here!"[17]

Pereira's predictions regarding the dawn of a new age were also proving correct in terms of the popular fascination with jet travel. A hit song in France in 1963, Gilbert Bécaud's "Dimanche à Orly," celebrates the novel ritual of the family outing to the airport. Although there had been plane watching before then, the jet age brought large numbers of families such as this one (fig. 0.6) to the airport in their Sunday best. It is an updated version of spending what in France used to be the ritual togetherness of passing a weekend day in the country. The older customs, such as relaxed lazing by a riverside, were replaced by riding escalators and using automated vending machines on the terrace of the newly redesigned airport—part of a high-tech ritual of participating in what would become a circuit of people-moving. The Orly terrace is one of the jet age spaces we examine here.

"Dimanche à Orly" is not the only song inspired by the period's novel passenger transport. When Pan Am began its regular jet service across the Atlantic in fall 1958, the association of flying with going far afield was already part of popular American consciousness.[18] In January 1958, Frank Sinatra released what would become a Grammy-winning album, "Come Fly with Me," whose cover prompted the singer to complain that it looked like a poster for TWA (fig. 0.7). The album featured travel-themed songs, including the title song with its repetitive referencing of far-flung places: Bombay, Acapulco, and Peru, while never mentioning the speed of travel.[19] Instead, the song emphasizes the quality of the jet's movement, promising that the lovers would "float down to Peru" and "just glide, starry-eyed." While the jet's speed may have made it the fastest form of commercial passenger travel available, if that were what defined the jet age, one could say we are still living in it, as no form of regular passenger transport can move any faster now than the jet did back then.[20]

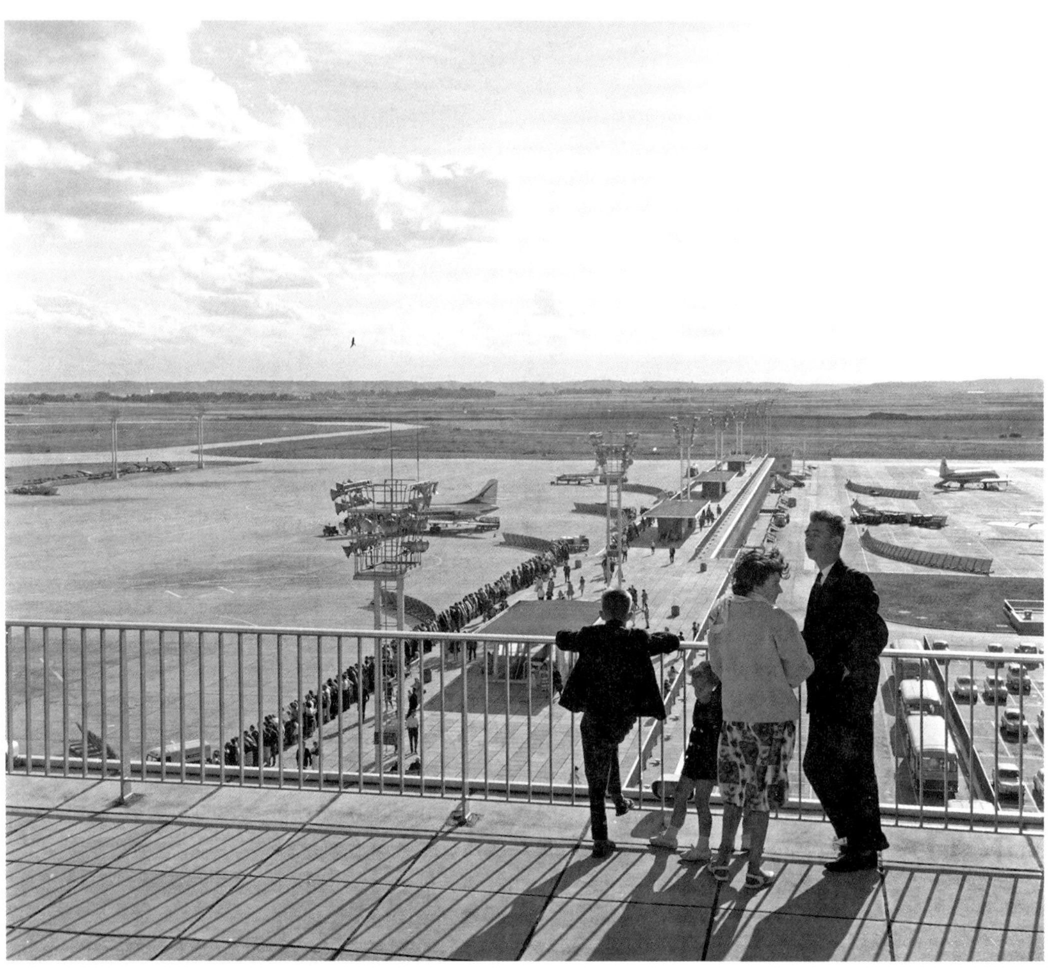

Fig. 0.6 Family visit to Orly Terrace, circa 1961–62. Aéroports de Paris

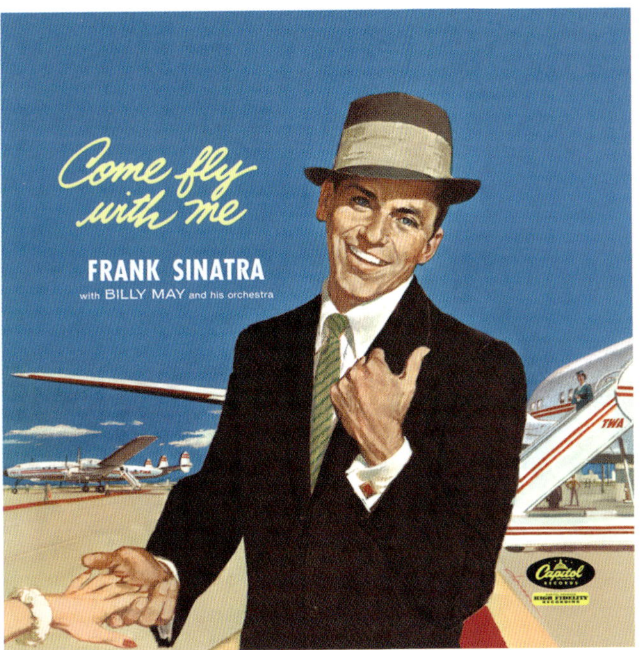

Fig. 0.7 "Come Fly with Me," Frank Sinatra album cover, 1958. Capitol Records Inc. Cover produced in cooperation with Trans World Airlines and featuring TWA Jetstream Superconstellation

If popular culture characterized the experience this way, intellectuals and designers also seemed to concur. When Roland Barthes wrote about the jet test pilot in 1955 in his essay "Jet-Man," he also underscored the lack of sensation one experienced: "The jet man is defined by a coenesthesia of motionlessness (at 2,000 km in flight no impression of speed whatever)."[21] Industrial designer George Nelson described what was modern about the jet as its passengers' encapsulation: "The prime characteristic of modern travel is that it tends to isolate one from experience. . . . In the move from open-cockpit planes to the noisy prop jobs to the near vibrationless and silent jets one has the impression of more and more layers of padding being applied. The old open elevators have become sealed tubes stuffed with Muzak. . . . Encapsulation is a good part of the price paid for speed."[22] The faster the vehicle went, the less the passenger experienced any sense of motion at all, thanks to the perfection of design that naturalized the jet's mechanically powered motion, extending—or perhaps, one could say, finally seemingly "perfecting"—the relation between human and machine movement so that their differences grew increasingly imperceptible.

Before the jet, planes flying at a relatively lower altitude had offered an important new perspective on the world in a form of visual "distancing." Aerial vision constructed and represented a God's-eye view as well as created a perspective of the landscape as an abstracted grid.[23] As the aerial view became part of everyday life after a half century of flying, however, the jet introduced new qualities to that visual experience. Passengers saw very little by looking out of the window from the heights at which jet planes flew for most of the flight's duration. Although at 30,000 feet one could hypothetically see a horizon that was 142,000 square miles, in reality, there was less to see than ever before. Windows on jets were smaller because of pressurization, and there was an increasingly smaller number of windows per passenger. The Boeing 707 sat four people across, so most passengers were quite far from the window or from any "view from above." In fact, the 707 offered the first airplane window with shades, and in 1961 TWA and United began to offer regular in-flight entertainment. The view on the jet was certainly turned toward the inside of the plane rather than outside it.

The jet defined an age because it was contributing to a transformation in subjective experience. On the one hand, its speed made the world that much smaller. On the other hand, the jet defined an age through the creation of a jet age aesthetic. That aesthetic addressed and managed the new subjective experience created by the circulation and mobility of the postwar world. The jet was not simply the new emblem of a complex transport infrastructure, but, in addition, its aesthetic situated it as a key element in a larger media culture that glamourized fluid motion. By navigating a combination of newly built spaces and contemporary media forms in the late 1950s to the late 1960s, jet age people learned to increasingly close the distances between physical space and time and also to toggle between the material and immaterial worlds, which is how globalization works on the level of subjective experience.

The moment became known as the dawn of an age in its own day because, like the motion of the jet, which promised to easily slip through space, jet age people did too, and to follow them, so did I. That jet age aesthetic does not simply consist of the familiar aspects of air culture, such as the decoration of jet interiors, the uniforms worn by flight attendants, the meals served on board, the ads promoting the new service, or the airport art. These constitute what one might call a design style because it generated symbolic meaning and value but is ultimately located in static forms and objects. This makes them not particularly well suited to explain how people traverse space and make sense of time in relation to technology and media forms.[24] To understand the jet's quality of motion as part of a period phenomenon requires journeying outward from the plane and the discrete spaces of transport history, the history of technology and aviation; traversing the borders of architectural history, design, and urban planning; entering the airspace of mobility studies, globalization, and tourism and leisure studies; circling over film studies, communications, art history, and the history of photography; and then coming in for a landing. The study of the jet age traverses borders and boundaries as much as the jet plane did the open skies. For example, we will see how transport became a form of media, because it played a fundamental role in altering subjective experience.

To imagine the jet age as having an aesthetic is a way of envisioning the period's creative and aesthetic force and drive. Fine art movements of the period such as kinetic art and spatialism also fit within its purview. But the footprint of the jet age aesthetic is far larger, shaping and encompassing the more general sensory regime of postwar culture. In *Atlas of Emotion,* Giuliana Bruno considers "sensuous cognition" and notions of psychogeographic journeys across a vast range of media forms, practices, and spaces. I also consider the senses both aesthetically and historically to focus on the connection between transport and media but with a greater focus on a specific period. Homing in on the decade of the jet is not accidental. Having given its name to an age in its own day, the jet apparently was seen from the start as able to define its moment. What the jet was thought to be, whether what it appeared to herald at the time was what it became, and what its long-term impact might have been are what drew me to study this mid-century object.[25] Having spent so much time in jets myself, I wondered what jet travel must have been like at the beginning, especially since the speed of flight and the plane itself in many ways have not changed that much. Was my experience the same? And, conversely, when the ride was a new experience, did it actually change how people felt and experienced such things as time and space?

To answer these questions regarding the experience of what I call "fluid motion" to capture the impact of jet travel is not as straightforward as tracking growth in tourism or considering laws regarding the sovereignty of air space. People we might consider aesthetic stakeholders, such as architects and city planners, mass cultural entrepreneurs, designers, photographers, and filmmakers, all participated in the moment's aesthetic of fluid motion by extending, promoting, and embedding the singular experience of the jet—as a value and as a sensory experience—to life on the ground. These people were in the business of mass media, so this is also a means to reach broad social experiences and the responses of ordinary people to these new spaces and cultural forms. Working on mainstream mass cultural production affords us a view into such popular reception, which is, in turn, also a form of cultural production.

Many media theorists—especially Georg Simmel, Walter Benjamin, and Marshall McLuhan—have correlated human sensory change to media technologies. I consider transport a medium and approach modern systems of mobility, transport, and mechanization as historical rather than autonomous forces.[26] I argue that transport and communication media did not just support each other; rather, they served the same end in one network by facilitating circulation. By connecting them to such commercial imagery as photographs, film, and television, and their distribution spaces, as well as to the built environment, such media formed a dense system that produced new forms of subjective experience. Although by the mid-nineteenth century the telegraph technically had separated transportation and communication (because information until then could travel only as fast as the messenger who carried it), there has been a continuing relation between communication and transportation, so much so that this connection suggests that they are virtually identical.[27]

In fact, when McLuhan was preparing to write *Understanding Media* (1962) he noted that "I expect to add . . . several media like money, railways, ships, and planes and cars—in fact, all of those externalizations of our bodily functions and perceptions which cause all human technology to exist in the ablative case."[28] This observation combines transport and media as sharing a dedication to motion, suggesting that during the period under examination here, transport and media became newly reconnected. The period's media ecology reconfigured both simultaneously, as well as perception itself—thanks to the central role played by the jet's fluid motion—working to dissolve the boundaries not simply between forms but also between the material and immaterial worlds. As McLuhan noted, the photograph created a world of "accelerated transience," and the age was one in which "travel differs little from going to a movie or turning the pages of a magazine."[29] This study decodes the meaning of such observations by looking back at the decade of the jet age and at several key sites and intersecting forms that allow us to capture that culture of media in motion.

My list is not the same as McLuhan's, but its impulse is. By examining certain paradigmatic jet age spaces that shared a dedication to fluid motion—such as new airports and the theme park in Anaheim built by Walt Disney that opened in 1955 and became known as Disneyland (the first obvious, the second I hope obvious after reading my description and analysis)—and through a careful examination of the period-specific history of the mass-media environment, the jet age aesthetic takes form in the pages of this book. The jet age was also the heyday of the photographic newsmagazine, and by considering new methods of making and taking pictures, and especially the explosion of color in photojournalism, I show how spaces and pictures worked in tandem and around a logic of circulation to mediate new subjective experiences of motion. Such experiences led observers not only to sense that they were living in a new era but also to feel the impact of new experiences of time and space. The pace had changed, and the future could be lived as fast as it could be visualized, as Pereira had noted. Translating such words into experience is what the jet age aesthetic did for ordinary people. This was significant in its own moment and also fundamental to the reconfiguration of how media shape our world, laying the groundwork, I argue, for the networked society we inhabit today.

Newsmagazines, often disparaged as vehicles of outdated consumerism, played an important role in the elaboration of the jet age aesthetic. They were never mere tools of such unfettered capitalism nor Cold War propaganda nor simple transmitters of such ideologies as the American Way of Life. These persistent scholarly views are caricatures that obscure their actual impact.[30] As art historian Shelley Rice observes: "Since its invention, photography has moved up and down the social hierarchy in all media-based cultures, and it has also substantially reorganized the relationship between the local and the global. The metamorphoses of objects and images are not by-products or accidents of communication; this mutability is photography's *raison d'etre.*"[31] Such mutability of form also related to mobility in ways that made "press" and magazine-format photography particularly important in this period and to this day (while its format has changed) as a part of a culture of media in motion. Such media, I believe, are the linchpin in discussions of modern experiences of motion, of experiences of speeding up of time and the collapsing of physical space. They also help us see how the jet can be thought to be a form of media in motion too. All that is treated in this book.

As a cultural history of how media facilitate globalization, my book is aimed at grasping changes in subjective experience rather than at the structural level of economics and politics, where such globalization is most often studied. Histories of globalization have focused almost exclusively on the large-scale circulation of people and goods, the bedrock on which the history of capitalism sits. Historians of globalization have considered such topics as trade, migration, and how goods have been transported, contained, stored in an attempt to give larger structural and sociological narratives more historical precision, making the drive toward "connectedness" seem less inevitable.[32] Such histories have been of recent interest because they help explain the neoliberal paradigm of the connection between globalization and the triumph of democracy and capitalism in the wake of the divisions of the Cold War. This offered a view of history with a "drive" not all that different from the old Marxist version of history, reinvented in the form of globalized or braided and connected forms of "world history," with trade, economics, and money still making the world go round.[33]

Although historians of transport have been attentive to how vehicles and infrastructure have altered physical spaces by studying, for example, changes in the landscape and urban morphology, they have been less interested in how such large projects have affected individual experience.[34] Although we associate globalization with the growth of travel and the history of the tourist industry, we have yet to pay enough attention to the process of journeying itself because we have been too preoccupied with its end: arrivals and departures.[35] Art history as a field has fortunately addressed questions of individual response or affect, but, in regard to globalization, the field has typically translated the primarily political and economic histories into the terms of visual and material culture with which it usually works: the objects of fine art, architecture, and the like. This has produced studies that treat subjects such as imperial iconography; the production of scientific knowledge through illustration; the iconography of plantation culture; human rights images; and the design and styling of transport—but often as reflections of such social forces more than their embodiment or as autonomous forces of creation.[36] Beyond the way such phenomena are represented in images, the field has also studied myriad topics related to mobility: the circulation of such images, the migration of art and artists, the influence of trade on style, and the rise of the art market. Such studies seek to show that visual and material culture are not mere byproducts or afterthoughts in global market culture but function as its driving forces as well. For example, entire cities can survive based on their status as art-fair hosts or because they are places where certain folk crafts or artworks are produced and then sold around the world.[37] Attention to the materiality of objects and images and their production and circulation provides a way to study what culture produces rather than what it reflects, which is an important step in the right direction.

People and objects that travel and circulate can tell us a great deal about how transit and transportability shaped and tested communities that were challenged by physical distance in earlier periods or that were connected through quick and easy travel in the jet age.[38] In its aesthetic of fluid motion and communication on a planetary scale, the jet age aesthetic, which dematerialized experience into a system of circulating spaces, people, and images, produced the condition of the digital age if not its actual technologies. Putting systems of transport into alignment with image production and reception gives us new insights into the relation between individual perception and the ties between transport technology, media, and their aesthetic expression as key forces in shaping social formations. Culture does not just reflect underlying political and economic systems. It is why I do not want to simply locate a "jet style" that functions as the cultural reflection or symbolic vehicle of the more "real" interests of, say, the airline industry, or that sees the industry as a stand-in for the forces of the "Americanization of the world" or of global capitalism in neat and I would suggest reductive ways. Humans create and extend meaning through the technologies they make, and the consequences are often unanticipated and not even fully absorbed and assimilated in their own time. That is what historians can be good for.[39]

Although transport history has served as a prism through which we have refracted the history of trade, state-building, nationality, and other such topics, it can also offer us an important source for the history of sensory experiences.[40] Wolfgang Schivelbusch, in his pathbreaking book *The Railway Journey* (1977/1986), blazed such a methodological trail when he turned to train travel to identify a new kind of vision in the nineteenth century. Using the view from the train window, he argued that the train's speed and relationship to the landscape constructed something called panoramic vision. He argued that this new train-induced somatic experience served as a key vector for new cultures of time, space, and human perception.[41] Schivelbusch's research ranged across national histories (mostly of France, Britain, and the United States) to describe general transformations in the experience of geography wrought by the new mode of travel known as the iron horse—and in the standardization of time. He noted that as passengers rode they could no longer distinguish between foreground and background. This novel experience so influenced them that they began to see the world as though they were looking through the frame of a train window. Schivelbusch argued that passengers looked through the apparatus that moved them and thus, he says, they likened the experience to that of nineteenth-century optical devices, apprehending the train ride as among the transformations that turned them into spectators. The train, a mode of transport, also worked as a form of media.[42]

What the train was to the nineteenth century, the car and the plane may be to the twentieth and twenty-first centuries. Scholars of the history of aviation, in particular, have written extensively about the early "heroic" period of flight, concentrating on what we might consider the powers and problems of Icarus, who was triumphant in flight but ultimately burned by the sun due to his hubris. At the same time, a growing body of literature about motion and mobility has extended the visual paradigm developed in *The Railway Journey.*[43] The impact of flight on visual perception ushered in a new perspective—the "view from above"—that had previously been derived only from standing on mountaintops or towers. Planes also afforded new kinds of surveillance that could aid military operations, promote commercial exchange, and expand scientific knowledge, which is why the vehicles are also associated with social control. Everything from the deployment of aerial bombs to drone warfare suggests how strategically important the view from above has been. For many cultural critics, most notably Paul Virilio, who associated the airplane with an entire apparatus of militarized technoculture whose logic has been speed, there could be no good associated with air culture.[44] Everything has functioned as a camouflage for the essentially nefarious goals of the view from above. Yet looking out the window of low-flying planes has prompted reflections on new forms of planetary consciousness. Some have located in that view a growing vision and awareness of urban infrastructure and argued that it afforded viewers abstracted and more structural views of the landscape. As we went farther into outer space, we could see the earth itself in photographs such as *Earthrise* and *The Blue Marble,* which have even been seen as encouraging environmental consciousness.[45] But no matter how many Stewart Brands and *Whole Earth Catalogue*s emerged from manned flight, for Virilio, flight is a fundamentally destructive force.[46]

The aerial view surely provided new forms of command and mastery, but the jet also flew so high that people mostly remarked that they could see nothing at all.[47] Why negatively essentialize the meaning of jet culture when there was hardly any view from above for most ordinary people during the ride in a jet? Further, I wanted to make sense of what people like this passenger, interviewed about flying in a jet in 1966, said: "The plane is really yourself, it is you, with wings."[48] This observation expresses the experience of fluid motion that defined the jet age aesthetic. Man and machine had become one. If Virilio condemned the jet and the cinema as well, as machines of war, I wanted to know why so many people fly and go to the movies. They must not feel that aerial culture is only about war and death.

Life pulses through systems of circulation. Understanding aerial culture through the aesthetic of the glamour of media in motion, we can see how the jet's quiet and smooth ride would be valued more than its speed. An airport artifact, from a decade before the arrival of the jet plane into service, heralded the promise of what the jet age aesthetic would create: subjects who interacted with technologies that traversed time and space

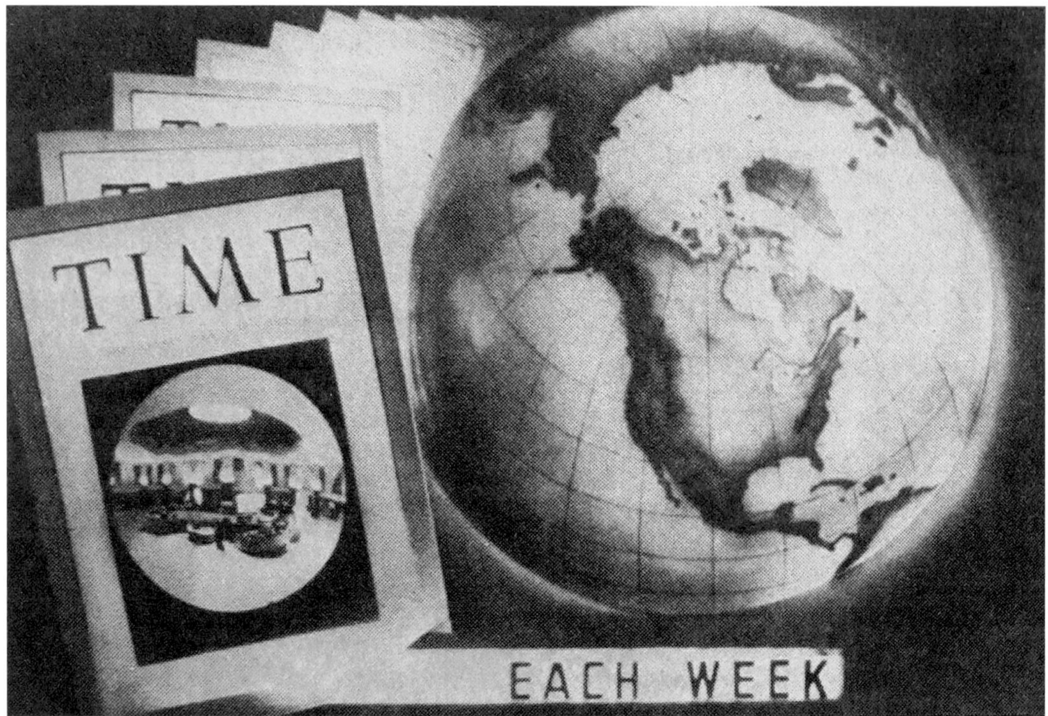

Fig. 0.8 The *Time* magazine 3D Airport Diorama, *FYI*, July 16, 1948

in new ways to dissolve the distinctions between the material and mediated worlds.

In the late 1940s, *Time* magazine created the 3D Airport Diorama, which hung in airports throughout the United States.[49] It measured four feet wide and seven feet high and was suspended with a hemispheric globe that curved out twenty-four inches at its central point (fig. 0.8). It was lighted from within. The display consisted of *Time* magazine covers made from thick Lucite and fanned outward and downward toward the observer. But instead of an actual magazine cover subject, the Lucite *Time* had a large curved mirror that reflected the terminal's moving crowds. The traveling sign beneath the globe read, "3.3 million travelers like yourself travel through time each week."[50] Mirrors were among the first media known to humankind. They taught people that their actual material bodies could be immaterially represented as pure image.[51] The Airport Diorama transformed magazine readers and flyers on the go into the subjects of world news. It also suggested that by being on the move they became spectators—not just of their own lives, but of the world that was also in motion. The *Time* display was an ad that collapsed transport and magazines and passengers into one system of circulation: from plane to airport to magazine but in a continuous loop. Magazines anticipated before the advent of jet travel what the jet would later accomplish, and the jet and magazines worked together to shape new experiences that allowed people to embrace the pleasures of such circulation and to see themselves, literally, in its mirror.

It is no surprise that images from and re-creations of the jet age kept appearing in twenty-first-century contemporary popular culture, in films and television series such as *Catch Me If You Can* and *Mad Men,* or that the TWA terminal is being turned into a luxury hotel. This is not just out of a nostalgia for the sleek look and optimism of another time, when the future seemed better and brighter. Rather, the presence of such cultural references reminds us that they are anchored in our own history, pointing to the world we came from. In an episode of *Mad Men* called "The Wheel," when protagonist Don Draper introduces an object that his client (a photography equipment manufacturer standing in for Kodak), calls "the wheel," his pitch begins by matching sentimental attachment and glittering technology. Although he speaks of nostalgia and calls the device a "time machine," the gadget he eventually dubs "the carousel" does not just go backward, as the nostalgic are compelled to do. It circulates, going "around and around." The device creates flow, a system of passing images that change seemingly automatically in an endless circle rather than being cast back in time.[52] *Mad Men,* the television series about the jet age, is no nostalgia trip. Today, we can still feel its flow. The internet is the most remarkable media form of sensationless fluid motion. It exemplifies the impact of the jet age and helps us understand why it makes sense to us that we can "surf" the internet and physically go nowhere at all. But for now, let's circle back to the jet age, and the creation of a glamorous experience of media in motion where we learned to navigate spaces on the ground as if we were still flying high in the jet.

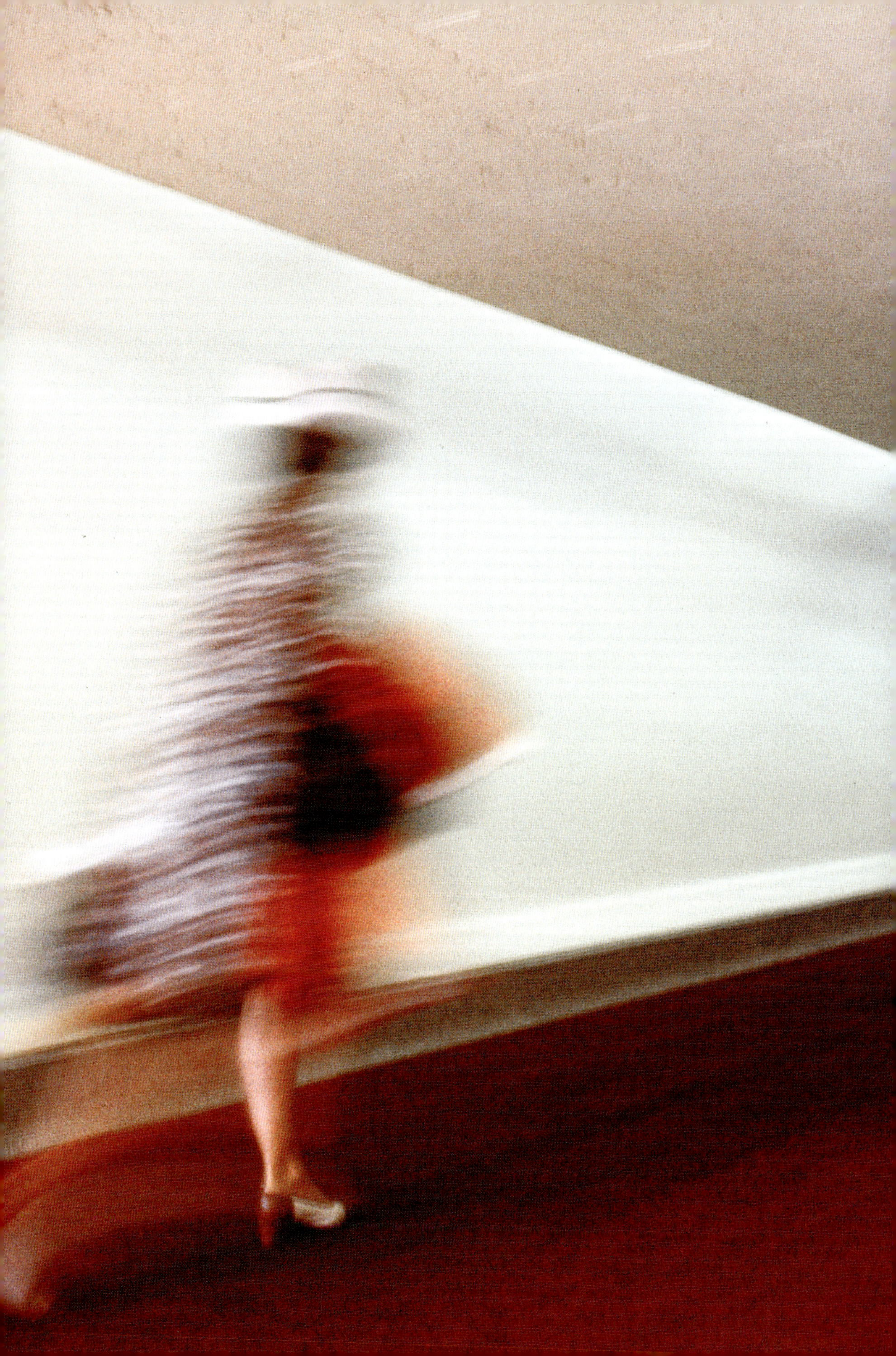

Fluid Motion on the Ground

Designing the Airport for the Jet Age

The most enduring symbols of the jet age are the many new and redesigned airports built to welcome jet service, and perhaps none is as iconic as the TWA terminal at John F. Kennedy International Airport in New York (fig. 1.1). The building, designed by Eero Saarinen, is no longer in use as a terminal but is so valued for its futuristic vision of airport life that no one can bear to part with it. It fronts the extremely hip Jet Blue Terminal behind it today, having been transformed into a hotel.[1] Such terminals symbolize the jet age, which put a global transport system into place and became idealized as sites where individuals could prepare to inhabit a future whose time had come. For the government authorities charged with designing and building them, airports were enormous public works projects, claiming vast material and symbolic capital. They can, in that way, be contextualized in a much longer history of projects in which governments and citizens alike in the western world have staked their power and prestige on their relative technological "modernity." One need think only about the fountains of Versailles to understand the power of state-sponsored technological spectacle in places such as France. For European nations especially, the imperialism of the nineteenth century offered an extensive laboratory for technological experimentation in transport, including track-laying, canal-building, and even spectacular car-racing that tested the limits of both speed and dependability.[2] The history of the jet age airport fits into this longer-term history and in fact extends the link between colonial development and transport: western powers built runways and eventually airports in the physical places they dominated and thus continued to exert and extend their spheres of influence, even into the period of decolonization.[3]

While providing the infrastructure that made the genuinely global expansion of travel by air possible, airports also were spaces for extending the experience of flight. The jet's special quality, aside from its unprecedented speed, was a ride that seemed to defy the ordinary experience of moving through crowded spaces on the ground. The sense of going nowhere fast provoked and challenged planners and architects who sought not merely to "symbolize" the experience of the jet in the new airports but also to design new kinds of spaces that would make the airport more like

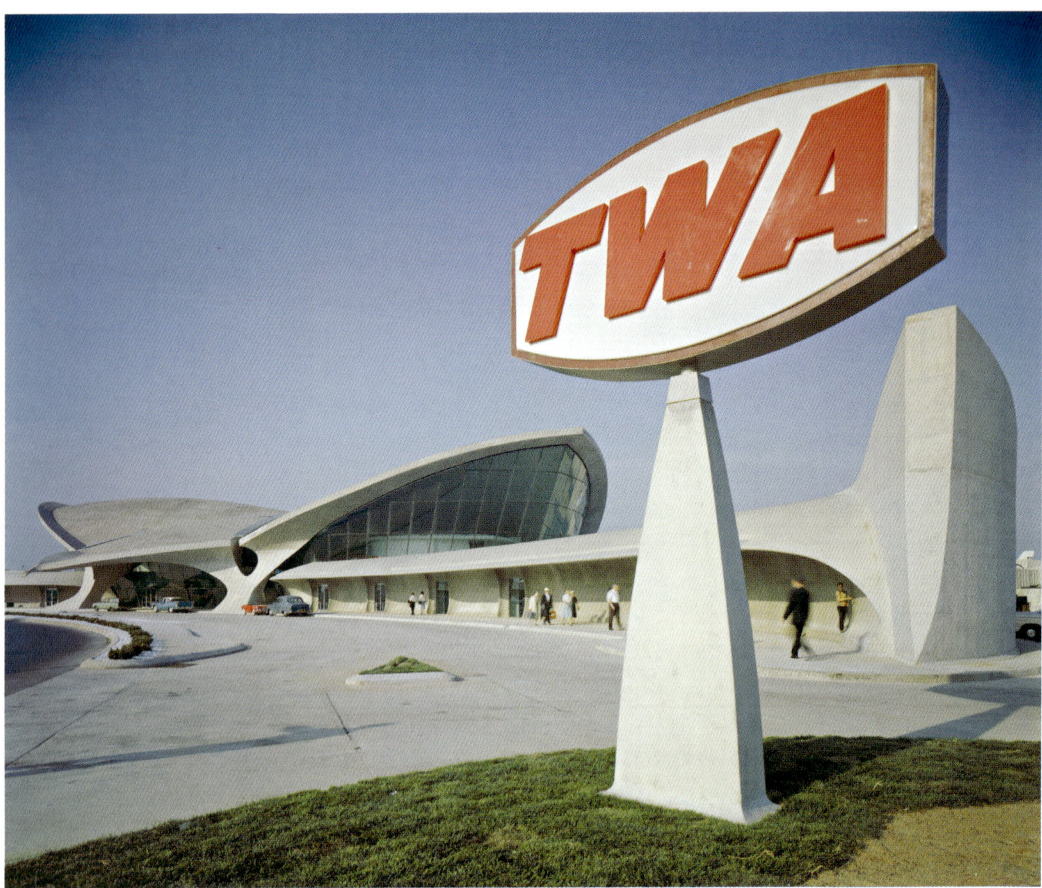

Fig. 1.1 Eero Saarinen, TWA Terminal, John F. Kennedy (originally Idlewild) Airport, New York, 1962. Photograph by Ezra Stoller. © Ezra Stoller/Esto

the experience of riding in a jet plane.[4] The airport also took the lion's share of attention because the jet plane's design became homogenous across the world and only interiors varied.

Although architectural historians have studied airports as distinctly twentieth-century features of the built environment, they have, for the most part, anachronistically concentrated on the terminal buildings. They have also considered them in the broader context of the work of such celebrated architects as Saarinen, Paul Andreu, and Norman Foster, who, in their careers, did much more than design airports. Although it may be tempting to study airports as though they are the cathedrals of the mid-twentieth century, they are not equivalent. Fixating on terminal buildings as if they were monumental gateways distorts a history that was neither imagined nor experienced that way by planners or passengers. From a transport history perspective, it may well be that the airport is to the mid-twentieth century what the train station had been to the nineteenth century and the port had been before that.[5] But as *Time* magazine explained in 1960, "Many of the new airports boast functional rather than beautiful buildings."[6] Architects, planners, and passengers had much more on their minds than the airport's terminals. Driven by predictions of rapidly expanded travel, airport planners built with the idea that no airport could ever be fixed enough to serve as a monumental gateway because airports must meet the challenge of constant expansion and change. If jet age airports monumentalize anything, it is the period's embrace of rapid growth and change, the new consumer-oriented focus on design (passengers and their movement), and a dedication to the idea that enormous building projects could be bound for obsolescence—all undertaken in order to keep people moving.

At the inauguration of the newly renovated terminal at 11 A.M. on February 24, 1961, the president of France, Charles de Gaulle, explained with pride to an audience of fifteen hundred people that the airport at Orly would stand as proof that France would play an important role in the present and future of global politics. He insisted that "in inaugurating this impressive work, we prove that we are not only capable of living our century but even more that in a certain way we are shaping and leading it." That evening five thousand invited guests toured the new terminal and danced the night away, knowing that, as the president had earlier said, "our country is made aware that all its limits have been pushed back."[7] Given the nation's extensive recent material and psychological war damage, the shiny new airport became a part of national recovery and a means to jockey for a leading status among nations. While such airport tales offer important insight into specific municipal and national histories, jet age airports also shared many broader qualities.

To address the expansion in air travel, airports responded to local demands with a variety of architectural and design solutions. George Nelson, however, reflecting on changes in travel-related architecture between 1947 and 1967, saw the value of uniformity. "The last thing the international airlines need is picturesque variations in terminal design. To run an airline with any possibility of reliable schedules and safety, every operational feature . . . has to be identical everywhere. . . . The universal architectural response to mass travel is mass modern."[8] Of course, airports did vary, and Nelson went on in the very same article to assess Saarinen's TWA terminal, which seemed to him less flexible than Orly, whose endless façade was built with expansion in mind. Nevertheless, if an airport offered mass modern as a style, its aesthetic also massively emphasized motion.

Although they were enormous infrastructural undertakings, the many airports built and rebuilt to accommodate the jet display a new architectural logic in which the technological and consumerist cultures of obsolescence and expendability extended to the built environment. Once introduced into regular commercial use, the Boeing 707 ensured that jet travel could more or less safely become a major mode of passenger transportation. To bring the experience of air travel to life on the ground, planners focused on fluid motion, transforming architecture in favor of the user and envisioning their own engagement in large projects of people-moving and planning as being as significant as their former charge to make monumental gateways.

The introduction of civil jet service inaugurated a period of global airport renovation, expansion, and construction. Between 1958 and 1962, new airports or redesigned and expanded ones opened in many places, including London (Gatwick), Algiers, Vienna, Copenhagen, Nice, New York (Idlewild), Brussels, Bordeaux, Marseilles, Montreal, Rome, and Los Angeles. Although it would not be until the end of the 1960s that frequent air travel in Europe and the United States extended to masses of travelers, the fact that the sparkling new Kingston airport in Jamaica is featured as a mark of James Bond's cosmopolitan life in *Dr. No,* the first of the Bond films (1961; released in 1962), suggests the extent to which people expected jets to knit the world together. The airport depicted in the film—a gleaming open rectangular passthrough—could have been anywhere until the moment Bond steps into the specificity of Jamaica's tropical climate. In other words, airports would be the herald of a truly global network that would transport not just occidentals but also people from such former British colonies as Jamaica. This network would bring the otherwise developing world into the metropole and well outside it, creating a new geography beyond core and periphery that the colonial era had established.[9]

Because the jet was certain to maintain its identity as the fastest form of travel for the foreseeable future, it also retained its cutting-edge status for a long time, even as it was in a constant state of flux owing to airport expansion during the period. Critics worried that builders could not keep pace with the changes jets would bring. "These bright new jets w[ould] operate in obsolete terminals," fretted one writer on the inauguration of Pan Am's Jet Clipper America service in 1958.[10] This comment was meant to urge rapid expansion of airports everywhere, but it also reflected the broader ethos of planning for change and growth that shaped the quality and character of jet age airport design. As M. Blackburn, the TWA pilot who flew the first New York–Paris flight in a Constellation in 1945 observed, "For fifteen years I have been through all of the world's airports; I have never seen a finished terminal."[11] Not only did the growth of air travel in the fifteen years since the end of World War II outstrip anything with which airports could keep pace, but the pilot's bemused tone also reveals what would become the accepted view of airport building: airports required expansion planning even as they were being built. The experience of walking through constantly changing terminals became an important way for passengers to experience the sense that the future had indeed arrived.

At the same time, from a functional point of view, the jet itself actually demanded relatively minor changes at airports. Because jets went faster and carried heavier loads, airports needed longer runways made to bear the greater weight and safely land the planes. The larger wingspan and length of the planes necessitated greater space at the plane's parking gates. Yet airport redesign went far beyond such basic renovations. Because the planes could also accommodate many more riders, jet age airport planners focused on the passengers rather than on the operational needs of the flying equipment. For the first time, the airport was about the people flying rather than the machines flying, which was also in keeping with the period's general orientation toward consumers, especially in design.[12] Airport designers focused on saving passengers from long walks and protecting them from the weather, the jet fumes, and the physical realities and challenges of moving human beings through space. Again, the goal was to replicate the sensationless fluid motion and comfort of riding in a jet.

Jet age airports, as contemporary critic Reyner Banham noted, were designed for "obsolescence."[13] When Charles and Ray Eames made a film as part of the planning of Dulles Airport, sited outside the capital of the United States in Chantilly, Virginia, and the first brand-new airport built from scratch to service the new jet planes, its title, *The Expanding Airport,* described a condition that assumed built-in obsolescence. Although some airport designs offered solutions that turned out to be better adapted to continual change than Dulles, the constant growth of air travel foreseen in such projects motivated planners to embrace the ideal of constant motion on the ground as part of the project of building in a state of flux.

In the wake of the inauguration of the new terminals, Banham's 1962 essay "The Obsolescent Airport" summarized the state of things. Banham observed that airports were like "demented amoebas" that had turned inside out to the point of the "disintegration of buildings." The initial yacht basin–like structure of the airport, with its compact cluster of buildings, had given way, he noted, to hidden tunnels, far-off gateways, and terminals that he described as mere passthroughs. During the first era of airport construction, in the 1930s, designs had developed away from the primitive landing fields to follow the general logic of other main transport facilities, in particular that of the maritime culture after which it had been modeled.

The jet age airport would differ. In the new airports Banham saw the logic of the techno-pop culture he sought to explain more generally as part of his critical design theory: "Like all monuments in a technological culture, they were by definition dead, superseded before they were designed."[14] Like the other members of the Independent Group in England such as Lawrence Alloway, Banham identified the reorientation of values in art and design to consumer taste. Airport planners, who hardly had the same cultural taste as these young critics, nevertheless shared the view that obsolescence and expendability should drive decision-making.[15] They aimed to make structures that could "disintegrate." Building for obsolescence attests both to the culture of rapid change associated with the speed of the jet and also to the notion that the feeling of speed needed to be lived on the ground. Airports changed in order to reinforce the promise that flyers would take the jet's airborne, fluid motion back to terra firma.

Deadening passenger sensation in favor of circulation became the raison d'être of the jet age airport, an extension of the plane ride. One British architect noted: "To us, the passenger is a package on legs—or more accurately a weak swimmer in the strong current of a Circulation Diagram—accepted, inhaled, sucked into a backwater, ejected, swept on . . . and finally

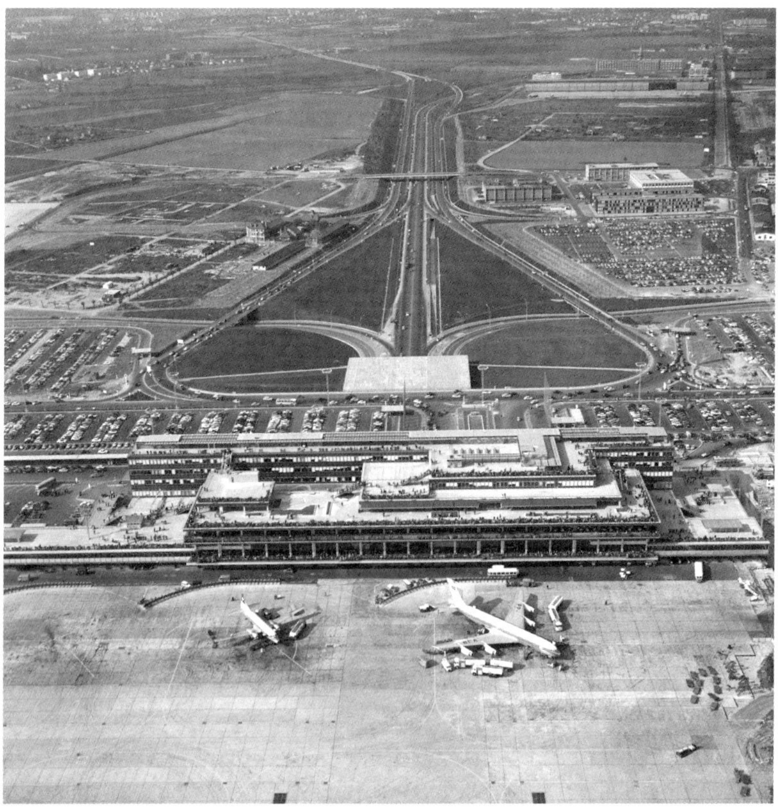

Fig. 1.2 Orly Airport, circa 1962. Aéroports de Paris

disgorged into some kind of streamlined transport, of which all kinds look increasingly alike. For this is a second curiosity—the effect of contemporary styling as sedative, bromide, antidote to feeling. . . . You deaden travel (which is drama) by . . . not allowing the passenger the actual moment of crossing the windy tarmac or the steep gangway."[16]

The jet nonexperience began with the passenger's journey to the airport. Jacques Block, director of planning and development at the Aéroports de Paris (ADP) during the 1960s, emphasized the idea that jets inaugurated an era of fluid and speedy mobility in the context of a vast transport network. He argued that airports needed to be sited near city centers because of the increase in the relative cultural and symbolic value of speed that jets would extend to all sorts of travel: "Because of the rapidity of air travel, passengers find delays in getting from town to the airport increasingly intolerable."[17] Thus, planners focused on efficient means of airport arrival, ranging from such realized plans as Gatwick's train station, which offered the first direct rail service to an airport, to the redirected highway underneath Orly airport (fig. 1.2), to Los Angeles International's unrealized plan for regular helicopter service. As new airports developed, they took up more space and were increasingly far from the cities they served, epitomized by Dulles, situated twenty-six miles from the capital, and O'Hare, eighteen miles from downtown Chicago.

Continuity of travel happened between modes of transport as well as within the airport itself. Banham observed that the new airports were unlike the train stations of the nineteenth century: "The emphasis lies increasingly on the continuity of the process of transport, rather than the monumental halting places along the way."[18] Desire for continuity of the journey also shaped transit strategy within airports, where everything from moving sidewalks to monorails to LAX's unrealized coin-operated aerial tramway, known as the Skylift, preoccupied jet age planners (fig. 1.3).[19] A 1967 report on a planned expansion of Los Angeles International Airport, its first since the initial one in 1961, summarized what an airport should be: "The airport . . . is dedicated to moving people in an orderly manner in the shortest time possible."[20] Moving people, not airplanes, defined the mission of the planners.

Infrastructural organization assured continuity of movement as much as any architectural element did. For example, as an American Airlines brochure explained, "At your destination terminal, you'll find the advantages of jet travel extend to ground service as well: thanks to American's Jet Flagships' new Baggage Expediter system, you'll be able to claim your bags and be on your way sooner than before."[21] At Orly, planners envisioned the trip to the airport as a seamless journey from home to the airport by car, even though most Parisians did not even own cars. The airport planners created

Fig. 1.3 Lockheed Aircraft Service, Proposal for Los Angeles International Airport Intra-Terminal Transportation System, 1960

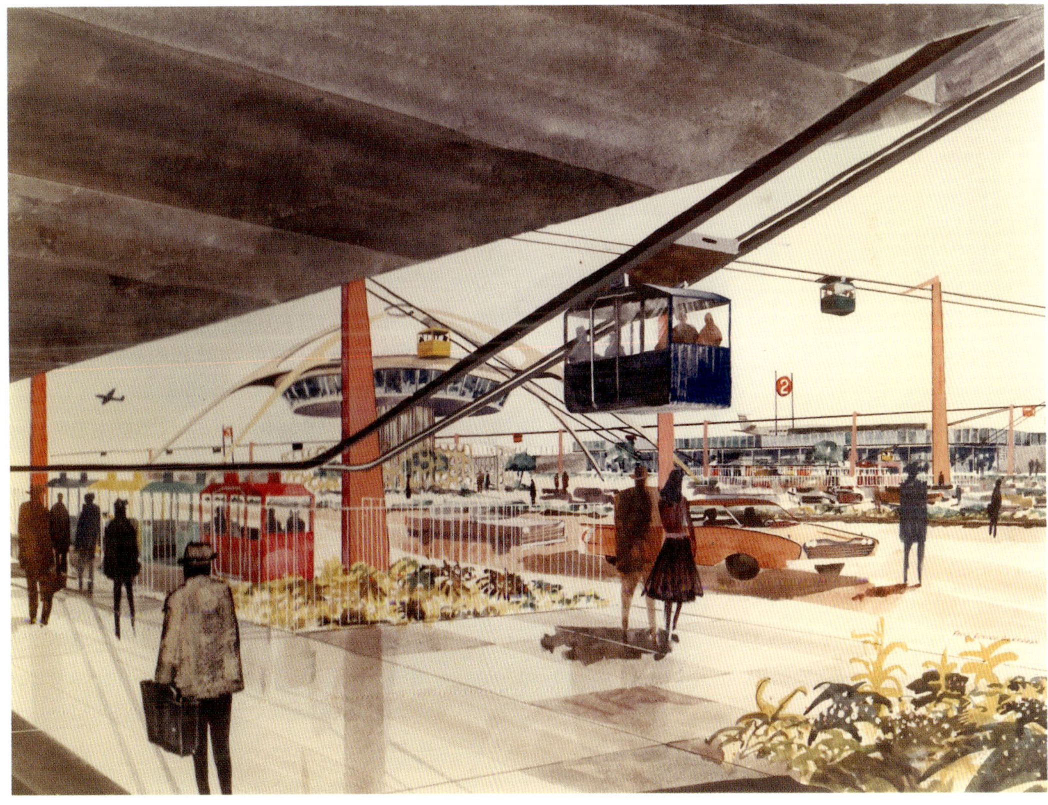

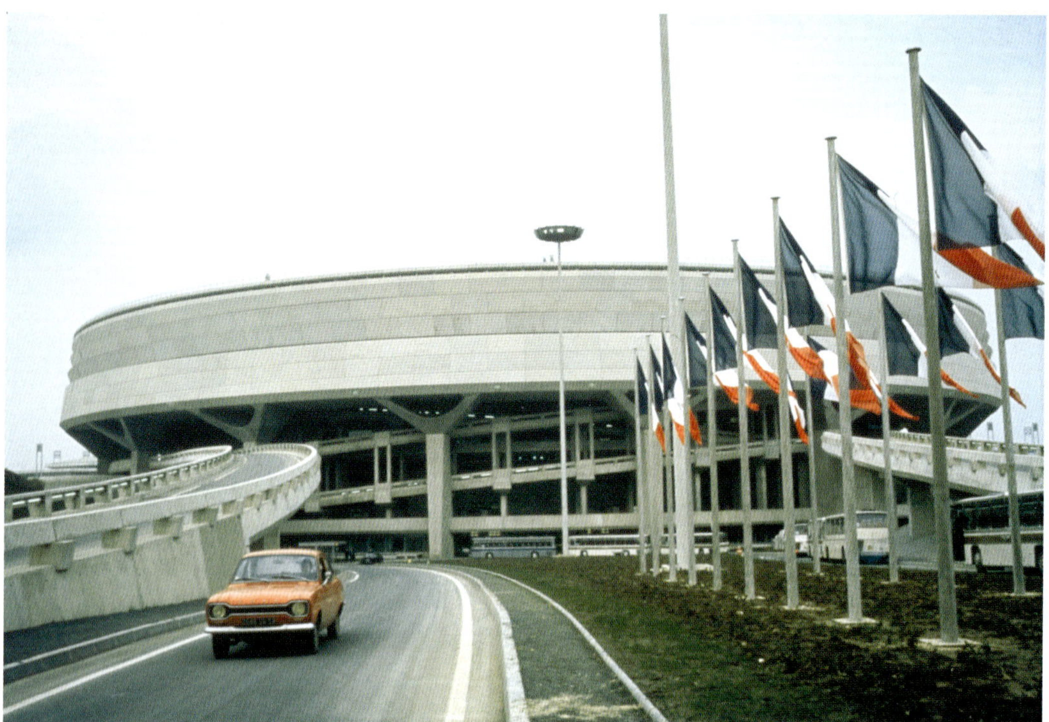

Fig 1.4 Paul Andreu, Terminal 1, Roissy-en-France, 1970. Aéroports de Paris

four thousand parking spaces, more than any other airport had at that time. Regardless of how passengers actually arrived, once inside the terminal they were treated to the new and efficient process that became known internationally as the "Orly-system" of handling bags and customs. Previously, passengers with Paris departures had arrived at the airport through a series of stops and starts. They were gathered at Les Invalides Terminal in town and handled as a group by flight, herded by a hostess. They presented their bags at the in-town terminal and then passed through customs and boarded a bus to the airport. The new system was, on the other hand, one-stop, awarding passengers new-found independence until the moment of boarding. Planners envisioned that passengers would now be able to move at a better pace, that the process would be faster and more convenient. Upon arriving at Orly, travelers individually presented their bags at check-in and passed through customs and passport control, a system that became the model at most airports worldwide.

Planners welcomed the speed and speed-up of travel by air as a challenge on the ground and were concerned with the passenger's experience. The speed of jet travel exacerbated the perception of the slowness of terrestrial travel in the minds of passengers. As Eero Saarinen explained at an airline presentation regarding his commission for Dulles, "It is also felt that with high-speed jet planes, the sense of 'standing around' and the slow processes on the ground will, psychologically, produce even more aggravation and annoyance than now."[22] An unpredictable but sometimes unavoidable slow-down of this class of people who embraced mobility

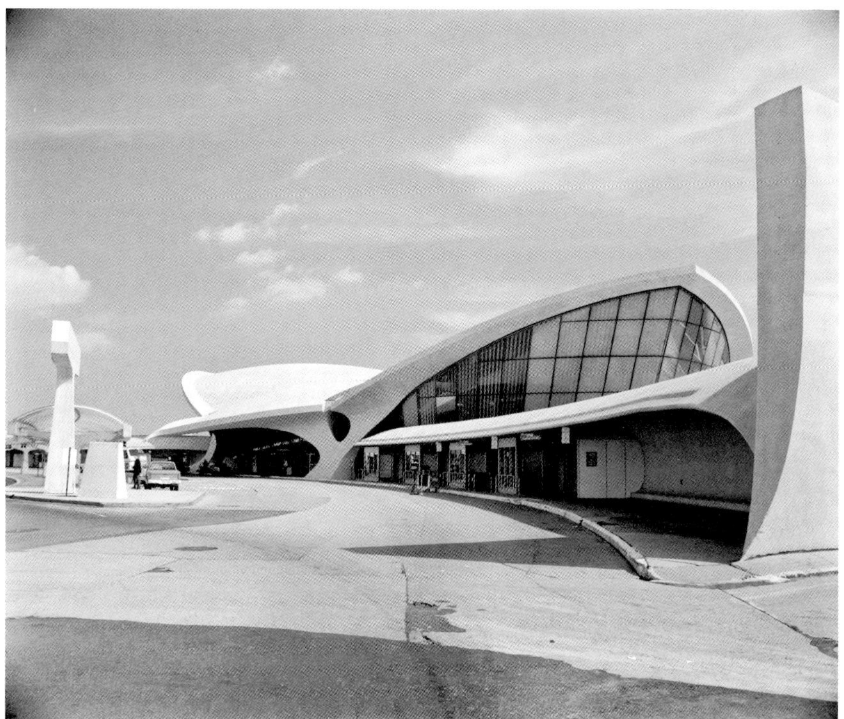

Fig. 1.5 Eero Saarinen, TWA Terminal, John F. Kennedy (originally Idlewild) Airport, New York, 1956–62. Photograph by Balthazar Korab

collided with what became an expectation of smooth and undisturbed travel. Speed was as much imagined as it was real, in other words. As one passenger explained, "From the moment when we realized we could go fast, we wanted it to go faster." Another dreamed that the airport soon would be "just a passthrough where we would never wait because the airplanes would be constantly taking off. We'd walk three seconds and suddenly be in the plane."[23] Employees were quick to note that passengers expressed frustration when planes were more frequently delayed than were trains, and they reported that travelers were especially vexed when nature and weather conditions wreaked havoc on their travel schedule. Despite these rising expectations and growing frustrations, Orly airport employees interviewed in 1965 suggested that airports were on the whole successful in achieving the effect of sensationless flow for their passengers. One interviewee described the airport as a place where passengers were put into pneumatic tubes at one end and spit out at their destination. The speed of travel even provoked observations that the idea of taking a trip or journey—*un voyage*—was being replaced by the notion of pure transit; one observer called this experience *déplacement,* which emphasizes movement itself as the key element in such travel.[24]

The most influential airport designer of the period immediately following the jet age, Paul Andreu, once said, "Any airport must be as much an interchange as a building." Andreu delighted when people likened his best-known airport, the circular Roissy-Charles de Gaulle, to a parking garage (fig. 1.4). He even quipped that no photos could represent his project because they could not "capture the image of movement, [as] they were indifferent to this temporal dimension."[25] His building projects are associated with what became the next wave of airport design in the jumbo-jet era of the 1970s, but Andreu insisted that planners already had established the values and vision of travel by jet that remained unchanged until security concerns arose with the hijackings of the 1970s. Andreu pointed especially to Eero Saarinen as his inspiration, and it was Saarinen, in the prime of his short but important and busy airport-building career, who stated, "An airport should be essentially non-static."[26]

If we have the jet age to thank for establishing the blueprint for all airports since, Saarinen's projects have come to represent the glamour and innovation of this first wave of jet age airport designs.[27] Saarinen did not live to see any of his airport projects completed, although Kennedy airport's TWA Terminal (fig. 1.5) and Dulles Airport were being built when he died in September 1961 from complications following surgery for a brain tumor discovered the month before. His third project, the foreign carrier terminal at Athens Airport, was barely even designed by 1961; Kevin Roche completed it in 1969. The circular shape of the first two projects, as well as Saarinen's creative use of concrete, helped to define a modernist architecture that has fallen in and out of critical regard several times since. Saarinen's reputation for having been complicit in fulfilling the vision of corporate clients had also been part of his critics' disdain for his work.

Despite the attention paid to his terminal buildings then and now, Saarinen saw in airport building something else entirely. In the midst of the Dulles project he wrote to Charles and Ray Eames, "We have not thought about what the building will look like, what the design will be. . . . Those are later functions that result out of what works the best. What works the best is partly what works best for the airlines, but it's also for what works the best for the passengers."[28] In other words, the building was literally the last thing on Saarinen's mind. Although no one had charged him with doing anything other than the "pure" architecture for the project, as he put it, Saarinen boasted that, along with the engineers and the economic consultant, "we created an entirely new system of passenger handling."[29] Saarinen formulated his passenger orientation by thinking of the entire trip and its continuity rather than simply designing a monumental gateway or thinking about where to land and park an airplane. Instead, Saarinen attempted to construct airports around a naturalized idea of how humans moved through space in order to keep them moving in ways he considered "unremarkable"—ways that would keep them moving like a jet. This is consonant with the era's larger inauguration of ergonomic culture. As Henry Dreyfuss, author of the key text *Designing for People* (1955), put it, "When the point of contact between the product and the people becomes a point of friction, then the industrial designer has failed."[30] For Saarinen and others who set about to design jet age airports, flow rather than friction became the goal.

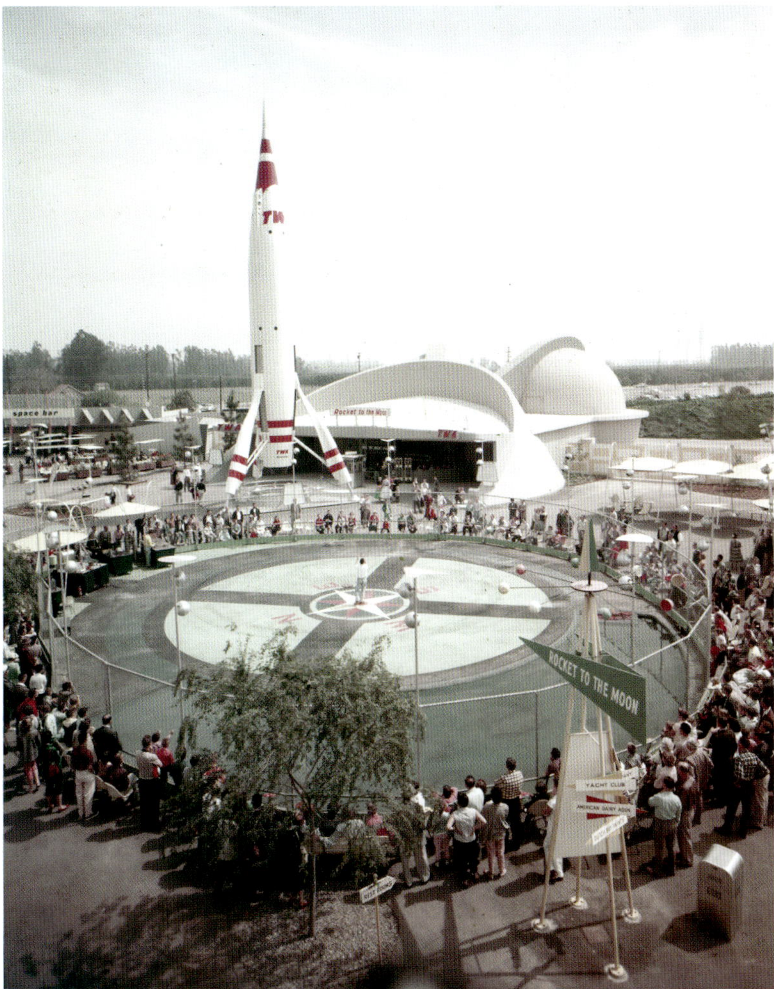

Fig. 1.6 TWA Rocket to the Moon, Tomorrowland, Disneyland, circa 1955–59. © Disney

Saarinen developed his ideas about the needs of passengers while designing the TWA Terminal and conceiving the entire airport project at Dulles. He first followed directions from the airlines, but he also conducted meticulous airport passenger usage studies in both places. During the design phase, he and his firm directly observed and measured how people moved through space rather than simply considering the needs of the airplanes. According to Roche, who worked with Saarinen at the time and later took over much of his architectural practice, "We would travel to airports and time planes taking on passengers . . . the time it took to go from sidewalk to ticketing, checking in your baggage, stopwatch timing all those things."[31]

The TWA Terminal became the iconic airport image due to the distinctive soaring look of the concrete, which people associated with flight or with a bird. Saarinen, however, denied this had been his intention: "The fact that to some people it looked like a bird in flight was really coincidental." The terminal was also made famous by the beautiful photographs by Ezra Stoller that the architect's wife, Aline Saarinen, commissioned when

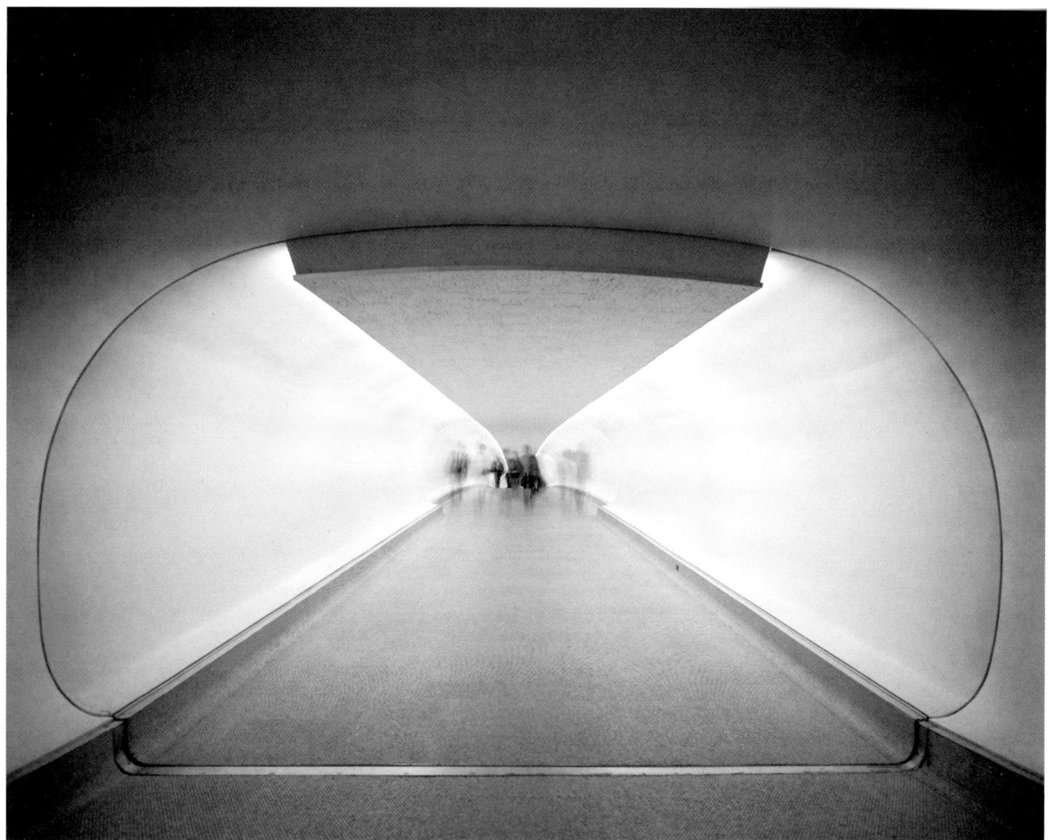

Fig. 1.7 TWA Terminal Tunnel, 1962. Photograph by Ezra Stoller. © Ezra Stoller/ Esto

the job was completed (see figs. 1.1, 1.7).[32] The building also no doubt successfully functioned as a branded object for TWA, and thus the external shell, where the logo appeared, has drawn great attention. Yet in its design and form it also suggests a great deal of visual continuity with Disneyland's TWA Rocket to the Moon ride, which opened in 1955, the year Saarinen received the terminal commission (fig. 1.6).[33] While the TWA Terminal may have been a classic "signature building," when recontextualized among the variety of simultaneous jet age airports, we can see that its interior, as well as the fantasy of fluid motion around which it staged the passengers' movements, was part of a larger vision of new airports. Inside the TWA Terminal passengers were to be handled with optimized precision on the model of the "smoothly functioning machine."[34] To Saarinen, getting through the building mattered more than what it looked like, inside and out. What he cherished, rather than the soaring concrete, were the tunnels and tubes, which made up the in-between spaces called jetways, and the automated luggage systems that moved passengers smoothly through space (fig. 1.7).

In the excitement generated by the TWA Terminal under construction, Saarinen next received a Federal Aviation Administration commission to design Dulles Airport. Guided, he said, by the following questions: "How should an airport terminal function? What is the best method? What

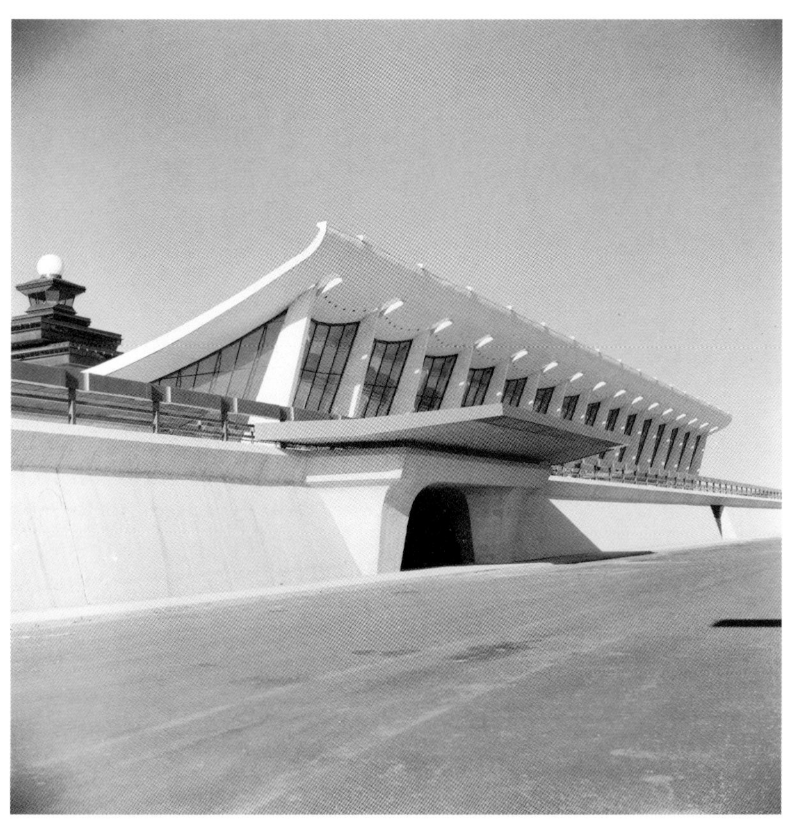

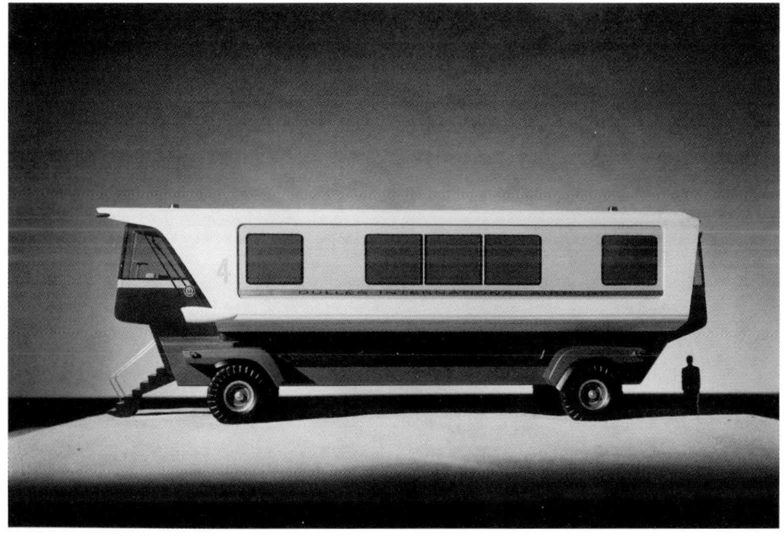

Fig. 1.8 Eero Saarinen, Dulles International Airport, Chantilly, Virginia, 1961–63. Photograph by Balthazar Korab

Fig. 1.9 Eero Saarinen, Dulles Mobile Lounge, model, 1958. Robert C. Lautman Photo. Yale University, Eero Saarinen Papers

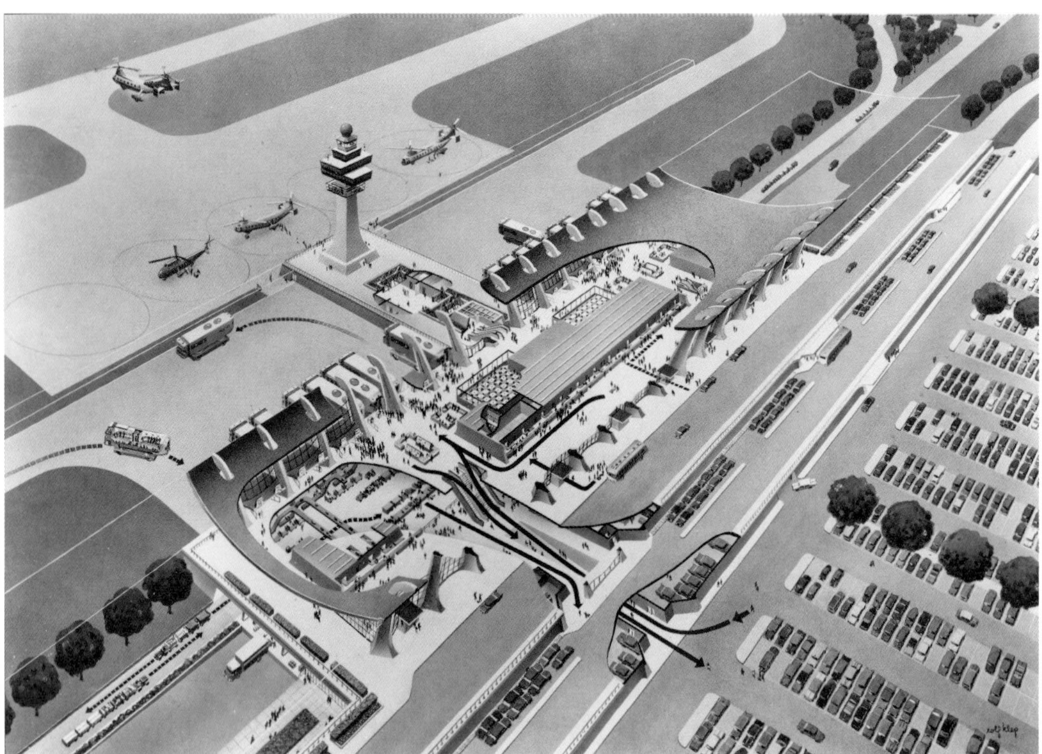

Fig. 1.10 Dulles Airport, Federal Aviation Administration brochure, 1961. Yale University, Eero Saarinen Papers

really happens in a terminal?" Saarinen imagined what was then known as Washington International Airport as "the best thing I have done." Not long after his death, his widow, Aline, confirmed that "my husband and his associates thought the latter [Washington International Airport] will probably be his masterwork."[35]

Saarinen's satisfaction with the project taking shape derived not from the spectacular terminal building that continues to stand for critics as the best interpretation of the airport terminal as "something between earth and sky" (fig. 1.8).[36] Rather, it was from the greenlighting of what he considered the most important of the project's innovations: the much-debated mobile lounge, which the *New York Times* noted was the "heart of the Dulles idea," as well as a "lumbering, awkward-looking land ferry" (fig. 1.9).[37] The lounge would serve as the ultimate both in people-moving devices and as part of the logic of expanding airports. It detached from the main terminal and took passengers directly to the airplane, which could thus be located as far out in the field as needed (fig. 1.10). In a brochure the FAA touted the new airport's use of the lounge: "The passenger has had the same priority as the airplane in the planning for the new airfield."[38] The FAA promoted the mobile lounge as a "dramatic solution to a jet age problem."[39] Although it might have been compared to the buses then in use in Europe to take passengers from the ticket counter to the plane, Saarinen, who thought a bus was a technological step down from the plane, instead asked, "How can one make something that is luxurious? Then it struck us: by combining the departure lounge and the moving vehicle into a single convenience, and by combining *that* with a covered gangplank which hitches directly to the plane."[40]

The lounge made a complete separation between the terminal buildings and the airplane possible. Passengers would board planes directly from the mobile lounge, a vehicle fifteen feet wide by sixty feet long that detached from the terminal and attached to the plane, and could remain in the field or at a servicing station, thus bypassing the need for what most planners, critics, and passengers considered the plague of expanding airports: the lengthy walks, often of more than a mile, from the main buildings to the gates. Saarinen's proud devotion to this project resided in assuring passenger flow rather than in building the monumental architecture for which most people know Dulles today.

Due to the cost and suspicion over the unusual concept, along with the logistical challenges it would entail, it took a great investment of time and energy to get the airlines to agree to the mobile lounge, even though Saarinen was adapting an FAA report originally commissioned in 1953.[41] So committed was Saarinen to this idea that he made an animated film to pitch the project. Finding his film ultimately inadequate, he also proposed to his partners in the project, Burns and McDonnell Engineering and Amman and Whitney, that he commission his good friends Charles and Ray Eames to make a different film to pitch the advantages of the mobile lounge, a film like the one the pair had made for IBM.[42] As Charles Eames explained, "Eero was having really a tough time with the official groups involved. . . . And he said, '. . . it takes three hours (to explain the lounge concept as the heart of the airport plan). And they just can't sit still for it . . . if we had a film that could state the concept of Dulles Airport . . . if we could state it in fifteen minutes, God, it would be great.'"[43]

Charles Eames claims that they spent a day with Saarinen in July 1958 to consider the project, although that seems unlikely, given that on July 7 Saarinen and Roche sent more than two-hundred-fifty pages of research to the Eames Office in California, including the script and slides of a presentation Saarinen had delivered to the airlines on July 1, which contained his unsuccessful pitch for the mobile lounge. Additional materials included a copy of the 1953 FAA report "Proposed Mobile Gate House," which had inspired Saarinen, and materials that appear to be passenger studies such as the ones that Roche said they used for the design of the TWA Terminal and that were, according to Aline Saarinen, the result of a "conscientious and intensive research program . . . undertaken by the whole staff. . . . The possibility of the mobile lounge and the research into its workability, etc. occupied an intensive three months—and was a seriously studied thing."[44] The materials charted airport research on the number of passenger steps, length of trips (timed by stopwatch) from passengers' arrival at the terminal to enplaning, as well as descriptions of the new problem of jet blast, which made it desirable to keep passengers and planes apart.[45]

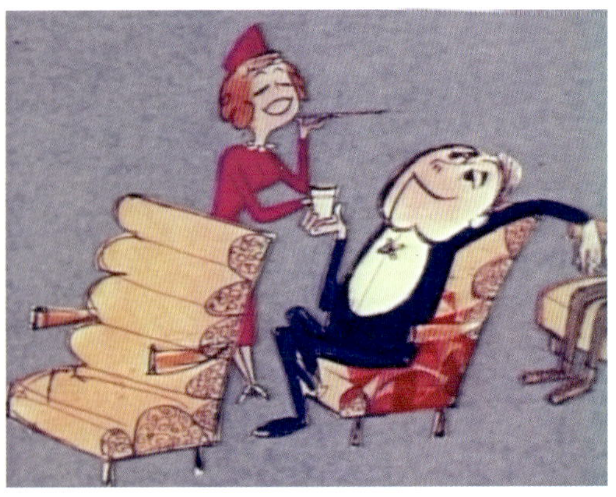

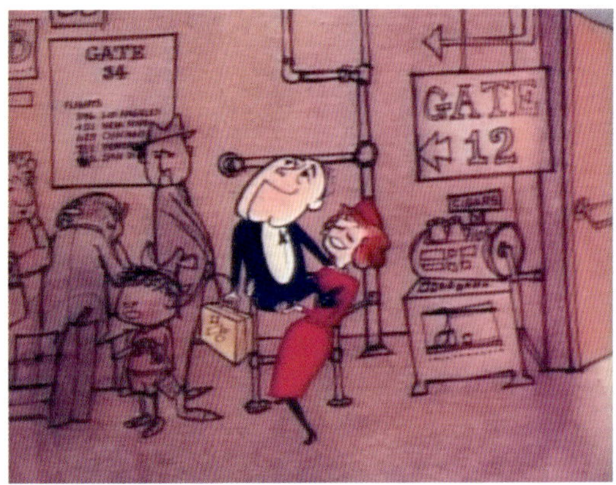

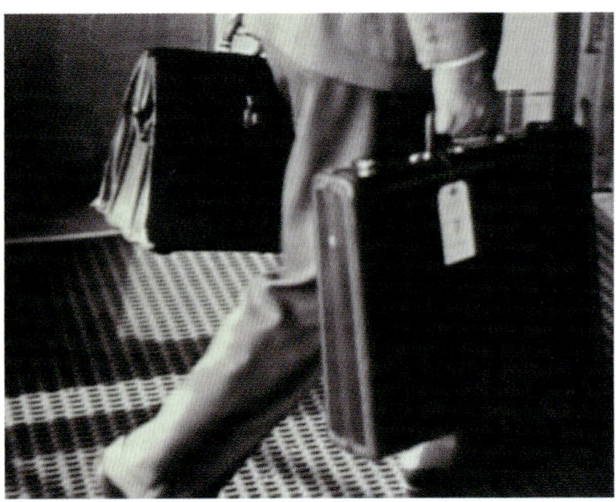

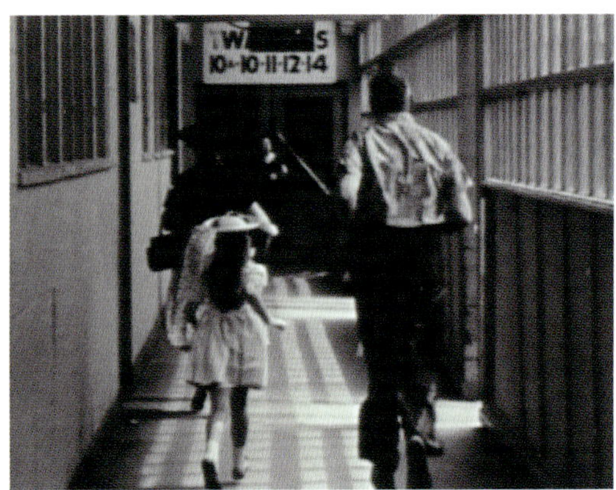

Figs. 1.11–1.18 From *The Expanding Airport: A Study of Service and Convenience for Washington International,* 1958, directed by Charles and Ray Eames. DVD screen captures

The film made by the Eameses, *The Expanding Airport: A Study of Service and Convenience for Washington International,* visualized the vast amount of data Saarinen provided and condensed it into an appealing form that was only nine minutes long. It used the familiar very flat and economical mid-century style of animated drawings penned by artist Glen Fleck, which were combined with photographs.[46] The film's narrative begins with a new-fangled jet plane emerging from behind the clouds, and then we enter a schematically drawn jet interior where a lounging male passenger is attended to by a stewardess (fig. 1.11). The comfort of life in the air is immediately and comically contrasted to the problems on the ground, where the flight attendant is forced to carry her passenger in order to continue the luxurious service and comfort offered in flight (fig. 1.12).

The problem of long distances and of the passengers' need to walk them is laid out in three effective ways. First, the total distance walked by all passengers is depicted graphically: a map of the United States is marked with black lines going coast to coast as the narrator announces that that distance is translated into one hundred cross-country journeys plus twenty walks around the world (depicted by a globe with black lines circumnavigating it), plus four round trips between the earth and the moon, depicted with the addition of a moon now tethered to earth with lines that represent a trip between the two

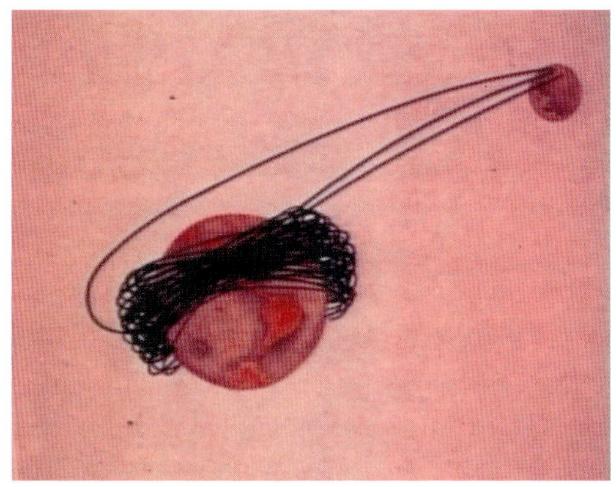

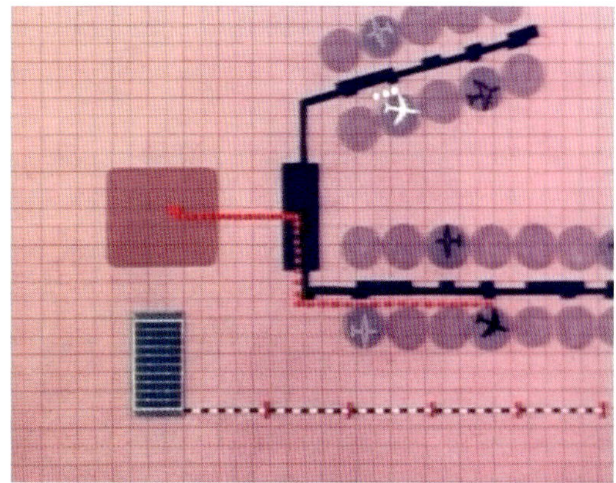

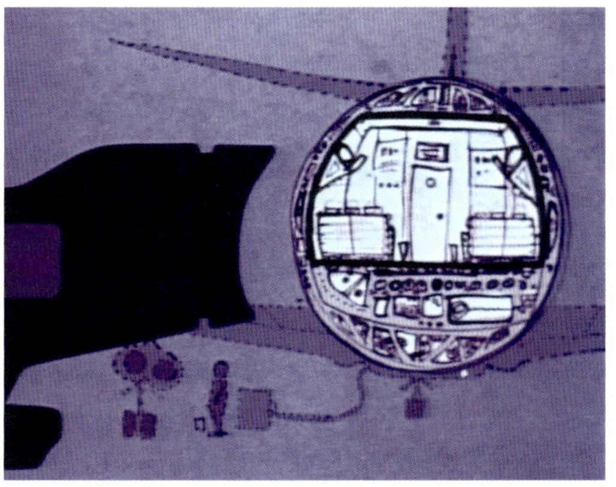

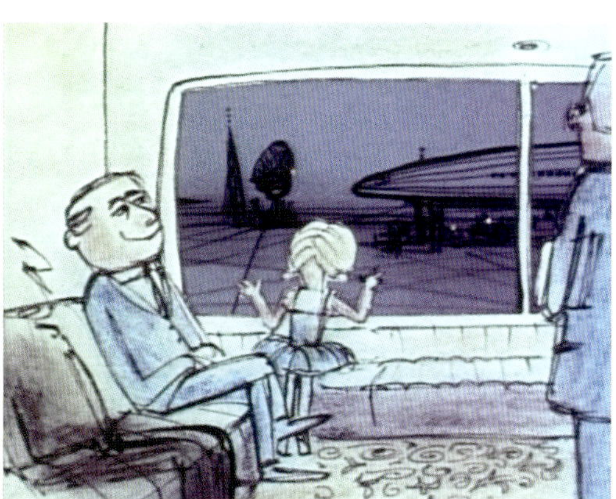

(fig. 1.13). The story is then told as that of the "average" passenger (a diverse group of passengers is melded into the silhouette of a businessman) whose journey is depicted in diagrammatic fashion as five times the length of a football field (fig. 1.14). The film warns that this problem will increase as airports expand to accommodate jet service. Here, the film changes visual idiom to great effect. To a soundtrack of stepping heels, the film cuts in quickly changing black-and-white documentary-style photographs of men, women, and children carrying their loads through long airport distances and getting more and more "irritated." The slowdowns brought on by high-speed flights have transformed a romantic adventure into a major chore (figs. 1.15, 1.16).

The film is designed to show that the passenger and his movement are the priorities in the new airport. It touts the mobile lounge—a "spacious room isolated from fumes and noise"—as offering convenience and luxury. In addition, there is great value in the "freedom and flexibility it gives to airport planning." In other words, today's luxury would be tomorrow's necessity, because the future had already arrived. There is little reference to the terminal building itself—the exterior does not appear once in the film—no doubt because it had not yet been designed. The terminal is sketched merely as a large central building from which the proposed solution, the mobile lounge, would detach.

The film predicts that the growing terminals would begin to shrink through the use of the lounge, as what used to be the fingers of the terminal would now detach and transport passengers to the plane, to which the lounge would seamlessly connect by virtue of a pneumatic door connection (fig. 1.17). This new process would also augment the airport terminal concessions, as passengers would patronize them in the main terminal before boarding the lounge, which would be open for only fifteen minutes. Additionally, the lounge addressed the challenges of constant change and the need for adaptation: "In the lounge, the passenger has started his trip and can be ferried to his aircraft from where it is most convenient from an operations standpoint" (fig. 1.18). The film closes against an airport where vertical takeoff jets and rockets represent the travel of the near future and whose introduction the new airport was already prepared to welcome.[47] The film helped persuade the FAA to approve the key element of the Dulles plan for at least two decades, until the lounges began to serve newly built midfield terminals, suggesting that the airport had not anticipated the developments of the future as effectively as it had promised.

It is, of course, impossible to predict the future, no matter the intentions of "planners" or the success they realized in designing for growth at airports such as LAX. While that airport's focus on functionality was hardly singular among projects oriented to meet the jet, it stands out from other airport renovations because its planners were so openly committed to building for change. Phased building would subsequently characterize all airport projects. But as early as 1960, the Los Angeles Department of Airports Annual Report explained, "We have learned that an airport system is never completed. Constant change is routine in airport operations; maintaining the status quo is synonymous with being 'out of date.'"[48] In a retrospective explanation of the design framework for LAX, Charles Luckman wrote, "We were then, in 1955, planning an airport to be constructed by 1960, which was to be large enough for 1980."[49]

Inspired by an enthusiasm for the radical changes in travel that the jet had made possible, which drew Los Angeles into closer connection with the rest of the United States and outward toward the Pacific, and given its special role as a center of aviation, it makes perfect sense that Los Angeles International Airport, once merely the Mines bean fields of Inglewood sandwiched between the ocean and the oil refineries of El Segundo, became a shiny new example of what a jet age airport might be. By the fall of 1961, after nearly ten intensive years of planning and building, Los Angeles opened the first American airport redesigned for the jet age. How far planners had come in just seven years from when a concerned journalist remarked, "It seems incredible . . . that Los Angeles, which is perhaps the greatest center of American aviation—the largest industry in the nation and the state—should in the year 1955 still be operating with interim airport facilities."[50] The airport's embrace of planning for obsolescence and expansion, its decentralization of terminals, and its emphasis on passenger movement aimed at "breaking the ground barrier" (the challenges of getting to the airport quickly), were innovations that set the terms for other airports. In fact, in the Dulles planning materials, Saarinen explicitly refers to the decentralized LAX plan, which he had consulted.[51] Prescient site planning meant that the Los Angeles airport would handle anticipated increases both in the number of arriving planes and in the numbers of passengers flying well into the half century after its jet age redesign. LAX is one of the most outdated airports around today precisely because its flexible design never required the kind of major overhauls that rendered terminals such as TWA's in New York so outdated as to be beyond use.[52]

Despite local challenges in obtaining funding for an airport renovation, the Los Angeles Department of Airports commissioned the firm of Pereira & Luckman to conceive a master plan in 1952. By that time, William Pereira, whose eventual contributions to the architecture and planning of Southern

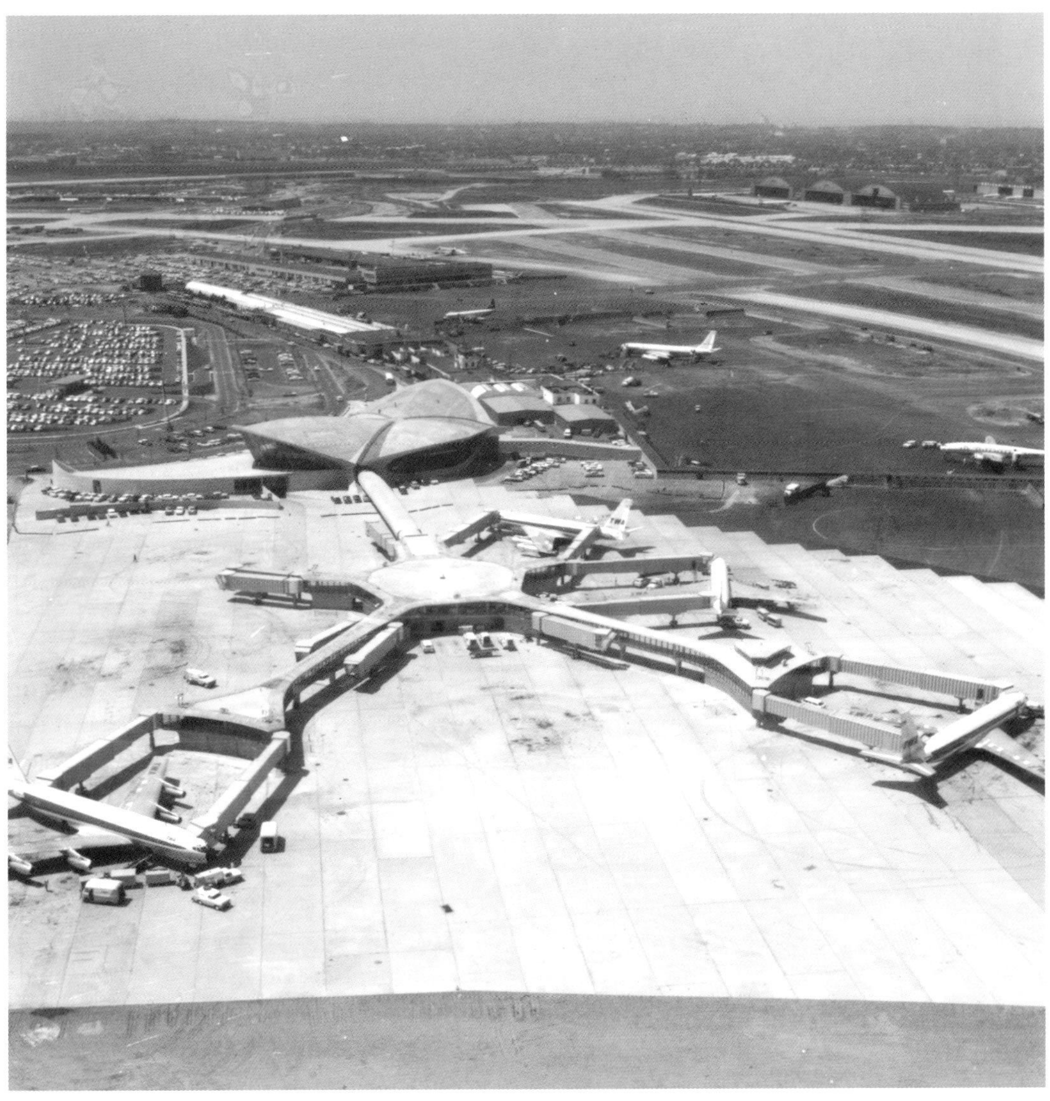

Fig. 1.19 TWA Terminal, circa 1962. Yale University, Eero Saarinen Papers

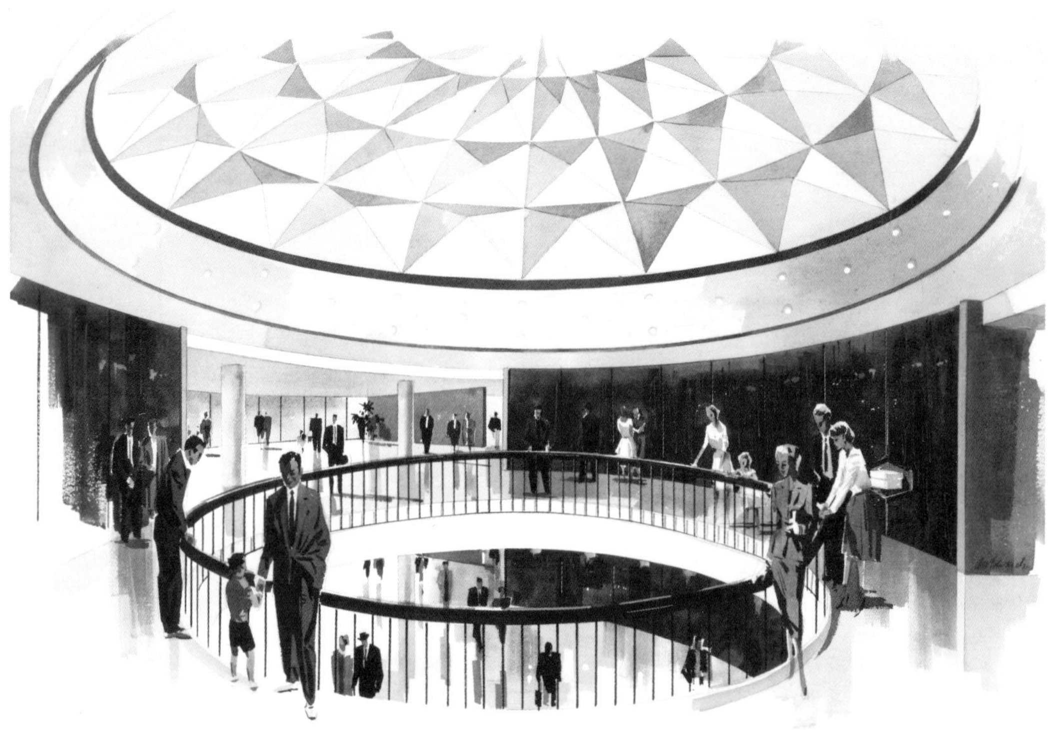

Fig. 1.22 Interior view of Satellite Rotunda from *Master Plan Drawings*

system of underground tunnels that led to satellite terminals. As Luckman put it, "The only way to solve the complex problem of a modern airport is to separate the people from the planes."[55]

Decentralization of the airport terminals was the linchpin in a vision geared to achieving better continuity in travel between ground and air for what the planners bet would be new masses of travelers. According to Grant Anderson, the chief engineer for the Los Angeles Department of Airports during the era of expansion, with such decentralization planners could better manage passenger growth: "There is a limit to how many people can be processed in a single building," he explained about the project in retrospect. The idea was to create a proliferation in the number of buildings that would separate check-in from departure, and such buildings would operate as interchanges rather than as holding places. Thus the designers gave particular attention to building tunnels that were 375 feet to 575 feet long, with "color, special lighting and decoration." The tunnels used lighting effects to make them appear shorter. Some members of the LAX project also recommended installing moving sidewalks within the tunnels to further automate and speed the process. In 1964, the Astroway opened in the American Airlines tunnel.[56]

The satellites themselves were elliptical, which enabled the planes to taxi right up to the edge of the building (figs. 1.20, 1.21). Each satellite boasted ten plane-loading positions; the removal of the fingers not only decreased walking distances for passengers but also gave the planes greater

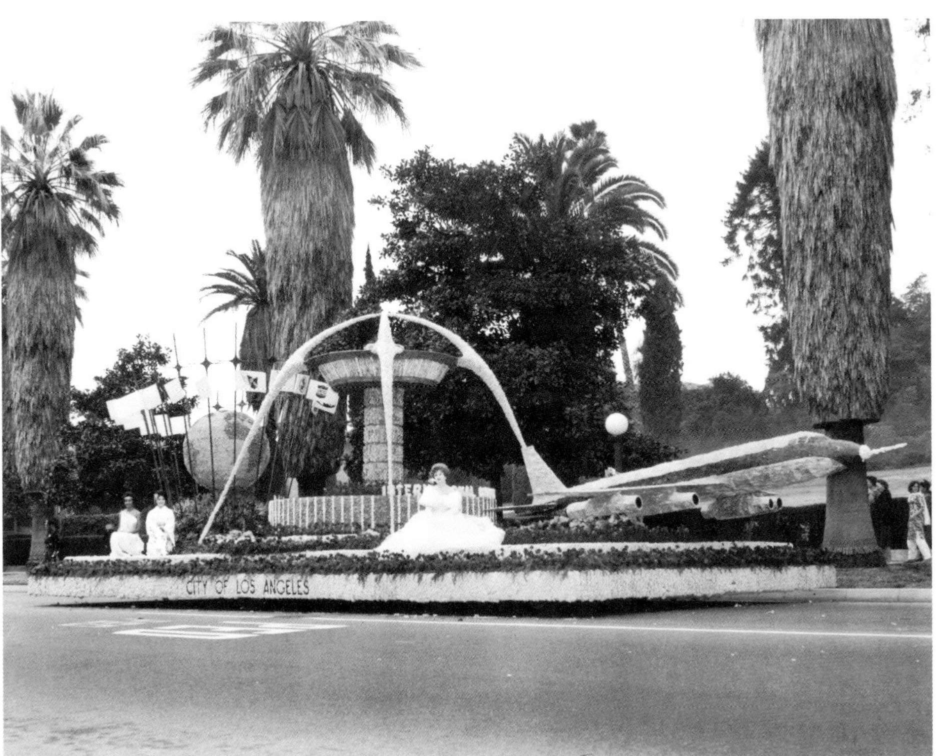

Fig. 1.23 Los Angeles Float, Tournament of Roses Parade, 1962

maneuverability. Passengers accessed planes in the two-story satellites by climbing a circular staircase lit from above by a glass dome (fig. 1.22). Each satellite could expand by a possible 50 percent with the addition of a mezzanine, an element that signals the expansion plans already imagined in the initial design. All of the satellites had restaurants with California themes, such as Old Hollywood and California Desert Flowers, managed by Interstate Host, a food supplier that specialized in concessions on toll roads and in steamship shopping centers.[57] The 1967 expansion plan, which Pereira designed after his split from Luckman, even proposed something he called a "holding gate" in the satellite buildings themselves, which consisted of a space in which enplaning passengers assembled. It was to attach and detach rather than act as a structural part of the satellite building. He called this a form of "mobile architecture" and was clearly influenced by the mobile lounge concept that had been introduced at Dulles in 1962.[58] For Pereira, the less permanent and durable the building structure, the better.

Although Pereira viewed architecture as a "series of contrasting spaces which solve specific functional and aesthetic problems," his work focused almost exclusively on creating functional and orderly spaces. For the airport, he and Luckman defined their challenge as moving people rather than planes. The "movement of people can be intercepted and diverted by architecture, just as a dam affects a river."[59] If a particular space required a passenger to slow down, Pereira simply proposed putting a rough surface on the floor. He wanted signs at the sides of throughways in order to divert people away from the main paths. In other words, not only did form follow function, it would expressly shape use and passenger mobility.

The lion's share of the design effort went into the work of moving passengers from their cars to their planes as seamlessly as possible. Such priorities, however, made for poor symbolism. Public transport buildings may have been evolving past the St. Pancras train station phase, but critics and visitors also yearned for such things as emblems in order to "see" the otherwise diffuse and mobile experience of being at LAX and in fluid motion. The Theme Building appears to have filled that role.

Airport planners did not initially envision the Theme Building as the airport's main symbol, since they reckoned that such a symbol would have to be explicitly functional. They imagined that the new control tower, the nation's tallest such tower, which housed not only the air- and ground-control operations but also the DOA's administrative offices, would stand in for their project. Its location at the airport's eastern and then main entrance (now the Century Boulevard entrance) meant that it greeted the majority of passengers and visitors. So clearly important was it that the Control Tower was used to illustrate the DOA's 1958 and 1959 Annual Reports. The 1958 report predicted that the "tower will be the identifying landmark of the airport and will serve a dual function."[60] The Flame of Freedom and court of flags were positioned in front of the 172-foot-tall building at the newly named address of 1 World Way. When the city of Los Angeles selected LAX to represent it in the 1962 Tournament of Roses Parade, the float featured both the control tower and the Theme Building (fig. 1.23). Additionally, when the airport put up its Christmas decorations, they lighted the tower with a cross, and the Theme Building, its whimsical partner, got its own Christmas tree atop it (figs. 1.24, 1.25).

The Theme Building served as a legacy from the earlier plan, which had conceived of having a central building; this is what was chosen to be built in its place. Many people had a hand in the final details of the design of the structure, whose 135-foot-high parabolic arches were initially scheduled to be clad in aluminum for an even more futuristic look (budget concerns determined the use of stucco instead). Having imagined the space as occupied by a building, the DOA set out to give it a purpose, but even the persistence of its generic name, the Theme Building, suggests its lack of mission. Ever mindful of the airport's need to pay its own bills, planners turned the building into a revenue-generating source: it would house a restaurant and an observation deck that charged admission (until the cost of maintaining it as a fee-paying space was not even worth the effort). It also housed Host's enormous kitchen, which serviced all the satellite restaurants and offered a commissary for employees, on the ground level behind the perforated concrete wall that surrounded the circular base.

The Theme Building eventually outshone the more pragmatic Control Tower. It was open to visitors who could overlook the airport from an eighty-one-foot-high observation deck (fig. 1.26). In its first month of operation, the deck drew three thousand people. It was open seven days a week

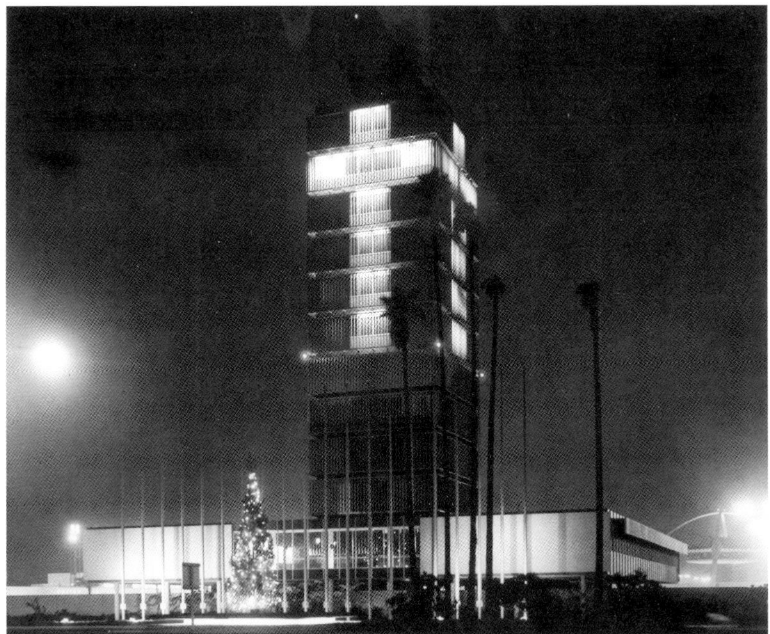

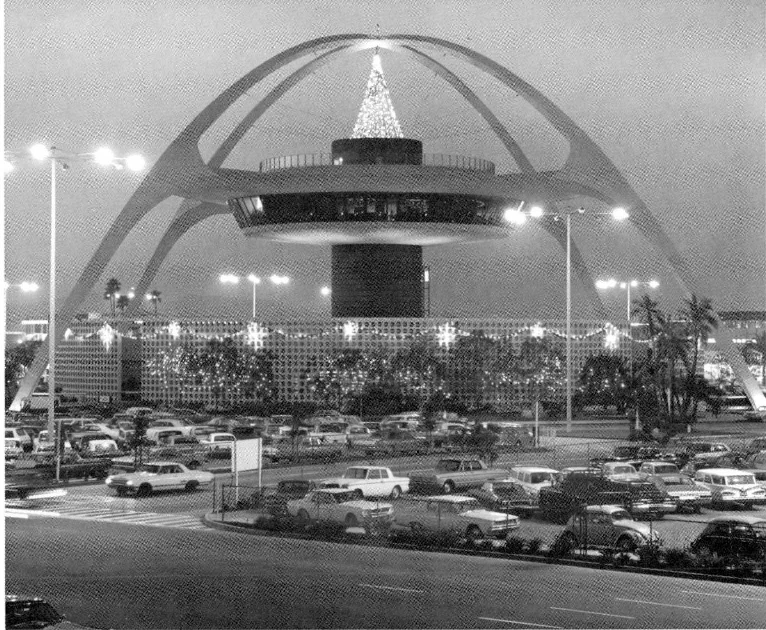

Figs. 1.24 and 1.25 Los Angeles International Airport, Christmas 1962. Control Tower and Theme Building

and would often host a thousand visitors a day during vacation months and on weekends.[61] The entrance featured a "Court of Stars"—backlighted panels of color transparencies of the heavens taken at the Mount Palomar Observatory. The restaurant became a destination for those flying as well as for others who simply wanted to visit to see the people who flew in planes, anticipating their own future trips.

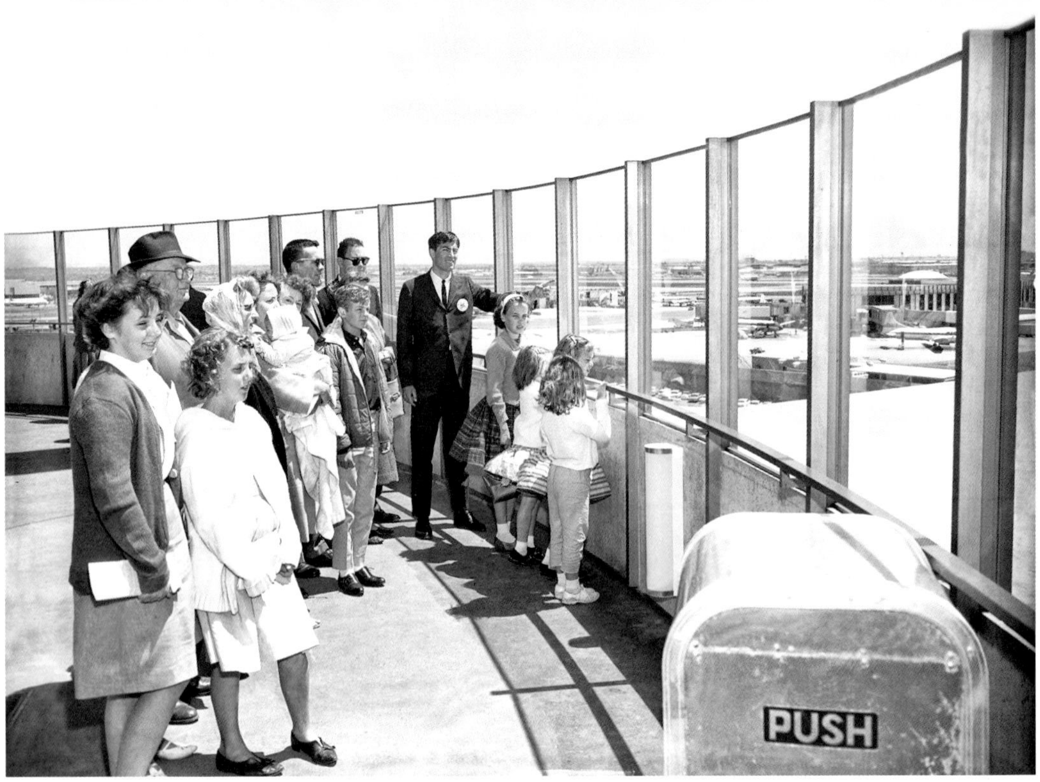

Fig. 1.26 Observation Deck atop Theme Building, circa 1963

Jet age airports often had as many visitors as travelers. In the Theme Building restaurant, international tourist sites decorated the murals, hostesses dressed in costumes from France, Japan, Scandinavia, and Spain, and the menu offered equally international fare, such as "Swedish meatballs," rather than local fare. At the Theme Building and the airport more generally, visitors could breach both time and space.

Most significant, the Theme Building's lack of apparent purpose fostered the idea that it should have "style," because style attracted visitors and defined the purpose of a jet age airport. The style that the architects chose clearly links the building to the broader landscape of Southern California's already well-developed "fantasy architecture" and its greatest contributor: Walt Disney. If the fantasy architecture of Los Angeles had multiple ties to the movies (and Pereira's earlier career as a film art director often is invoked to better grasp his design principles), an even tighter circle of designers connects the airport to Walt Disney, linking entertainment culture and urban infrastructural projects such as the airport.[62]

In the Theme Building we can see a link between Welton Becket, Pereira, Luckman, and Walt Disney, whose own career in the movies had recently been eclipsed by the phenomenal success of his major planning project, Disneyland, which opened in July 1955 and was itself directly responsible for a great deal of the traffic increase at LAX in the period.[63] The airport and Disneyland were also linked in public discourse. In a preview article, the *New York Times* called the airport a "Disneyland for adults."[64] When the airport opened in 1962, FAA chairman and California native son Najeeb Halaby quipped, "You will have the first airport terminal area specifically designed for the jet age and it well may achieve some of the world-wide renown, some of the international acclaim as—who knows?—Disneyland."[65]

By the time the planning team decided on the look of the Theme Building, Becket was already known for his "total design" concept, which characterized such projects as Bullock's of Pasadena and the Capital Records Tower. Although there have been many ways to describe the concept, author Chris Nichols put it well when he explained that it involves "clear story-telling of an environment that is art directed to be both authentic and idealized, is visually calming, emotionally directive and effectively creates the feeling of stepping into another world."[66] The airport's iconic building and its flying saucer look was designed the year Disneyland opened. Becket and Disney knew each other well as neighbors in Holmby Hills, and Becket and Pereira, linked in the LAX joint venture, had worked together on the flagship theater of the Pan Pacific movie theater chain in the 1940s. Walt Disney, in the initial design phase for Disneyland, commissioned Pereira & Luckman to offer a preliminary study.[67] Despite his rejection of their theme park plan, Disney hired Pereira & Luckman to design the Disneyland Hotel in Anaheim from 1954–55, the same period in which they worked on the airport. The projects share a design dedicated to people-moving rather than to monumental architecture (fig. 1.27).[68]

Fig. 1.27 Disneyland Hotel with tram and iron beams, 1957

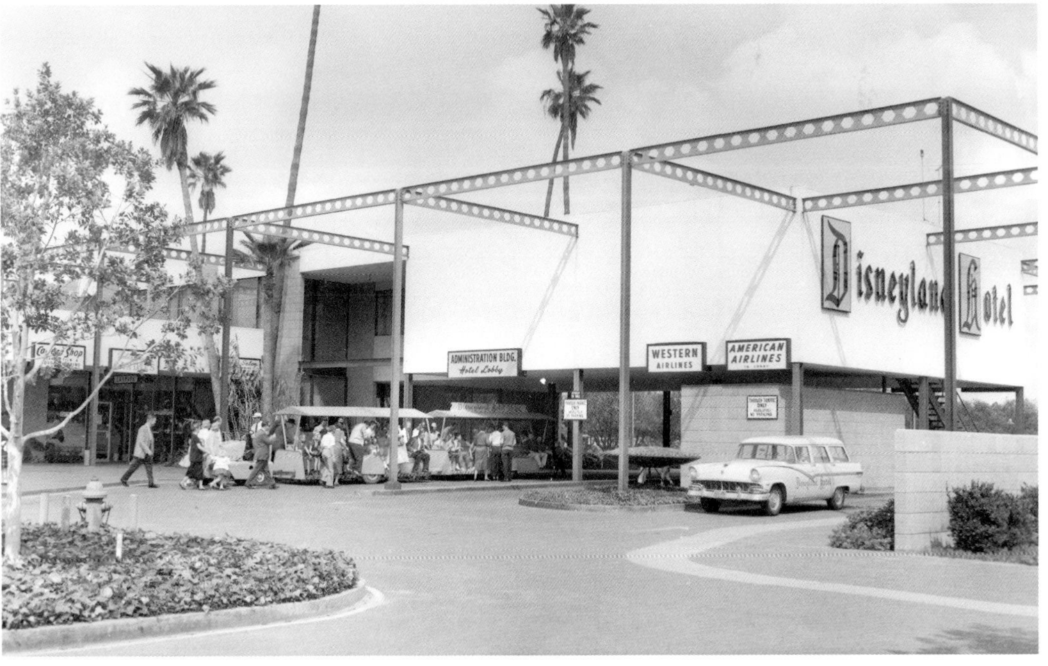

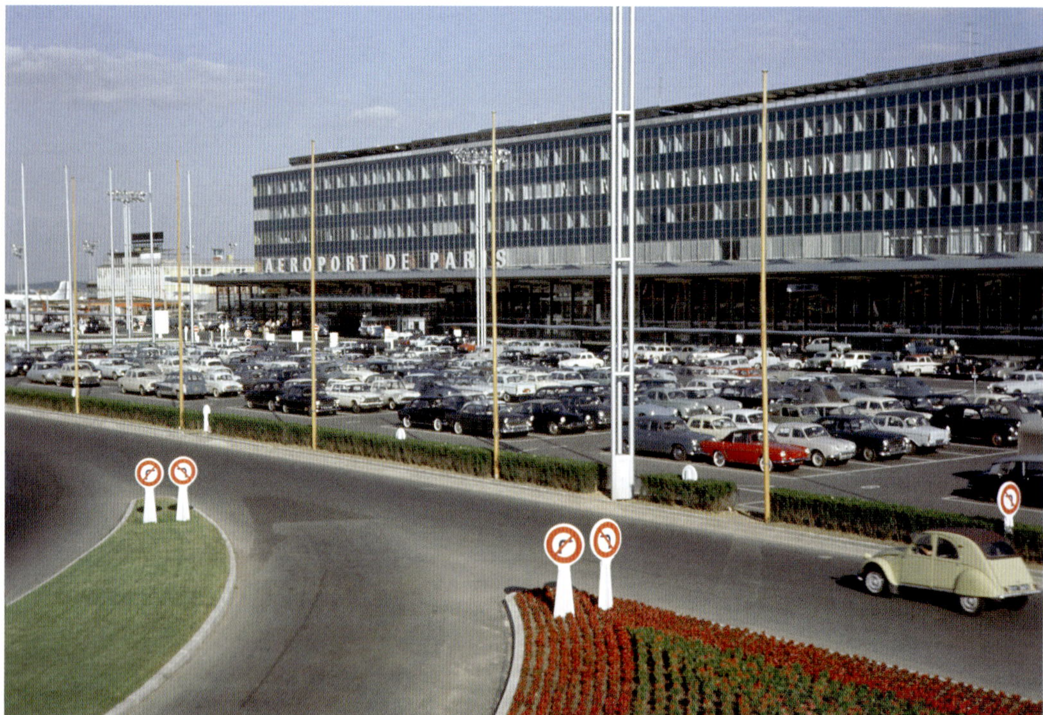

Fig. 1.28 Façade of Orly Airport, near Paris, 1961

For reviewers and patrons alike, eager to interpret the airport, the Theme Building reinforced that one aspect of fantasy architecture is its futurism. As *Life* put it in an article about California, which included praise for the state's many "free-wheeling shapes with a feel for the future," the Theme Building at LAX is "all future, no past."[69] Airport public relations materials observed that the building denoted the airport's "futuristic theme."[70] The Theme Building's lack of function also assured that it was destined to last. The old Control Tower became so outdated that it was closed, and only the DOA offices remained there. A new air-traffic control tower, located much closer to the Theme Building in the middle of the field of operations, opened in 1996.

Armed with a vision that airports would always be obsolescent, the team led by Pereira & Luckman succeeded in defining jet age airport planning as antimonumental and in a constant state of becoming even while creating an icon. The Theme Building would stand as a symbol of the once-optimistic moment when airports produced what seemed like the future in the present, and to extend, for the first time, the wonder of jet motion to the mere mortals left to navigate the challenges of moving on the ground.

If an icon such as the Theme Building gave symbolic weight to a largely functionalist airport scheme such as that at LAX, Orly turned such airport functionalism into a kind of monumentalism of its own. It turned the airport almost into an exhibition.[71] Orly not only offered the spectacle of being technologically up-to-date but it also emphasized watching jets come and go, which helped make the sensationlessness of travel by jet an all the more remarkable accomplishment of the moment in air travel.

As much as any other airport, Orly defined the new jet age facilities and service. It had the most traffic of any continental airport and was second only to London's Heathrow among airports outside the United States in jet traffic throughout the 1960s. More important, it offered proportionally more jet service than any other airport in the world during the early jet age and thus became associated with the plane's novelty.[72] Pan Am's continuous jet service began with trips between New York and Paris in 1958 with service into Le Bourget, north of Paris (where Lindbergh landed in 1927), although the newer airport at Orly would expand to welcome the jets. While Boeing and Pan Am led the way in transatlantic jet travel, the French plane manufacturers and airline were not far behind. Sud Aviation introduced its Caravelle, which became a staple of middle-distance trips. When United Airlines purchased twenty Caravelles that year, the supply of planes became a thoroughly transnational affair, with France, one of the few airplane-producing nations other than the United States, supplying the U.S. for the first time. Air France also offered the largest air network, in terms of miles, by a single airline.

The Aéroports de Paris (ADP), an Association de 1901 (a private organization in the public interest), created in 1945 in the wake of the reversion of airports to civil traffic from military use in World War II, directed the renovation of Orly. The site required enormous reconstruction because bombs had all but destroyed the airfield.[73] Orly had originally served as Paris's second airport when it opened in 1932 as a landing field after the main airport Le Bourget opened in 1919. It stood just thirteen kilometers from the city's southern entrance at the Porte d'Italie, which spurred fantasies of speedy arrival to the center of town. Between 1949 and 1960, passenger volume at Orly quintupled from 720,000 passengers to 3,638,000, making it the world's fourth-busiest airport after New York, Chicago, and London.[74] Orly had been built to handle 4 million passengers per year and would expand to serve twice that number. The renovation also included a plan for a second expansion in the form of a second terminal, which opened as Orly West in 1971.

Orly looked like a big-box store; its enormity and emphasis on function created an antimonumental kind of monumentalism, especially by virtue of the length of its single façade (fig. 1.28). Despite Orly's plainness, its scale impressed observers. As one analyst noted, "We understand the necessity of large-scale airports. . . . It seems important to magnify the image of the plane and man's technological power."[75] The main terminal consisted of a six-story structure above the ground and two stories below. Designed by architect-engineer Henri Vicariot, it was made of glass, aluminum, and stainless steel, which created a contemporary look and simplified maintenance (although the head of the ADP explained that they did need to devise a purpose-built machine with which to wash the windows). Pierre Boursicot, head of the ADP's administration, described the terminal as "elegant, without wasteful

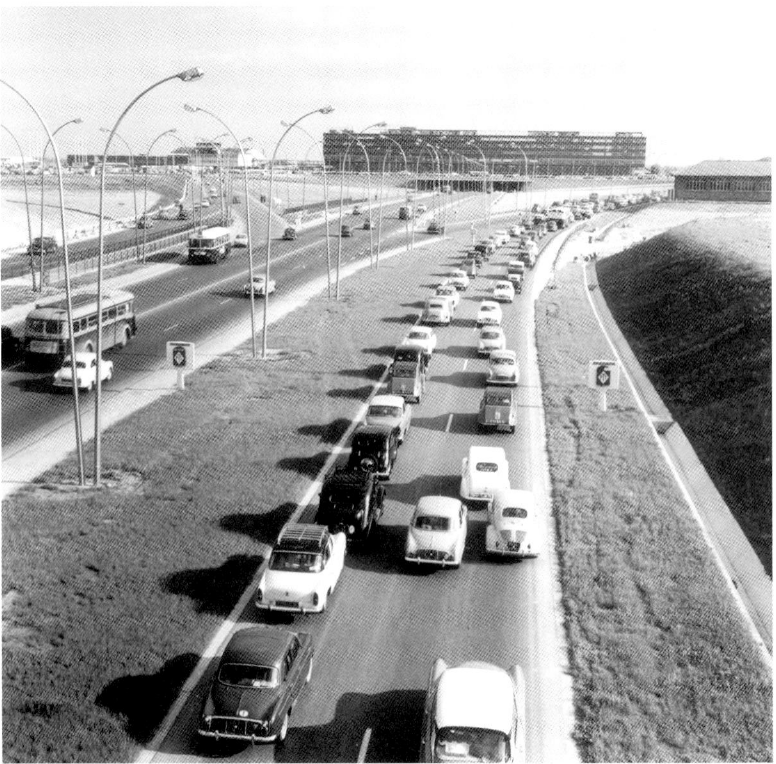

Fig. 1.29 Autoroute to the Airport, circa 1961

luxury, but dressed nevertheless in noble materials that highlight the purity of their line and practical, practical above all else."[76] The airport did not need beautiful decorative schemes; it impressed with its comprehensive offerings and its ability to process the numerous people going through it, which began with its link to the autoroute (fig. 1.29). Although planners boasted that the airport was the biggest building project in France since Les Invalides under Louis XIV in the seventeenth century, and that its length was the distance from the Opéra to the Louvre, they also celebrated the fact that the maximum distance passengers would have to walk would be no more than four hundred meters—about the length of a train platform.[77]

As a node in a system of travel, Orly functioned as a passthrough for passengers. Yet the airport also introduced elaborate non-flight-related facilities that we associate with the "aerotropolis" of today.[78] Orly became a rival city of the future, host to a large number of passengers laying over and waiting to board, passengers with time to spend before their flights departed since they now arrived at the airport on their own. Promotional material noted that the airport would feature a modern hotel with televisions in each room; a Hilton eventually opened at Orly, with ground broken in 1963 and an inauguration in 1965.[79] The airport boasted three restaurants on the third level, each of which could be accessed from the terraces. One of the restaurants was named Les Trois Soleils (The Three Suns) after the title of the enormous commissioned artwork that decorated its wall: a modern tapestry by Jean Lurçat, the key figure of the tapestry revival.[80] The airport had, additionally, a huge bar,

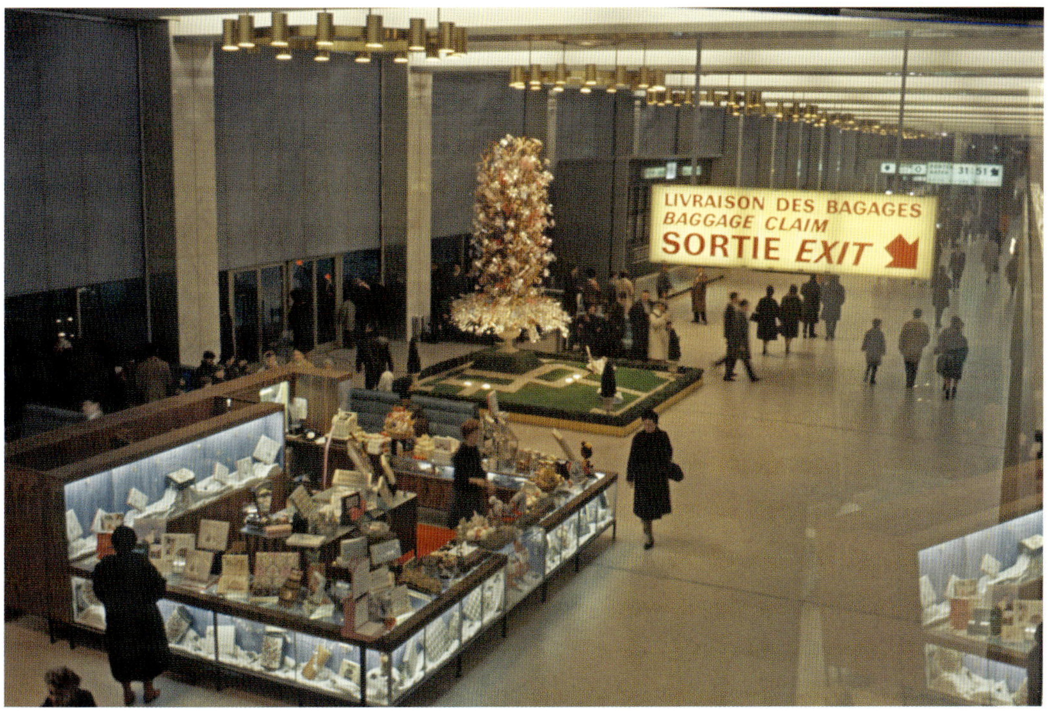

Fig. 1.30 Orly, Christmas 1965

a three-hundred-fifty-seat cinema, and exhibition space for art shows. The following year, 1963, Félix Potin opened one of their first "super-marchés" at Orly. Publicity materials boasted that the store would be open seven days a week and noted that it was ironic that the airplane had given new life to the "centre commercial"—such early malls actually had been associated with automobile culture.[81] Orly's role as a shopping destination would be further developed during the holiday season when, starting in 1962, the stores and restaurants offered late-night hours and free parking. Adorned with seasonal decorations, like department stores in the city, Orly envisioned itself as the new town square and even hosted midnight Christmas mass in the main hall starting that year (fig. 1.30).[82]

The new Orly incited such enthusiasm among Parisians that it became one of the most visited places in Paris from the late 1950s through the following decade.[83] Road signs boldly instructed drivers, "Visitez Orly," making clear that the airport was a destination in itself (fig. 1.31). An ADP film made in 1961 to promote the airport announced, "Anticipation is no longer a fiction. Today is the rendez-vous of progress."[84] This positive vision of Orly as the future that had already arrived could also take a dystopic turn, as is evident in Chris Marker's well-known 1962 film *La Jetée,* which begins on the terrace at Orly. The film depicts a post–nuclear holocaust Paris where life has come to a standstill—even the images no longer move (his film consists of still images in sequence) (figs. 1.32 and 1.33 are the terrace in contrast).[85] Such avant-garde depictions as Marker's function as a telling

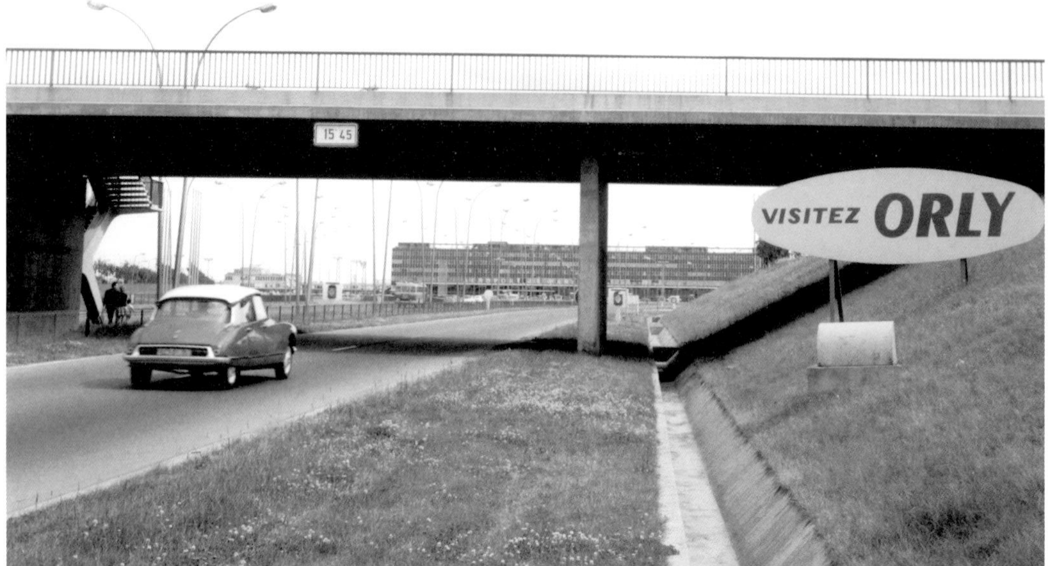

Fig. 1.31 Sign encouraging drivers to visit Orly, early 1961

counterpoint to the mainstream culture detailed here, in which great enthusiasm for the jet age's future present was promised, choreographed, rehearsed, and delivered in airports such as Orly.

Orly witnessed an enormous boom in visits in the years leading up to its renovation and upon the arrival of the jet. Between 1954 and 1957, the number of visitors to the terrace at Orly went from 32,321 to 647,563. In 1960, slightly more than a million people visited the airport and no doubt also saw the new terminal going up. In the year of the opening of the renovated airport and the new terminal, 3.5 million people paid to enter the terraces. Visits peaked at 4 million in 1966. Sundays, holidays, and summertime proved to be the busiest times, and as many as 40,000 people would visit daily. Between 1956 and 1966 the terrace at Orly became the second-most-visited tourist site in Paris, behind only Versailles (the Eiffel Tower, by contrast, had almost 1.8 million paid visits yearly). The architect speculated that visitors were mesmerized by the "the charm of the incessant movement of arrivals and departures."[86]

The terminal's design, in fact, had anticipated such visitors. From the second through the sixth floors of the building, visitors could access public terraces that overlooked the tarmac. The new airport terminal offered 35,000 square meters in total of public terrace, most of which could be visited without even passing into the terminal building, confirming that the airport expected to host people who were not at Orly only to travel outside

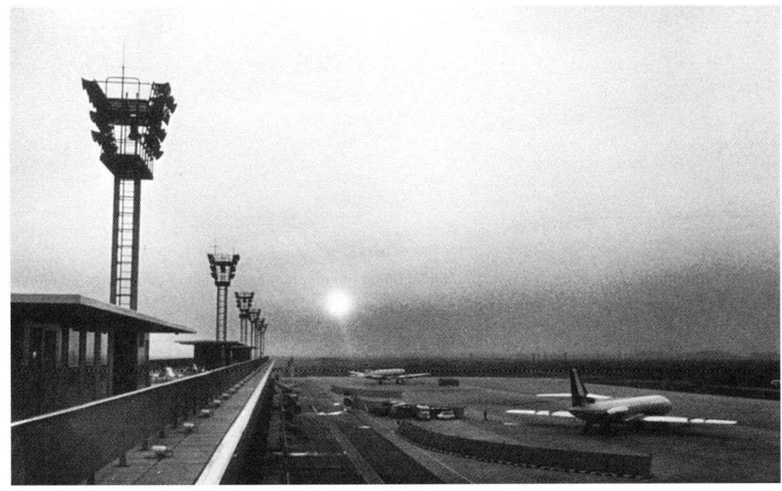

Fig. 1.32 *La Jetée*, 1962, directed by Chris Marker. Argos Films/RTF. DVD screen capture

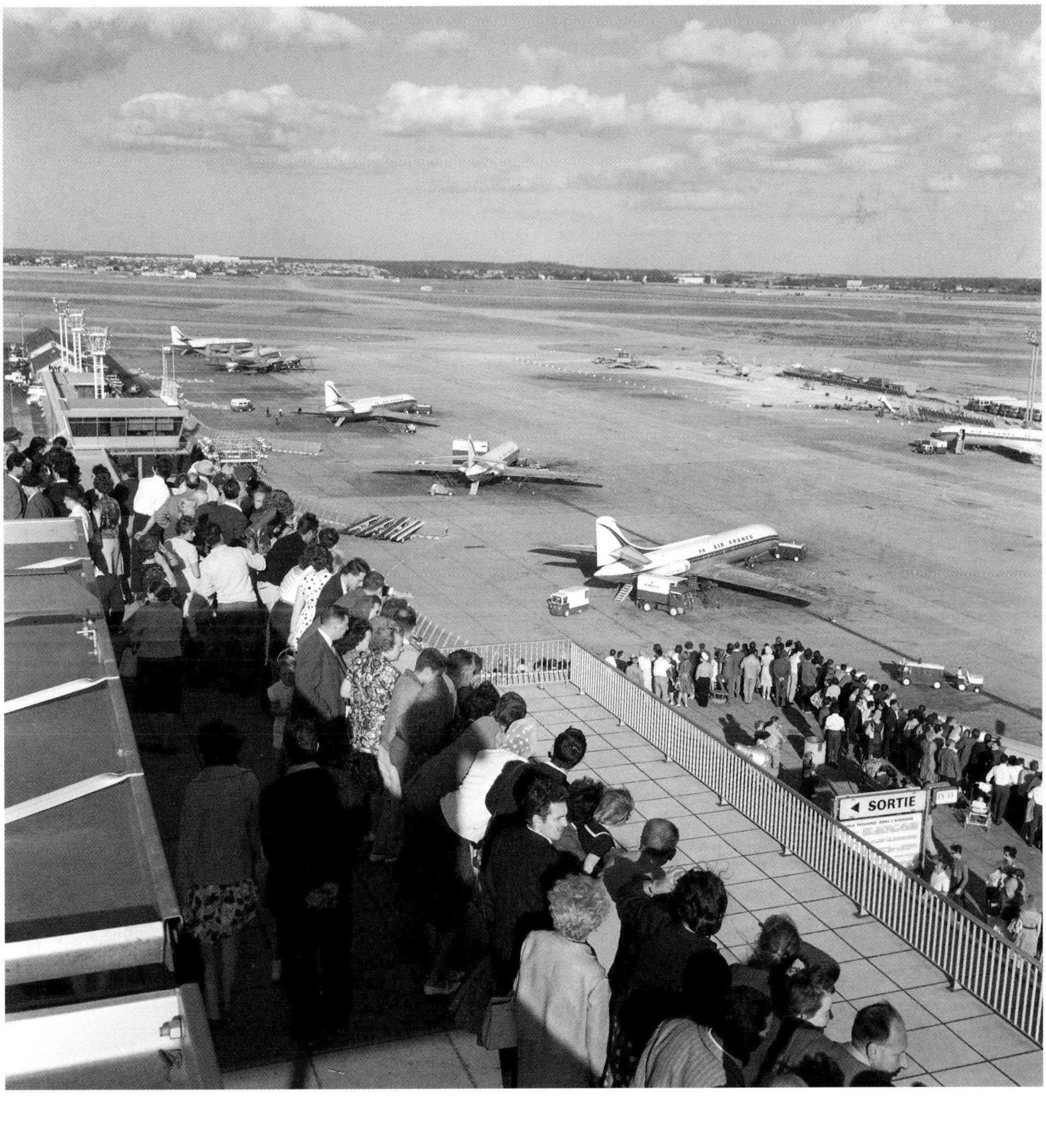

Fig. 1.33 Observers on Terrace at Orly, circa 1961

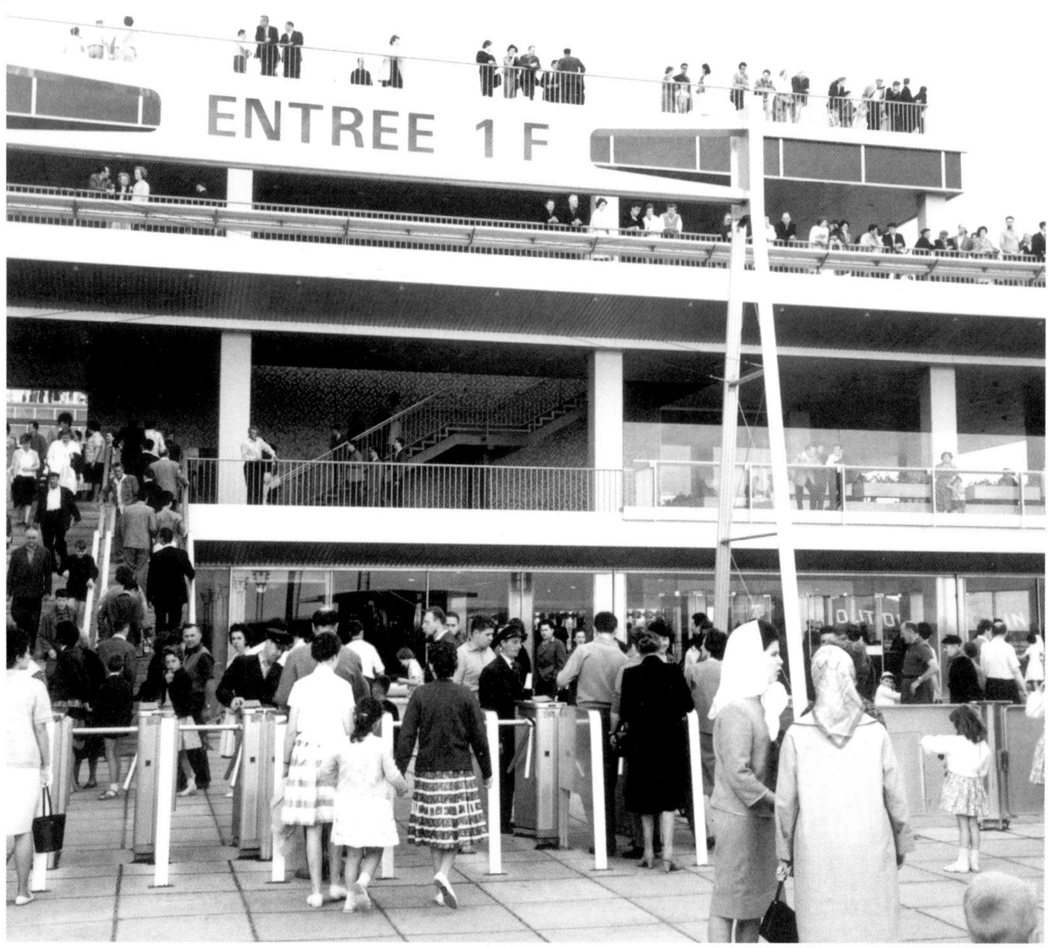

Fig. 1.34 Terrace external entrance, 1961

of Paris by plane. In addition, the airport was listed among the attractions in the *Officiel des Spectacles* in the 1960s, a guidebook to the French capital. For the cost of one new franc, which was half the price of admission to a museum, visitors could pass through turnstiles and be admitted onto the busy terrace, where they could watch the planes land, load, and unload, all accompanied by loudspeakers describing the activities (fig. 1.34). Such features as sound walls were built on the strip close to the terminals to shield people from the shriek of the jet engines. These were no doubt installed with onlookers as much as deplaning passengers in mind, since the onlookers would have been exposed to much more plane traffic than would a passenger exiting his or her own plane.

The terrace offered much more than plane-spotting. It became a sort of a jet age family picnic ground. While on the terrace, family members could eat crêpes, drink coffee, and sit on comfortable chairs and benches among well-chosen plantings. Children played in sandboxes (fig. 1.35). New-fangled vending machines on the terrace sold items for every member of the family: candy, ice cream, drinks, and even nylon stockings. The experience of making the purchases by vending machine was as important as consuming the goods, because it reinforced the futuristic and cutting-edge novelty of air travel, of the airport, and of being on the terrace itself.

For an additional fee visitors could take a guided tour of the airport, which included a bus ride around the airport to the hangars as well as a trip through the inside of the terminal itself, including descending all the way down to the belly of the heating and cooling rooms. Between 1957 and 1962, the ADP also offered a maquette of a Caravelle jet that was decked out in the exact interior of a real plane so that visitors could experience the thrill of sitting inside an airplane. During that early period, travel by plane, let alone by jet, was still limited to a relatively small group of French elites.[87]

The airport authorities also functioned as if they were running a tourist attraction as much as an airport. A 1962 film made by the ADP about Orly spent most of the nineteen-minute run time on a virtual tour of the establishment, exploring the airport's viewing facilities in particular. The camera lingered on the turnstile entrance, showed youngsters playing on the escalators, and filmed from within the restaurant looking out over the terrace and onto the tarmac.[88] This perspective is also evident in a series of management memos. They note that visiting the airport was so pleasant and so popular that the admission fee should be increased for the first time since 1961, when the terrace price rose to one franc from half a franc. (The lower price dated back to the start of paid entry, 1954, before jet service had even begun.) "Visitors benefit from a very pleasant location that is also very comfortable: plenty of seats, excellent facilities, air-conditioning, and being able to be a part of the airport ambiance." In April 1968 the management pointed out that it was much cheaper to visit Orly than other rival tourist attractions, such as the Eiffel Tower, the Arc de Triomphe, Unesco, the Musée Grévin (the most expensive entry fee of all), and the major art museums. The admission fee hike thus made prices more in keeping with the cost of admission elsewhere in Paris.[89]

Admissions figures alone cannot complete the picture of the experience of such visits. A writer for *Le Figaro* described the atmosphere as something out of a Jacques Tati movie, which may well be why Tati opens his film *Playtime* at the airport. He noted that people amused themselves by incessantly going up the down escalators and elevators. For this reviewer, the airport had too many visitors and the wrong kind at that. He complained that they turned the continent's "most modern airport" into an "amusement park like that of the glory days at Luna Park."[90] The crowds at the airport irked other visitors as well. As one Dr. Jacques Meuley from Reims griped in a letter to the ADP in September 1966, he had come on a visit with his children to find the guided tours were already full and that the next tour was not leaving for two hours.[91] Crowded, chaotic, and alive with the excitement wrought by anticipation, Orly became a vitrine of how the future of cutting-edge technology was being lived already.

One visitor described the airport as "a world apart . . . richer, more international, where you rub elbows with extremely exotic people, people of all colors . . . you have luxury items, you have escalators, you have bars . . . you grasp that here you have everything . . . everything that a person, that man could desire."[92] This giddy visitor did not even mention the promise of far-flung travel. Instead, the airport was a glamorous, high-tech bazaar, a place where all anyone could want was already on offer. Observers envisioned, in this way, the airport of the mid-twentieth century in ways that very much resembled the department store or the World's Fair in the nineteenth century. It is no wonder, then, that the airport also drew on these earlier models to become a spectacle in its own right.

As the jet age gave way to the era of the jumbo jet, it became apparent that it was difficult to anticipate and manage growth, and traffic jams to and in the airports ensued the world over. And the hijackings of the 1970s made clear that fluidity of motion could also be easily assaulted because it rests on a sense of liberal consensus about the value of free circulation. This, no doubt, previewed many of our current dilemmas regarding the costs of a world economy, the flow of information over the internet, and the new forms of global nomadism across a connected world. But this reality should not diminish our understanding of how people experienced the dawn of the jet age—a decade whose enormous technological optimism and embrace of rapid change and obsolescence in even the most permanent of spheres, architecture and the built environment, allowed people not only to take to the skies but also to reorient themselves in time and space through technology.

Nineteenth-century spectacles may have turned the universe into a garden. They had been monumental and iconic. The jet age airports, on the other hand, created not only a world that was actually smaller—to the extent that people could be transported around it more quickly than ever before—but also a world that changed how people moved on the ground. Such airports helped create a new kind of relationship between the built environment and the material world it stood for, and people's relation to them, by shifting the focus of such spaces to how people might move through them. The jet age may have initiated a new culture of travel and even a culture of perpetual motion, but it is the fluid quality of that motion—of going without feeling—that characterized the aspirations of the jet age. That those involved in designing the spaces in and around air travel might extend that fluid motion to the ground, I have argued, was fundamental to how the jet age offered an aesthetic rather than simply a new mode of travel. That architects and planners who worked on jet age airports were able to transform their practices and embrace new values regarding how people related to the built environment in light of these changes is the complex story that needed telling. Although I have located this aesthetic as close to the jet as one might get, for the remainder of the study we will range, like the jet, farther and farther afield. I argue that the jet defined an era and did so by reconfiguring communications via ideas of transport and experiences of motion and mobility. Although the jet age airports described here were visited by millions in the period under consideration, by 1962 not one of them had as many yearly visitors as the place to which we now turn, and which remains the period's outstanding purveyor of jet age aesthetics: Disneyland.

Fig. 1.35 Terrace with sandbox, Orly, 1961

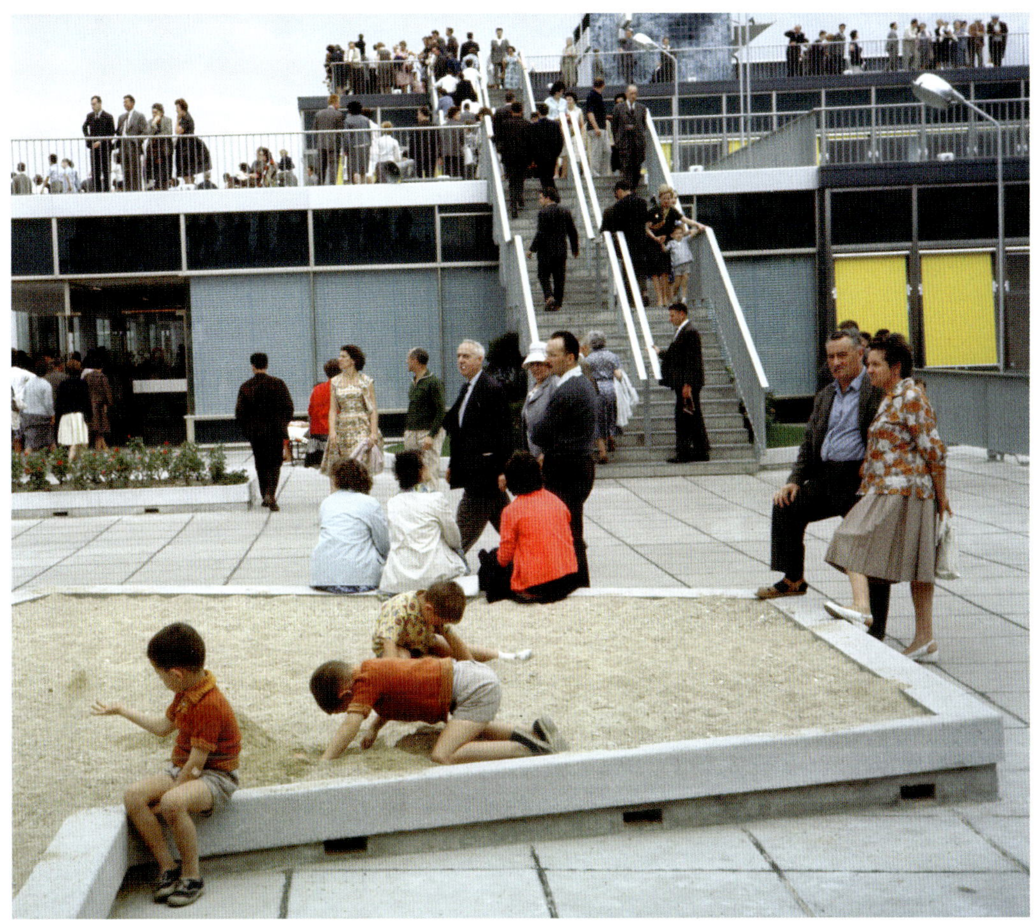

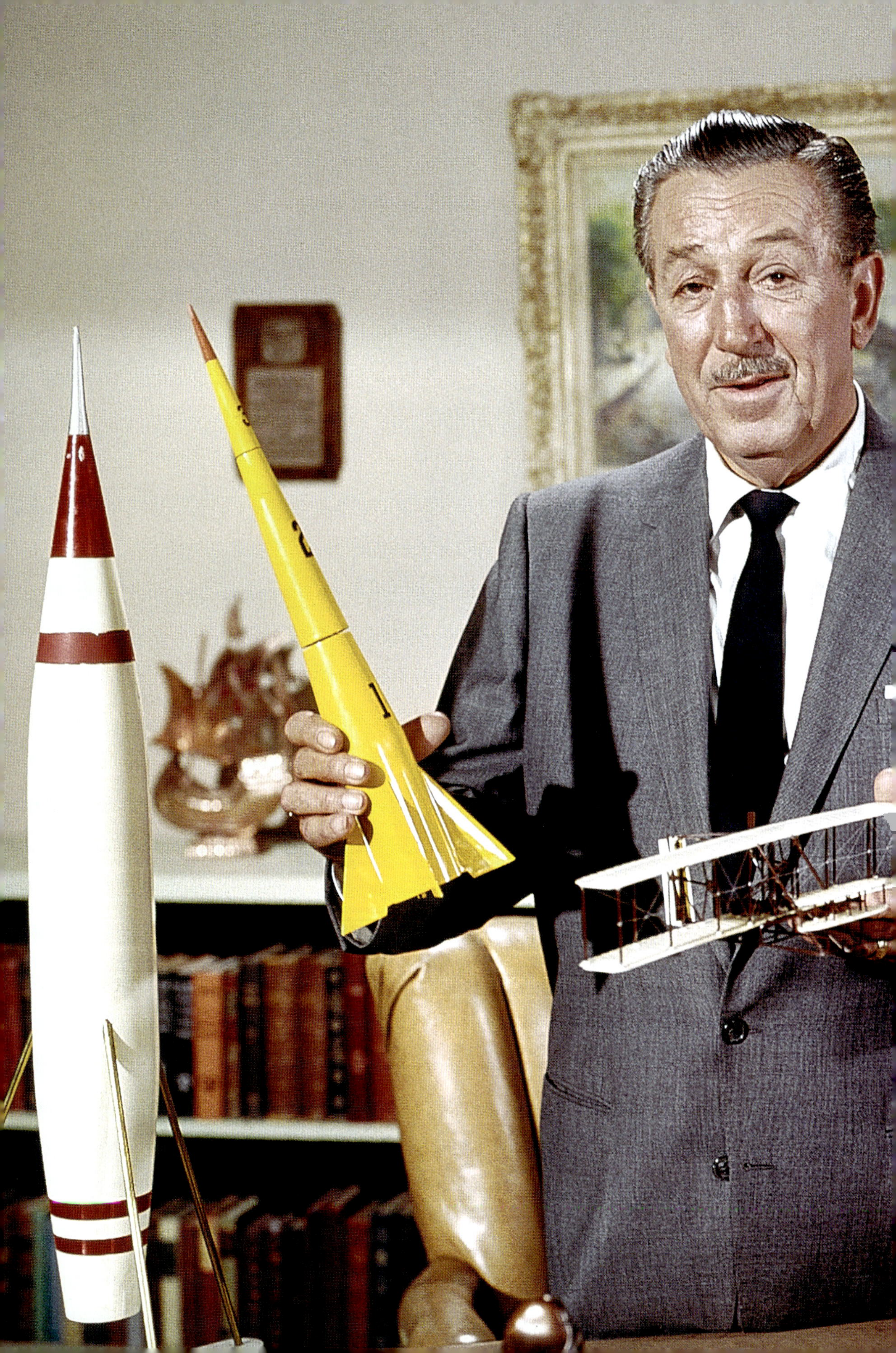

CHAPTER TWO

Disneyland and the Art of People-Moving

The tendency toward speed—the acceleration of our age—is reflected in the entertainment world as in every other area of modern living. . . . Disneyland . . . [has been] designed to effect a pleasant and exciting outlet for the sense of adventure, for exuberant energy, for imaginative play in physical action.

—*Walt Disney, 1959*

We don't have an edifice complex. We want our community shaped not around buildings, but around people. This will be a community for and about people.

—*Walt Disney, 1966*

In a climate of cultural innovation dominated by youthful technologists, it may be hard to imagine that, despite the many firsts for which Walt Disney and The Walt Disney Studios are known (synchronized sound cartoons, Technicolor cartoons, full-length animated features), the man himself was over fifty years old when the tractors arrived in Anaheim to break ground on what many consider his greatest legacy and unsurpassed accomplishment: Disneyland. Disney explained what he valued most about the place that would give rise to a new entertainment form, the theme park: "Disneyland is something that will never be finished. It's alive. It will be a living, breathing thing that will need change. A picture is a thing. . . . I wanted something alive, something that could grow." Disney called the park "my latest and greatest invention," and his enthusiasm made great sense. In his training as an animator he had learned to make inanimate objects seem alive (as in *Pinocchio*). He emphasized the park's organic qualities: "Not only can I add things, but even the trees will grow and become more beautiful each year."[1]

Disney may have invoked the park's many trees, but even they were carefully planted and pruned, and the park's artists were known to improve upon them when necessary.[2] Planning, designing, and executing the growth of systems "dedicated to the happiness of people" preoccupied Disney from 1953, when he began in earnest on the Disneyland project, until his death in 1966, when he and his team at the company named for him, WED (Walter

Elias Disney), were planning the "Florida Project," or Walt Disney World Resort.[3] For something as complex and successful as Disneyland, it would be foolish to imagine that any one aspect explains the whole. Yet by contextualizing Disneyland as a project that both embodied and shaped the culture of media in motion, we see that Disney's focus on the aestheticization of "people-moving" was central to fostering the "happiness of people" when the park opened in 1955, at the dawn of the jet age.[4]

In this chapter, I examine Disneyland from its emergence and execution to the projects completed or planned by Walt Disney himself and the company he established to create the park: WED Enterprises. Workers at WED, who became known as Imagineers (they executed "imaginative concepts in design, architecture, engineering and entertainment"), were dedicated to the art of people-moving, as well as to making people-moving into an art.[5] The qualities of fluid motion, circulation, and mobility that planners and architects introduced into airport culture to mimic the movement of the jet—and which became functional problems as airports grew and air travel expanded—found a more satisfying course at Disneyland. People merely went to the park in Anaheim to experience the pleasure of jet age fluid motion, and, through technology and planning, the journey was rendered into a purely aesthetic experience. Disneyland's significance and impact in its first decade had as much to do with its role in disseminating the jet age aesthetic as with the more familiar aspects of the park. The Disney parks, including sites in Europe and Asia, continue to draw millions of people. And they continue to renew themselves because, whatever their content and iconography, they are founded on the formal and structural principle of the technological aestheticization of fluid motion, which is how the jet taught us to see and feel and which remains essential to media culture.

By the early 1950s, The Walt Disney Studios had already taken the art of animation—of making inert hand-drawn images move—to new levels of aesthetic and technological accomplishment. But within the context of Disney's corporate history, few moments approach the importance of Disneyland's creation. The often-told tale of the park's history begins with Walt's artistic vision being met by his brother's skeptical and conservative business attitude, an attitude that was eventually bested by the dreamer's determination. But the truth is, both men helped shape the success of the enterprise, and there is little doubt that Disneyland stands as one of the most successful innovations of the jet age.

Disneyland received a barrage of press attention when it opened in July 1955, including the most extensive live-television coverage of a single event until that time. But analytical studies of the park were initially few; press coverage was mostly celebratory and in the travel-writing and tourist literature vein.[6] When scholars finally took pen to paper to analyze the park they unwittingly adopted those very genres and so wrote about their own Disneyland moment, paying little attention to the actual history of "historic" Disneyland. Among the most memorable of these accounts are the ones made by a trio of European semiologists in the late 1970s and early 1980s: Louis Marin, Umberto Eco, and Jean Baudrillard, who offered tendentious ideological critiques of the United States that masqueraded as semiotic analyses of Disneyland. They provided a series of ethnographic essays in a period when it was still rare to turn such a critical eye on the rituals of modern western culture.[7] These left-leaning European intellectuals analyzed Disneyland in order to see the flaws of the United States and its consumer capitalism. In their different ways they were each bemused and skeptical. They focused on the park's technique of simulating the real world, which they identified as a peculiar American condition of "hyperreality," claiming this quality as a ruse intended to make visitors and natives alike believe that the rest of America was real "when in fact all of Los Angeles and the America surrounding it are no longer real, but of the order of the hyperreal and of simulation."[8] Eco called Disneyland's representations "masterpieces of falsification," the Sistine Chapel of the hyperreal U.S.A.[9] Such perspectives now seem antiquated, since by 2007, a mere fifteen years after opening Disneyland Paris, the park in Marne-la-Vallée had already overtaken the Louvre and the Eiffel Tower among the most-visited tourist destinations in Europe. [10] So at least some Europeans have welcomed the Disney culture of simulation in the heart of cultural authenticity, or perhaps it only proves a larger point about Disneyland as the greatest evidence that American leisure culture has a truly global reach.

Since the 1980s, when the concept of hyperreality often accompanied discussions of postmodernism, other scholars of western modernity, by taking a much longer view—whether by focusing on the periods since the Renaissance, since the eighteenth century, or since the nineteenth century—have established that the culture of simulation was hardly the result of a diabolical American genius of inauthenticity. Indeed, they have traced the concept to earlier times and to other places.[11] There is not now nor has there ever been a hyperreal United States and an "authentic" Europe, for example. Disneyland, after all, incorporates many elements of the world's fairs, those spectacular commercial and industrial events that began in Europe in the nineteenth century. In fact, the critic Walter Benjamin had called Paris "the Capital of the 19th century," referring to the seeming mastery of spectacle associated with consumer culture in Paris at a time when many Americans were still managing the challenges of crossing the prairie in covered wagons. The Eiffel Tower displayed the wonder of Parisian modernity—the world's tallest tower had been built in a record two years—in time to celebrate the centennial of the French Revolution for the Exposition of 1889. The first projected moving images shown in public played in that same city in 1895; they were produced by the Lumière Brothers, who specialized in the manufacture of photographic materials, another modern technological artform born in the City of Light. Although Disneyland's emergence is specific to its cultural time and place, neither its representational aesthetic of simulation nor its spectacular culture of display is without precedent. It is part of a longer history of mass culture that emerged in the mid- to late nineteenth century in the western world.

Not long after Walt Disney's death, the first historically oriented studies, such as Richard Schickel's *Disney Version,* began to consider the Disney enterprise in general and to focus on the park in an analytical and interpretive way.[12] Although *The Disney Version* can also be understood as the first of what would become the standard anti-Disney positions among cultural critics after Disney's death, Schickel's views regarding Disneyland were, in fact, much less negative and extremely prescient. Writing in 1968, he called it "one of the best mixed media shows ever devised" and pointed to it as an example of Marshall McLuhan's "global village," already grasping that Disneyland would not be reduced to "Americana" and that its use of physical space, technology, and people-moving made the park part of the communications revolution that McLuhan described and for which I suggest the jet age aesthetic helped prepare the way.[13]

In the decades that followed, American scholarship about The Walt Disney Studios and Disneyland increased substantially. Such research has been constrained by limited access to archival materials, especially regarding the creative process at WED and the history of general park operations.[14] Scholarship about Disneyland falls into three general orientations: one group of scholars approaches the park from the perspective of its content (symbols and myths), which it interprets as a performance of ideology; another locates the park's history within the context of the business of the entertainment industry; while a third regards the park as a spatial expression. The first orientation emphasizes the very American qualities of Disneyland that the European semiologists did, focusing on such themes as nostalgia; American expansion; consumerism; the racial constructions of whiteness, racism, and racial exclusion; and the perfection and conformity of the environment. To these critics Disneyland is a very dangerous place indeed, especially because it performs its content as ideological mystification with a smile on its face to an unwitting audience.[15]

For scholars interested in the economic dimension of Disney's larger corporate strategy, the park exemplifies the power of branding and the diversification of the company into tourism and leisure, and its early and continued leadership in the field of product development. These studies are focused on how the park works as part of Disney's corporate strategy. Disneyland is a venue where products are sold; it is a brilliant embodiment of corporate synergy: characters inhabit the rides, appear on products in the gift shops, visit guests in the restaurants, and are represented in the myriad experiences throughout the Disney environment. Activities, experiences, and products are monetized into generations of family life and spending in the park and on Disney products.[16]

Such readings of Disneyland are too general, seeing the park as an embodiment of cultural expressions that also operate elsewhere in the culture (and thus imply that Disneyland did not cause these cultural values).

Simultaneously, they are too specific because they simply assert that Disneyland is important in the history of the entertainment industry. Disneyland is much more important than that.

Studies of Disneyland's spatial organization have been some of the most significant interpretations of its history and impact, contextualizing it within a broader history of gardens, parks, and utopias, as well as within a history of urban planning. Such approaches understand Disneyland as a brilliant amalgamation of earlier practices—building on traditions of gardens, tivolis, world's fairs, and amusement parks (complete with water elements, the domestication of real and robotic animals, industrial displays, and the corporate management of formerly public spaces). More locally, the geographic and spatial dimensions of the park's history have also been grounded in other forms of mid-century American planning, particularly as they relate to the development of Southern California's regional culture, including suburbanization and the development of malls, planned living communities, and industrial parks.[17]

Diverse as these approaches are, they all invoke the park's "theming," beginning with the creation of different "lands" that created a sense of overall design through Imagineering's aesthetic of "detailism"—coordinating all aspects of the artificial environment in which structures also help tell stories. The built environment is not monumental, but it is conjured to be enlisted as part of a narrative.[18] Yet such places are also constructed in order to be traveled through. Observers point to the park's hyperrealism, which one might consider a form of realism for which there is no literal original. The lands are designed to evoke in visitors a variety of emotional responses: nostalgia on Main Street, U.S.A., the thrill of empire in Adventureland, discovery in Frontierland, and the wonder of the transformation from the flat world of Disney cartoons to three dimensions in Fantasyland. In Tomorrowland, this very detailism often presented a challenge: conjuring a utopian frontier that had never been encountered. The narrative works only because the visitor moves. As Imagineer Marc Davis explained of Walt Disney's Enchanted Tiki Room (initially sponsored by United Airlines), the attraction that introduced one of WED's signal technologies, Audio Animatronics, lifelike moving and talking automata, or animation in three dimensions, "Rides should be what people don't expect them to be, and it doesn't have a lot to do with continuity of story. It does have to do with the entertainment value of surprise and seeing things you can't see anyplace else."[19] Disneyland is not, in fact, merely a simulation; it is often pure moving spectacle, and when it is narrative, that narrative unfolds because of visitor motion. It is no accident that an image of Walt Disney surrounded by modes of air transport dates from this period (fig. 2.1).

By building on these ways of looking at the park, I examine Disneyland's aesthetic in which the media and technology of its mid-century moment not only shaped how the park came to be but also explains why it resonated so profoundly at the time it opened. Disneyland is pure jet age

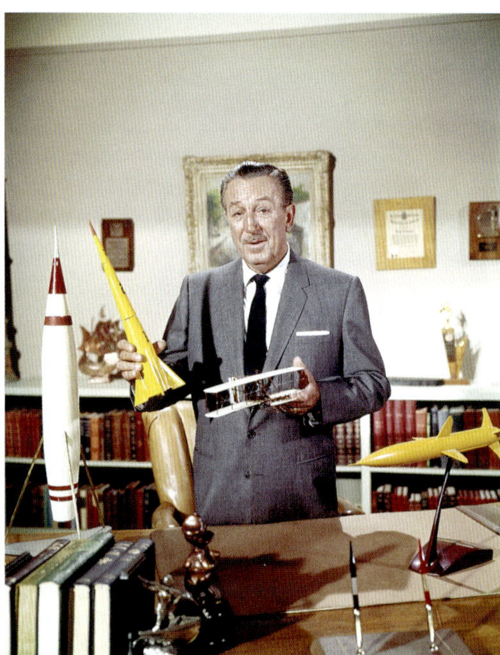

Fig. 2.1 Walt Disney's Introduction on *Disneyland Television Show*, "Fly with Von Drake" episode, 1963. © Disney

because its underlying formal work, as a place of profound visual and sensory design and intention, offered visitors a chance to enact the new form of the jet's highly valued positive quality of movement: its fluid motion. Like the jet age airport, Disneyland also made the experience of motion itself into something beautiful, pleasurable, and easy. That motion became an object to see and simultaneously hardly feel—like riding in a jet; the thrill of Peter Pan's Flight is in its smooth and easy path over London.

Disneyland's emphasis on motion as a beautiful and joyful sight and the park's successful people-moving made it a place where visitors participated in jet age aesthetics. While inside the park and in constant circulation, people learned to toggle between the material and virtual worlds, aided by new forms of media and technology. Disneyland organized, ordered, and aestheticized kinesis and "transport" itself. It is not merely in obvious symbolic artifacts, such as Tomorrowland's ostentatiously sponsored TWA Rocket to the Moon, that Disneyland can be seen as part of the jet age moment (fig. 2.2). At Disneyland, as has been noted by others and as many of the Imagineers have explained, filmmaking was also transferred to three-dimensional space.[20] But the entire place operated under a vision in which Walt Disney engaged his jet age interest in people-moving, turning transport into the story that connected the different lands while making a function into an attraction, narrated as the driving tale of human progress, written on the American landscape. The constant movement of the attractions and of the guests themselves defined a visit to the park, which was intended to be an experience more than a show. Disneyland also helps us better understand that this experience of toggling between the material and virtual worlds,

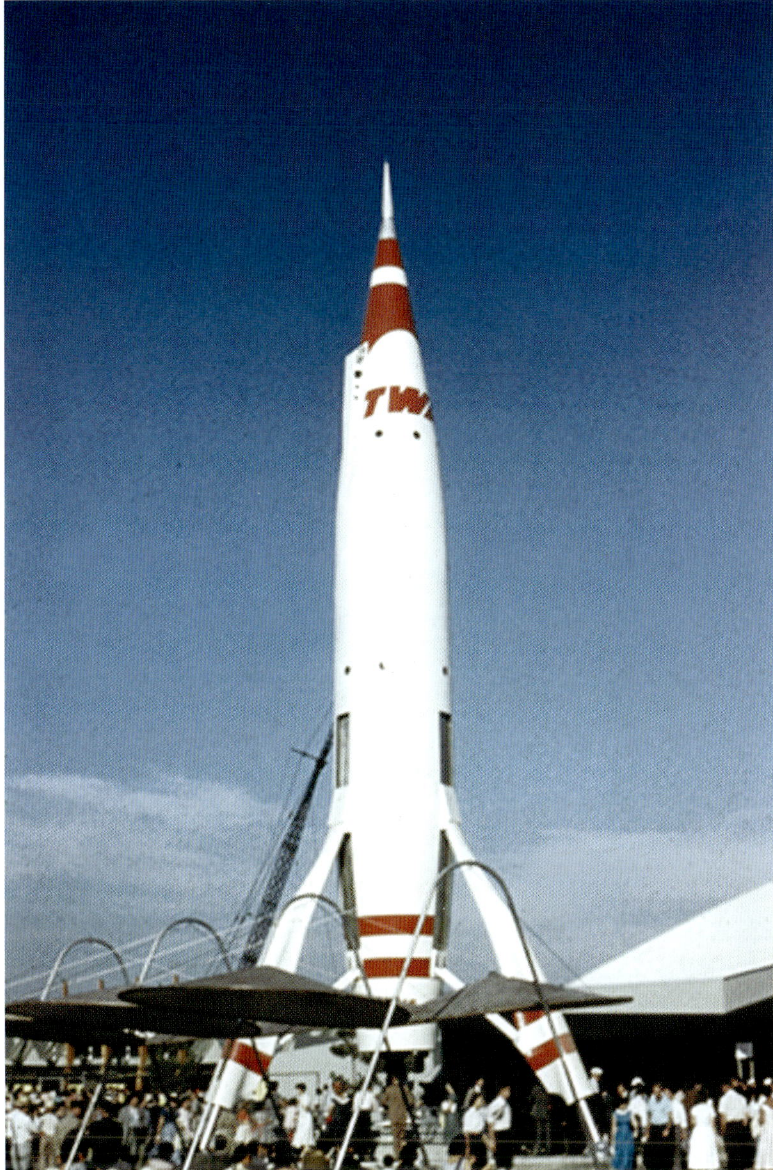

Fig. 2.2 TWA Rocket to the Moon, Disneyland, circa 1956. © Disney

rather than fast travel, is why the jet created an age that made such an impact and of which the park is an important part.

When Disneyland opened, visitors parked their cars only to be transported all day long. Rather than a series of different lands, the park was a series of roads, tracks, and skyways that ultimately narrated journeying and offered a history transport technology as the key element in a larger history of progress. Visitors experienced the transformation of a functional activity (transport) into a beautiful attraction. Transport defined the space in every land from the moment of arrival, when guests encountered the whirring train at the Disneyland Main Street Station (fig. 2.3).[21]

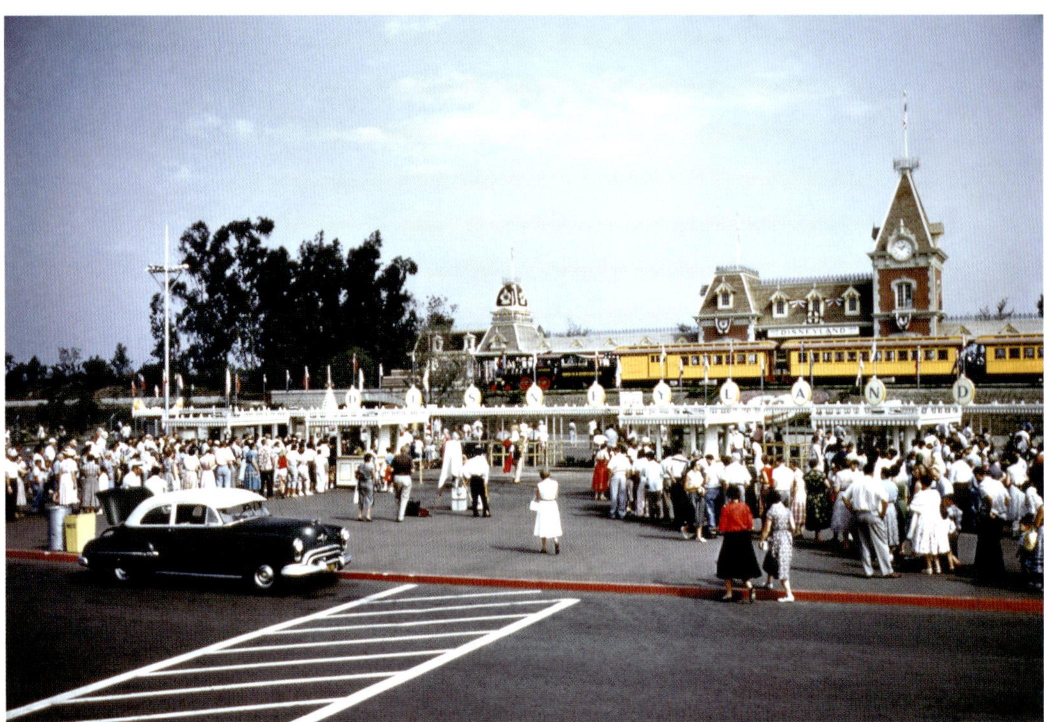

Fig. 2.3 Disneyland Main Park Entrance, with train, circa 1950s. © Disney

Although one could argue that nothing like Disneyland had ever existed, it was not entirely unprecedented. Its originality inhered in its recombination of familiar experiences in spaces devoted to exhibition and spectacle combined with the repertoire of Disney film narratives and their associated characters and themes. Disney called it a "combined amusement park–public wonderland–fair–carnival–showplace of magic and living facts, wondrously devised for the visitor's participation."[22] Although we tend to focus on the importance of fictional narratives as the center of Disney storytelling, Walt had become increasingly aware of the value of information to the entertainment business. Perhaps the Studios' wartime work for the government (making instructional films and propaganda such as *Victory Through Air Power*) had raised his awareness, but judging from his commitment to expanding the repertoire from animation to live-action film and into documentary with the True-Life Adventures and People and Places series, Disney began to cast his venture as being in the business of visual communication as much as entertainment—"infotainment" before the fact, one might say. In a 1953 memo he mused that the "motion picture screen has become one of the major sources of popular information. . . . The screen must now devote a substantial portion of its time and showmanship to factual matters."[23]

By extension, Walt saw Disneyland's mission as extending well beyond being a mere pleasure zone. When his team visited multiple amusement parks to research working models in 1954, they were most impressed with the Chicago Museum of Science and Industry, which they reported was an "extremely excellent combination of education and entertainment."[24] Another press release for Disneyland called it "a world's fair, a playground, a futuristic city and a tropical park all rolled into a permanent landmark."[25] Simple categorization failed because the park was not exactly like anything else, even as it drew on familiar European exhibition practices that engaged in the best of industrial and corporate design, updating them technologically by adding the moment's relentless preoccupation with transportation and motion, mobility, and circulation.

Disneyland also emerged from a more local and practical problem: Walt Disney's desire to respond to the public's interest in touring his studio. He had experimented with satisfying this curiosity by making a studio tour film called *The Reluctant Dragon* (1941). The film showed how the studio made animated films, and it offered audiences a vicarious visit to the new studio in Burbank.[26] Designed by Kem Weber, this state-of-the-art studio had features that would become signature elements at Disneyland: purpose-built furniture, thematic coherence throughout the buildings, and a heavily choreographed space mixing a campus environment with streets bearing whimsical names, such as Dopey Drive and Mickey Avenue (the sign for this intersection was created for *The Reluctant Dragon;* figs. 2.4, 2.5).

The Burbank studio, opened in 1939 on the heels of the wild financial success of *Snow White and the Seven Dwarfs* (1937), is notable for its planned space, which was designed to house the specialized work to be done there, as compared to the hodge-podge development of the original studio on Hyperion Avenue.[27] As part of the vision for Burbank, Disney also began to imagine a small park and train ride on land he owned across the street, a place he considered calling Mickey Mouse Park.[28] In various iterations it would be used by employees or visitors to the Studios. That park plan never came to pass, but it laid the foundation for some important thinking about the place that would eventually become Disneyland.

Simultaneously, Southern California, already home to the creative side of America's major media and communications industries in its movie studios, experienced two significant revolutions in transport. First, the American interstate highway system began to take shape, and its expansion and postwar freeway-building connected the Los Angeles basin to the rest of the country. In the mid-1950s the growing national highway system threaded Northern and Southern California, opening the region to a national network of drivers. Southern California had also been the heart of a developing aviation industry, both military and civil. After World War II, jet travel would place such seemingly remote places as California and Hawaii within reach of the East Coast of the United States and Europe.[29]

Such changes prompted a greater contemporary consciousness about transport's impact on history, which in turn fostered a nostalgic train fad in America. Animators at The Walt Disney Studios, who had the talent and resources, responded by building working trains for their own backyards.[30] Among them was none other than Disney himself. In 1949 he opened the

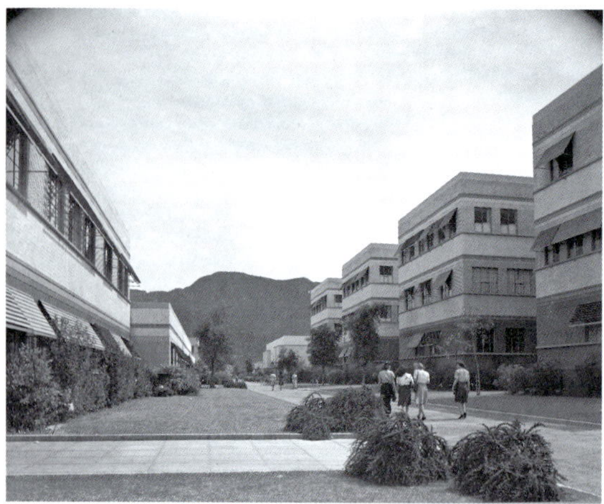

Fig. 2.4 Burbank Studio, The Walt Disney Studios, circa 1940. © Disney

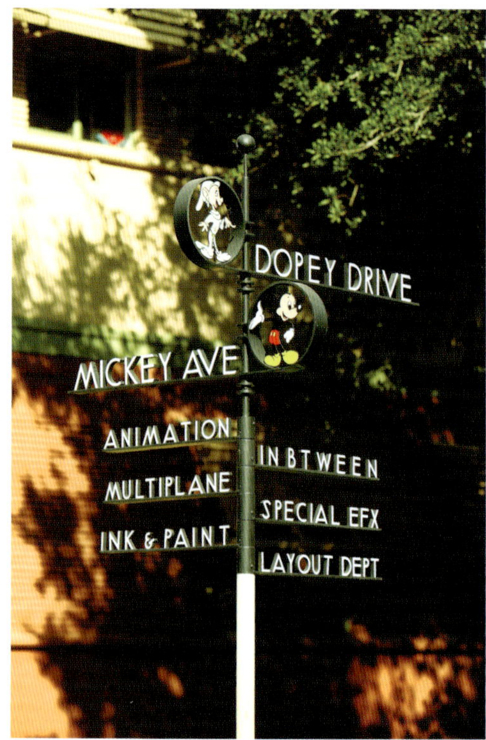

Fig. 2.5 Street sign erected for *The Reluctant Dragon* in Burbank at The Walt Disney Studios, circa 1939. © Disney

Carolwood-Pacific Railroad, which ran through his own backyard in Holmby Hills (fig. 2.6). As plans for a park took shape, Disney always intended that a train would circle around it. Like the one through his own backyard, as well as the one originally sketched for the park across the street from the Studios, the train would be enclosed inside a berm so that those seated on the train could not see the world outside; the train would circulate along the perimeter of a "make-believe" world. Vehicles that moved people defined space, but constant motion would eventually shift the emphasis from such defined spaces back to simply moving through them.

The broader public interest in trains extended beyond tinkerers and people who had the means to build model trains. In 1948, Disney, who had sold papers on the Santa Fe line as a boy, accompanied by the animator Ward Kimball, attended the Chicago Railroad Fair, an enormous months-long event that commemorated a hundred years of the railroad west of that city. There they saw many things that they would later adapt for Disneyland, such as Indian villages and a re-creation of French New Orleans. The Railroad Fair also framed American history as a history of transport and technology in ways that shaped Disney's view of the past.[31]

While the particular role of trains for Disney and their appearance in the park may link them directly and anecdotally, virtual voyages and vehicles had been vital to the cinema and to expositions and amusement parks. Whether one considers such early attractions as Hale's Tours, in which passengers boarded fake trains and watched a cinematic landscape go by, or whether one goes back to actual train passengers in the mid-nineteenth century, whose window views seemed to prefigure the experience of the moviegoers' experience of time and space (as has been argued by Wolfgang Schivelbusch), the convergence of such train rides at Disneyland locates the train within film history and the history of world's fairs and other amusement parks, even as it relocates the train within a transport context of the 1950s.[32]

Although the idea for Disneyland had thus been percolating for some time, the actual financing and building of the park became a relatively speedy project by 1953. The key dimensions of this often-told tale include the fact that the Disney brothers did not agree on risking the Studios' assets in order to finance Walt's wild idea, and so it became an independent project. After liquidating a great deal of his personal wealth, he had to raise still more cash, and, as he would later say, "ABC needed the television show so damned bad, they bought the amusement park."[33]

In exchange for agreeing to broadcast a weekly television show, the third-place network, desperate to make a splash, financed the park with $500,000 and became a 35 percent owner. It also guaranteed another $4.5 million in loans for a project that would cost $17 million to build.[34] The network had bet on the right horse. Disney's need for cash had significant long-term consequences for movie studios, including Disney's leading the way to the kind of cross-platform synergy that today characterizes the entertainment

Fig. 2.6 Walt Disney and children riding the Carolwood-Pacific Railroad in his backyard in Holmby Hills, circa 1950s. Photo, Disney Family Museum. © Disney

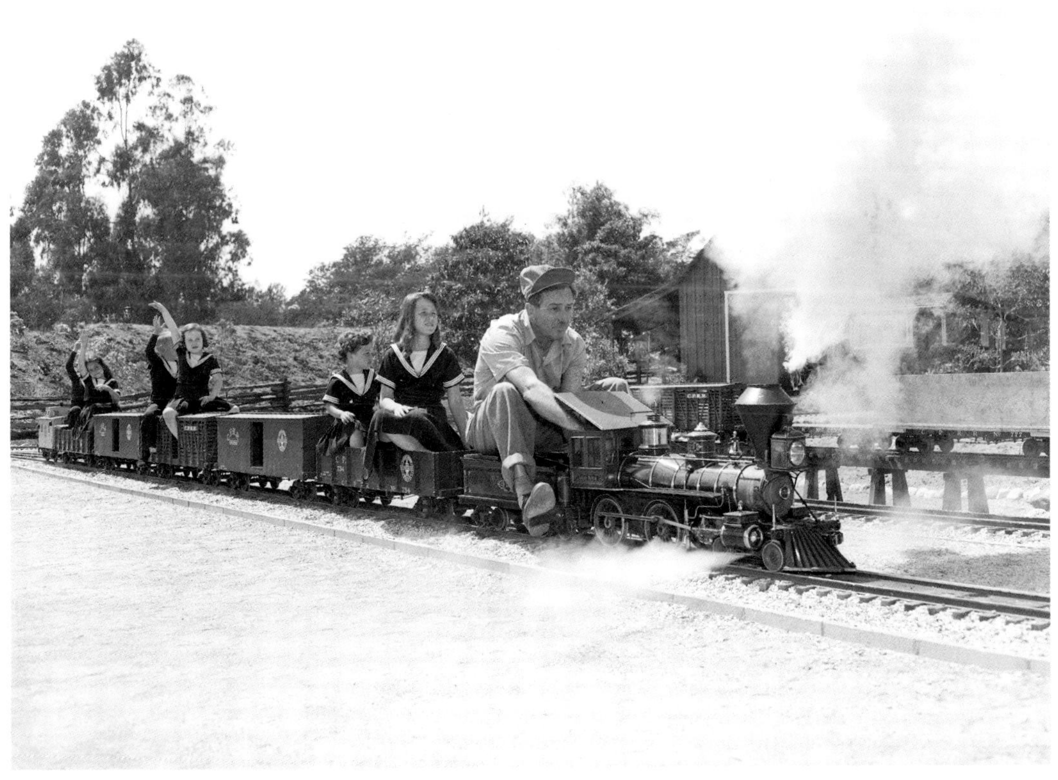

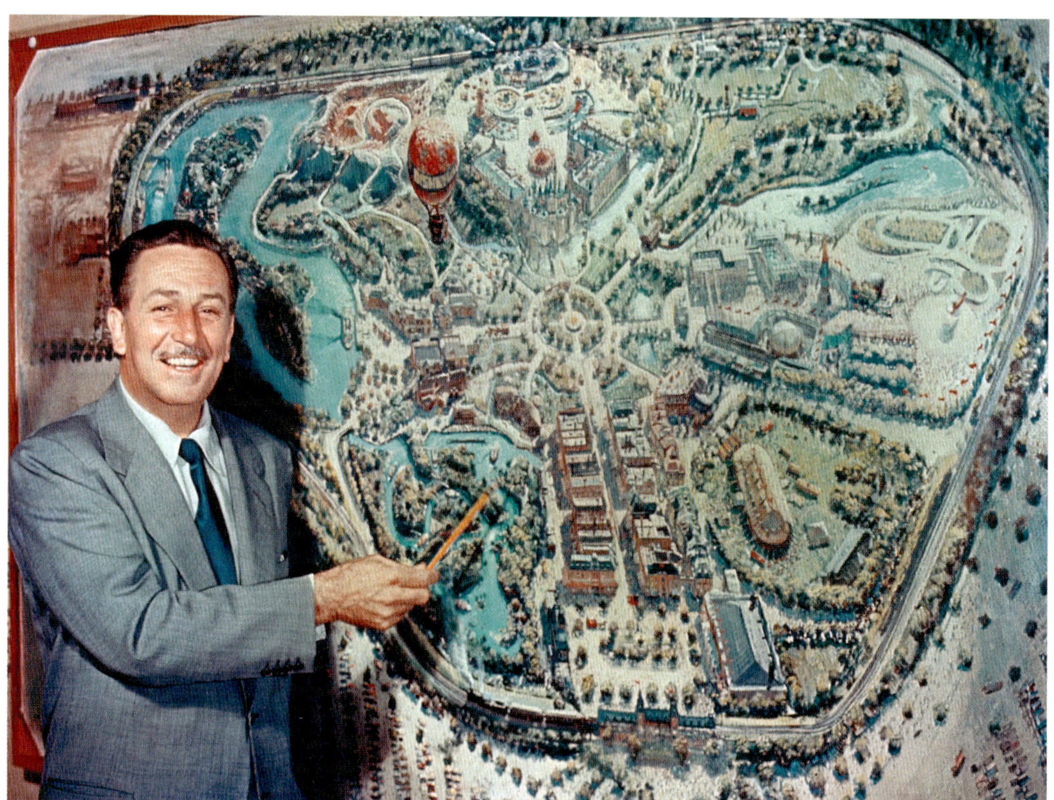

Fig. 2.7 Walt Disney in front of a map of Disneyland illustrated by Peter Ellenshaw, circa 1954. © Disney

industry more generally. At the time it established two things: First, it showed that television could be productively used by movie studios, which had initially considered the medium as competition. Second and more important at the time, *Walt Disney's Disneyland,* the television show, functioned as a ten-month advertisement for Disneyland, the place. As Walt explained in the first episode, "Disneyland the place and *Disneyland* the show are one and the same."[35] Television's antigeographical space made it easy to foresee the Disneyland geography, in which different lands would be juxtaposed around a hub, as Karal Ann Marling has observed. The discontinuous park geography even resembled the channels on a television dial.[36]

Disney himself had conceived of the park's basic shape, with the spacious hub that allowed visitors to both circulate freely and be easily oriented (fig. 2.7). The hub also visualized Disney's main preoccupation in designing the park: moving people through space and turning that motion into something to look at and simultaneously experience. Disney prioritized circulation and the "flow" of people who would be "transported" through the park by the movement of their own two feet, by purpose-built vehicles, by themed ride environments, and by engaging in a form of "three-dimensional story-telling art that places guests in the story environment."[37] The remarkable achievement of creating an artificial storytelling environment has preoccupied interpreters of the park, while visitors' movement through the space has seemed relatively insignificant. Analysts and observers, I would suggest, have unwittingly naturalized this movement in the same way that viewers do not see the camera movements in classic Hollywood films, and they have thus failed to see the vehicles and spaces of flow as the park's major aesthetic experience and intent.

Such movement also participated in an antimonumental logic. As the epigraph from this chapter attests, "We don't have an edifice complex. We want our community shaped not around buildings, but around people." In the same period that Walt Disney was working on opening Disneyland, airport planners were working on antimonumental airports that met the demands of the jet age. With the same approach to building spaces, they also sought to account for how people "naturally" or seemingly unconsciously moved through space. Disneyland was designed to anticipate change and growth with flexible, modular, and evolving spaces. As Disney explained, one of the appeals for him was that "Disneyland will never be finished."[38] Such change also suggested that culture would be improved and forever in a state of progress. In airports and at Disneyland, planners, architects, engineers, animators, and ordinary consumers glamourized and aestheticized such change and flux. Motion also denoted a sense of moving through time and represented the idea of progress itself. At Disneyland, visitors would participate in the speed of the age by seeing how far they had come by virtue of how fast they would be going tomorrow. But like the jet age itself, the future had already arrived.

It should come as no surprise that, to realize this jet age vision for his project, Disney assembled a team with close ties to actual jet age planning.[39] The people he hired from outside the Studios came from his circle of friends, who were often guests at his home and who specialized in orchestrating highly aestheticized spaces dedicated to moving large numbers of people. Welton Becket, his Holmby Hills neighbor, was already known for designing Bullock's department store and was working on the Beverly Hilton and beginning the Capital Records Tower at the time Walt was planning Disneyland (fig. 2.8). Becket would design the Theme Building at LAX (see fig. 1.20) the year Disneyland opened, and he would later work on several Disney projects, including the Ford Magic Skyway at the New York World's Fair of 1964–65 and Disney's Contemporary Hotel at Walt Disney World Resort (complete with a Monorail running through the lobby) (fig. 2.9), as well as Century City in Los Angeles. Becket convinced Walt to forsake using architects and have his own animators design the park.[40]

Among those rejected architects were the well-known team of William Pereira and Charles Luckman, who were introduced to the Disneyland idea at a party at Walt's house and who subsequently wrote him, explaining that they had gone "hook, line and sinker for Disneyland." Disney rejected the initial plans that he had invited them to submit. They did advise him early on regarding certain key principles, such as having only one entrance to the park, which they believed would reinforce the public's orientation, advice that Disney took and that distinguished Disneyland from its competition.[41]

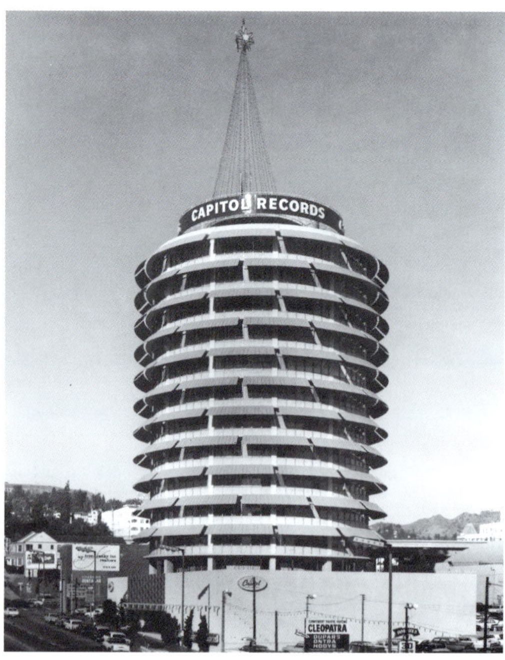

Fig. 2.8 Welton Becket, Capitol Records Building, Los Angeles, circa 1955–56. Dick Whittington, photographer

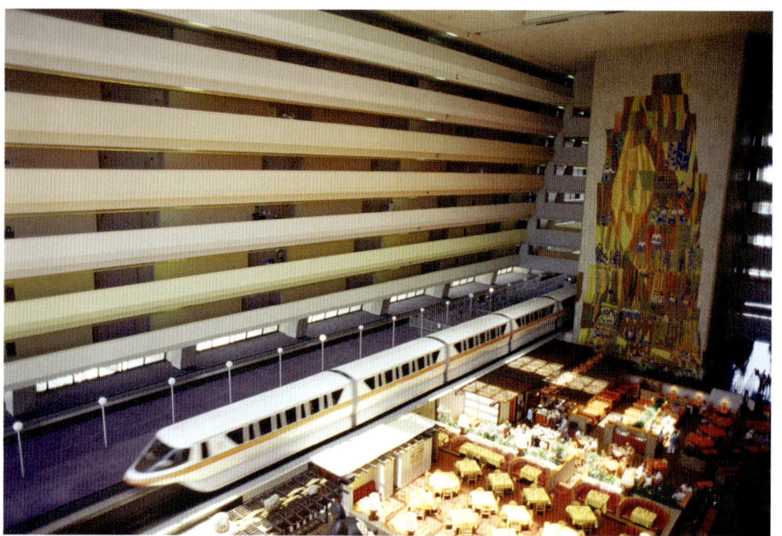

Fig. 2.9 Welton Becket, Disney's Contemporary Hotel, Walt Disney World, 1995. © Disney

In fact, Disneyland was so different in design from other parks that when its planners pitched the concept to the heads of the most successful amusement parks in the country, they proclaimed it would be dead on arrival.[42] The Pereira and Luckman team was offered a consolation prize, however: designing the Disneyland Hotel, operated independently by Disney's friend Jack Wrather, in 1954–55, the same period when they were working on the new master plan for LAX. Both projects shunned monumental architecture in favor of unremarkable rectangular buildings that could be added to or moved. Instead, each project, though notably different in scale, would be distinguished for the way it could be connected to and moved through.

They were not destinations but passthroughs for people on the way to somewhere else—repeating the hub as a concept if not formally re-creating its design (fig. 2.10).[43]

Disney's relationship with Pereira and Luckman, whose own partnership did not last very long, left another vital legacy for Disneyland. In 1953 Charles Luckman introduced Disney to the work of the Stanford Research Institute (SRI). Disney met C. V. Wood, the aviation engineer he would hire away as Disneyland's first general manager. Disney and Wood then hired retired Naval Admiral Joe Fowler to help supervise construction. Van Arsdale France, also from the aviation industry, eventually joined the team. Perhaps most significantly, Disney met consultant Harrison Price at SRI. Disney hired SRI and "Buzz" Price, who managed such things as site selection and is credited with inventing the term Imagineering. He consulted for WED into the years of the Florida Project and shaped Walt Disney's final and very personal project—Cal Arts—serving on its board of trustees for many years. Price epitomized the rational planning approach that Disney would embrace in building the park.[44]

The SRI consultants and the company Price built, called ERA (which had one major client: WED), have often claimed that they made invaluable contributions to Disneyland's success. In particular they believed that they had

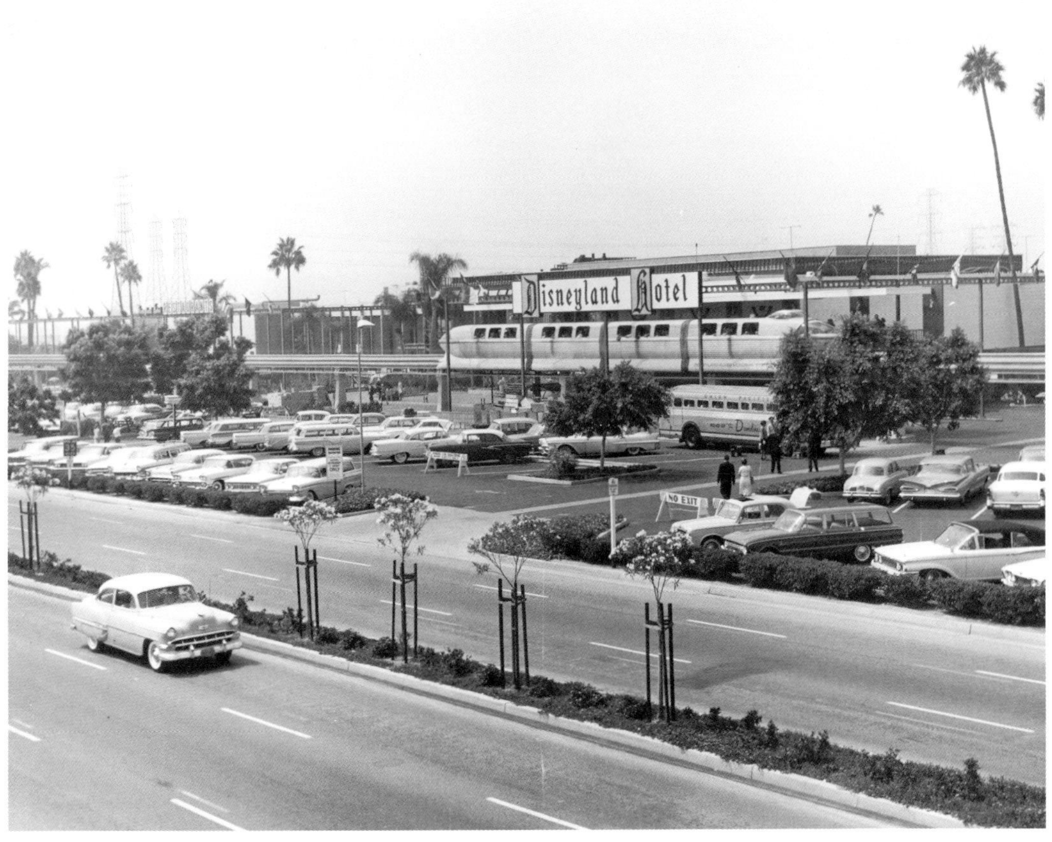

Fig. 2.10 Disneyland Hotel, Anaheim, circa 1959

taught Disney about people-moving by using scientifically managed and quantifiable information to shape planning and decision-making regarding park building, growth, and attraction design. No doubt Disney wholeheartedly endorsed the rationalized form of knowledge-gathering undertaken on his behalf. He needed the research he paid for, if only to bolster what he planned to do anyway, which required enormous capitalization and thus risk-taking and buy-in from his brother Roy and eventually the Disney board of directors after WED became part of the Studios in 1961.[45] What is less clear is the extent to which SRI and ERA really could generate data that were any better than Walt's and the Imagineers' anecdotal observations, which they gathered by simply watching how people used the park spaces. They made changes and projections based on those ethnographic and qualitative observations.

For the Imagineers themselves, the success of the park derived from something else entirely. John Hench, who began his career as a Disney story artist, argued that Disney's sense of the flow of people was a "know-how" that "developed in the Studio and from making films, because it really is, basically, to relate an idea with another idea, to control this relation. And this is what films do. It's really a theatrical problem to relate ideas in sequence with some kind of concept in time." This theatrical problem had to be adapted to three dimensions in the park. Hench described working with Disney early in the process of creating the park: "[Walt] would tell us to watch people. See how they behave; don't force them down artificial paths. You'll have to study people."[46] Disney also spent lots of time in the park once it opened to observe how guests used the spaces. When a maintenance director explained that they would have to fence in a flowerbed because people kept walking across it, according to Hench, Disney resisted: "When guests make their own path, they probably have a damn good reason for doing it."[47] Disney's view was very much in keeping with the times. This was, after all, the era of the rise of ergonomics. As noted earlier, Henry Dreyfuss explained, "When the point of contact between the product and the people becomes a point of friction, then the industrial designer has failed."[48] In a 1966 film describing ten years of success at Disneyland, the echo of such principles stands out: "In the planning and building there were no standards to follow; whatever worked became the code. Whatever failed to meet the public need was changed, replaced by a better idea." Perhaps Disneyland's singular success can be attributed to its founder's knowledge, experience, and investment in both forms of knowledge: the rational planner who was also steeped in the theatricalization of cinematic storytelling. Disneyland, as Walt said at its opening, seemed to embody the contradictory logic of being dedicated to the "ideals, dreams and hard facts that have created America."[49] What may have been unusual and unusually insightful about Disney was that he did not see a contradiction in employing both of these forms of knowledge.

The park concretized and spatialized this ambitious vision by offering interconnected transport modes. Freestanding transport, as much as the

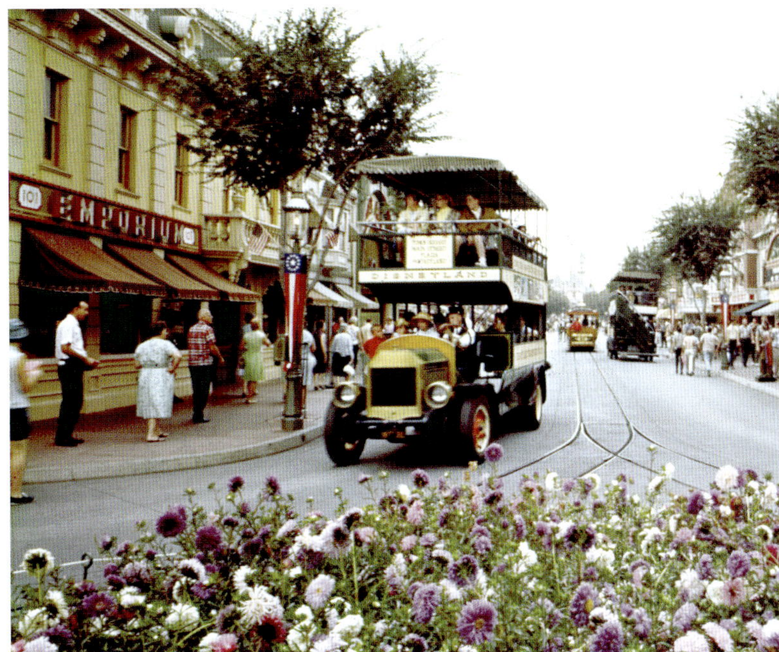

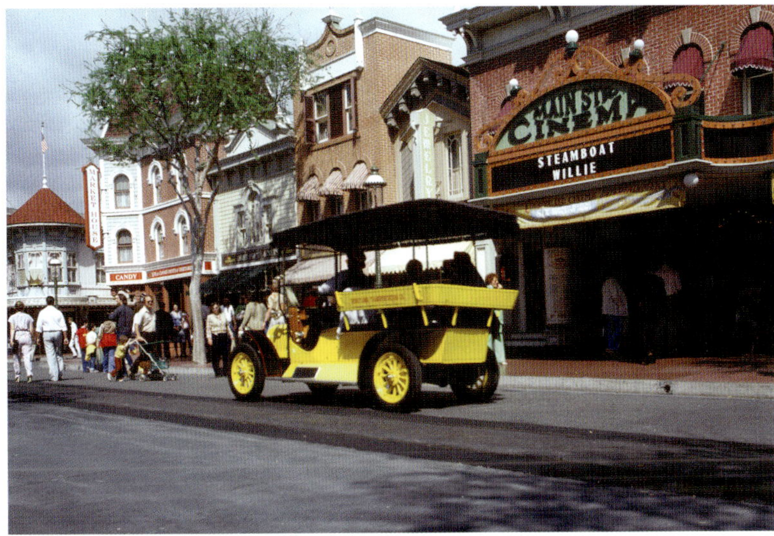

Fig. 2.11 Main Street, U.S.A. Vehicle, Disneyland, 1966. © Disney

Fig. 2.12 Main Street, U.S.A. Vehicle, Disneyland, 1973. © Disney

themed ride-throughs, offered riding itself as an aesthetic experience—for those on the ride and for those who watched. At the same time, guests journeying through the park experienced an overall narrative of historical progress through transportation.

At the park's one entrance, guests looked up at the Main Street Station to find the train that traced the park's perimeter (see fig. 2.3). From there, Main Street, U.S.A., teemed with old-time vehicles such as omnibuses, delivery trucks, horse-drawn streetcars, and surreys designed for Disneyland by Bob Gurr, a car designer without an engineering background (figs. 2.11, 2.12). As visitors made their way to Frontierland they encountered a

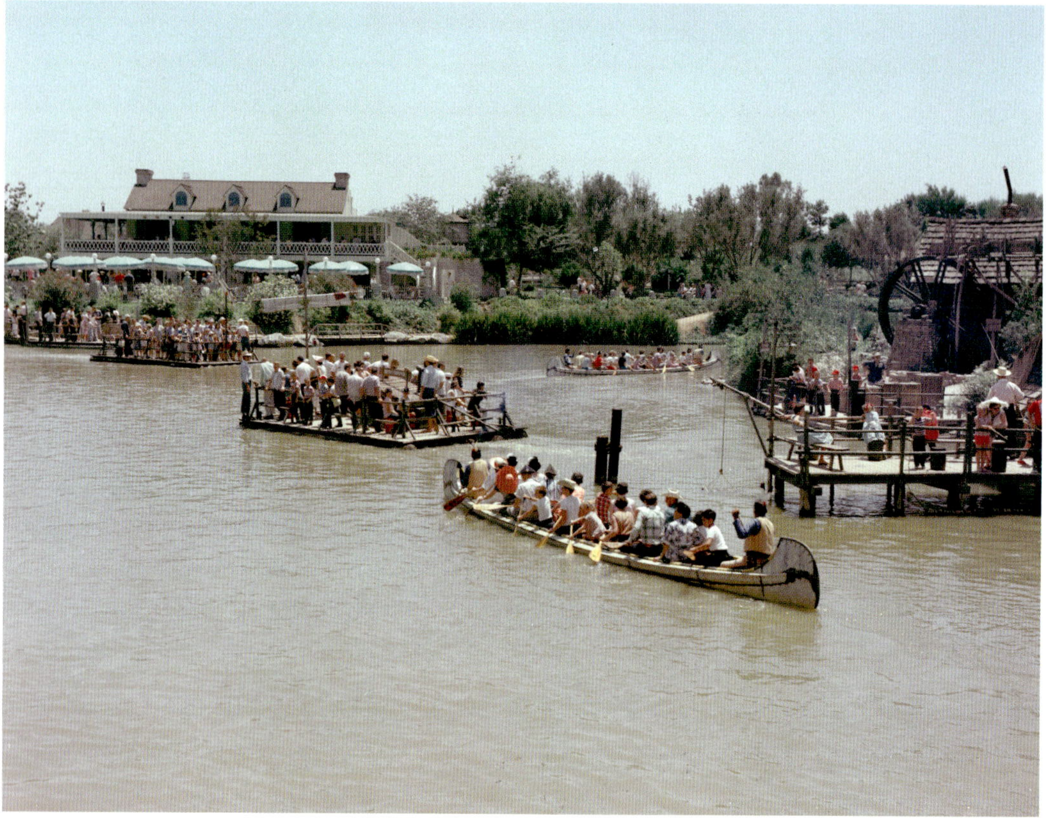

Fig. 2.13 Indian War Canoes and Rafts to Tom Sawyer Island, 1959. Rivers of America, Disneyland. © Disney

Fig. 2.14 Indian War Canoes, 1956. Rivers of America, Disneyland. © Disney

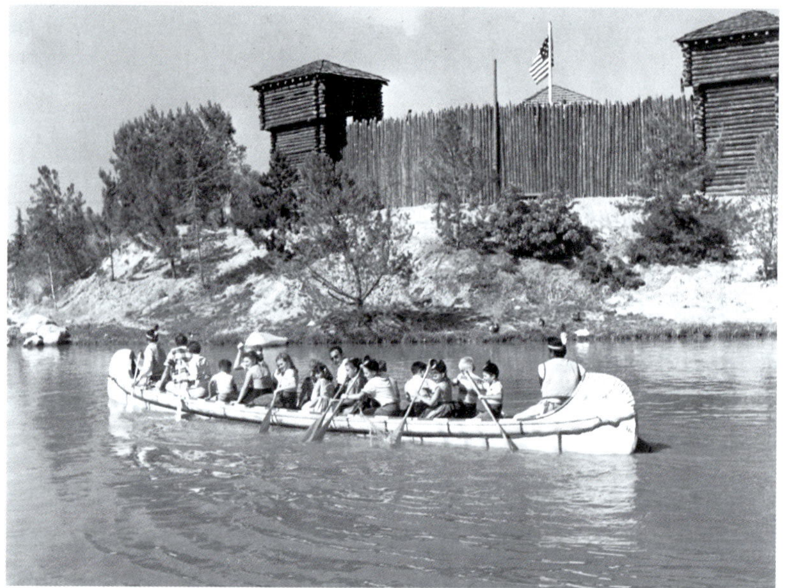

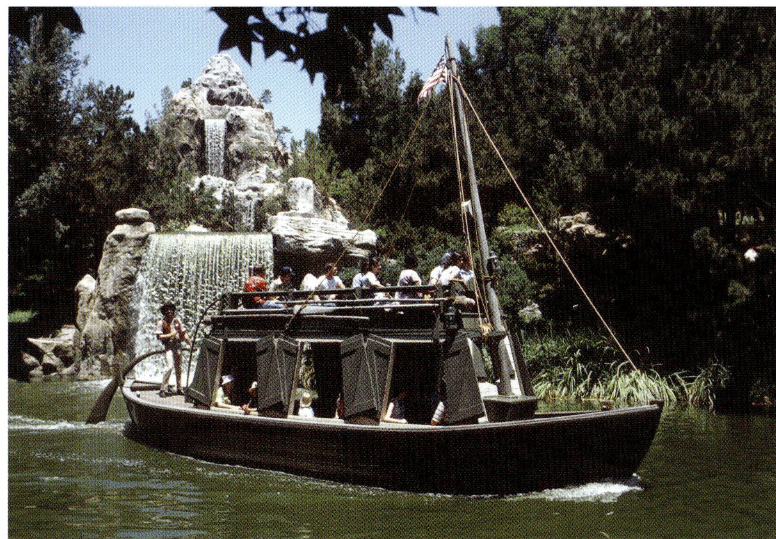

Fig. 2.15 Keel Boats, circa mid-1970s. Rivers of America, Disneyland. © Disney

Fig. 2.16 Columbia Sailing Ship, circa 1970s. Rivers of America, Disneyland. © Disney

Fig. 2.17 Mark Twain Riverboat, 1979. Rivers of America, Disneyland. © Disney

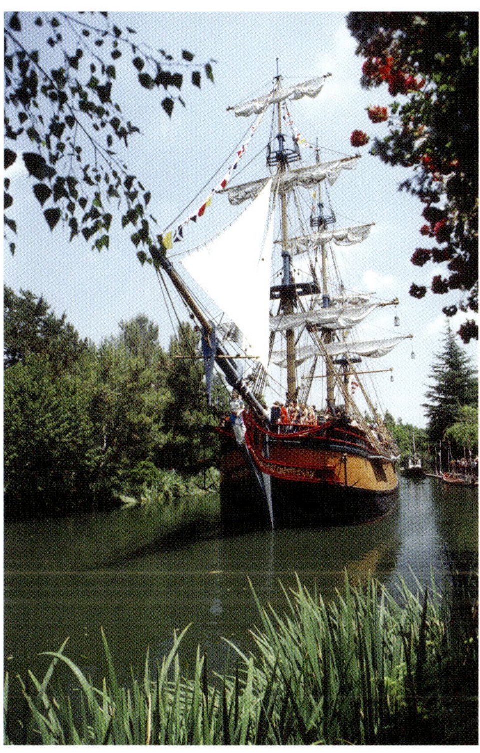

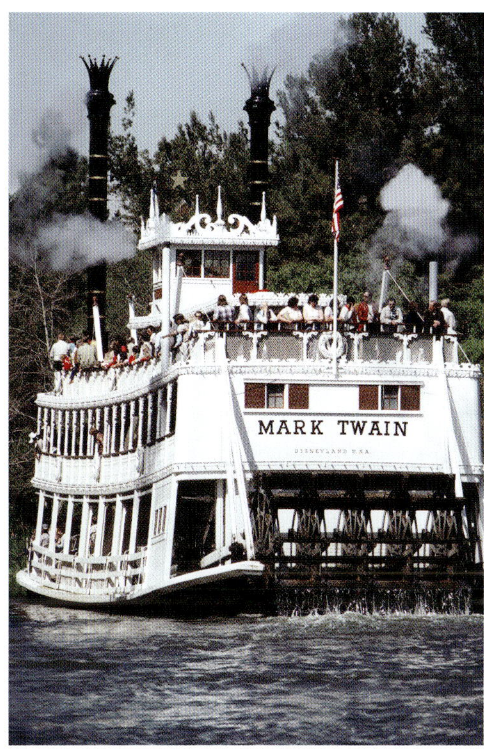

variety of watercraft on the artificially constructed Rivers of America, defining westward expansion. These craft were set in an evolutionary relation to each other, from the simplicity of the Indian War Canoes and the Mike Fink Keel Boats (which had also been featured on the *Disneyland* show's hit *Davy Crockett* series), to the sophisticated beauty of the three-masted Sailing Ship Columbia, added in 1958, to the Mark Twain Riverboat, a working steamship built for the park (figs. 2.13–2.17).

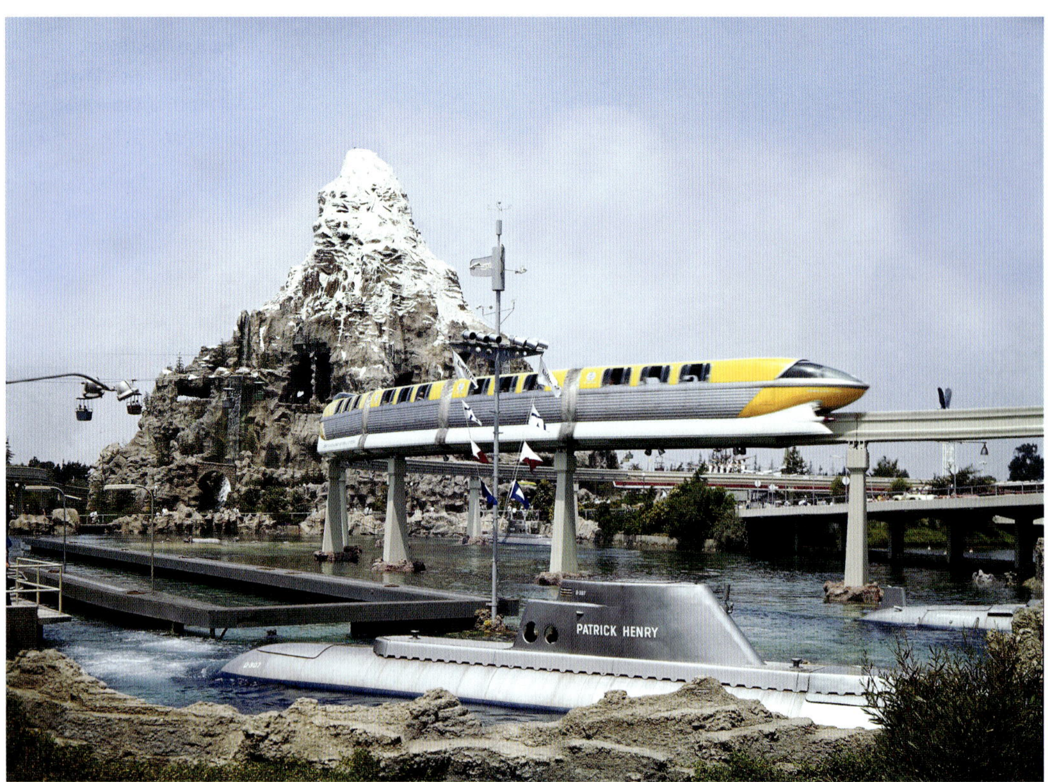

Fig. 2.18 Monorail, 1959. Disneyland. © Disney

While Tomorrowland's Autopia represented a play freeway with gas-powered cars that guests could drive, newer and more experimental modes of transport, such as the Skyway (a Swiss innovation redesigned for Disneyland) and the Monorail (a German-American innovation called the "highway in the sky," the first of its kind operating in the Western Hemisphere when it opened in 1959), directed guests' attention skyward, leaving the ground for walking (fig. 2.18). The Monorail offered "silent, electric-powered travel high above the Magic Kingdom," and the Skyway actually never fully stopped running to load its passengers.[50] A circle through the park would eventually lead visitors to the future of transport in the Rocket to the Moon in Tomorrowland.

The challenge of presenting the future and keeping it from feeling dated plagued Disney so much in Tomorrowland that they left the area quite underdeveloped in the park's first iteration (fig. 2.19). According to Dick Irvine—an art director at Disney who had left to go to 20th Century Fox and then came back to Disney and was responsible for the developmental oversight of all the park's attractions, the 1964–65 World's Fair Disney projects, and was named WED's chief operating officer in 1967—Walt said, "The minute we do Tomorrowland, it's today and it's past."[51] In fact, it originally was set a mere thirty years in the future, to 1986, when Halley's Comet was expected to return and when it was envisioned that supersonic travel might inaugurate an age of space travel. Tomorrowland's iconic entryway "weenie" (as the "landmarks" were called), the Clock of the World, an hourglass-shaped tower that showed

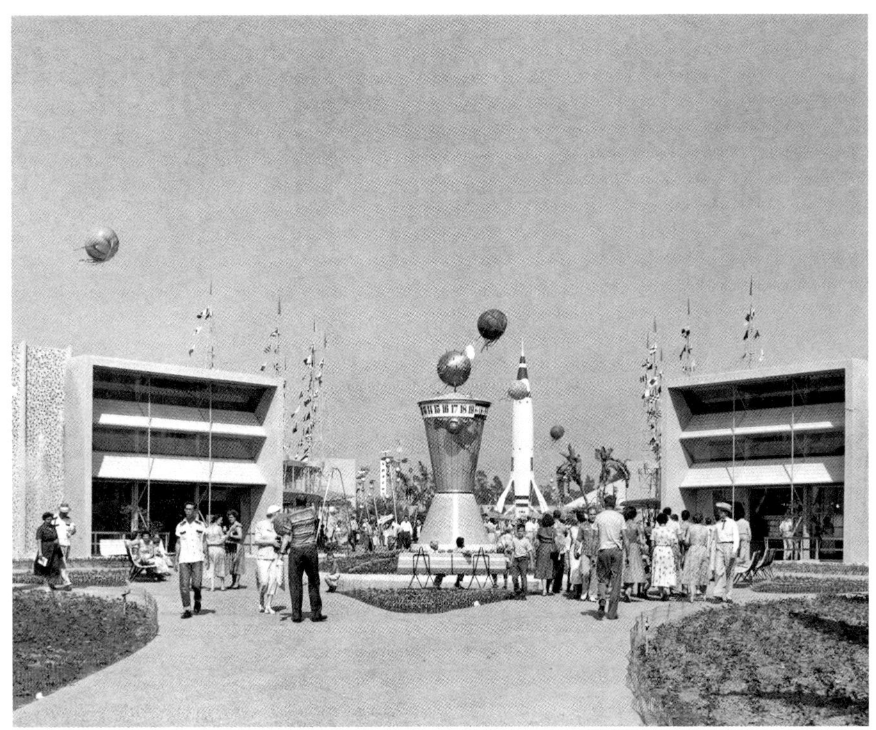

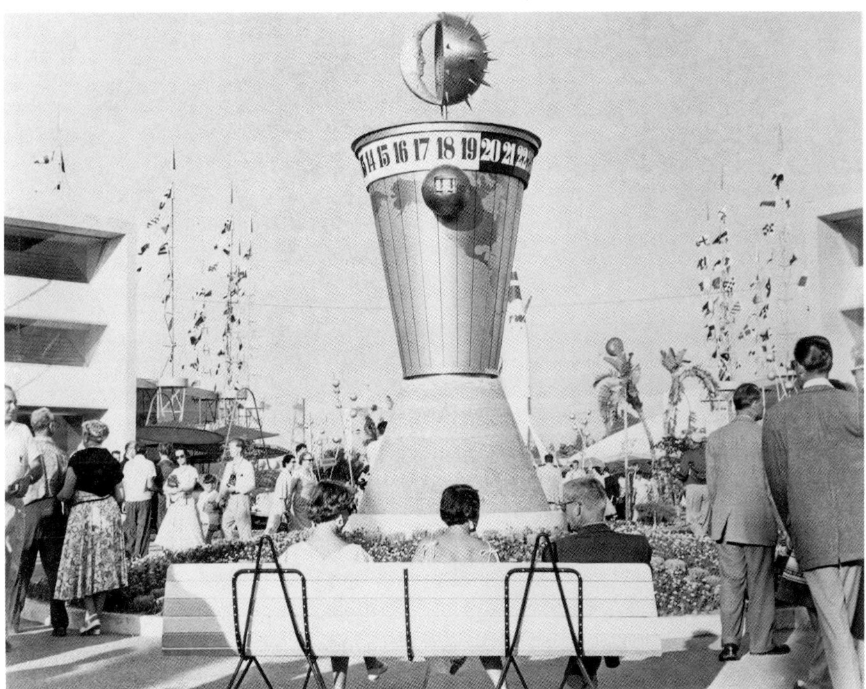

Fig. 2.19 TWA Rocket to the Moon, Tomorrowland Entrance, 1955. © Disney

Fig. 2.20 Tomorrowland Clock of the World, Disneyland, 1955. © Disney

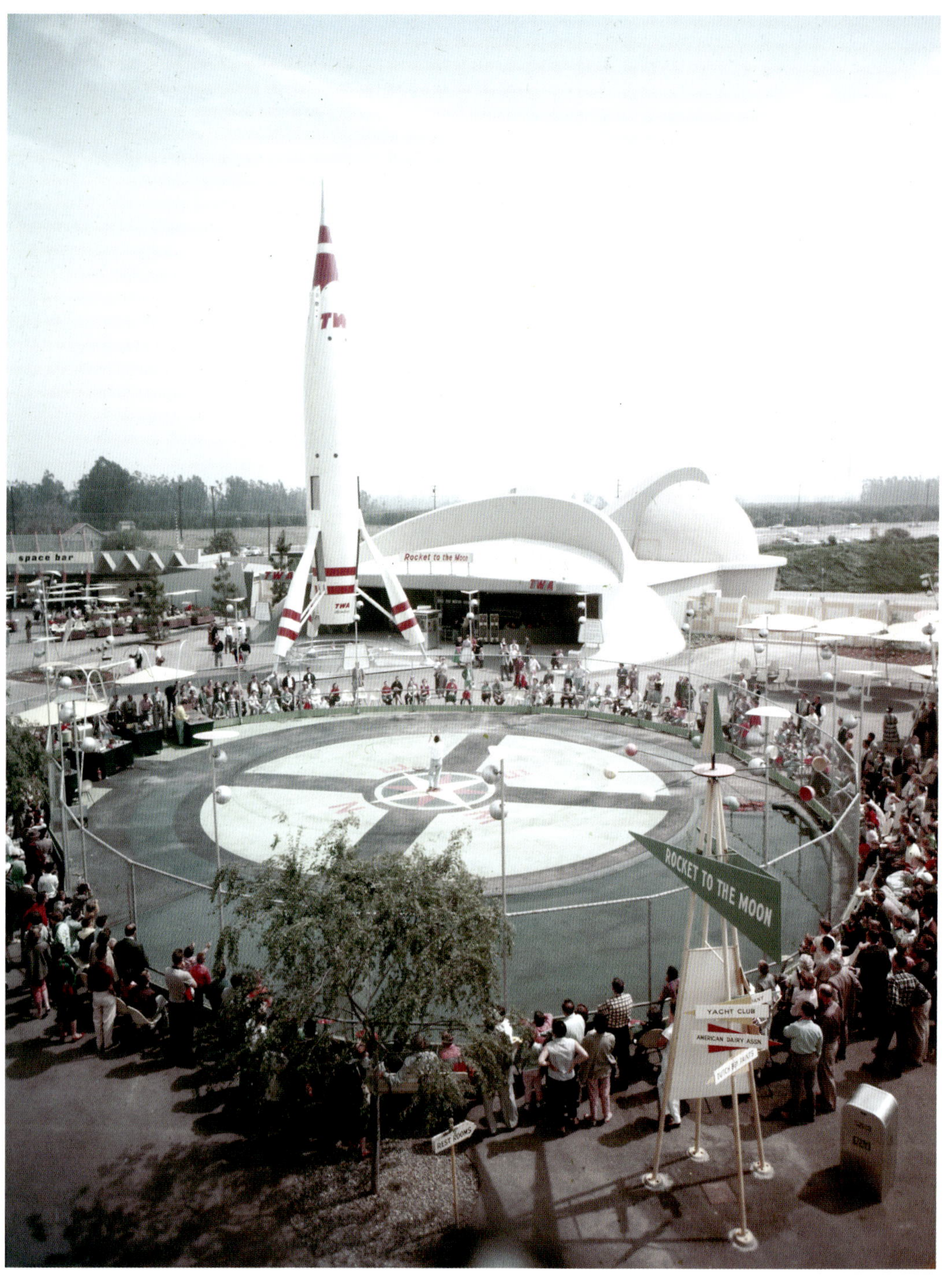

Fig. 2.21 TWA Rocket to the Moon, 1955–59, © Disney

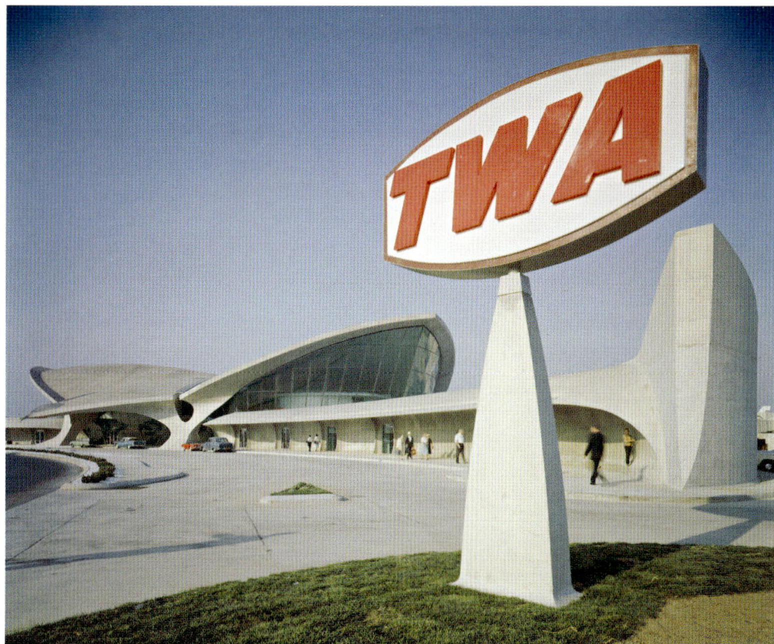

Fig. 2.22 TWA Terminal, JFK, 1962. Ezra Stoller, photographer. © Ezra Stoller/Esto

what time it was everywhere in the world simultaneously, hardly pointed to that interstellar future. Instead, it betrayed its jet age consciousness of increasing simultaneity of time across space, which served as a visual shorthand for the jet's time-space compression (fig. 2.20).[52] Nothing could have seemed more 1955 than that. In fact, Tomorrowland seemed so associated with the jet age that one observer concluded that it even looked like an airport: "It called for a huge concrete shell to cover the entire area. . . . It looked not unlike the TWA Terminal at Idlewild in New York."[53] This undated comment, found in the Walt Disney Archives, had to have been made in retrospect, because the TWA Terminal did not even exist when Disneyland opened. In fact, it might have been more apt had he noted that the iconic TWA Terminal, designed by Eero Saarinen, who received the commission in 1956, the year after Disneyland opened, looked a lot like what had been built at the theme park the year before. One cannot help but wonder if TWA had asked Saarinen to consider what had already been built in Anaheim, a project into which a great deal of corporate identity had already been poured (figs. 2.21, 2.22).

Since Tomorrowland represented a jet age idea of a future that closely resembled the present, it always needed updating to be "futuristic." In 1964, planning began for a $22 million renovation, which opened in July 1967 as New Tomorrowland. The park's vision of the future was now seen less through such symbols as rockets and interplanetary travel than through abstraction: the sight and experience of fluid motion, a spectacle of a networked system of people being moved on planet Earth. It was touted as "A World on the Move" in a press release. "The new land is alive with whirring wheels, jet propelled travel and exciting sights and sounds on every side. Architecturally, the new land is designed to facilitate movement of large numbers of people along an

Fig. 2.23 Disneyland's "New" Tomorrowland, concept drawing, circa 1964–65. *Disney News Magazine*, Summer 1967. © Disney

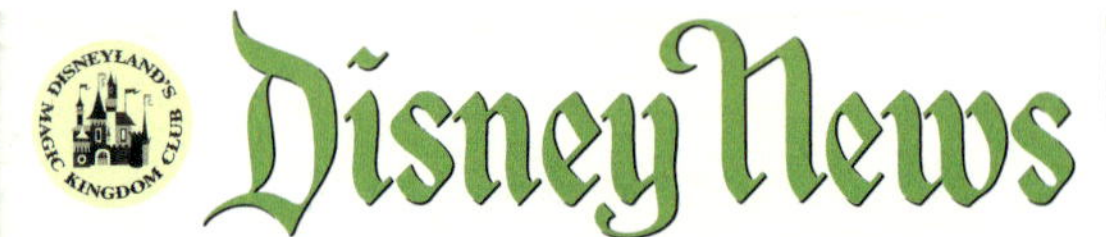

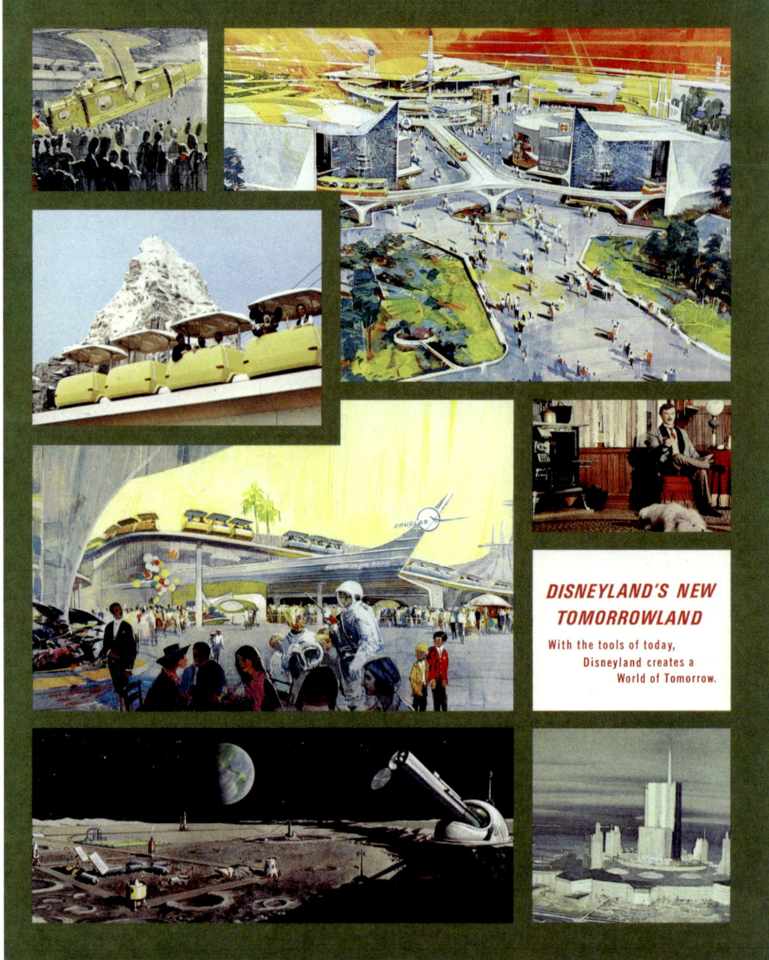

exterior corridor and through its colorful pavilions—conveying a constant impression of movement and activity."[54]

Fluid motion and a naturalized choreography in which nothing actually stops defined New Tomorrowland (figs. 2.23, 2.24). Gone was the Clock of the World, replaced by the PeopleMover, designed by WedWay Transportation Systems and dubbed a new concept in transportation for High Density Traffic Flow Areas. Another press release emphasized that the PeopleMover was a "series of vehicles that never stop moving, even when passengers are boarding or debarking . . . vehicles that can't collide, compartment doors that open and close by themselves."[55] In other words, the name finally said it all: the vehicle, like the vision, was about people-moving (fig. 2.25).

The PeopleMover improved the belt technology that WED had developed for the Ford Magic Skyway at the 1964–65 World's Fair; Disney's original

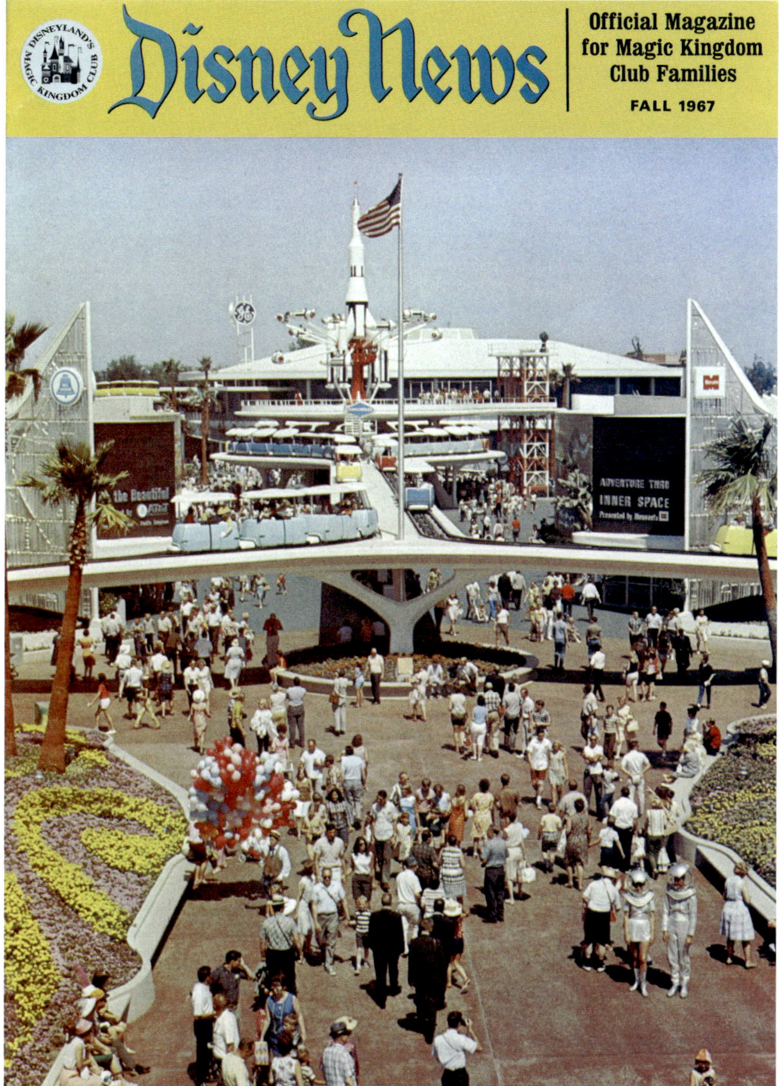

Fig. 2.24 Disneyland's "New" Tomorrowland, circa 1967. *Disney News Magazine,* Summer 1967. © Disney

inspiration had been the way people moved through buildings at the Swiss National Fair of 1964 in Lausanne.[56] Of the many renovated and new attractions, it ran through New Tomorrowland as its pulsing beat. The park promoted it as an automatic and all-electric point-to-point shuttle service, although in reality it merely offered a "scenic tour" through Tomorrowland. The park promoted it, however, as if one day it would be an actual working form of transport. Additionally, WED developed the Omnimover vehicle for the Monsanto-sponsored Adventure Thru Inner Space attraction. The Omnimover was a continuous chain of constantly loading vehicles (called Atomobiles—still in use in the park in such rides as the Haunted Mansion, where they are known as Doom Buggies), and the vehicles had the ability to rotate 360 degrees and "aim" passengers at particular areas for viewing, directing their gazes in a three-dimensional show, an improvement over the more

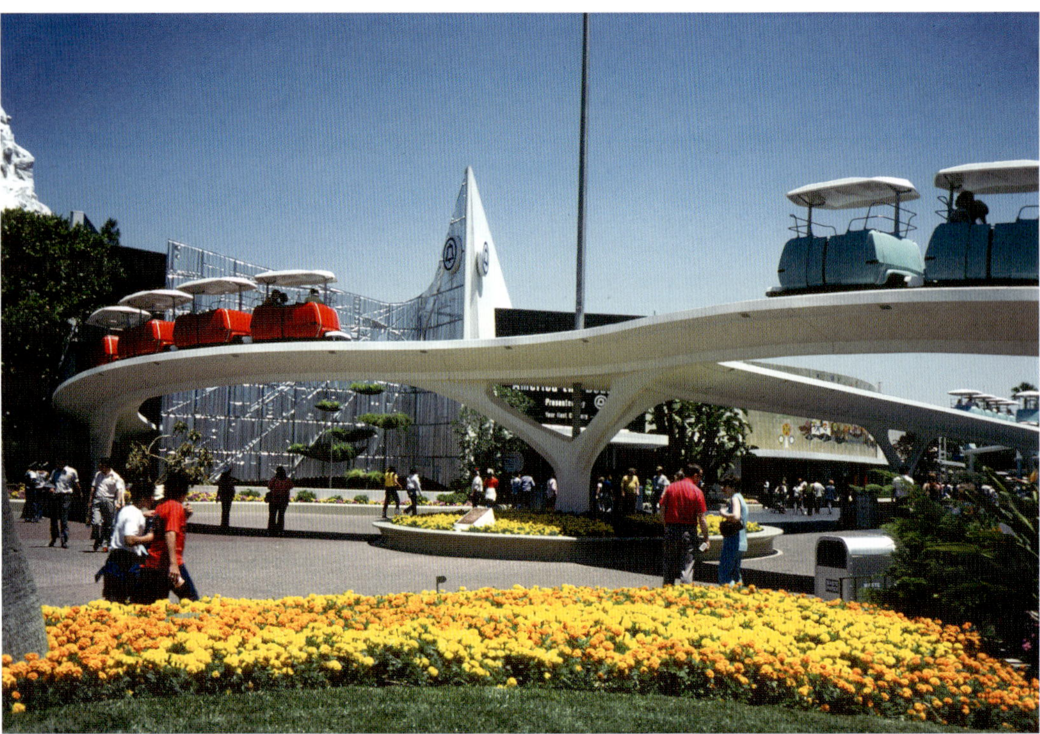

Fig. 2.25 PeopleMover at Entrance to "New" Tomorrowland, 1974. Disneyland. © Disney

limited control of the viewers' gaze in films, where such directed attention was achieved only through camerawork.

The impact of such change in 1967 started to clarify for more astute observers that Disneyland's genius lay in its infrastructure and system of flow. As the architect Peter Blake wrote in 1972, "The *real* Tomorrowland is the vast infrastructure that no paying customer ever sees. . . . The *real* Tomorrowland is also above grade: the grid of trains and other earthbound vehicles, and of skybucket aerial vehicles (none of which pollute the atmosphere). . . . And the *real* Tomorrowland is also an electronic communications network . . . a jet-engined power plant that provides all the needed juice and much, much more."[57] Blake was writing on the heels of the 1971 opening of Walt Disney World, when New Tomorrowland could be understood with even greater clarity in relation to the park in Florida. It was placed in relation not just to the history of Disneyland since its opening but also with regard to Disney and WED's 1964–65 World's Fair work, which itself had led to the planning for Walt Disney World and EPCOT, the place that Disney imagined and proposed publicly as the culmination of his vision of fluid motion in the month before he died.

Blake understood why one of the greatest urban planners of the century, Robert Moses, president of the 1964–65 World's Fair, sought Disney's participation in what he hoped would be the most successful fair of all time. Of course, Disneyland was already a major phenomenon. To give a sense of its impact: six years after the park's opening, 25 million people had already visited. In a survey, 99.9 percent of Disney visitors said they would recommend a visit to a friend. Interestingly, for every child who went to the park, four adults attended.[58] In Disney, Moses saw a master planner, a designer, and a man who was as accomplished in the art of people-moving as he was in providing amusing and entertaining content. As Welton Becket, who worked at the fair designing the Ford Magic Skyway, noted, the tables had turned regarding Walt's relation to architecture and planning. Whereas Disney had picked the brains of architects such as Pereira and Luckman when he was planning Disneyland, it was now Disney who was in the position to explain to architects how to "design public space for optimal use, including such things as where to locate the concessions, the toilets and ticketing."[59]

Moses sought out Disney based not just on the success of Disneyland, but also because Disney had already applied his knowledge more broadly, at the 1960 Winter Olympics in Squaw Valley. In 1955, the International Olympic Committee selected the California location for the VIII Olympic Winter Games. It would be the first purpose-built site to host an Olympic Games (including the construction of the first Olympic Village). Walt Disney, who had been an early investor in the Sugar Bowl ski resort in the Donner Pass, became the head of the Pageantry Committee. Within five years the WED team took over many planning activities beyond designing the opening and closing ceremonies, for which they were initially hired. Imagineer John Hench redesigned the Olympic torches and the relay, and he oversaw the creation of colossal ice sculptures (fig. 2.26). Disney designed the main ceremonial stage with flagpoles and giant aluminum crests of the participant nations, all underwritten by corporate sponsors. Additionally, and perhaps most significantly, WED consulted on such aspects of the event as ticketing, parking, and the organization of crowd movement.[60] During the games, Disneyland Cast Members even came to the site and entertained athletes.

Moses initially had hoped to ask Disney to install a working monorail on the fairgrounds. In 1962 he wrote to Martin Stone, head of the Fair's Industrial Division, to remind him that "we are bending every effort to get the Walt Disney monorail" to the New York fair.[61] Eventually Moses abandoned the plan for the Disney system as too expensive and complex, and he sought a less ambitious monorail by AMF, a recreation company best known for making bowling alley equipment, but he persisted in enlisting Disney's creative energies. Disney, in partnership with several sponsors (three corporate, a state government, and UNICEF) organized four extremely successful attractions that were visited by 91 percent of fairgoers: the GE Pavilion's Progressland, featuring the GE Carousel of Progress; "it's a small world; Great Moments with Mr. Lincoln; and the Ford Magic Skyway. The skyway alone accounted for visits by more than 15 million people.[62]

Disney embraced the opportunity to participate in the fair, and not simply because he was flattered by having the premier urban planner of the age seek out his advice. He had his own business reasons to venture east of the Mississippi. Within the Disney organization, various parties struggled over

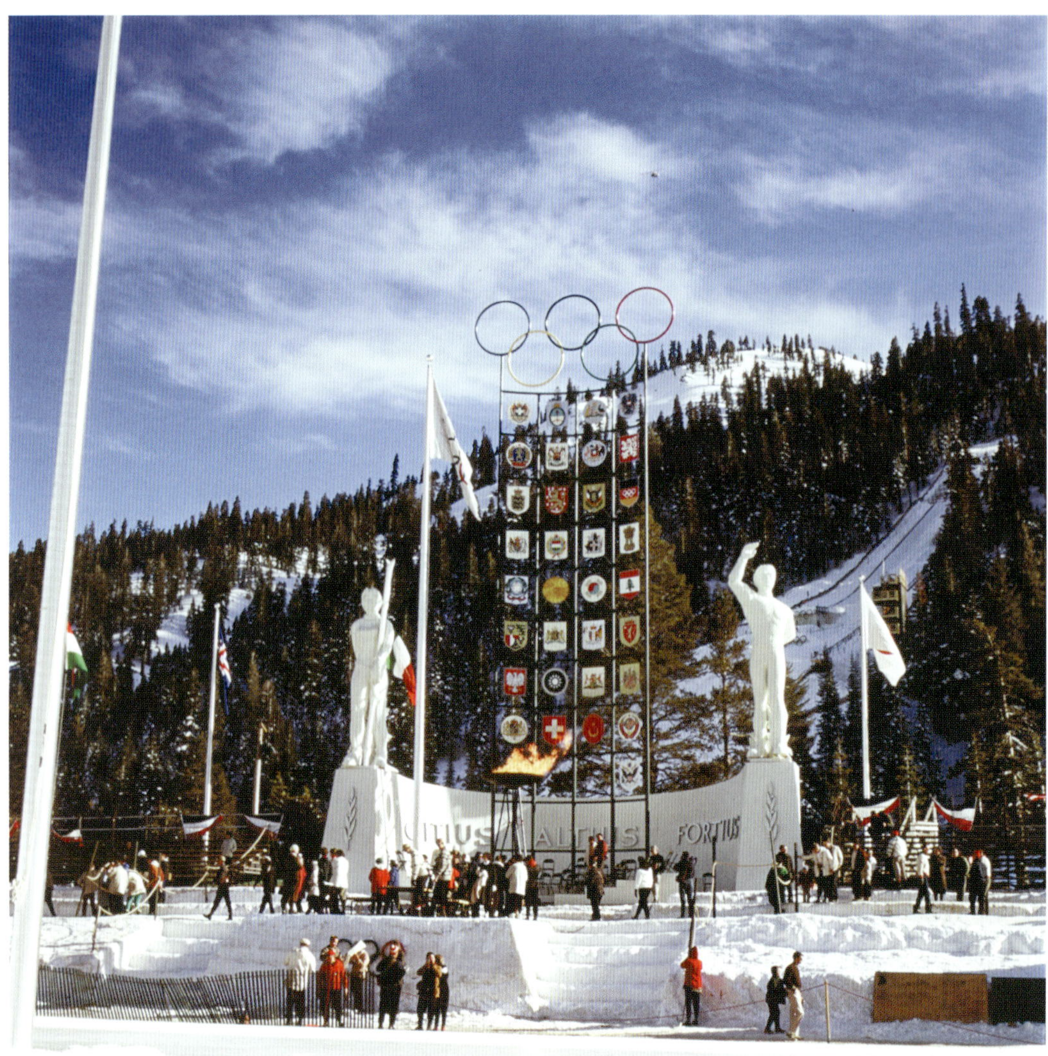

Fig. 2.26 Ice sculptures at Squaw Valley Olympic Village, 1960. Bill Briner

what might motivate their involvement, and they carefully considered exactly what value they brought to the fair. On the one hand, in an October 1960 memo, the organization tried to define and differentiate their business: "The Disney organization owns and operates Disneyland Park, which is a combination amusement and recreation center and permanent exposition. . . . We are not in the business or profession of industrial or exhibit design and we do not seek employment in that field as such."[63] But in a letter from Disney consultant Harrison Price dated October 5, 1960, to Dick Irvine, Price defined "Imagineering" as "imaginative concepts in design, architecture, engineering and entertainment." It seems hard to separate this neologism from what people had begun to call industrial design, a field highly involved in world's fairs. In other words, it seems that the Disney people were undeniably in the business of industrial design. Imagineering is simply what they named it. Price described "institutional, expositional and show design" as part of Imagineering's mission, and then explained that WED had devised a theme for its client, an institutional story that would be incorporated into shows or exhibits, along with a budget, and then had implemented the engineering and construction phases.[64]

Two aspects, however, stand out as distinct from the charge of ordinary industrial designers: WED emphasized their expertise in traffic flow and people-moving and their ownership of the work they produced. Industrial designers may have been interested in lighting and ergonomics, but the sorts of elements that Price liked to enumerate—turnstiles, ticketing, parking, and walkways—seemed to fall into the bailiwick of landscapers and engineers. WED's interdisciplinary team handled this diverse charge on its own. Additionally, Price explained that while it had been customary that the "designer's" creation would eventually belong to the client, WED retained ownership of the content. The company worked as cosponsor on every project and reserved the right to bring everything it designed back to Disneyland.[65] This commitment to product ownership can even be gleaned from general publicity. Marty Sklar, who wrote many of the early Disneyland scripts as well as the *Disneyland News,* noted in a 1963 letter regarding a story for *Popular Science*, which Ford was trying to arrange, that "we are hopeful that we can do so [be featured in the story] without revealing any mechanisms for which patents are being sought."[66]

From WED's perspective, the fair allowed the company the unprecedented opportunity to seek funds for research and development of new attractions that would debut at the fair in New York and then be brought to Disneyland. They were happy to tell the GE story, for example, because the "content" really amounted to the design of the experience—the carousel, the Audio-Animatronics figures—as much as the story of progress through electricity and the GE message that "progress was their product." Although Walt Disney Imagineers crafted the narrative content and managed the corporate story, they also understood the attractions as vehicles for the display of the Disney exhibition systems.

Corporations sometimes struggled with the flash proposed by the Disney packaging, fearing that their own product would be buried by the attraction itself. This explains why it proved hard to find a sponsor for the show originally called "One Nation Under God," initially imagined as an Audio-Animatronics hall of presidents but that eventually featured only one president: Abraham Lincoln. As Harold Sharp, vice president of Coca-Cola, wrote when declining to sponsor the attraction, "We certainly would like for every visitor to be subjected to this awesome spectacle but we would also like for him to go away with some kind of first-rate and enduring impression of the delicious and refreshing qualities of Coca-Cola."[67] The show had nothing to do with soda, and so the company felt the connection was simply too remote for Coca-Cola to sponsor.

The fair opened doors for Disney, presenting opportunities for the company to enter into new relationships with more corporations, many of

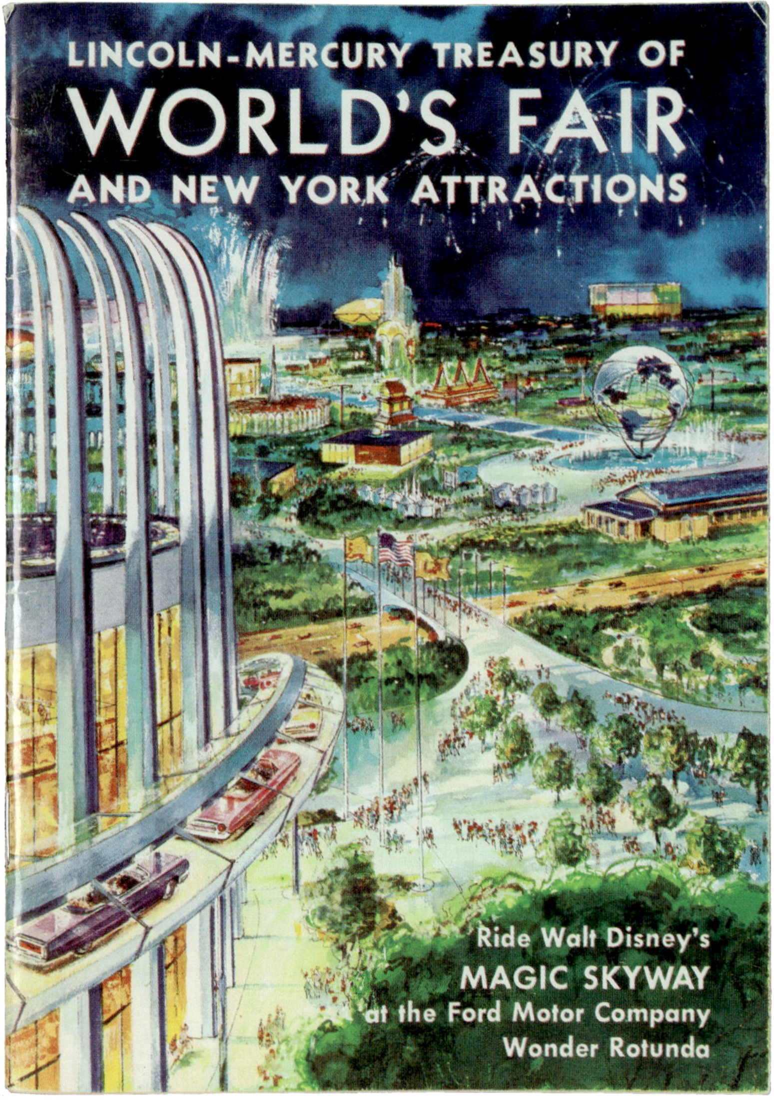

Fig. 2.27 Welton Becket, Magic Skyway, Ford Pavilion, New York World's Fair, 1964. Brochure: Lincoln-Mercury Treasury of World's Fair Attractions

which might be more inclined to partner at the world's fair than in the park in Anaheim. For example, it gave Jack Sayers, in charge of leasee relations for Disneyland, an excuse to reach out to such corporations as American Airlines and IBM, although preexisting relations between such companies also shaped who would or would not work with Disney. For example, as Sayers reported in a memo, "IBM feels their competitive position with GE would preclude any World's Fair development." Conversely, Ford was eager to get involved with Disney in 1964 because "they are determined to have a better show than GM at this Fair following GM's domination of the 1939 World's Fair with Futurama."[68] And, in a sense, Disney did produce for Ford the "Futurama" of the 1964–65 World's Fair: the Ford Magic Skyway.

Relations with the Ford Motor Company had begun much earlier, when Disney had hoped to install a hall of presidents at Disneyland and had discussed it with Henry Ford II when he visited the park in July 1960. The project, however, shifted gears to creating a $2.5 million fair attraction, still undefined as of May 1961, when the opportunity to work together presented itself. What is interesting to note is that from the start Disney sold Ford not the content of a show but rather WED's expertise in crowd management: "From the standpoint of handling capacity crowds, Disneyland Park has provided a laboratory for experience that cannot be duplicated anywhere. All our technical and management experience in taking care of large attendances will be available to you."[69] They also pointed out that the crowd at Disneyland was 80 percent adult with above-average incomes and job status and who also owned more than one car per family. Such demographic information also probably helped them settle on a very adult Ford Magic Skyway exhibition at the fair.

More than 15 million people visited the Disney/Ford exhibition, which consisted of two large buildings designed by Becket, whom Disney himself selected for the job (figs. 2.27, 2.28). After a walk-through of miniature dioramas of different places where Ford made cars, as well as a presentation of a history of Ford told through a series of equally small dioramas, visitors passed through a comical orchestra made from car parts. All this led them up to the physical space of the Magic Skyway, which fairgoers had already previewed outside on the fairgrounds—a classic Disneyland method of teasing by showing some of an attraction from the grounds outside. Riders entered via cars, especially the highly touted new Ford convertible, the 1964 Mustang, mounted on one of the ingenious technological aspects of the attraction of which WED was proudest: a belt on which the cars were affixed and which moved passengers at a uniform speed (figs. 2.29, 2.30). The automatization of the loading process reduced wait time and soon became part of other Disney attractions back in Disneyland. The eleven-minute journey began via a time tunnel to "the dawn of time in the animal kingdom, (where mammals without benefit of mind) destroy themselves" (fig. 2.31).[70] As Walt Disney explained, the Ford Magic Skyway continued

Fig. 2.28 Ford Pavilion at the World's Fair, New York, 1964–65

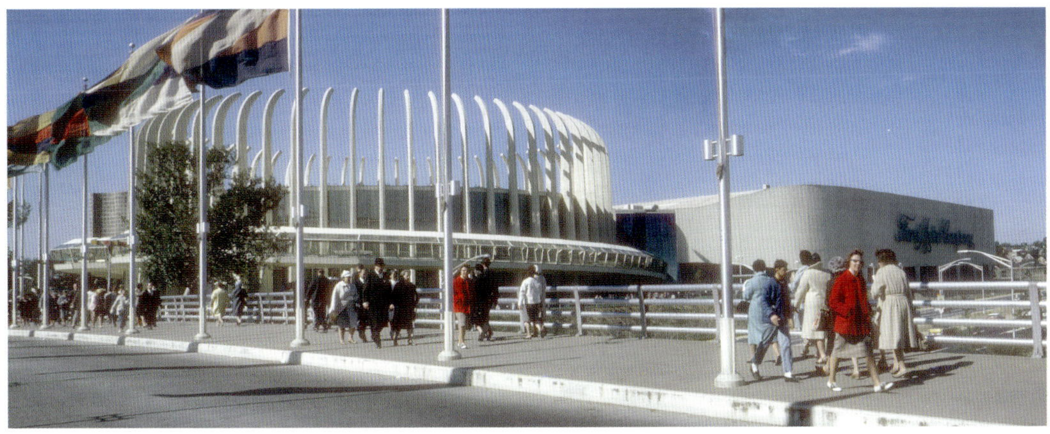

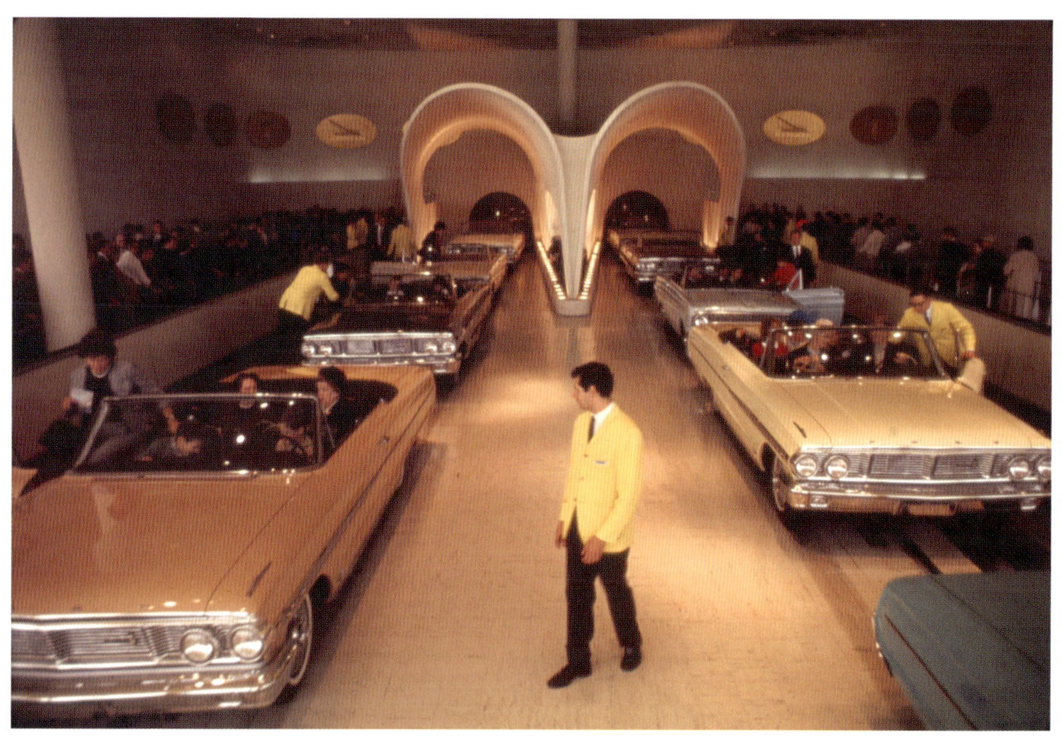

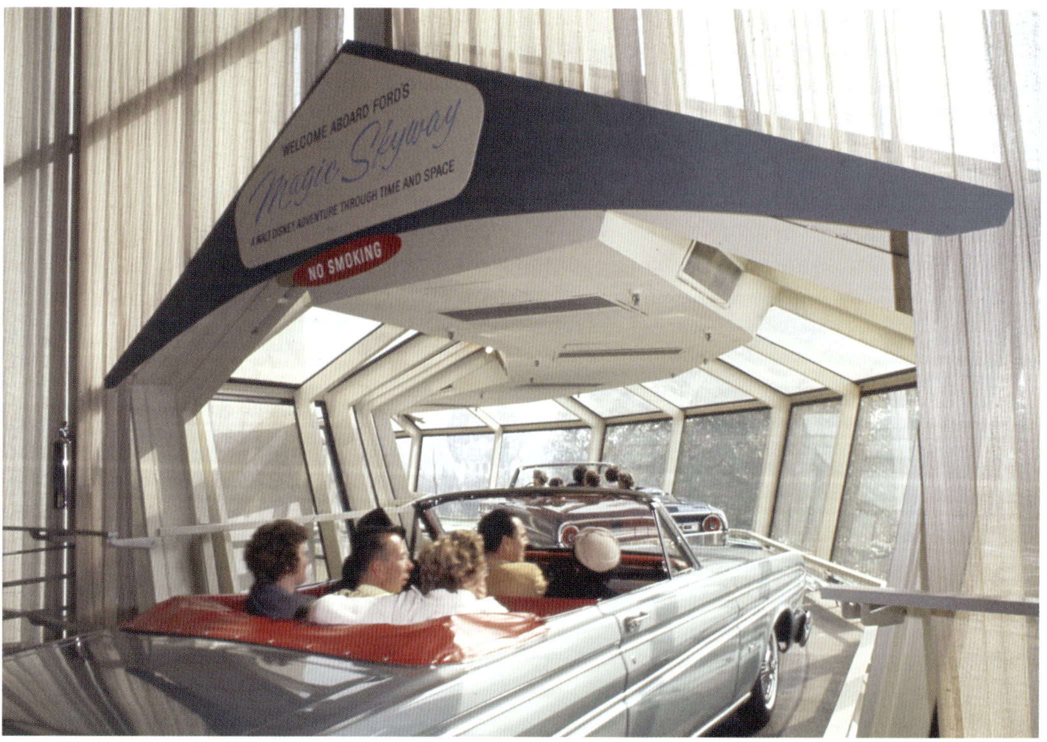
WELCOME ABOARD FORD'S
Magic Skyway
A WALT DISNEY ADVENTURE THROUGH TIME AND SPACE
NO SMOKING

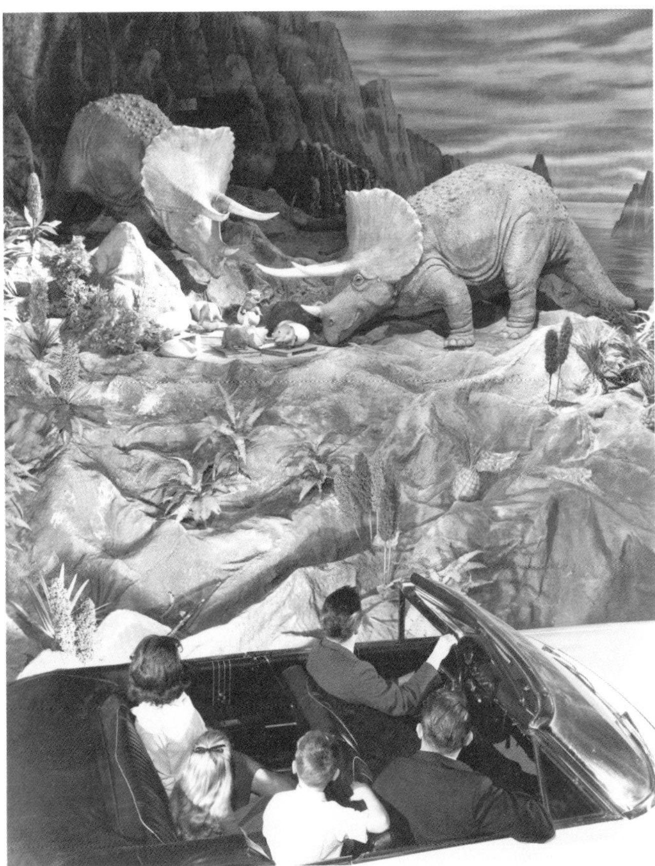

Fig. 2.29 Loading area for Magic Skyway, Ford Pavilion, New York World's Fair, 1964–65

Fig. 2.30 Entering the transparent tunnel, Magic Skyway

Fig. 2.31 Primeval Earth Diorama, Magic Skyway

the plausible implausibility of such attractions as Walt Disney's Enchanted Tiki Room, but here with relatively simple Audio-Animatronic dinosaurs: "What we want to provide guests . . . is an entirely original experience, something no one had ever seen or done before. It could never happen in real life . . . but visitors feel they have lived through a wonderful once in a lifetime experience."[71] The attraction's catalogue explained, "The ride then moves to man and his dominion through ingenuity—with particular reference to the invention of the wheel. The illustrative scene in this section is man's challenge to move an elephant, and thus how man's conquest of transportation problems is achieved."[72] Through a second time tunnel, passengers arrived at Space City, a City of Tomorrow, where the taped voice of Walt Disney himself urged them to explore the world where Disney's jet age temporality promised that "tomorrow was created today."[73]

If transportation as progress was the attraction's manifest narrative, the mode of transport was as meaningful as its content. A booklet describing the Ford Pavilion emphasized comfort, convenience, and the fact that no effort would be required of passengers whose "engineless" cars were powered and guided by a central control panel. The ride would seem as if the vehicle were moving "on a cushion of air like the experimental Ford Levacar. Will it also fly?" it asked.[74] In other words, history progressed through

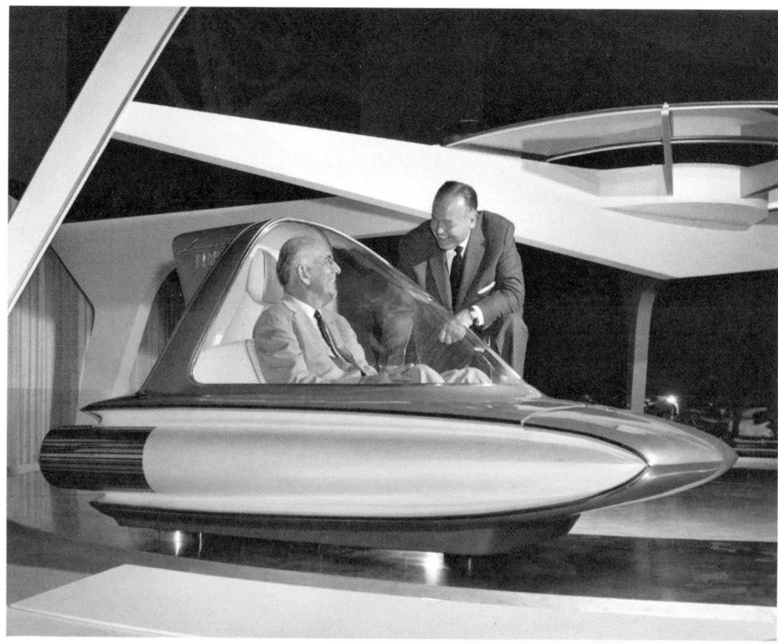

Fig. 2.32 Levacar Mach 1 Concept Car, Ford Rotunda, 1959, Dearborn, Michigan

transport technology and soon, driving in a car, which already seemed as smooth as flying in a jet, might actually take flight (fig. 2.32).

The final Disney attraction organized at the fair, "it's a small world," took passengers on a boat ride that was also updated for the jet age. Promotional material explained that the "boats will be propelled at the rate of two feet per second by silent, hidden jet streams beneath the water line of the channel. This WED system will eliminate vibration, noise and engine fumes."[75] In other words, given such "attributes" as fluid motion, even a little boat took on jet age qualities. Additionally, although passengers journeyed in a boat, the jet, its advocates promoted, led to a greater harmonization of cultures around the world. To design the attraction, Disney turned to Mary Blair, a former employee, and asked her to return to work for him after a long hiatus that included extensive experience in advertising and in doing illustrations for Golden Books. He was firm in seeking her style for the attraction's overall design and for its interior artwork.[76] Because Blair had been a children's book illustrator, she ably used that format's big blocks of color, transforming the art of the flat page by blowing it up, tipping it in many directions to achieve a pop-up book effect. Toys, wrapping paper, and scenic backdrops were displayed against iconic tourist posters–like settings. Elaborately costumed Audio-Animatronic dolls moved electronically, but the sense of fluidity was aided by glitter everywhere—on the costumes, on the backdrops and props. Blair described her work as creating a "theater in the round" and explained that "the audience moves, the performers move, and everyone . . . seems to have a grand old time."[77] The use of bright colors throughout and careful use of specific colors for certain places (tartans in Scotland; a frantic, mismatched noisy palette for Latin America; heavy blues for the South Seas) cedes in the

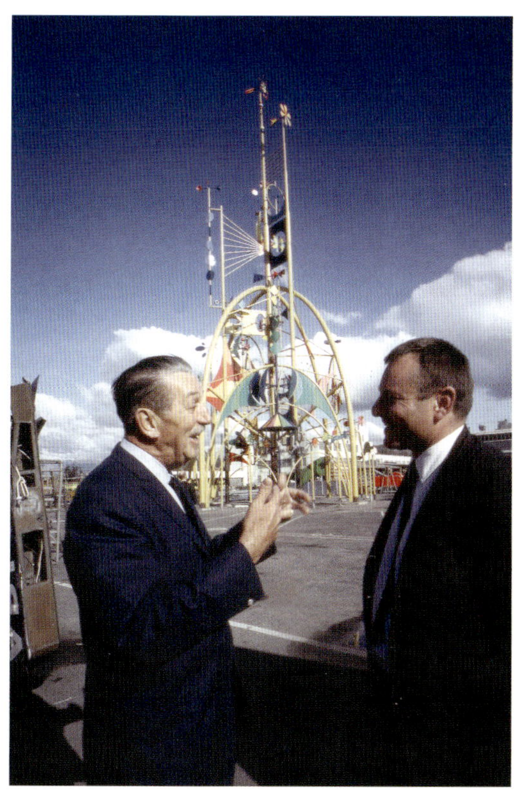

Fig. 2.33 Walt Disney and Rolly Crump in front of the "Tower of the Four Winds," 1964. © Disney

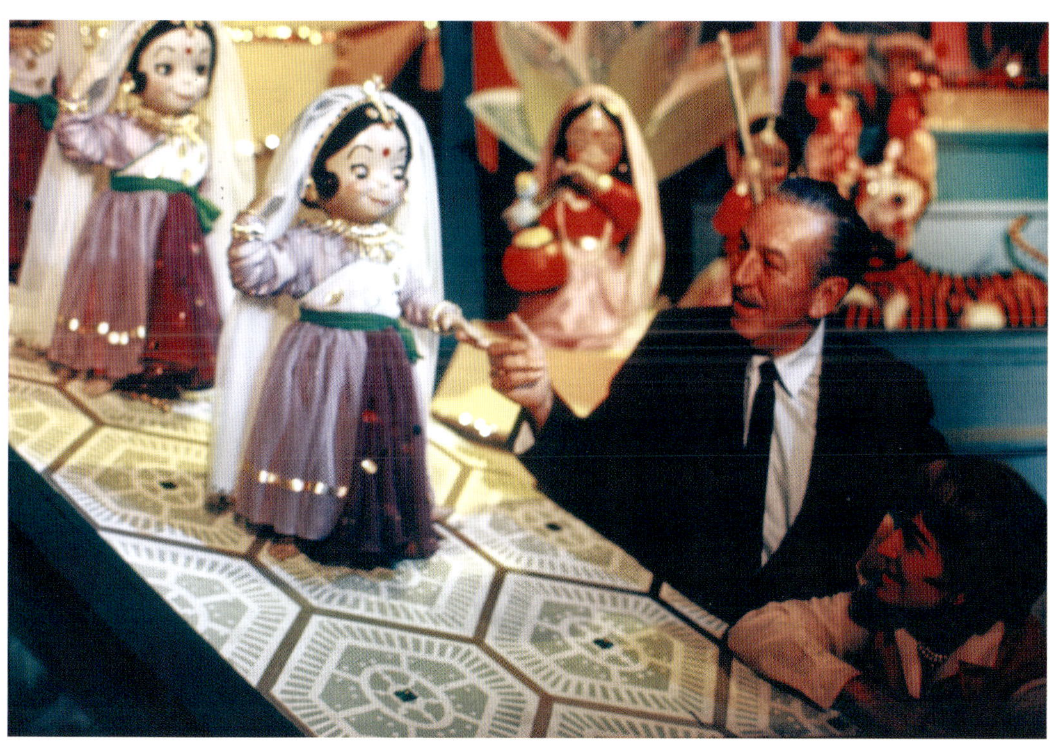

Fig. 2.34 Walt Disney and Mary Blair with "it's a small world" dolls, circa 1964. © Disney

final scene to unity through the filtering out of all colors other than white and gold. As WED's description noted, "With the finale, all boundaries have been removed; the hosts on this tour are simply children who share the common bonds of friendship, imagination, purity and understanding."[78] The attraction "which tells the story of 'The Family of Man' at a child's level," was from its inception destined to return to the park in Anaheim where it would be part of a new land, International Land.[79]

Although "small world" had to be built at breakneck speed in New York, Disney insisted that it also include a showy "marquee," as did many of the Disneyland attractions, which drew visitors in and established mood—here of color in motion.[80] Rolly Crump designed the Tower of the Four Winds according to Disney's vision, which Crump translated into a 140-ton tower of mobiles, which included fifty-two wind-driven elements.[81] A press release described the tower as a "graceful, soaring landmark . . . with over one hundred multi-colored elements spinning and swiveling on it. These include miniature carousel with stylized animals from several countries; figures of birds, flying fish, winged dragons, butterflies and bees; propellers of varying sizes and shapes—all in perpetual motion."[82] Ten million people visited the attraction at the fair, which is still in operation today at Disneyland in Anaheim (figs. 2.33, 2.34).

The GE exhibition also showcased motion and progress but emphasized circularity rather than linear form. Disney had been working with General Electric to tell the story of progress through electricity since 1958 when they hoped the firm, whose slogan was "Progress is our most important product," would invest in the development of Edison Square, which would present a turn-of-the-century cityscape in Disneyland featuring the genius of Thomas Edison and his centrality to the story of American progress in several dioramas connected in a circle. The final scene would be set in the future, where people lived on an "island in the sky" full of GE products such as "space scanners and sky views."[83] By the time it became part of the world's fair Disney attractions, the circular design of the original four tableaux had evolved into a theater where the audience was automatically rotated around the stage rather than the other way around. This allowed the show, called the GE Carousel of Progress, to run constantly for four audiences simultaneously, but it also "transported" the audience through time by moving them, even if only in a circle. Real people in the audience would circle through time in a form of history in which the structures are the same: families with new and improved appliances facing a "great, big beautiful tomorrow as the attraction's song explained."[84] The Disney show's circular form of time, like the jet age notion of the future arriving in the present, was made possible by the aesthetic of constant circulation that collapsed transport and media in the park. Constant and efficient circulation also characterized the novel technology all four attractions shared: Audio-Animatronics, whose potential was thought to have reached its apex in the Lincoln figure, which the State of Illinois eventually sponsored.

Like the GE attraction that had been in development for years before it came to the fair, an environment dedicated to American heritage had been in the works for Disneyland since 1956. A press release that year even announced Liberty Street, which would feature "operating shops and a show . . . related to aspects of the founding of our nation" and would highlight the role of American enterprise, a "living experience" rather than a show. Its centerpiece would be two life-sized sailing vessels used in trade on a waterfront that faced a Hall of the Declaration of Independence and a Hall of Presidents. Early discussions about the fair limited the attraction to "One Nation Under God" (which was not produced), featuring the Constitution and the presidents who led the nation. The Disney people urged Robert Moses to come view the model in California, where he could visit Disneyland and the show prototype "at the studio,"[85] because they also intended the show to include the "most astonishing development in animation and theatrical technique."[86]

WED called Audio-Animatronics a "breakthrough in three-dimensional animation that is quite properly a product of the Space Age. It utilizes many of the same equipment that controls our satellites, rockets and missiles in space" and would "bring President Lincoln to life before their eyes."[87] Not only did Audio-Animatronics reanimate a dead president, but the speakers that had been carefully placed throughout the auditorium gave the audience a greater sense of immersion and participation; the intent of the attraction was for guests to "actually feel themselves present at one of Lincoln's speeches."[88] The cost of the exhibit and the richness of its content made finding a sponsor difficult. When the State of Illinois finally stepped up at the last minute, the other presidents disappeared from the venture in favor of Lincoln. As WED employee Jim Algar explained, "This is the way Walt would work. He would do whatever idea could be brought to fruition. If the whole thing couldn't be had, do the Lincoln part, later do the *Hall of Presidents.*"[89]

Although the fair gave a big boost to Audio-Animatronics, fairgoers and Disney alike were equally attuned to WED's other achievements in people-moving, and Audio-Animatronics were just a part of that. As a post-fair customer survey noted with pleasure, one respondent liked best the "the Magic Skyway Ride and the use of the automobiles to transport people through the show." The survey summary also remarked on comments about the "good handling of crowds."[90] Back in California, WED had been planning a pirate walk-through using Audio-Animatronic figures during the period of the fair. But when it came time to build the attraction at Disneyland, Walt wanted people to be transported instead: "We've learned too much from the Fair about moving people with vehicles, we can't leave this as a walk through."[91] People-moving clearly animated Walt Disney more than Audio-Animatronic pirates.

As Disneyland continued to succeed by every metric imaginable (number of visitors, profitability, worldwide visibility), WED's growth preoccupied

Disney more than Disneyland per se and more than the Studios' filmmaking did, even though this was the period when *Mary Poppins* was in production. Experiences such as the world's fair emboldened Disney to undertake an expansion east, and that became his full-time preoccupation. As Marty Sklar retrospectively explained, "As it turns out, the Fair was one of the stepping stones to Walt Disney World."[92] Others concurred. The success of the Disney attractions in New York not only offered WED capital investments in research and design to develop new attractions but also "set the stage for our being able to move ahead in Florida and have the confidence and the backing of not only the world of potential exhibitors but the financial world."[93] Thus, empowered by the success of the New York attractions, work accelerated in a secret room in Glendale at the WED offices on what they discreetly referred to as the Florida Project.

With the Florida Project, WED would do more than build a theme park in the East. Instead, in its planning and vision, the forty-three-square-mile parcel of land ("twice the size of Manhattan," as Disney would boast) sixteen miles southwest of Orlando, Disney's aims regarding people-moving would reach another level entirely.[94] Disney sought to build a whole complex, eventually known as Walt Disney World Resort, complete with an airport of the future, a theme park, an industrial park, and a centerpiece he called EPCOT—a Disneyland without the themed lands, without Audio-Animatronics, without the characters. EPCOT would be about the beauty and pleasure of moving people and things practically and efficiently.

EPCOT, an acronym for the Experimental Prototype Community of Tomorrow, would be a place where new technologies and living-working experiences would be prototyped and put on display and, like Disneyland, "will always be in a state of becoming."[95] As Hench put it, EPCOT would "show how many of today's city problems can be solved through proper master planning," and in that way, of course, Disney would fold entertainment into a form of utopian systems planning underwritten by a beautiful transport network of circulation and mobility. [96] Disney's vision for EPCOT was not entirely new. It combined the turn-of-the century utopianism of Ebenezer Howard's Garden City model with the more newfangled radial plans of Victor Gruen, whose book, *The Heart of Our Cities* (1965), was definitely on Disney's reading list. Disney was aware of Gruen's work at least as early as May 1960, when he read an article in *Horizon* written by critic Ada Louise Huxtable describing Gruen's eventually unrealized plan for the 1964–65 World's Fair in Washington, D.C. Gruen had proposed a reusable plan for a circular, climate-controlled city, which is exactly what Disney would propose in Florida.

Disney lived long enough only to offer his vision in a movie made to persuade the legislature of Florida to agree to various government concessions to The Walt Disney Company and to muster additional corporate sponsorship for the project. It would be one of his final filmed appearances. The EPCOT project was Disney's; the film's script was an interpretation of his vision written by Sklar, and the visual renderings were in part drawn by Herb

Ryman, the same artist who had visualized Disneyland in its earliest stages. Disney had originally asked Becket to draw up a plan, but he refused.[97] Filming began in late October 1966 and went into early November; Disney died December 16.

The film, which was first screened in February 1967 in Winter Park, Florida, captures in verbal and visual narrative not only a vision of what EPCOT would be, but also summarizes what Disneyland had already achieved in its more than ten years of operation. It is a story of transport and people-moving. The film's entire twenty-five minutes offer only furtive glimpses of Disney characters (the first in the shape of Mickey's head in plantings at the park entrance in an aerial view, the second a quick view of the spinning Dumbo attraction). There is not a single reference to the park's different lands or to use of theming and detailism within the lands to create a total environment. Rather, the film's first five minutes, which are dedicated to the retrospective analysis of Disneyland and its success, consist of quick-paced cuts to inventory the park's many modes of transportation. As the narrator explains, "People and vehicles are constantly in motion at Disneyland. Here people travel aboard almost every method of transportation man has ever designed," adding that Disneyland's 340 million passengers have traveled in both "comfort and speed."[98]

The film is more than a Disneyland travelogue, however. It also promotes WED Enterprises, which it describes as a "design organization" made up of designers, architects, and engineers skilled in the "Disney way." The organization included fine craftsmen and technicians who used their creativity and technical knowhow both inside the Disney organization and beyond it, such as at the world's fair. The film positions WED as much more than an entertainment company by citing praise from the well-known urban planner James Rouse. In 1963, at the graduation of the Harvard School of Design, Rouse called the park the "greatest piece of urban design in the United States today." Specifically, he noted that Disney had lifted the standard of the amusement park to entirely new heights by concentrating on its respect for people and by fulfilling "all the functions it sets out to accomplish, unselfconsciously, usefully and profitably to its owners and developers."[99] After establishing Disneyland as a place in motion, an ideally planned place that works for the people who use it, the film pivots to the studio—"a little bit of Florida, here in California"—and to the presenter, Walt Disney, who, after more than ten years of hosting his television show, was quite skilled at pitching his ideas on the screen. Dressed in a fine suit, he stands in a large room filled with maps and people hard at work and proclaims, "We know what our goals are." And he explains that planning is under way for the "Disney World Project."

Before an enormous map, he describes a venture that is "tied together with a high speed rapid transit system" and centered on something called EPCOT, which would "always be a showcase to the world of the ingenuity and imagination of American free enterprise. . . . Everything in EPCOT will be

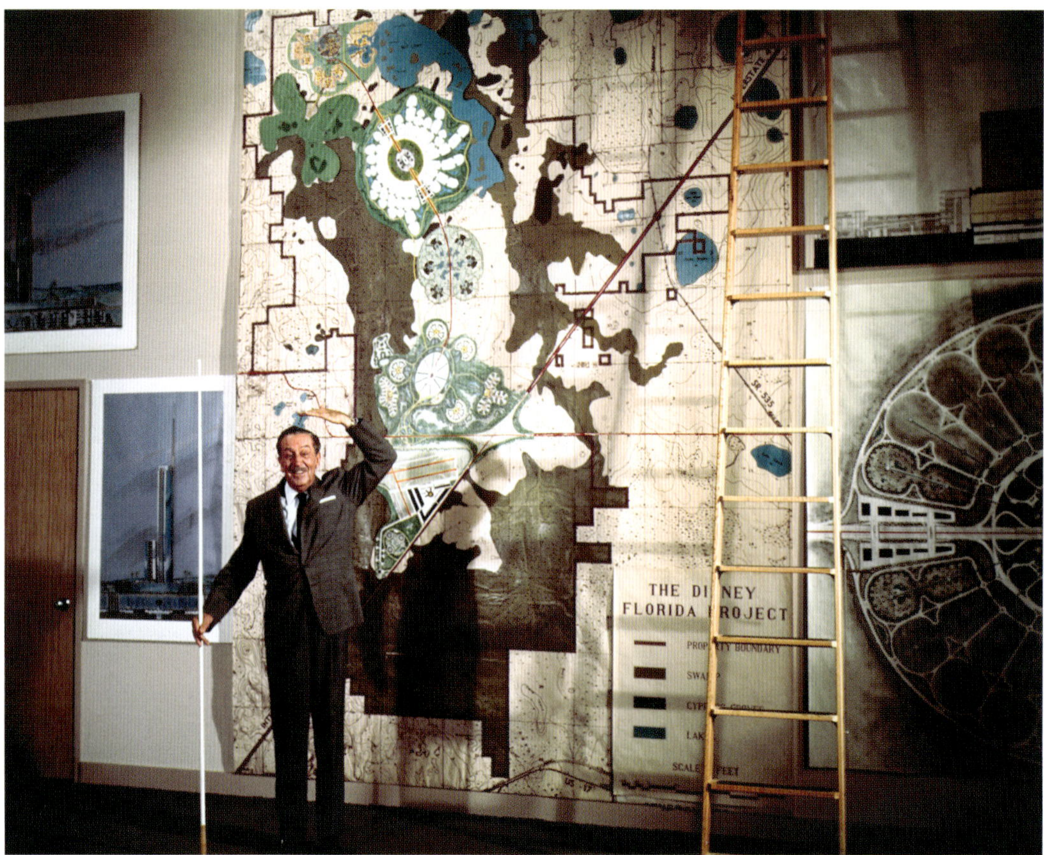

Fig. 2.35 Walt Disney introduces the Florida Project in *The EPCOT Film*, 1966. © Disney

dedicated to the happiness of the people who live, work and play here, and those who come here from around the world to visit our living showcase." The film transitions to an animated film of renderings—beginning with the premise "No city of today will serve as the guide for the city of tomorrow." The notion of creating something unprecedented is exactly what had guided the construction of Disneyland almost fifteen years earlier (fig. 2.35).[100]

EPCOT emphasized the multimodal flow of people and vehicles on which the airports of the jet age were also being constructed. One might think of EPCOT as a combination of Le Corbusier's radial city and Disneyland's hub structure with Walt's commitment to keeping infrastructure out of sight by operating such unsightly necessities as garbage and delivery trucks in underground tunnels. It additionally integrated many of Gruen's notions, such as parking cars outside the main commercial zones, which would be ceded to pedestrians (something already practiced at Disneyland). EPCOT's transport was part of an arterial system of silent circulation. All motorized vehicles would run underneath the city, with trucks on one level, cars on another, while electric powered vehicles, already part of the Disneyland ecosystem, like the Monorail and the PeopleMover, would glide above pedestrians on rails: the latter, they boasted, would be a "silent, all-electric system that moves non-stop."[101] The nonstop operation meant that there would be no breakdowns and no traffic jams. The film then cut to Disneyland, where the PeopleMover and Monorail could be seen efficiently and fluidly crisscrossing each other.

If EPCOT were to be an experimental community, Disneyland's Tomorrowland would now serve as a lab for EPCOT. Specifically, Imagineering would now begin to see Tomorrowland as WED's three-dimensional test space, where they could try new modes of transport that they would develop and send to Florida. At the same time that the Florida Project was getting under way, WED was taking on the transformation of Tomorrowland into New Tomorrowland. Disney himself found enormous inspiration in linking the two projects. The press release for New Tomorrowland envisioned the WedWay Transportation Systems as the "potential means of tomorrow's transportation for large numbers of people at jet age airports [and it is in fact installed in Houston], fashionable shopping malls, sports stadiums, parking facilities, sprawling new universities and other institutional and industrial land residential areas."[102]

What the never-realized plan for EPCOT makes clear is that transport in Disneyland was no simple thematic motif. The rise of a connected, technological, fast-moving world happened not at the expense of aesthetic experience but largely because of the central role played by people such as Walt Disney and the WED Imagineers, who embraced and advanced a form of techno-aesthetics in which images were transformed into places and experiences through technology—in which inert objects did not simply appear to move, they actually did. The idea of organizing spaces around a perpetual and naturalized form of fluid motion not only sets Disneyland apart from the jerks, spins, and hijinks of the turn-of-the-century amusement parks from which it may have descended, but it also locates its origins in its own period of the jet age—for which Disneyland may well stand as the era's crowning achievement. Disneyland, Walt proudly explained, as we noted earlier, "is dedicated to the dreams and hard facts that have created America with the hope that it will be a source of joy and inspiration to all the world."[103] Dreams and hard facts—the seamless interchange between the mediated world and the material world became the centerpiece of Disneyland's kinesthetics, which embraced and advanced the jet's fluid motion in singular fashion, at once defining a jet age aesthetic in its most popular period form while also embracing and advancing the epistemological terms by which most entertainment as well as all media have functioned ever since. Circulation rather than simulation kept things flowing at Disneyland and has kept people moving in, out, and through at Disney parks, now all over the world, in one glorious, seemingly continuous ride.

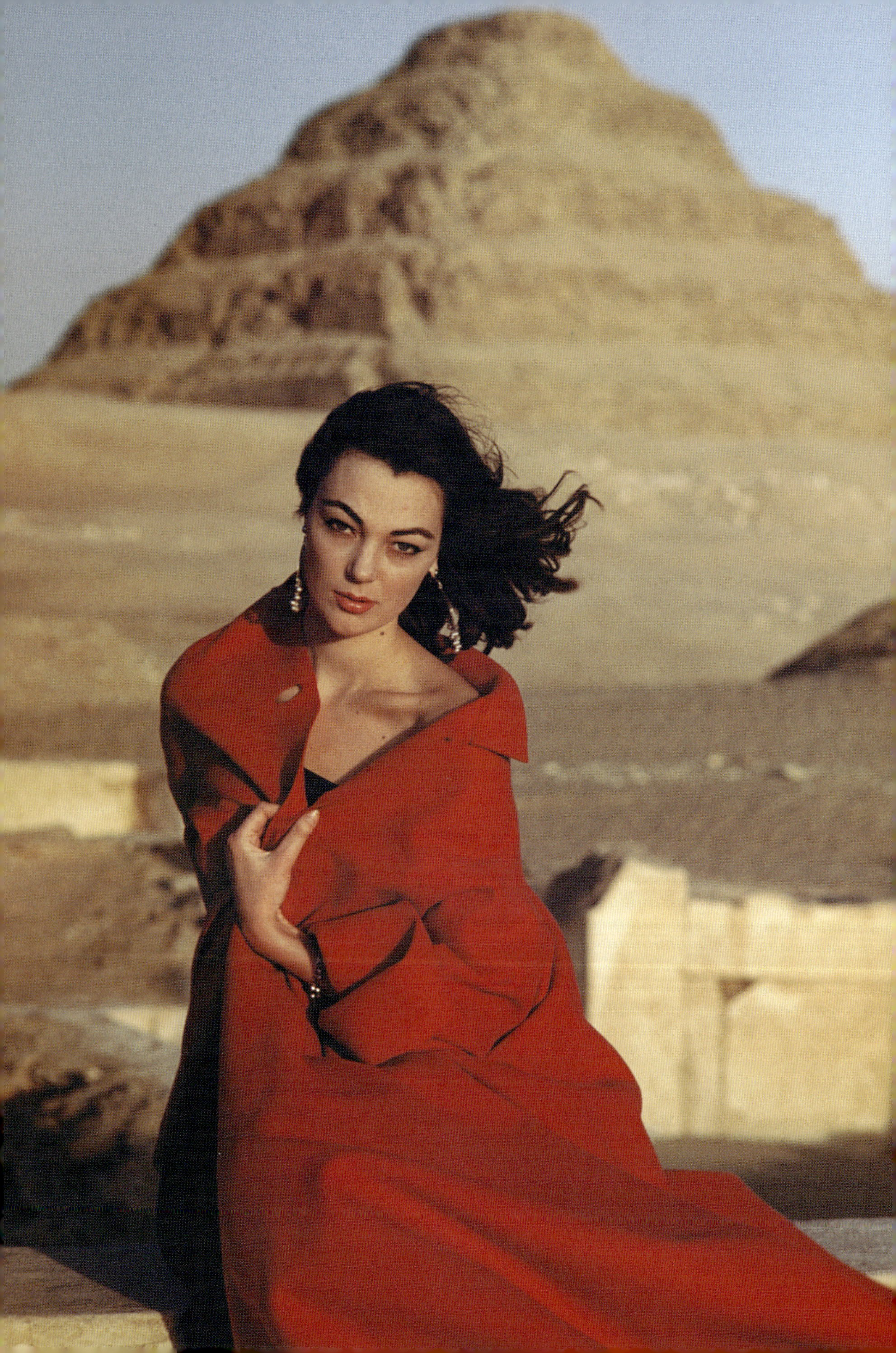

CHAPTER THREE

Arrivals and Departures

Photojournalism and the Making of the Jet Set

The camera, like the airplane, is in a state of dynamic growth.
—*Wilson Hicks, executive editor,* Life *magazine*

The photographer is the contemporary being par excellence.
—*Berenice Abbott, photographer*

In 1963, audiences broke records at the Empire Leicester Square in London and all across the United States in theaters showing *The VIPs,* one of the highest-earning films of the year. As its trailer exclaimed, the film would depict the "famous and the near-famous" in a very modern crisis: stranded at the airport because their transatlantic flight was grounded by weather. The film starred Elizabeth Taylor and Richard Burton, whose real-life affair, recently begun on the set of *Cleopatra,* had made them the most infamous couple in the world, exhaustively covered in the tabloids. The film's publicity underscored its "real-life" drama by using a red and white *Life* magazine–style banner for the film's title in its trailer (fig. 3.1).

The VIPs was not casually set in an airport. These VIPs were part of an incipient social group so closely identified with the jet that they became known as the jet set. It was shaped by a culture of photo magazines that had itself resulted from the development of such modern modes of transport as trains, cars, and ocean liners. Jet transport created a life dedicated to arriving and departing, defining this new elite. In this chapter I consider the origin of the jet set, which, as depicted in the film, was as much a loose assemblage of images as made up of actual people. The grounded passengers, juxtaposed in no particular order, shuffled around like pictures in a magazine, were a mere depiction made possible by visual media as much as they were a sociological category or lived identity. The jet-setters' mobility was as dependent on the circulation of pictures in magazines as it was on the jets that took them from place to place and on which they had come to rely. In this chapter I describe the importance of circulation and the temporality of the news, and the relation of both to the history of magazine photography and its production to argue that it was their intersection that produced the jet set.

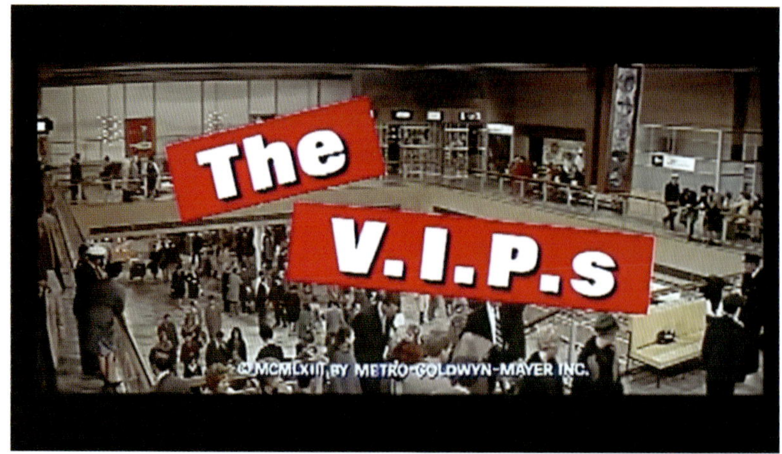

Fig. 3.1 Trailer, *The VIPs*, directed by Anthony Asquith, 1963. MGM/Warner Bros. DVD screen capture

The press and especially the photo magazine had long evolved in sync with modern modes of transport, but air travel imposed a complex relation between the material changes of the "modern" world and its experiences, sensations, and new forms of mobility and their representation that led photographers to play an important new social role. Magazines, which were themselves a product of a culture tied to circulation, glamorized people who were mobile, and they also used a pictorial culture deeply connected to mechanized transport to extend experience to readers. The press also aestheticized motion in a number of ways. By taking a close look at this moment, perhaps the last time the photo magazine would wield such singular influence, and situating it in relation to other media, such as film and television, we will see how magazine images that could obviously circulate more easily than people played a key role in the creation of a jet age aesthetic. While claiming to connect to the real world through their news content and through their relentless ambition to present the present, they did not just "thematize" ideas about the jet age but also became a mechanism by which viewers could toggle between the pictorial world on the page and the material world through which they were being asked to move with greater fluidity.

Great care went into the construction of the set for *The VIPs,* a double of the newly opened Terminal 3 at Heathrow Airport. The film's screenwriter, Terence Rattigan, had proposed *International Grand Hotel* as the film's alternate working title, to make clear that this film "updated" an older one. In *The International Nomads,* published a few years after this film debuted, public relations man Lanfranco Rasponi noted that airports had become what grand hotels had once been. "It did not take me long to discover that the Ritz Hotel bar is no longer the place to feel the throbbing pulse of people in motion but Orly Airport. There in the space of an hour, one runs into numerous members of this shifting society, either arriving or departing."[1] The film follows an unconnected group of orphans in the storm who represented the kind of international nomads about whom Rasponi wrote, reinforcing the notion that the jet life was a glamorous

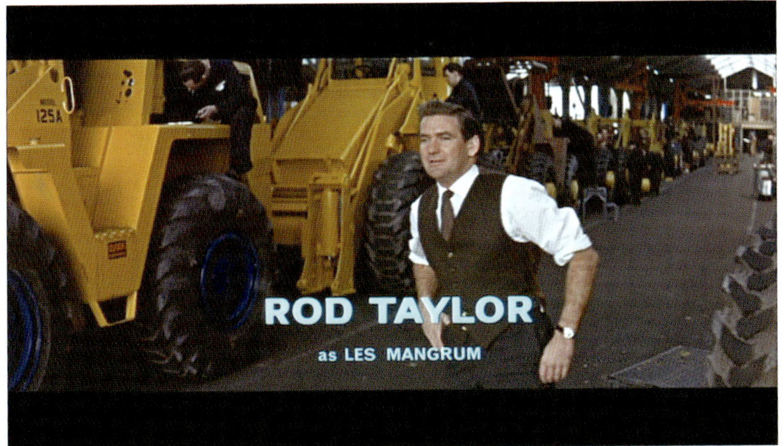

Fig. 3.2 Rod Taylor from opening titles, *The VIPs*. DVD screen capture

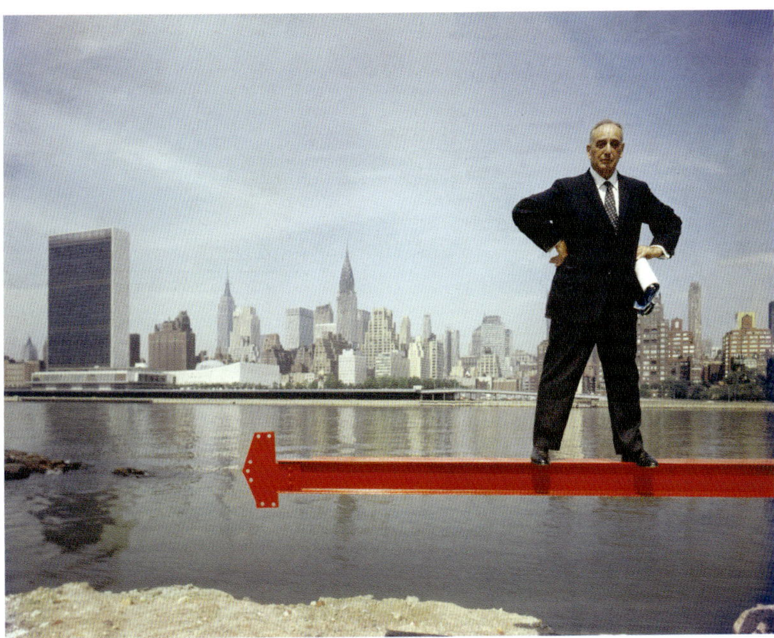

Fig. 3.3 Environmental portrait of Robert Moses, 1959. Arnold Newman, photographer

one, except when nature might trump the facility and ease of the best new-fangled systems and technologies. Such were the perfect plots of jet age melodrama.

In the cast assembled, as well as in the characters they played, the airport became a New World crossroads. Orson Welles played a Hungarian (read Jewish) tax-dodging film director who needs to keep moving for financial reasons. He is accompanied by his Italian starlet, played by Elsa Martinelli. Louis Jourdan plays Elizabeth Taylor's French lover. Taylor and Burton depict a British couple. The Australian Rod Taylor is cast as a troubled businessman helped by his loyal English secretary, played by the then unknown Maggie Smith. Finally, there is a characteristically penniless British duchess played by Margaret Rutherford, who was in the colonial service on her last trip out of the country. Here she is to take her first flight in order to assume a job at a hotel in Miami Beach so that she can afford to run her ancestral home in the Old Country. Even the aristocracy must take to the road for New World glitz if they want to save the old manor. There is no staying anchored and rooted forever.

The publicity campaign framed the film as a contemporary "real-life" drama. Its trailer opens with a series of newspaper headlines followed by magazine covers flashing across the screen. These images capitalized, no doubt, on the real-life notoriety of Taylor and Burton's romance. The film's credit sequence also unfurls slowly, as if cut and laid out from a newsmagazine. The film begins by introducing its stars. Each major player is photographed in what might be referred to as environmental portraiture, framed in an appropriate setting: Taylor in a tiara and fur collar on a yacht with Burton (her husband) on a phone; Jourdan as the playboy-lover surrounded by women in a casino; the businessman, a proud captain of industry, assuming a pose as he receives a delivery of a group of his tractors. The opening credits evoke the kind of magazine photographic work of Arnold Newman, who had taken the sensational portrait of Robert Moses suspended over the East River in 1959 in what became a quintessential example of the genre (figs. 3.2, 3.3).[2]

After the introduction of the cast, a red carpet unfurls, thus symbolically welcoming the audience to a VIP "movie" experience, but the magazine analogy visually persists as the credits continue to invoke a mid-century modern magazine layout. Against sleekly stark saturated rectangles of color, the credits continue and découpéd luxury objects associated with advertising oriented to a mobile elite appear. In the first sequence, a Rolls-Royce grille pops onto the screen front and center, is multiplied, and then a photo of the latest Mini is added as a fourth vehicle over the name David Frost, the young British television personality (fig. 3.4). The next sequence looks like an ad for liquor or cigarettes: it features anonymous male and female legs hanging beneath barstools with briefcases at their feet, framed on top by a saturated band of red (fig. 3.5). The image introduces those who travel for work and leads to a series of flashes of saturated color followed by several frames of press cameras flashing in and out. The next several frames consist of furs, Champagne magnums on ice, airline bags lined up on a carousel (fig. 3.6), a top hat, crowns, a martini glass, a box of cigars.

As the credits end and the film begins, the music indicates a shift in pace. A speed-up and frenzy sets the tone as we view a car from behind approaching an airport terminal and its departure sign. Rather than one of the luxurious cars we have already seen, a late 1950s Cadillac Fleetwood Limousine, series 75, with aerodynamic fins (a car that creates a jet effect) delivers chauffeured clients greeted by a pack of photographers jostling one another for a photo of these important arriving passengers (fig. 3.7). They are the movie director and starlet. As they exit the car and enter the terminal, she stops to pose with the terminal as decor. On one side, newspaper and magazine vendors hover behind her: W. H. Smith and *Time*'s brightly lit signs directly flank one side of the airport (fig. 3.8). The camera photographs the actress from the opposite angle to reveal that across from the press purveyors, airlines announce themselves: El Al and Qantas—denoting such far-flung and exotic places as Israel and Australia. The film's dialogue moves to an agent who serves as a VIP handler for the British national carrier, BOAC, helping manage the flight that will be the film's subject. Above the BOAC counter a world map depicts Heathrow as a global air hub in a connected air network.

The film may have struck a chord in 1963 not simply because of its airport setting and plot, which seemed right for its moment, but also because it established its narrative by using visual devices that linked the film to the photo magazines that had become the most pervasive mode of representation for visually narrating contemporary society to an eager general public. Although the cinema's ubiquity had, by mid-century, made it a master storytelling idiom for all kinds of narratives, the magazine's periodical nature and its tie to the press model of consistent and regular delivery of current events kept it more tethered to ideas of novelty, contemporary life, and the latest trends than did film, which covered a broader range of times and places.

This chapter links the history of the production and circulation of magazine images with the creation and glorification of this new group of international nomads: the Beautiful People. The jet set's identity was amorphous, though, in that it did not really exist in any measurable or structural way; rather, it was depicted photographically, and those images were arranged and rearranged in alluring glossy newsmagazines. Such pictures were hardly simple portraits, nor were they high-end postcards from the places they went. Magazines did not offer a form of armchair tourism; they were not merely vehicles through which to create social aspiration while promoting the sale of airline tickets.[3] Instead, the jet set invoked a new social type as part of the glamorization of motion itself. In the process, it placed a premium on Nowism—which is to say, on a sense of living in the moment, which news photography enshrined.[4] The jet set constituted a newly physically mobile elite who symbolized what it meant to be the latest, the hippest, and the most of their moment—they were the social cutting edge in the way that the jet age denoted the technological cutting edge. For the first time, being a social elite meant being one step more in the present than others, while simultaneously acknowledging that such a distinction might be ephemeral. Although we may think of photography as capturing a moment for all time, magazine photography, despite the enormous capital investment in it, relished its ephemerality and its sense that it would be of its moment, and then be replaced by the next issue, the next fashion. It would move on to new people and topics, which is precisely why magazines have become so useful in historical research. The key is to not look right through them but rather at them, which is what people in the jet age started to understand.

Although in the nineteenth century Charles Baudelaire had already called the sketch reporter Constantin Guys the "painter of modern life," by

Figs. 3.4–3.6 Opening titles, *The VIPs*. DVD screen capture

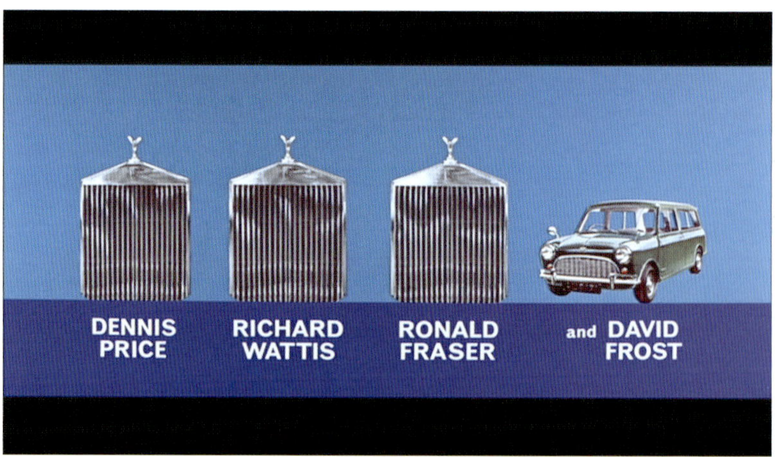

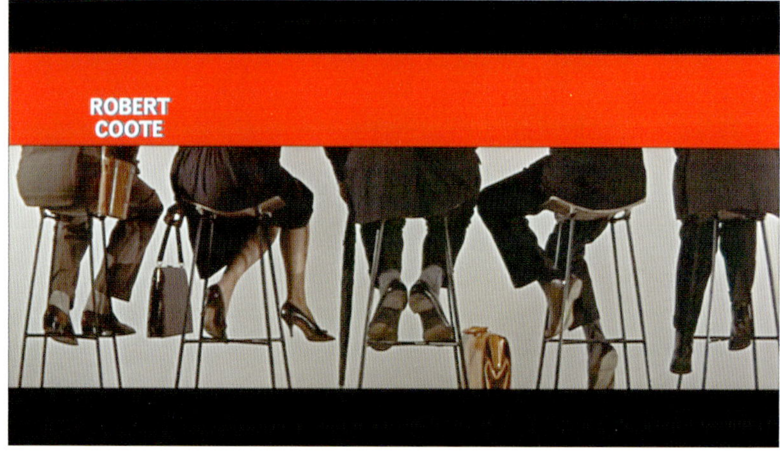

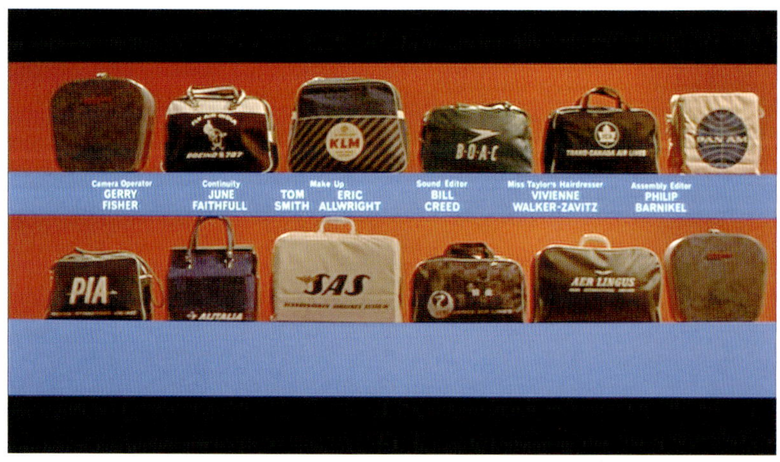

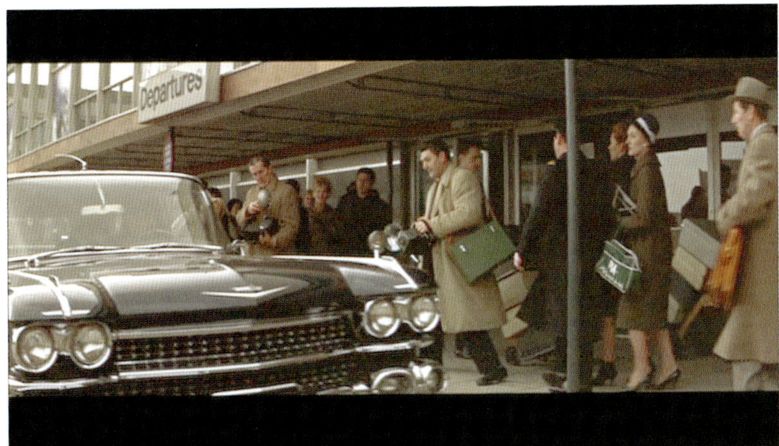

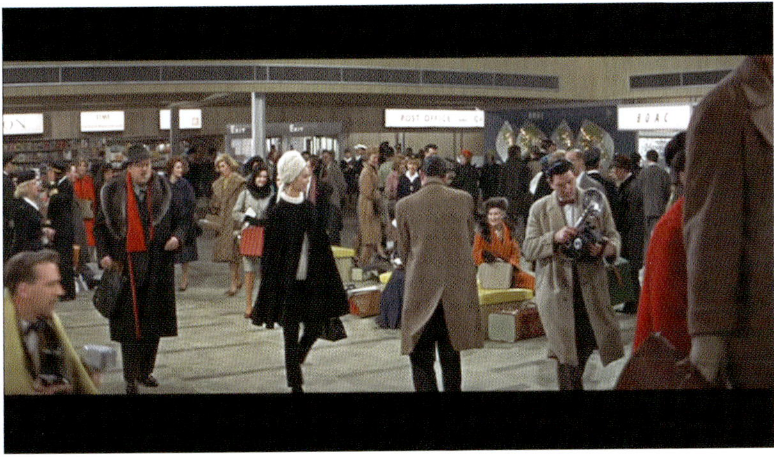

Figs. 3.7 and 3.8 Terminal, *The VIPs*. DVD screen captures

the mid-twentieth century magazine photojournalism had become the most up-to-date mode of depicting "modern life," not only because it presented the news on a regular basis but also because it projected the dynamic quality of contemporary life, especially by giving a sense of movement to its photography and layout. Airplanes and eventually the jet—the mode of transport par excellence that had sped things up as "the latest" in technology—produced a consistent flow of news by materially changing the production of magazines, transforming key photographic practices. Additionally, while migration and mobility had characterized much of the history of the western world since the mid-nineteenth century, never had red carpets welcomed the displacement or movement of peoples. At the same time that planes and magazines were glamorizing both images and mobility, the social status of photographers themselves, who lived like the international nomads they photographed, rose as they joined the new elite whose image they had helped to create.

Longstanding social hierarchies dissolved during the period after the Second World War, as did longstanding ideas of social deference. For some observers, the culture of the mass press played a fundamental role in such transformations. In his 1956 book *The Power Elite,* C. Wright Mills observed that "printer's ink has replaced blue blood." Mills mostly looked at institutions like the military and corporations as responsible for such changes, but he also described the emergence of other kinds of elites and especially noted the rise of celebrities whom he described as "the somebodies who are held to be worthy of notice: now they are news, later they will be history."[5]

Press photography played more than an incidental role in these developments. Even before the war the press had begun to erode the privilege of traditional elites by subjecting them to the invasive roving eyes of their photographers, as the takedown of Edward VIII over his relationship with Wallis Simpson right before the outbreak of the war had made clear. This episode—and King Edward's eventual abdication of the throne in order to marry the divorced American—was not only a turning point in the history of the monarchy, in which the photographic image contributed to the downfall of a king, but it was also a fundamental moment that reflected how photography more broadly had been key in the democratizing force of the press and its general erosion of social privilege. Additionally, physical access to the elite itself via the photographic image became hotly contested, and press photographers were themselves subject to public discussion and scrutiny. They were alternatively treated as folk heroes and as voyeuristic social menaces, as Peeping Toms wielding blinding flashes in the battle to construct the modern category of the "intimate stranger."[6]

While the press helped remake social hierarchies through its fundamental contribution to creating a more democratic and accessible public sphere, intellectuals also began to consider "low culture" as a realm for serious scrutiny. Between 1955 and 1962, many pathbreaking studies regarding the power of mass media, and especially its image culture, were published on both sides of the Atlantic.[7] In France in 1957, such intellectuals as Roland Barthes, whose columns for *Les Lettres Nouvelles* were collected as *Mythologies,* and Edgar Morin, who published *Les Stars,* made film and photography the subjects of critical and sociological scrutiny. In England, young critics such as Lawrence Alloway and Reyner Banham at the Institute for Contemporary Art analyzed mass culture as well and went beyond Marxist notions of understanding such culture as merely reflecting the relations of economic production. In his essay "The Long Front of Culture," Alloway identified what he called a cultural continuum or flatbed visual field, which he saw as replacing older forms of cultural hierarchies and becoming an "expendable multitude of signs."[8] As a flatbed visual field, the mass arts could be considered to be spatially laid out the way images were laid out in magazines.

Within this developing discourse, one study stands out as a landmark. In the United States, Daniel Boorstin's *The Image: A Guide to Pseudo-Events in America* diagnosed with insight the changes wrought by mass-media society. Boorstin, a professor of history at the University of Chicago, had made his name writing about American politics and went on to write the Pulitzer Prize–winning book *The Americans*. Though working in a traditional field, and later known as a conservative for renouncing his early leftist leanings and naming names before the House Un-American Activities Committee, Boorstin was in the 1960s remarkably ahead of his time as an historian. He had identified the central role played by media technologies in shaping every arena of modern life, no doubt owing to his early Marxism, which led him to focus on technology and the material dimensions of how ideas are produced and disseminated.

Boorstin's book received a chorus of mixed reviews on its publication in 1961, yet it has never been out of print. *The Image* offers the kind of critique of mass-media society that could be shared by people across a broad political spectrum. In what amounted to a condemnation of contemporary culture whose inauthenticity, Boorstin argued, had been created by a revolution in print and graphics, he asked readers to contemplate the changes wrought by numerous technological developments in representational media in a short period of time. He marveled at what he established as the basic framework: that the country had witnessed, "in less than a century," the advent of everything from the daguerreotype to the color television.[9] The study has been largely undervalued, and certain important aspects disregarded; when the text is examined closely, however, we will see how even during the period, connections between magazine images and the jet could be made and how this link came to play a critical role in fabricating the jet set.

Boorstin's analysis narrates the rise of the mass media and especially press illustration, which in the early 1960s were undergoing transformations. Television combined the absolute immediacy of radio transmission with the pictorial storytelling of photojournalism and newsreels. The illustrated press in nineteenth-century Europe and America, as well as the influence of photography since the advent of the halftone, had played crucial roles in shaping not only what people knew about the modern world but also how fast they could obtain that knowledge. By the time Boorstin was writing, something had changed so fundamentally that critics could start to think of the world as being not so much reported by the image as being produced by it.[10] In particular, Boorstin identified the role the press played in illusion-making, coining the term "pseudo-event." He argued that "we risk being the first people in history to have been able to make their illusions so vivid, so persuasive, so realistic that they . . . are the very house in which we live; they are our news, our heroes, our adventure, our forms of art, our very experience."[11] As he put it, "The power to make a reportable event is the power to make experience."[12] Boorstin also saw in the condition of modern media the potential for an extreme form of democratization via the image, and he argued that images desacralized power through their dissemination in the press; in that way he shared views with such contemporaries as Mills.

Although it may seem odd to twenty-first-century readers, Boorstin made such arguments about illusions and images without referring to actual pictures. He employed the term "image" to mean any representation—something that was visible or to be looked at and seen—but he did not analyze actual pictures or the act of making them. At the same time, he carefully explained such media revolutions as the printing press, the daguerreotype, and the halftone (which reproduced photography in news media), and he even went so far as to denounce photography as a form of "narcissism."[13] While he thus appeared to understand that the history and problem he identified were pictorial in nature, he had neither the tools nor the inclination to address what was specifically visual.

But this was the age of photojournalism, and Boorstin was also clearly alluding to its power. Magazines became a major mass-media vehicle in what Wilson Hicks, *Life*'s picture editor and subsequently executive editor, from 1937 to 1951, called the Age of the Visual Image.[14] Hicks's phrase was not just self-serving guff. Museum professionals also understood similar forces to be at work. The curator of prints at the Metropolitan Museum of Art, William M. Ivins, wrote *Prints and Visual Communication* (1953), in which he had already argued that images alone could express certain ideas and that their exact reproducibility in print was the basis of their power as vehicles of communication.[15]

The notion that the image had come to dominate the age had been evolving over the course of a century—since the advent of reproductive technologies such as lithography and photography—and had taken on new power in the twentieth century with the rise of advertising and public relations, on the one hand, and wartime propaganda, on the other. It was not just that more images could be more readily disseminated. The artists and intellectuals associated with the New Bauhaus who had made their way from Central Europe to the United States also argued that thought itself was visually organized, as had been promoted by Gestalt principles as early as the 1920s.

Boorstin seems to echo press insiders and intellectuals about the pictorial fabrication of the news rather than its mere reporting. While contemporary academic reviewers disagreed on what was most important in Boorstin's study (some praised his emphasis on technology and others his overall pessimism at the condition of America), all agreed that he had more or less keenly caught the spirit of the times. None, however, noted or complained about his generalized and metaphoric use of the term "image." They, after all, used the term in the same way.

Additionally, none of the reviewers addressed what, in retrospect, is the striking originality of his discussion of the rise of tourism. Today we may understand the link between tourism and the mass media, but in 1962 the two were not as obviously linked.[16] Boorstin counted tourism as part of the host of pseudo-experiences that he described. He was one of the earliest critics to observe that the mass development of travel homogenized experience. He linked the circulation of people with the circulation of images, arguing that image culture reified experience, so that by the time people visited the real thing they could judge it only in relation to its familiar picture.

But even more interesting than this early observation regarding tourism as a part of commodity spectacle, which goes as far back as Victorian armchair travel, Boorstin also tied this reflection specifically to the advent of jet travel and even more so to the experience of flying in a jet. Like many period observers, he noted how little experience one had in a jet plane. Jets, he said, deprived those who flew in them of sensory experience. "The newest and most popular means of passenger transportation to foreign parts is the most insulating known to man. There is nothing to see but the weather; since we had no weather, nothing to see at all. I had not flown through space but through time. My passage through space was unnoticeable and effortless. The airplane robbed me of the landscape."[17]

The nonexperience described by Boorstin is more than mere midair boredom. Airlines had already begun combatting the tedium with a variety of distractions such as meals and lounges, and in 1961 they began showing feature films on board.[18] He proposed that rather than seeing the world framed as a picture below, which the "aerial view" had done, the jet created significant consequences regarding passengers' experiences of time and space. Boorstin observed that travel through space served as the universal metaphor for change, and without a sense of moving through it, individuals would not experience the passage of time or of change, thus depriving them of a sense of the past itself. "No longer do we move through space as we once did," he explained. "Moving only through time, measuring our distances in homogeneous ticks of the clock, we are at a loss to explain to ourselves what we are doing, where, or even whether we are going." He believed that we would eventually simply be measuring time against itself. He concluded, "We look into a mirror instead of out a window, and we see only ourselves."[19] Not only did the jet condemn people to live without history, but they would be increasingly condemned to live as narcissists as jet travel increased.

The myth of Narcissus haunts Boorstin's study because he also put responsibility for the negative condition he analyzed on individuals. Unlike many other interpreters of his era, he did not blame capitalism, the press, advertisers, and press agents—people that sociologists such as Vance Packard had identified as manipulators, as the creators of these contemporary problems.[20] Instead, Boorstin focused on the individual reception and response to the Graphic Revolution, suggesting that individuals were personally responsible for valuing, consuming, enjoying, or rejecting the culture that the media offered up as a matter of taste that they could control themselves.

No group of individuals seemed to stand for the enjoyment and pleasures of the era as much as the jet set. Although they would seem to represent exactly what Boorstin was worried about, their very mobility functioned as an antidote to his concerns by offering a contemporary and utopian recasting of the ancient cautionary tale of Narcissus on which Boorstin had fixated. These colorful individuals became a loose social configuration; a "set" who, like the jet, were of the moment, and came and went at a moment's notice. The jet literally gave this "set" wings by flying them around the world. To be a part of the jet set meant to be always arriving or departing. Magazine photography played an important role in creating this identity by circulating it in a form that emphasized mobility. By depicting them they would never end the way Narcissus did: frozen, motionless, and dying, transfixed by their own reflections. Like so many pictures in a magazine, and the photographers who took them, they were always on the move and in circulation.

THE MOBILE ELITE

Igor Cassini, brother of fashion designer to First Lady Jacqueline Kennedy, Oleg Cassini, is credited with introducing the term "jet set" into general use. There are a few uses of the phrase before Cassini made it part of the lingua franca, but those early examples refer to the idea of being airborne and swooping in from above rather than to being a part of a newly mobile social elite. Cassini was a faded Russian aristocrat turned society columnist for Hearst publications who regularly reported on the activities of the group he helped christen.[21] Cassini had boasted that his newspaper column could stand as useful evidence of how a "certain part of life was," should an atom bomb drop and people find the column a thousand years later—he was chronicler and participant in one. Another observer was less kind, arguing that "if you took a year's supply of them [Cassini's columns] and put them on a pair of old-fashioned scales against a piece of tissue paper, the tissue paper would weigh more."[22] In 1962, the *New York Times* credited Cassini with inventing the term "jet set" and summarized the qualities of the group: "The jet set is people who live fast, move fast, know the latest thing and do the unusual and the unorthodox. . . . The jet set has no fixed rules and standards."[23] The jet set might have been a class, except that they broke the rules of class, rules and customs that had been as impenetrable as the castles and estates that aristocracy had inhabited for centuries. They might instead be thought of as a modern tribe bound by shared rites, habits, dress, rituals, and migration patterns.

Although pundits may have named them, defining exactly who belonged was a struggle because nothing about them seemed particularly stable. Instead, most chroniclers agreed that what jet setters shared was related to the way they defined the changing times. They stood as evidence that now Old World elites would mix with and be reconstituted through the best that the new-fangled nomadism had to offer. The definition of the group was mobile as well: it was unsure, in flux, and variable. The jet set was known to be on the go, leaving town in search of such things as better weather. This was not a frivolous pursuit; it defined the powers that moderns had at their disposal. As Mills described in *The Power Elite,* "All over the world, like lords of creation, are those who, by travel, command the seasons and, by many houses, the very landscape they will see each morning or afternoon they are awakened."[24] Older elites had punctuated their rhythms seasonally, much like all people in traditional societies, and they left their cold homes for milder climates in winter (which is how places like the South of France first become resorts—in winter), but that meant decamping for months at a time. The jet set came and went as it pleased because its members were never stuck in any place or weather for long; being stuck at the airport in a storm unleashed enough of a crisis that one could build a narrative around it, as *The VIPs* depicted. As one observer joked, the jet set always risked arriving somewhere and phoning their friends to learn that they had gone elsewhere. The *New York Times* could describe them only as a motley, if elite, group: "businessmen and people with titles, models, social climbers, people successful in the commercial arts and touted as geniuses, foreigners and everyone with a nickname: Meet Kiki, Gigi, Ollie, Foozie, Flukie, Susie, Squeekie, Shugsie and Soupy."[25] As social observer Philippa Pullar noted, "There was a new class image. . . . The whole of society was mostly made up of restless, rootless people with no connection to the soil."[26] Or, perhaps, to the ground. The jet had introduced the idea that nomadism was appealing and even glamorous, which was a boon to people without old money and estates, or even without money at all: talent and genius, performers and pretenders mixed in a way that was possible only because of the random encounters of a nomadic and rootless culture.

The jet set would not exist without the press and people like Cassini. They had easy access to old elites and constantly met new people. Before the war and the jet, reporters had written for the closed world of "class publications" such as *Vogue* and for society gossip columns. Cassini himself had been part of the generation of White Russian emigrants whose Russian-Italian family fled to Italy after the revolution in 1917; he then made his way to the United States and into wealthy marriages. Another such PR man was Lanfranco Rasponi, the son of an Italian aristocratic father and an American mother, raised in Italy but educated at the University of California at Berkeley in the 1930s. Rasponi wrote two books in the 1960s: *The International Nomads* (1966) and *The Golden Oases* (1968). Cassini and Rasponi ended their careers amid financial scandals, in part because they had no real basis from which to make a living in a post-aristocratic society.[27] Rasponi's disdain and anxiety regarding money is clear in his justification for the importance of books such as his own. He explained that because of the changing media environment of the times, "two-thirds of our knowledge of that past has come down to us through letters. Of our era, all that will remain will be the reporting in the press, radio and television. . . . Archives of families will be strangely empty except for the bills and bank statements, and future Stendhals will find nothing of interest."[28] Rasponi indicated a great deal in this observation. He implied that elites no longer corresponded through letter-writing, a practice that previously had afforded glimpses into how they lived. But it is not only the time and space that separated them that was changing in the jet age, but also the intimacy and audience. Whereas families and small circles of friends once operated in entirely closed worlds, Rasponi suggested that they would now be known, even to their descendants, only if their actions or lives had been publicized or the subject of media coverage. With that justification, Rasponi set out to paint a collective social portrait.

Jet setters might come and go as they pleased, thanks to jet transport itself, but many who would be identified as jet setters were also geographically displaced to begin with. They had been "put on the road" by circumstances beyond their control. They represented the glamorous high-end of the remarkable migration in Europe and across the globe that had put some 40 million people in transit after World War II. They were not described as refugees, even though many had left home for good. Their status as transients was not only part of their celebrity and cachet but also the basis of their own social interconnection.[29] They were people like Rudolf Nureyev, who would go on to become the century's best-known male ballet dancer. Nureyev made a spectacular leap to worldwide fame at Le Bourget airport in June 1961 when at the age of twenty-three he refused to go with his KGB bodyguards, who had been instructed to take him back to Moscow from the Kirov tour in Paris.[30] Nureyev had been aided in his defection by another jet setter, a young woman he had just met in Paris: Clara Saint, the daughter of a wealthy Chilean artist living in France. Just a month before, she had suffered the loss of her fiancée, Vincent, the son of the French minister of culture, André Malraux, when he and his brother died together in a car accident. Saint later went on to work in promotion for yet another jet setter, fashion designer Yves Saint-Laurent, and was a close friend of Andy Warhol, who, of course, in 1967 said everyone would be famous for fifteen minutes but also admitted that he was "embarrassed that I don't like to fly because I love to be modern."[31]

Among those people associated with the jet set were wealthy expatriates who were members of the ruling classes adrift in a decolonizing world. They simply chose not to repatriate to "mother" countries they hardly knew. Instead, they met each other in different "exotic" locales. We might call them "cosmopolitans." For example, John Paul Getty II, who moved to Rome from Los Angeles, married one such figure: model-actress Talitha Pol (fig. 3.9). Pol was born in Indonesia to Dutch parents and imprisoned in a Japanese detention camp during the war; she grew up in London. She counted Nureyev among her very close friends in the years after his arrival in Europe (he had said he wanted to marry her). She and Getty were also close with Saint-Laurent and his lover and business partner Pierre Bergé, as they often visited each other in Morocco, where they all had houses. Pol died in Rome of a heroin overdose in 1971. As Bergé put it, "People like Talitha, Rudolf, Yves have the same flair—the same perception of life, more or less the same behavior. It's a decadence, a mix of Burne-Jones and Rossetti. For these people the rest of the world is square" (figs. 3.10, 3.11).[32] Although Bergé may have anchored his references in an earlier age of aesthetes, what could have been more of his moment than to label the rest of the world as square? That their hipness involved a good deal of drug use was unmentioned, but it ended Pol's life and nearly ended Saint-Laurent's several times; drugs no doubt provided one of the many appeals of jetting around to places such as Morocco, where they were easier to come by than in the metropole.

If the jet set consisted of displaced people who never really settled in one place, they also cultivated idiosyncrasy ("the rest of the world is square"), which combatted the supposed standardization that the era of mass media had created. And of course many of them, such as the fashion designers and photographers, were themselves instrumentally involved in creating that style. In 1956, Americans may have been discussing the joyless social conformity described in William H. Whyte's *Organization Man* and Sloan Wilson's novel *Man in the Gray Flannel Suit,* but the men of the jet set were anything but colorless and conformist. They weren't gray; many were gay—aesthetes, eccentrics, and dandies who cared about how they looked and what they wore. They were an antidote to the homogenization and standardization of culture that so many critics feared democratization was creating. As period chronicler Anthony Haden-Guest fretted in 1965 about the standardization of contemporary travel, "[We] reduce the actual traveling time to a well-lubricated circuit of airline terminals, customized limousines and internationalized hotels so that the individual characteristics of the country in question flatten out, emerge as a brightly-colored backcloth, identifiable only by examining the currency with which the steaks and Scotch are paid for."[33] To such notions, Alexander Plunket Greene, husband of London fashion designer Mary Quant, offered himself and his wife as counterevidence: "We spend money more on traveling, spending weekends in the obscure places of the world."[34]

"Obscure" is hardly a precise geographic term, but the jet set did come and go in a nonchalant manner to and from places that might have once seemed impossible journeys. This notion of obscurity also preserved the idea that such places somehow remained remote enough that people who wanted to "get away from it all" could do so and then quickly return to their busy lives. One could argue that the idea of the jet set articulated a vision of the world that in some sense extended colonial living during the era of decolonization. Jet access to most places that were "obscure" ran through former colonial routes, where certain infrastructural preconditions existed. For example, Air India was the first all-jet airline of a non-American carrier. Other airlines, such as Royal Air Maroc, bought a number of French Caravelles in the 1960s, although the distance between France and Morocco hardly called for jet service. Morocco, which had been a French protectorate

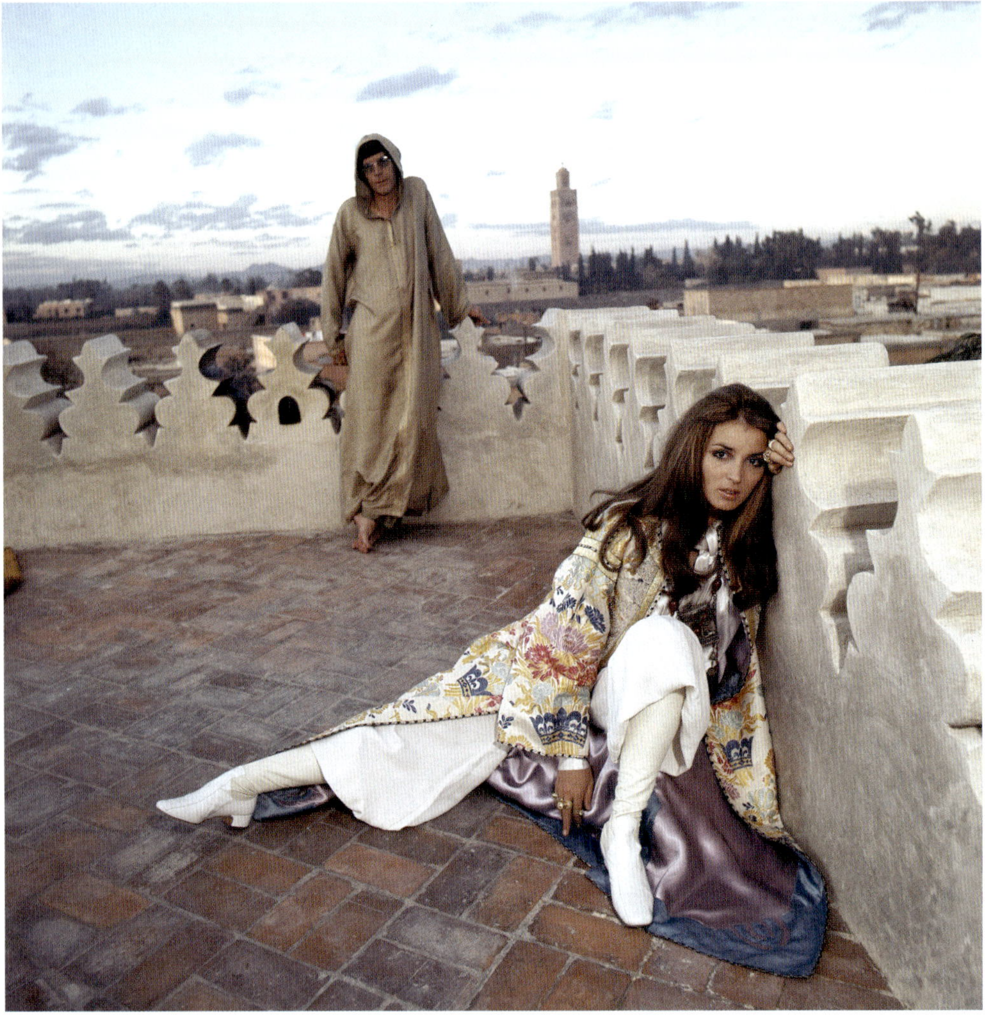

Fig. 3.9 John Paul Getty II and Talitha Pol, 1969, Marrakesh. Paul Litchfeld, photographer

Fig. 3.10 Yves Saint-Laurent and Betty Catroux in Marrakesh, 1960s

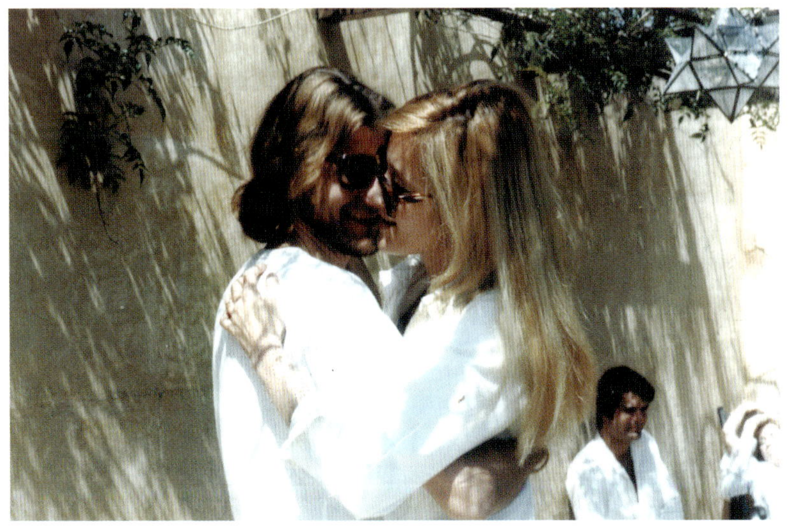

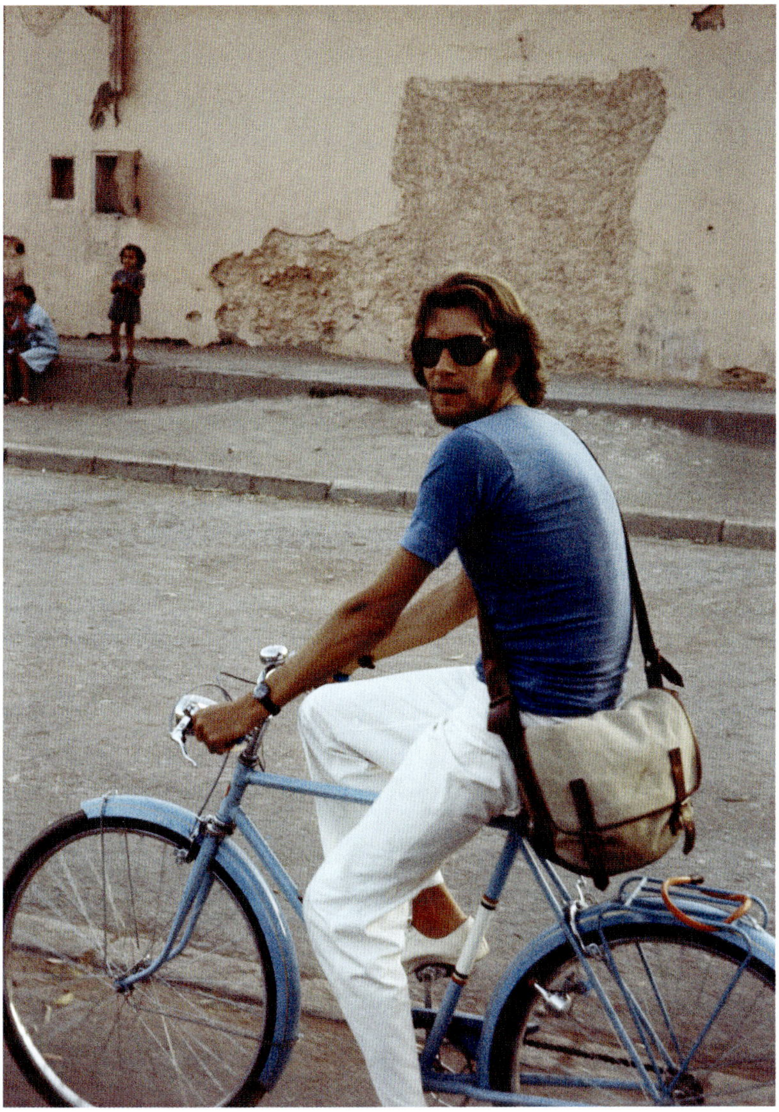

Fig. 3.11 Yves Saint-Laurent on bicycle in Marrakesh, 1960s. Photo by Pierre Bergé

since 1912 and became technically independent in 1955, cultivated French and Francophone visitors. Their numbers grew after the Algerian War sent over a million people from Algeria to France in 1962, including the family of Yves Saint-Laurent, who was born and raised in Oran. He and Bergé began going to Morocco in 1966, and Saint-Laurent spent the rest of his career shuttling between Paris and Marrakesh. It reminded him of Oran, he said, a "cosmopolis of trading people from all over."[35] In other words, he valued the idea of being in a place that represented an international crossroads, and he never spoke of the place as if it were different, exotic, or as having "Oriental" qualities, for example. He felt very much at home there, and that is the point about what it means to be a member of the jet set.

The jet set determined the social pace by being wealthy and nomadic. As fashion writer Marylin Bender put it, "To be in fashion means to be on the go. . . . The important thing is to keep moving, to arrive after everyone has heard of the place but before everyone has been there: Acapulco, Antigua, Gstaad, Hawaii, the Greek Islands have all had their moment of glory."[36] To be fast meant getting there, anywhere, first. But the jet age made remote places such as islands easier to access—not only because one necessarily "flew in" but also because jets, as we have seen, were part of a larger network of transportation. One could afford the time to sail to Capri if one had first flown from Rome to Naples. By virtue of the ever-shifting nature of their social composition and their youth and their association with the cutting-edge of culture, jet setters were utopian and forward-looking rather than decadent. As Arthur Herzog offered with a bemused tone, "Here were people who knew what to do with free time: jet setters found new places, invented new pastimes and generally had a ball. Perhaps the jet set is the forerunner of the leisure-time world of tomorrow in which problems of distribution and consumption have been solved and everybody can begin to dance."[37]

The jet set came into focus in images that turned their hedonistic mobility into an object for consideration as magazines showcased beautiful people in far-off beautiful places. Magazines extended the experience of the photographers' circulation with that of their subjects', and a vast image culture propped up this class of jet setters, as "beautiful people." That term is attributed to a copyreader working with Diana Vreeland, who had become editor of *Vogue* in 1962 after years of working at rival publication *Harper's Bazaar.* Bender, citing Vreeland, selected the name for her own book, *Beautiful People:* "We mean people who are beautiful to look at. It's been taken up to mean people who are rich. We mean the charmers but there is no harm to be rich."[38] Rasponi had included such people in his list of jet setters, noting, "Mannequins and cameramen are forever traveling. Clothes have become so dull that they are again and again no longer photographed in a studio but against Inca ruins of Machu Picchu in Peru, the teeming bazaars of Marrakesh."[39] But such models were the most "of their moment" as well. As Bender explained, "To be in fashion means to try hard to make the clock stand still. Arrested development is the essential of pop fashion." The jet set demanded that every moment be the present so they could always be in fashion, in both senses of the phrase; the meaning of "beautiful people" was both literal and figurative. Magazine photography gave them form and perpetuated their seemingly easy mobility into another type of seemingly easy mobility: physical circulation as pictures in magazines.

As the film *The VIPs* depicts, airports had become the new points for arrivals and departures, and the more important one was, the more frequently one would be in one. Photographers lurked at airports hoping to snatch images. Celebrities mostly cooperated. As Mary Quant explains in her memoir, the chief steward spoke to her as their plane was about to land in Washington, D.C.: "We have received a radio. . . . They have asked that you should be the first to step off the plane so that the television cameras and photographers can get pictures."[40] The airlines also benefitted from the presence of their well-known passengers and created press operations whose sole function was taking photographs on the tarmac. A selection of images from the Air France press archive suggests how such photos could "elevate" the person being pictured, despite their already elevated status. The photos capture the fact that the celebrity would, like a god, ascend to and descend from the skies. Such images emphasized the arrival or departure rather than transit itself. These are stopped images of a life that seemed otherwise always in motion, thus making the person special. Additionally, the prominence of the plane itself allowed viewers to appreciate the beauty of the new-fangled transport vehicle while associating travelers and such new technologies. As the genre developed, judging from the archive, images evolved in style from a basic portrait of a celebrity at the opening of the plane door, as in a 1957 photo of Yves Saint-Laurent (fig. 3.12), to compositions that became more visually sophisticated and playful, as in a 1965 image of Maria Callas with the airport in the background (fig. 3.13). In 1966, Françoise Hardy seems to be enveloped by the wings of the plane and its jet engine (fig. 3.14). Airports accommodated the culture of arrivals and departures by establishing press lounges, where stars would be interviewed upon arrival. In fact, Brigitte Bardot never left the airport in New York in December 1965 when she did a press appearance for the Louis Malle film in which she costarred with Jeanne Moreau, *Viva Maria!* (fig. 3.15).

Even before the era of security threats, airport authorities needed to establish press operations to control paparazzi and the mobs of fans waiting to catch a glimpse of someone famous. In other words, airports had become photo-op venues. One early example of jet age airport mobbing happened when the Beatles came to the United States in 1964. Their first visit, in February, was to New York. As one of the flight attendants put it, there were "thousands of fans awaiting us . . . 5000–15,000. I am not good at judging numbers, but it was a giant sea of people."[41] On the Beatles' second visit, that summer, the Los Angeles Airport authorities decided that there were "not enough police in all of Southern California to control the thousands who were planning to come to the airport." An internal memo described "three B-days" in 1964 that "touched off a James Bond thriller as airport officials plotted to separate the fans from their mop-topped idols."[42] Airport authorities begged the Beatles' manager, Brian Epstein, to use a charter and not announce the arrival. Having lost that battle, the airport managed the three entries and exits as undercover missions, and only the first leg of their arrival, on a Pan Am flight, included a press conference. The Fab Four were shuttled off their flight on August 18, 1964, through immigration, and to a "remote corner of the lower level where 75 members of the press, ready with cameras, questions and teen-age assistants to properly record this historic event . . . the first formal press conference for the Beatles on U.S. soil." An hour later they headed to San Francisco. The second arrival happened at 3:45 A.M. to avoid the mayhem, and their departure was from an undisclosed terminal. The memo concluded, "The mission was successful. No

Fig. 3.12 Yves Saint-Laurent at an open plane door, 1958. Photo by Roland Briens

Fig. 3.13 Maria Callas boarding a plane, 1965

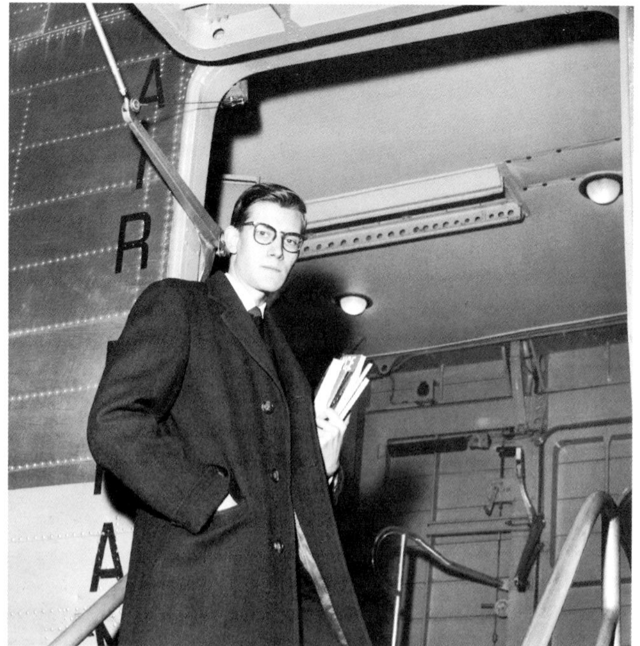

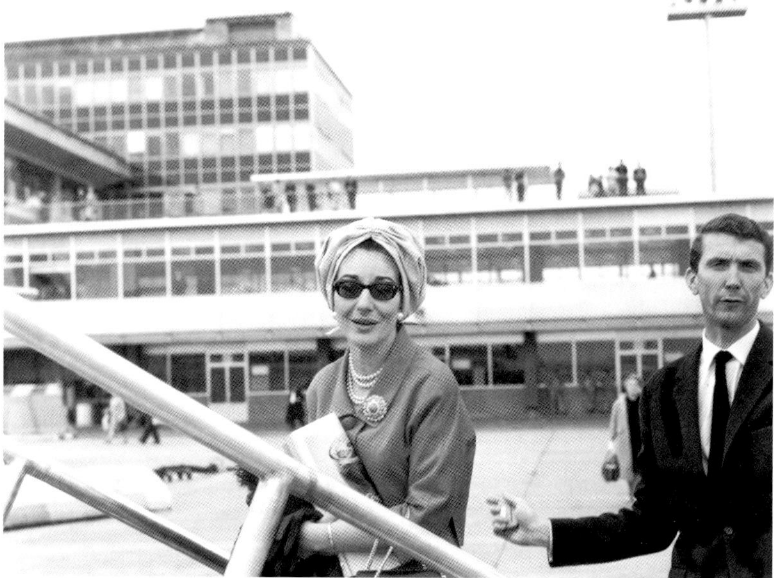

crushed ribs. No children crowding onto runways." It boasted that New York authorities had adopted the same method of separating fans from the Beatles "and have made this a permanent procedure for handling of highly publicized celebrity arrivals and departures which characteristically attract large groups of young people, sometimes numbering thousands, and endanger the public." In other words, suppressing a photo opportunity became as important as producing one. Suppressed or published, pictures of the new mobile elite meant that there was someone on the other side of the camera on whom the subjects depended: the press photographer.

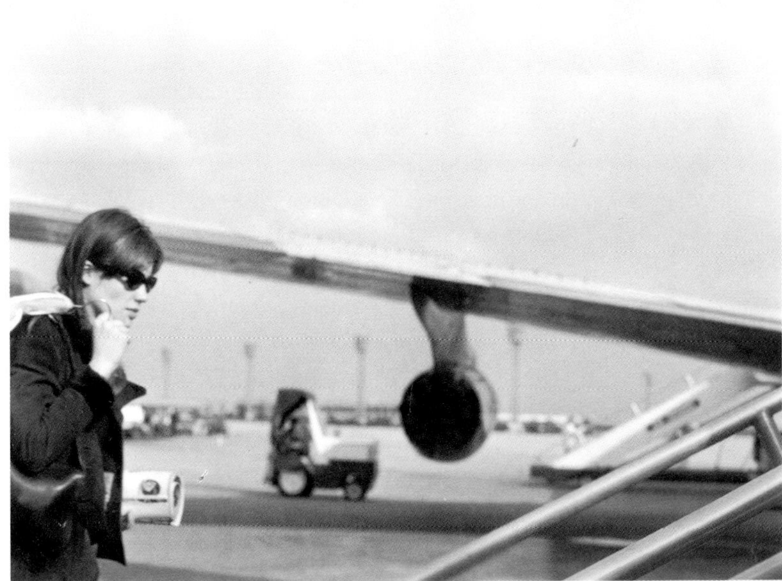

Fig. 3.14 Françoise Hardy enveloped by a plane, 1965

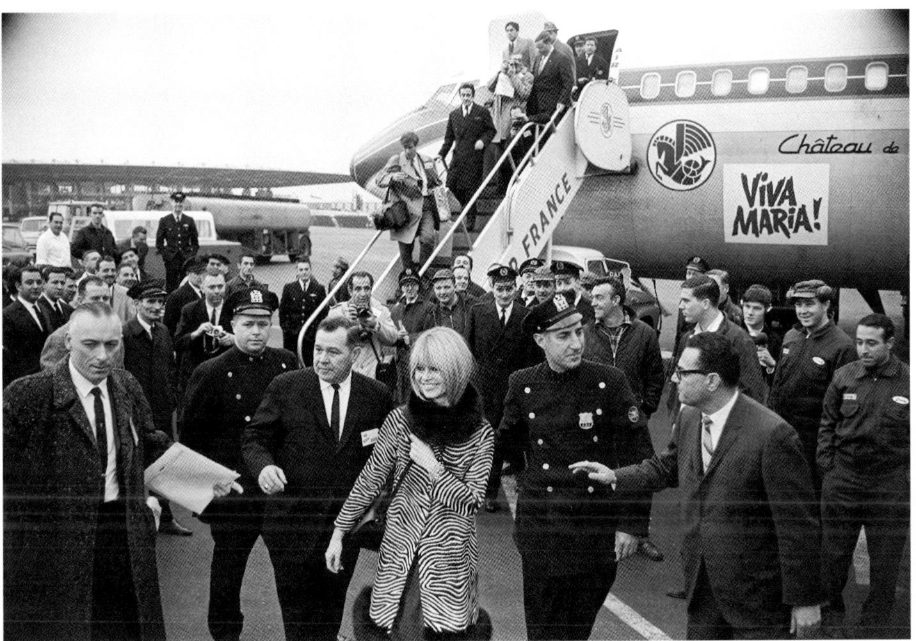

Fig. 3.15 Brigitte Bardot arriving at JFK Airport for *Viva Maria!* tour, 1965. Photo by Patrice Habans

THE PRESS PHOTOGRAPHER JOINS THE JET SET

Photography, of course, has a significant history independent of magazines. But as Mary Panzer has argued, magazines, with their "big shiny pages," exposed and disseminated photographs of many kinds—fine art, advertising, and news—before there were many other venues where they could be seen as such, although photography was already ubiquitous as a form of illustration in brochures and books, and in film strips.[43] Until recently, the study of the visual dimension and production of news pictures has been dedicated less to understanding magazine images per se and more to canonizing "great" photographers, whose magazine work is often viewed in the context of his or her broader artistic output or as an (often formative) moment on the creative journey. Instead, it is important to consider that a vast network of people produced magazines. The paper trail left by such institutions as the cooperative photo agency Magnum, for example, sheds light on the central role played by photo editors, like Wilson Hicks of *Life,* in creating photo essay ideas, assigning photos, and laying out pages. Many people were involved in producing the images we see in magazines, not just the photographers.[44]

Photographers were constrained in terms of what they could photograph because of the cameras they used, how fast they could get somewhere, and what lab conditions existed for reproducing images. Thus, production history, the history of picture-taking and picture-making, puts the literal travel of both the photographer and his film on display as much as it depicts the position of the eyewitness reporter through images. Robert Park, the Chicago School sociologist and early theorist of the value of the news, observed in 1940 that the press served "to orient man and society in an actual world"; one could rephrase this point to say that photo news functioned to establish that man's place was all over the world.[45] Mass visual media such as the photo press did not simply offer vicarious travel, they also transmitted to viewers a form of physical displacement—displacement by the image of the reporter, who had been moved or displaced by speedy transport.

Images are a way we know the world and are not simply a mirror of it; they are a tool for grabbing hold of it, however imperfectly. Wittgenstein's powerfully enigmatic "picture theory of meaning" reminds us that images are crucial to any and all forms of knowledge. Wittgenstein's metaphor was that a picture "reaches right out" to reality; that "it is laid against reality like a measure."[46] Vision and interpretation are themselves embodied and kinesthetic.[47] They are extensions of human actions and experiences. Thinking of the image as a form of embodied knowledge while also detailing the social and collective histories of photojournalism allow us to comprehend the materiality of images in magazines. That materiality is not simply attached to the photographic object; in addition, its circulation is tied to mechanized transport. Finally, those images are also the experiences of the people who journeyed to make them. They do not simply offer "virtual voyages" for readers, however, what would be the dangerous mirrors that Boorstin described in his conception of jet age tourism. The way images work to extend experience and the key roles played by speed, circulation, and mobility attest to the notion that, rather than false reflections, the jet age offered new arrangements for experiencing the material world and its representations.

Speed and pace have always been a fundamental part of the story of the modern press. As it regarded the production of images, however, the faster the news cycle, the harder it was to produce quality images, and so speed became as valuable to the news image as it was to the daily news report itself. One way that newspapers addressed the challenge of producing news images was to offer their own illustrated weeklies and pictorial supplements; other publications, what we would call magazines, either weeklies or monthlies, expanded the reportorial and expositional horizon of illustration of all kinds, from caricature to sketch reporting to photography. In compensation for a slower news cycle, they created "higher" visual production values.

The mobility embedded in news photography has its historical roots in such important nineteenth-century transformations as the mechanization of transportation. While the era of European expansion that had begun in the late fifteenth century introduced a degree and scale of travel previously unknown, no one would say it was speedy. Mechanization enhanced and promoted the value of speed. Such summary nineteenth-century images as Currier and Ives' "The Progress of the Century," made for the Centennial Exposition in Philadelphia, portrays the dynamism of mechanization in which communication and transport are tied, complete with a metaphor of the transparency of an "open window" (fig. 3.16). The image emblematizes many of the well-known technological advances of the century. The mechanized printing press (first used by *The London Times* in 1814) revolutionized the speed and volume of the printed newspaper. At the same time, the establishment of the telegraph in mid-century (featured prominently here with a tape of homilies about national unity as well as peace on earth—already a global vision) transcribed signals into words.

The history of communication was especially complicated as it relates to the distribution of images. Photographs in the early decades of the medium's history could neither be printed in newspapers nor transmitted otherwise. Most historians focus on the advent of the halftone process of the late 1870s and 1880s as a turning point for photojournalism, but it would be a long time before the London-based *Daily Mirror* became an all-photo illustrated paper in 1904. Exposure times were long in early photographic processes, and thus anything that moved would not even appear in a photo. Developing images was a complicated and delicate operation; the wet plate process used until well into the 1870s required photographers to have their own traveling darkrooms (fig. 3.17). Images made at a distance could not be transmitted until the Bélinographe in 1914; radiophoto served as a proto-fax in the 1940s. None of these technologies of photo delivery at a distance was good enough for reproduction without massive retouching and enhancement, and this process did not, in any event, mitigate the photographer's journey.[48]

Baudelaire had also identified the mobility of the modern observer in his "Painter of Modern Life" essay, as noted earlier. Of Constantin Guys, the sketch artist, Baudelaire wrote that "he wants to know, understand and appreciate everything that happens on the surface of our globe" and that his goal was "to see the world, to be at the center of the world, and yet to

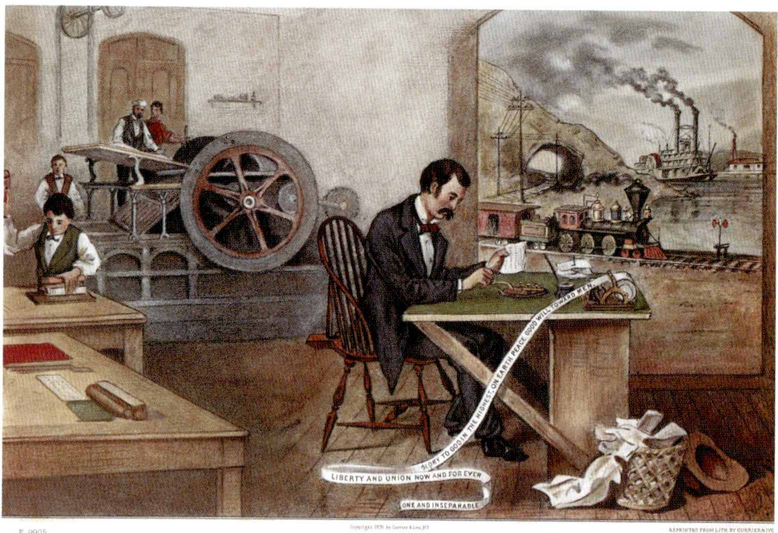

Fig. 3.16 Currier and Ives, *The Progress of the Century*, 1876. Color lithograph. Library of Congress

remain hidden from the world."[49] Photojournalists, however, did the opposite—testifying by proximity—which is why photojournalist Robert Capa became associated with the phrase, "If your pictures aren't good enough, you're not close enough."[50] As the Magnum photo agency's executive editor John Morris explained, "Unlike a reporter, who can piece together a story from a certain distance, a photographer must get to the scene of the action. . . . He must absolutely be in the right place at the right time."[51] Henri Cartier-Bresson boiled it down to this: photojournalists needed "an eye, a finger and two legs."[52] In other words, while images might circulate and breach distance, they also stand in for the photojournalist's mobility, and the photographer, in turn, stands in for the viewer.

A photographer's mobility depended on changes in equipment as much as on modes of transport. Photography became a more portable medium after the invention of smaller lightweight cameras, such as the Leica in 1925 and the Rolleiflex in 1929. By using perforated film rather than light-sensitive plates, and wider aperture lenses and flashbulbs, photographers could make more spontaneous news photographs.[53] Photographers could move more easily and quickly, and capture more action with their cameras. Such portability was linked, above all else, not simply to a notion of breaching distance and getting closer to the object worth photographing but to capturing and reproducing the news more quickly.

But such proximity and mobility required mechanized transport. As Capa's friend and collaborator in the field, Irwin Shaw, put it, "He always rode towards the sound of the guns."[54] There are, not surprisingly, many photos of Capa posed "en route" (fig. 3.18). As the profession of photojournalism developed, the mobility of both the image and the photographer remained at the heart of the news picture narrative and of the narratives related to their production, which were always part of news reporting itself. For example, in the 1940s, the celebrated crime and street photographer Weegee (Arthur Fellig) boasted of his specially equipped car (fig. 3.19). In Europe, when the term paparazzo first came into use, such photographers always seemed to ride motor scooters (fig. 3.20). American paparazzo of the next generation, Ron Galella, perhaps best known for his lawsuit against Jacqueline (Kennedy) Onassis, referred in interviews to a "paparazzo traffic lane," which he identified as the rightmost one, used for making quick turns in vehicular chases.[55] Until the digital era rendered the production and dissemination of the physical photographic image immaterial, photojournalists depended on modern mechanized transport. Nevertheless, even with technological changes, nothing has challenged the value attributed to the physical displacement and mobility of the news photographer to get the picture—even as surveillance cameras have rendered the photographic news record automatic.[56] Greater attention to the automatic nature of digital photography has led us to consider the centrality of concepts such as mediation, but such attention to the position of the photojournalist offers us a way to think more seriously about how transport helps to define media and mediation.

Fig. 3.17 The photographic van with Marcus Sparling on the box, 1855. Roger Fenton photographer. Library of Congress

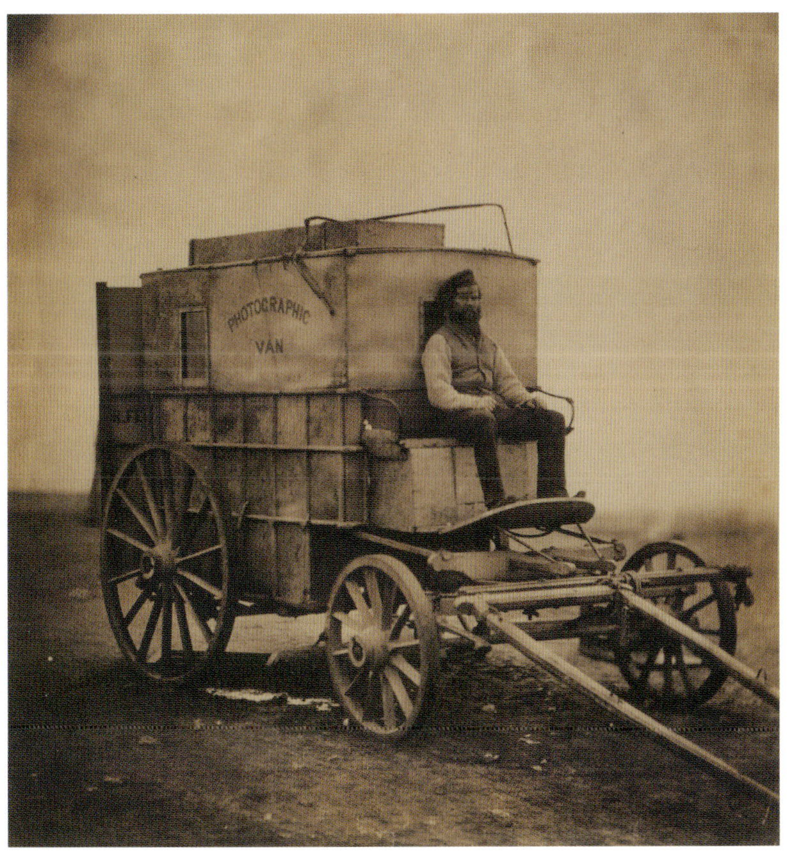

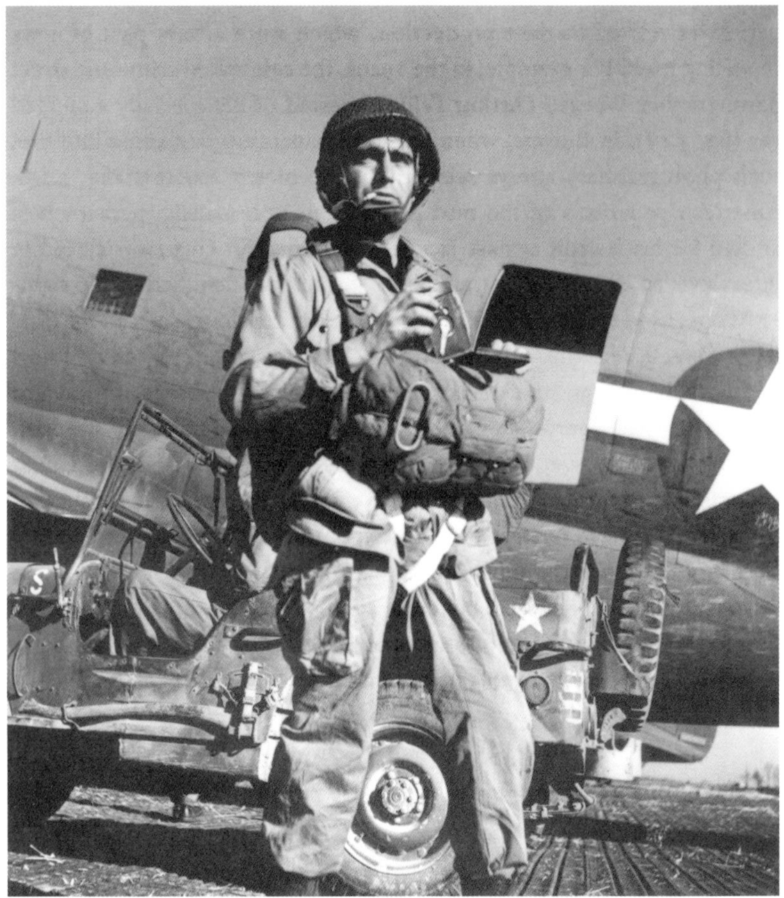

Fig. 3.18 Robert Capa before parachuting into Germany with American forces, March 23, 1945

Transport played a key role in facilitating the travel of photographers and their exposed film. As A. J. Ezickson, a photo editor, wrote in *Get That Picture!* (1938), successful reporting hinged on the way publications got the "cameraman to the scene and back with the pictures to the office."[57] They used various time-saving tactics: giving the film to a stranger on a train, who would be met at the station by someone from the newspaper, or meeting a suburban train with a motorcyclist who could rush the film to the newspaper office—every moment counted. The advent of airmail in 1927 resulted in faster speeds and new routes. Although telegraphic relay, on which the written press had long relied, could not translate high-quality photographic images, it was used to produce fast images for "hot news" items. Ezickson described the escalation of the speed of film delivery as critical to pictorial journalism's rise:

> From the first days of the news picture, the newspapers and picture syndicates have utilized every means of conveyance to bring the reproduction of the event before the eyes of the reader: from the interior of China the donkey and jinrikishaw have brought the flood and famine pictures; the carrier pigeon carried the film in Japan;

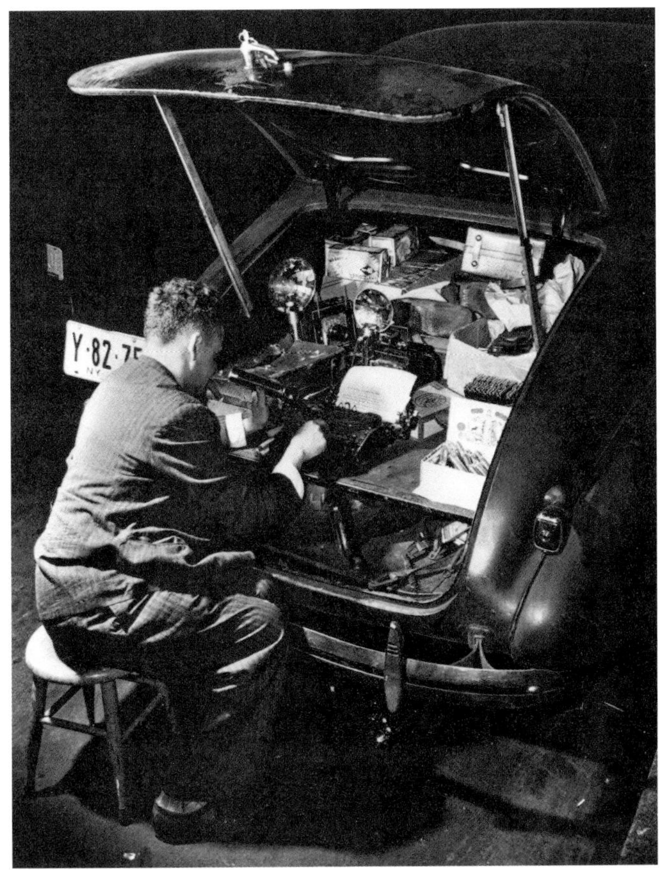

Fig. 3.19 Weegee's special car, circa 1940

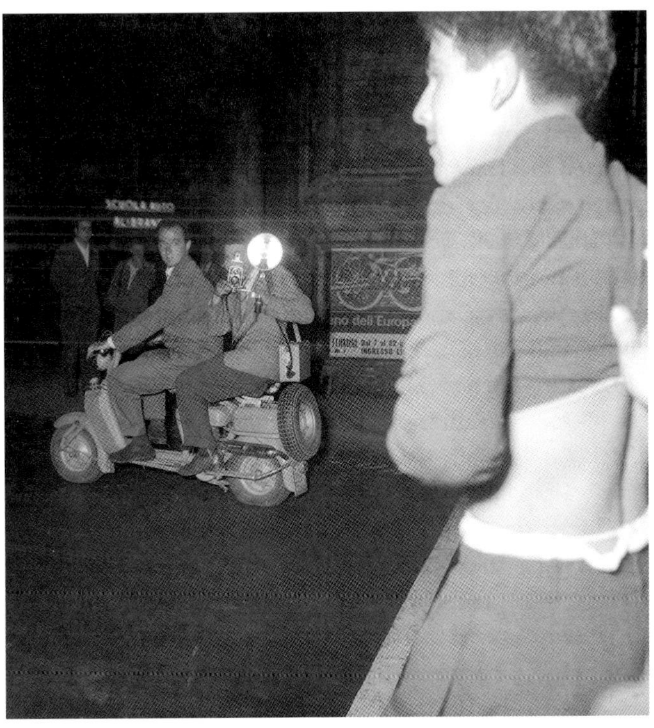

Fig. 3.20 Tazio Secchiaroli and Luciano Mellace, Rome, 1952. Franco Pinna photographer

> native runners brought the pictures from the jungle interiors; dog sleds bore the negatives from the Arctic wastes; every known vehicle in Europe and America has expedited the photograph, the automobile, train, speedboat, airplane, dirigible, motorcycle . . .[58]

According to this history of the profession, chartering boats and trains became common for one reason alone: "Speed, speed, more speed became the shibboleth and battle cry of a score of editors."[59] The picture became the proof of a fast journey as much as a depiction of the news.

When planes became the fastest form of transport, even before the advent of the jet, journalists were early adopters. Photojournalists used strangers as couriers for photos and undeveloped film, as they had on trains. They would hand the materials over, and couriers would be met at the other end by representatives of a publication or agency who would then rush the packages to the appropriate labs, or to editorial offices for story layout and mock-up. Redistribution for printing and publication would follow, then further redistribution to subscribers and newsstands. *Life*'s picture bureau, for example, was responsible for chartering the plane for and negotiating the price of the rushed photos of film star Rita Hayworth and Prince Aly Khan's 1949 wedding in France.[60]

Magazines and agencies worked behind the scenes so that photographers could be among the first group of frequent flyers. As Margot Shore, director of Magnum's Paris office, wrote to photographer Ernst Haas, dispatching him to Pakistan in 1954 for the celebration of the Aga Khan's jubilee, "Magnum is great friends with Air India, both through Werner's [Bischof] work there last year, and through the fact that Susie [Marquis] has given them pictures they wanted. So perhaps for the film shipment it would be best for you to talk to AIR INDIA soon as you get to Karachi, make a date and a place where you will give them all you shoot and have it well arranged in advance."[61] Eventually, photo agencies such as Magnum contracted a standing service with multiple airlines.[62]

Planes also changed the organization of picture-taking in the field. They made it possible for an international group of people to work together by sending personnel and material into the field before wireless signals made the transmission of images truly possible.[63] Agencies complained when photojournalists did not comply with directions to use prescheduled flights. As one Magnum memo writer griped, "Sometimes, the photographer, in spite of detailed, carefully worked out schedules prepared by the office, will be tempted into following last-minute inspirations about the best way of shipping the story: as poor Marc Riboud did in the case of the Coronation of the King of Nepal when, instead of airfreighting as we had specified, he gave his film to a rival reporter-photographer who deliberately held them back until all his own material had been distributed."[64] Eventually, the increasing efficiency of air transport led big magazines such as *Life* to reduce the number of staff photographers. As John Loengard explained, as he considered changes in the field of photojournalism, "The ubiquity and reliability of jet aircraft . . . allowed photographers to reach most places on the globe within twenty-four hours, and meant that free-lance talent, concentrated in New York and Paris could move anywhere with ease and speed."[65]

Planes also played a role in one of the great media spectacles of the midcentury period: the coronation of Queen Elizabeth II on June 2, 1953—the first such ancient ritual televised for a mass audience—20 million people in Britain alone.[66] Although the coronation has been singled out for this TV first, by reinserting it into a system of media that produced the "spectacle of the Coronation," and thereby focusing on the connection between transport and the speed and quality of image production, we can see how a larger system defined the meaning and shaped the look of the coronation itself, not just the television broadcast.

Television transmitted only in black and white, and only those hundreds of thousands of dedicated onlookers who lined the coronation path could take in the full colorful spectacle. This gave magazines the opportunity to step into the breach and communicate the event in all its colors. They would vaunt beauty over speed. If magazines specialized in distributing high-quality images, especially compared with the images in daily newspapers, once television came on the scene magazines would continue to mark their comparative advantage and distinction as being of high visual quality, this time by adding color to the mix. The movie industry had also begun to combat the competition from television, real or imagined, with a similar formula by embracing Technicolor and a host of widescreen formats to distinguish the movies from the fuzzy pictures on the little box in people's homes or in town bars. *Paris Match,* for example, printed news of the coronation twice—once in an article that also reported that it had been televised in a sort of reportorial mise-en-abyme in black and white images and then two weeks later in color. The periodical's editors eagerly sought to exploit their advantage over the American press, with whom they regularly competed for photo scoops; the Americans' distance from the place of the coronation meant that they had to fly the film across the Atlantic, and no matter how fast that transit was in relation to the boat, European publications would be able to publish images before the Americans could.

Life, operating with the same "lemons into lemonade" logic, decided that it would turn its own production challenges into news stories.[67] Editors engaged readers in a drama about whether they would be able to break the magazine's own records by using the power of air transport to produce color images faster than they had ever done up to that time. The June 8, 1953, issue of *Life* inserted a rather hastily pasted together announcement promising an attempt for next week's issue with a map route from London to various air stops (Gander, Newfoundland, for refueling, and then Boston, the closest point in the United States, followed by New York, Chicago, Los Angeles). The pieces of the magazine would be flown to those cities in

Fig. 3.21 "In Next Week's Life," map of coronation film route, *Life*, June 8, 1953

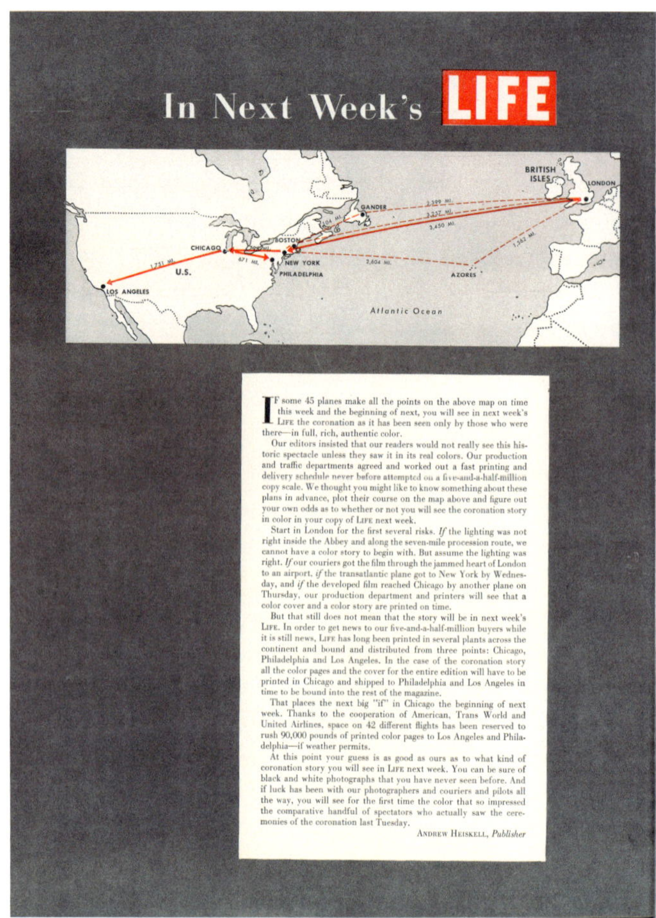

In Next Week's LIFE

IF some 45 planes make all the points on the above map on time this week and the beginning of next, you will see in next week's LIFE the coronation as it has been seen only by those who were there—in full, rich, authentic color.

Our editors insisted that our readers would not really see this historic spectacle unless they saw it in its real colors. Our production and traffic departments agreed and worked out a fast printing and delivery schedule never before attempted on a five-and-a-half-million copy scale. We thought you might like to know something about these plans in advance, plot their course on the map above and figure out your own odds as to whether or not you will see the coronation story in color in your copy of LIFE next week.

Start in London for the first several risks. *If* the lighting was not right inside the Abbey and along the seven-mile procession route, we cannot have a color story to begin with. But assume the lighting was right. *If* our couriers got the film through the jammed heart of London to an airport, *if* the transatlantic plane got to New York by Wednesday, and *if* the developed film reached Chicago by another plane on Thursday, our production department and printers will see that a color cover and a color story are printed on time.

But that still does not mean that the story will be in next week's LIFE. In order to get news to our five-and-a-half-million buyers while it is still news, LIFE has long been printed in several plants across the continent and bound and distributed from three points: Chicago, Philadelphia and Los Angeles. In the case of the coronation story all the color pages and the cover for the entire edition will have to be printed in Chicago and shipped to Philadelphia and Los Angeles in time to be bound into the rest of the magazine.

That places the next big "if" in Chicago the beginning of next week. Thanks to the cooperation of American, Trans World and United Airlines, space on 42 different flights has been reserved to rush 90,000 pounds of printed color pages to Los Angeles and Philadelphia—if weather permits.

At this point your guess is as good as ours as to what kind of coronation story you will see in LIFE next week. You can be sure of black and white photographs that you have never seen before. And if luck has been with our photographers and couriers and pilots all the way, you will see for the first time the color that so impressed the comparative handful of spectators who actually saw the ceremonies of the coronation last Tuesday.

ANDREW HEISKELL, *Publisher*

order to construct the fastest color news story ever delivered by *Life.* After explaining the complex variables and factors with a series of contingencies and "Ifs," the note from publisher Andrew Heiskell warned, "At this point, your guess is as good as ours as to what kind of Coronation story you will see in LIFE next week" (fig. 3.21).[68] By using airplanes, the magazine reduced what normally took seven weeks to just ten days for its post-coronation black-and-white printing (although the cover date was June 15, almost two weeks after the event, the actual date of the coronation was never mentioned). The magazine accomplished this by shooting exclusively in Ektachrome film (rather than in 35mm color, which would have taken longer to develop) and through a record-breaking transfer to metal engraving and printing in Chicago. But a story later published about the successful timely production pointed out that the two key moments of shooting and transfer had hinged on the overnight plane transport of the Ektachrome rolls and their delivery to the *Life* offices at 7:00 A.M. the day after the coronation. The speedy delivery made it possible to immediately develop the transparencies and create the layout, followed by the rapid airborne transfer to Chicago. The article also details the unprecedented airlift of the color photo sections from the plant in Chicago; these sections were usually sent by rail to be joined to the black-and-white sections printed in Los Angeles and Philadelphia. Instead, with the help of TWA, United, and American Airlines, the color photo sections were transported over three days and on ninety-one flights so that the magazine could be assembled and distributed as "fast news" (figs. 3.22–3.24). *Life* printed reader appreciation two weeks later: "After reading, June 8, about all the odds against getting the color pictures into the next issue, I could not help but cross my fingers. . . . They just had to come through. It wouldn't have been *Life* if they hadn't." From another reader: "No stretch of the imagination could color the radio or television portrayals as do these clear and brilliant pictures of such an inspiring and heart-warming occasion."[69]

The June 15, 1953, issue of *Life* featured the story of the coronation (fig. 3.25), and only in passing, in the editor's note titled "Dangerous Living by Editors and Climbers" (about the coronation and Mount Everest), is there a mention of the gamble they had taken by promising what amounted to a miracle in printing.[70] Perhaps to extol the value of magazine coverage, *Life* also printed a comical article recounting the various false starts and failed attempts by American television in covering the event.

Airplanes were thus the latest way that transport had revolutionized where photojournalists could go to get a picture and how quickly readers would see that image. Airplanes may have sped the pace of magazine production, but they did so at a time when it was obvious that television would eventually deliver the news more quickly than print magazines would be able to—although a difference in pace had always distinguished weekly and daily photo work.

The jet may have improved upon the actual speed of the airplane, but its impact on magazine photography went well beyond the possibility of getting photo-reporters, their film, and their magazines around the world faster. The same quality of motion that made the jet so seductive and that produced the jet set was what made the postwar magazine the ideal venue for supporting this flimsy and beautiful new social world. Lifestyle magazines emerged as sites for the glorification of international nomadism, and photographs circulated with greater ease as they were delivered more quickly. The increased physical mobility of both image and image-takers elevated photojournalists into the glamorous new crowd of jet setters they had helped to create.

Postwar lifestyle magazines such as *Holiday,* founded in 1946, became forces for innovation and displays of cultural trends. One might even consider that publications such as *Holiday* were largely responsible for creating what journalist Horace Sutton would describe in a 1967 special issue of the *Saturday Review* dedicated to developments in travel over the preceding twenty years as going from "Motion to Mobilism."[71] *Holiday* reported on Europe's slow recovery from war and, over time, its more glamorous elements, such as ski resorts, Paris fashion, the Riviera.[72] It also reported on many American destinations, addressing an audience that it presumed would be on the move.

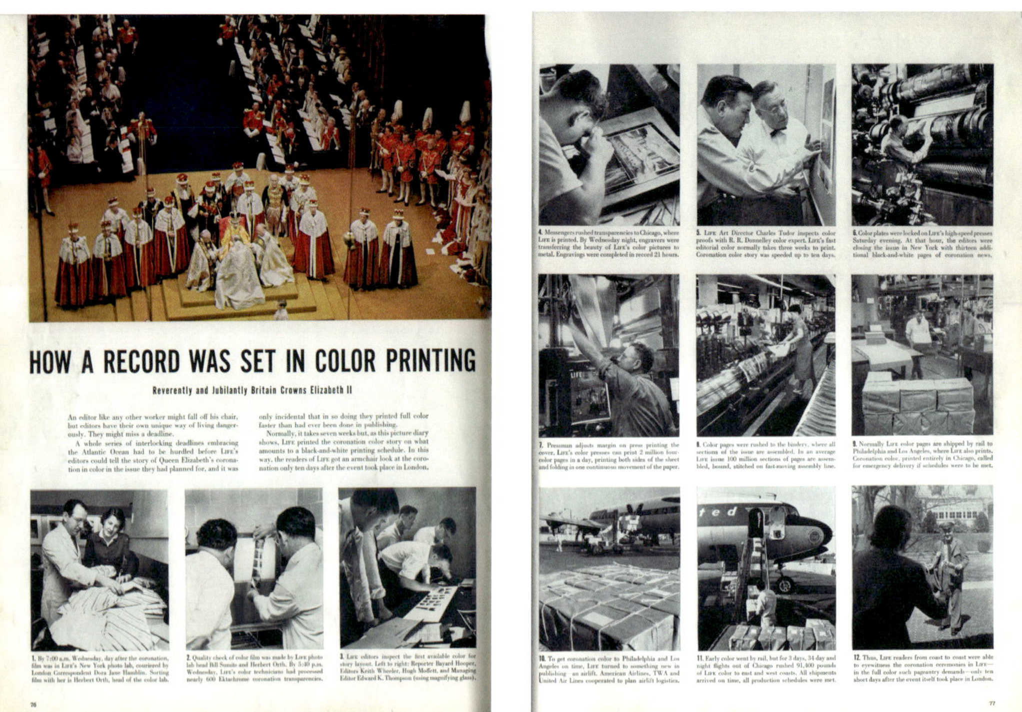

HOW A RECORD WAS SET IN COLOR PRINTING

Reverently and Jubilantly Britain Crowns Elizabeth II

An editor like any other worker might fall off his chair, but editors have their own unique way of living dangerously. They might miss a deadline.

A whole series of interlocking deadlines embracing the Atlantic Ocean had to be hurdled before LIFE's editors could tell the story of Queen Elizabeth's coronation in color in the issue they had planned for, and it was only incidental that in so doing they printed full color faster than had ever been done in publishing.

Normally, it takes seven weeks but, as this picture diary shows, LIFE printed the coronation color story on what amounts to a black-and-white printing schedule. In this way, the readers of LIFE got an armchair look at the coronation only ten days after the event took place in London.

1. By 7:00 a.m. Wednesday, day after the coronation, film was in LIFE's New York photo lab, couriered by London Correspondent Dora Jane Hamblin. Sorting film with her is Herbert Orth, head of the color lab.

2. Quality check of color film was made by LIFE photo lab head Bill Sumits and Herbert Orth. By 5:40 p.m. Wednesday, LIFE's color technicians had processed nearly 600 Ektachrome coronation transparencies.

3. LIFE editors inspect the first available color for story layout. Left to right: Reporter Bayard Hooper, Editors Keith Wheeler, Hugh Moffett, and Managing Editor Edward K. Thompson (using magnifying glass).

76

4. Messengers rushed transparencies to Chicago, where LIFE is printed. By Wednesday night, engravers were transferring the beauty of LIFE's color pictures to metal. Engravings were completed in record 21 hours.

5. LIFE Art Director Charles Tudor inspects color proofs with R. R. Donnelley color expert. LIFE's fast editorial color normally takes three weeks to print. Coronation color story was speeded up to ten days.

6. Color plates were locked on LIFE's high-speed presses Saturday evening. At that hour, the editors were closing the issue in New York with thirteen additional black-and-white pages of coronation news.

7. Pressman adjusts margin on press printing the cover. LIFE's color presses can print 2 million four-color pages in a day, printing both sides of the sheet and folding in one continuous movement of the paper.

8. Color pages were rushed to the bindery, where all sections of the issue are assembled. In an average LIFE issue 100 million sections of pages are assembled, bound, stitched on fast-moving assembly line.

9. Normally LIFE color pages are shipped by rail to Philadelphia and Los Angeles, where LIFE also prints. Coronation color, printed entirely in Chicago, called for emergency delivery if schedules were to be met.

10. To get coronation color to Philadelphia and Los Angeles on time, LIFE turned to something new in publishing—an airlift. American Airlines, TWA and United Air Lines cooperated to plan airlift logistics.

11. Early color went by rail, but for 3 days, 34 day and night flights out of Chicago rushed 91,400 pounds of LIFE color to east and west coasts. All shipments arrived on time, all production schedules were met.

12. Thus, LIFE readers from coast to coast were able to eyewitness the coronation ceremonies in LIFE—in the full color such pageantry demands—only ten short days after the event itself took place in London.

77

Figs. 3.22 and 3.23
Production history of the coronation told as "How a Record Was Set in Color Printing," in Stanley Rayfield, *How Life Gets the Story: Behind the Scenes in Photo-Journalism* (New York: Doubleday, 1955), 76, 77

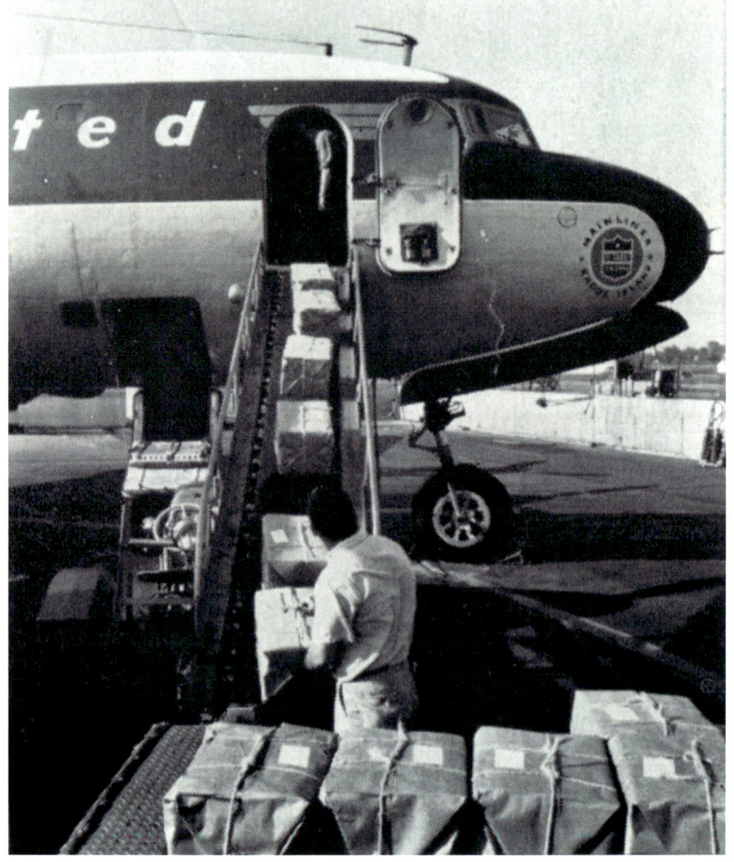

Fig. 3.24 (detail of fig. 3.23)
"Early color went by rail, but for 3 days, 34 day and night flights out of Chicago rushed 91,400 pounds of LIFE color to east and west coasts. All shipments arrived on time, all production schedules were met."

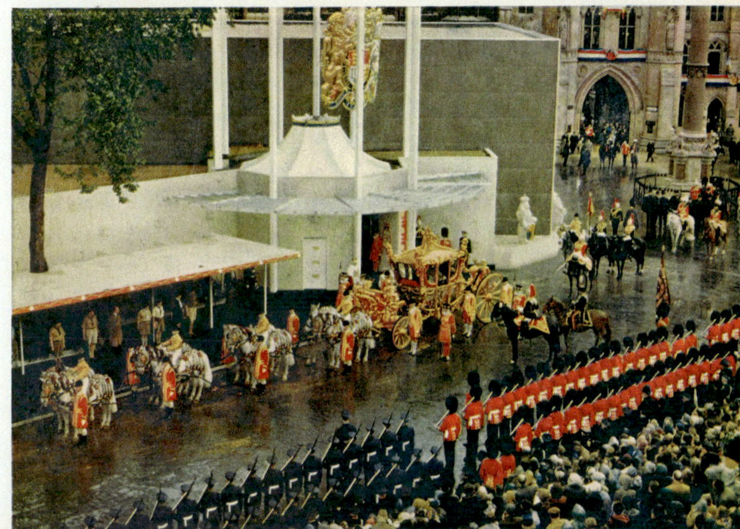
RECEIVING HOMAGE, queen hears Archbishop of Canterbury swear "faith and truth" as Bishops of Durham and of Bath and Wells kneel at either side. Coroneted bearers of regalia in crimson and ermine robes are ranked across dais. At back on both sides are foreign representatives. At right are heralds and peeresses.

LEAVING THE ABBEY, the queen has entered the golden state coach drawn up before the doorway to Abbey's temporary annex. Her maids of honor stand at the coach door, and mounted officers wait to escort her. Ranked in the foreground stand contingents of Royal Air Force (*at left*) and Brigade of Guards.

Fig. 3.25 Coronation photograph of Elizabeth II explaining the sped-up pace of production. From Rayfield, "How a Record Was Set"

Holiday seemed to have no actual generic precedent, which has led photo historian Mary Panzer to describe it as "part-*Fortune,* part-*National Geographic,* part-*New Yorker,* and part-*Gourmet.*"[73]

Holiday's main editorial staff had been Madison Avenue types involved in the Office of War Information who then transitioned back to magazine editing as their peacetime work. Powerhouses of prose such as E. B. White, Ernest Hemingway, and John Steinbeck wrote articles for the publication, which were sometimes illustrated by the photographs of well-known photo-reporters such as Robert Capa. Magazines such as *Holiday* would pay expenses and then some as photojournalists developed their own stories from the European recovery as well as from emerging conflicts—the wars of decolonization and independence, and civil wars in the Middle East, India, Asia, and Latin America.[74]

The design and style of lifestyle magazines were as important as their travel content. Many analysts of magazine culture reduce magazine aesthetics to their status as vehicles for advertising, but magazines have functioned that way from their inception, so it is not as simple as saying that they became a richer and more varied venue for sales over time. Instead, such periodicals increasingly became vehicles for the work of art directors, photo editors, and photographers due to an increasing sense of the power of visual communication in the wake of the Second World War.[75]

Yet magazines such as *Holiday* are part of the longer history of what publisher Condé Nast dubbed "class publications" at the turn of the century. As he explained in 1913, "A class publication is nothing more nor less than a publication that looks for its circulation *only* to those having in common a certain characteristic marked enough to group them into a class."[76] Nast had made *Vogue* into the "society" publication par excellence—one written by and for the four hundred people who would fit into Mrs. Astor's ballroom in New York. In 1913, William Randolph Hearst bought *Harper's Bazaar* and created a rivalry with *Vogue* that more or less continues to this day; it is a rivalry whose history is also a lesson in the early competition and distinction through visual style and graphic design—what we might call branding. Nast believed that advertisers were much better served by niche marketing than by casting about for the vague and perhaps even then unimaginable common tastes of a "general audience."[77] Subsequently, general weekly photograph driven newsmagazines developed in Europe in the late 1920s and 1930s with their storytelling capacities and audiences primed, I would suggest, by the development of the movies.[78]

The fashion press is as old as the periodical press itself and was dominated by illustration from the start. It shared with the news a logic of novelty and a need for reportorial accuracy via illustration. Images in the fashion press were in effect drawn to be used as guides for copying the clothing.[79] While early fashion periodicals made sophisticated use of illustration, they also turned to photography early and often. Deeply invested in the consumer culture associated with "capitalist modernity," yet socially elitist, the magazines were no doubt precursors, especially formally, of how photographic magazines would serve and be in dialogue with the dynamic world of the spectacular fashion shows on which they reported, vexed no doubt by whether the rise of cinema would eventually replace them altogether.[80]

Perhaps nothing changed, and saved, fashion magazines more than the course of World War II. The Occupation of France meant the end of the fashion business as it had been known; the exchange between France and America on which the industry relied was dramatically impeded; and the wartime conditions of bombing and rationing in London also checked opulent spending. Publications such as *Vogue* turned to American fashion and also, with their vast expertise and network in Europe, to hard news, reporting on wartime conditions overseas.

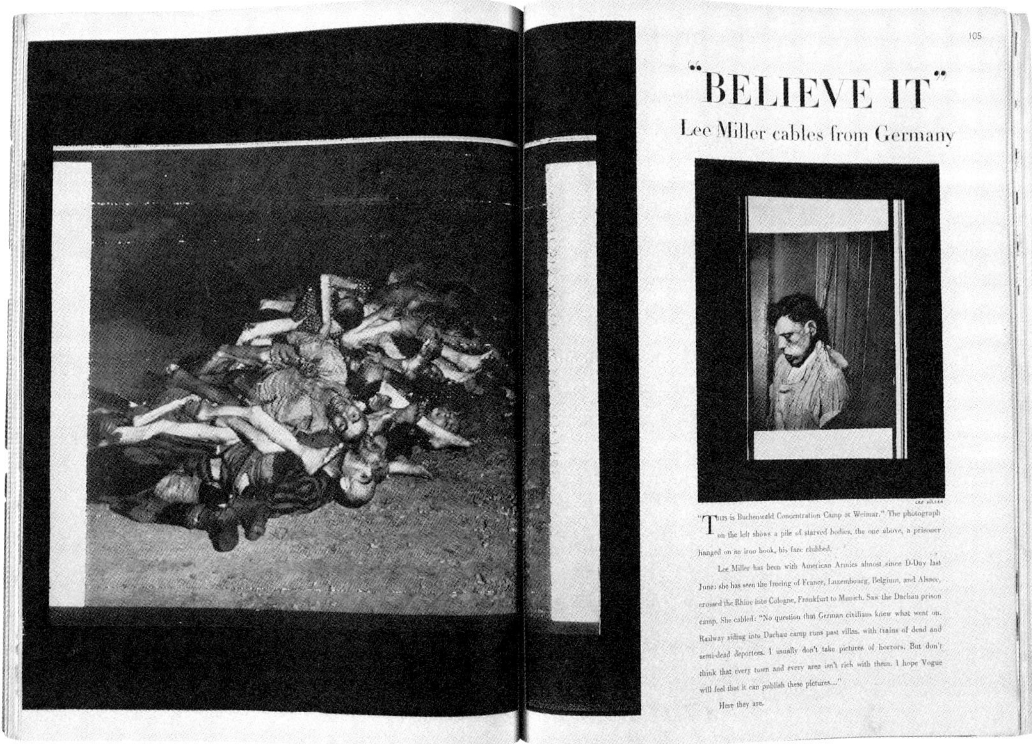
105

"BELIEVE IT"

Lee Miller cables from Germany

"This is Buchenwald Concentration Camp at Weimar." The photograph on the left shows a pile of starved bodies, the one above, a prisoner hanged on an iron hook, his face clubbed.

Lee Miller has been with American Armies almost since D-Day last June: she has seen the freeing of France, Luxembourg, Belgium, and Alsace, crossed the Rhine into Cologne, Frankfurt to Munich. Saw the Dachau prison camp. She cabled: "No question that German civilians knew what went on. Railway siding into Dachau camp runs past villas, with trains of dead and semi-dead deportees. I usually don't take pictures of horrors. But don't think that every town and every area isn't rich with them. I hope Vogue will feel that it can publish these pictures..."

Here they are.

Fig. 3.26 Lee Miller, "'Believe It' Lee Miller Cables from Germany." *Vogue*, June 1945

The work of model-turned-photographer Lee Miller is a flashpoint for the exceptional photojournalism generated during the war. Although some of her early war coverage in London suggests the sensibility of someone who had trained with the Surrealist Man Ray, her images from behind the lines are the sort of grainy news images associated with the best wartime photojournalists. The apex of her reporting came in June 1945 in her "Believe It" cables from Buchenwald, the Nazi concentration camp: "I hope *Vogue* will feel that it can publish these pictures." The magazine was among the few to publish the photos of piles of corpses and a prisoner hanged (fig. 3.26).[81] After the war, *Vogue* went back to its primary business of fashion, helping orchestrate the "recovery" of France, including Christian Dior's "New Look." Yet the war had produced a greater link between seemingly disparate kinds of magazines. Fashion magazines had covered the concentration camps. This increased overlapping and blurring of magazine genres was dominated by an aesthetic that embraced and reinforced what photography did, what magazines did, and what the jet did—and, importantly, what the jet set embodied: a world where people and things were on the move in a form of constant and seemingly unimpeded circulation and flow: arriving and departing with ease.

This chapter has shown that the content of photojournalistic images was as often the story of the pace of their delivery, the way that the complex technologies of photography and transport and magazine production combined, or the interrelation between media forms. This photographic content also extended to the identity of the person taking the picture, whose very mobility was a fundamental part of the picture's content and the viewer's connection to it. In the 1950s and 1960s, to be known as a photographer meant working as a magazine photographer on the move. Of the list of ten of the world's best photographers, compiled by *Popular Photography* in 1958 from a survey of "critics, teachers, editors, consultants, and working photographers," only two were not regularly engaged in press photography: Ansel Adams and Yousuf Karsh. The latter, a portrait photographer, nevertheless had published twenty *Life* covers and therefore was hardly a stranger to the magazine world.[82]

Photojournalism's significance was as much about the physical position of photographers as it was about the subject they photographed. In 1950, in the pages of *Portfolio,* a twenty-six-year-old Richard Avedon called photography a "double-sided mirror: the one side reflecting my subject, the other reflecting myself."[83] Such mirrors provided viewers a self-conscious opportunity to look at the photographer and his work. Magazine photography allowed viewers to experience the world through pictures and the operations behind photographic production, especially the constant circulation and mobility of photographs and photographers, eased by the fluid motion of the jet age.

To the editor of *Holiday* magazine, Ted Patrick, the cosmopolitan photographers of the Magnum photo agency epitomized "truly international, truly modern men who had the world not only as their beat but as their living room. They were at home, sympathetically at home, wherever they opened their cameras and suitcases."[84] As *Life* photo editor Ray Mackland echoed, "It is indeed glamorous, but make no mistake about it, it is a job. He is the envy of all of us for the places he visits and the people he meets."[85] The photographers' prestige, like that of the other jet setters, inhered in their association with far-flung places, even though they had to work when they were there. As Frank Zachary, art director of *Holiday* complained, "Our photographers turn down assignments because they're not far away enough. They always want to go to Africa or Burma."[86] *Life* staff photographer Eliot Elisofon boasted of how lucky photographers were to enjoy the lives and work they did: "Who but photographers meet the people we do, go to the places we do, control situations the way we do. . . . I am rich beyond belief, not in money but in friends, in places I've seen, experiences I've had. And I think that is an opportunity open to anyone. . . . Practically the only new professions are nuclear scientists and photojournalists."[87]

The very public marriage of the magazine and portrait photographer Antony Armstrong-Jones to Princess Margaret in 1960 also elevated a photographer—by catapulting him into the royal family. Cecil Beaton, who had been the royal family photographer for many years, had been annoyed when the young Queen Elizabeth commissioned Armstrong-Jones, a man of her own generation, to take her family photographs. But Beaton, having introduced Jones into the royal household in the first place, seemed relieved regarding the marriage. He assumed that the marriage would mean the end of

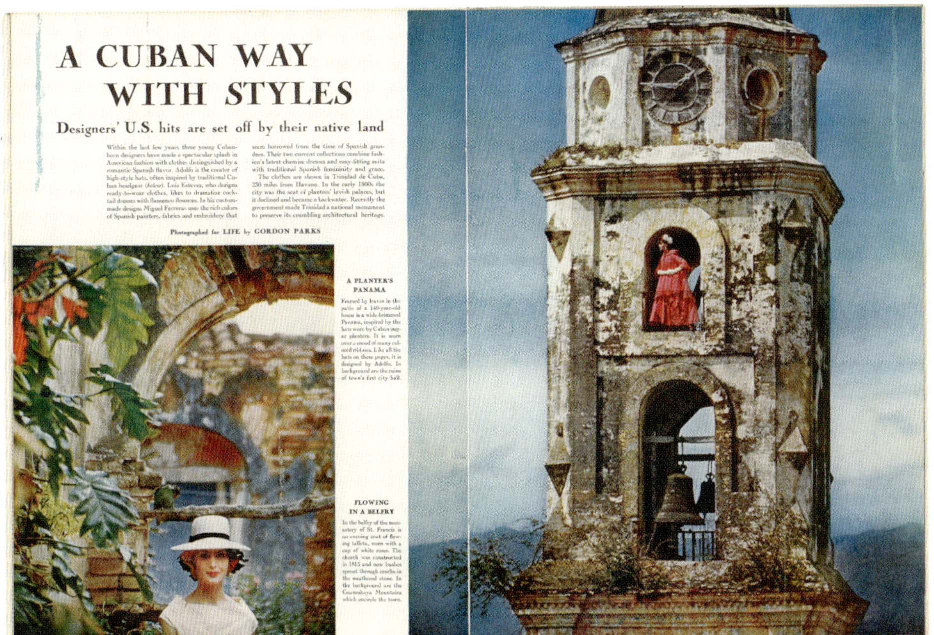

A CUBAN WAY WITH STYLES

Designers' U.S. hits are set off by their native land

Within the last few years three young Cuban-born designers have made a spectacular splash in American fashion with clothes distinguished by a romantic Spanish flavor. Adolfo is the creator of high-style hats, often inspired by traditional Cuban headgear (*below*). Luis Estevez, who designs ready-to-wear clothes, likes to dramatize cocktail dresses with flamenco flounces. In his custom-made designs Miguel Ferreras uses the rich colors of Spanish painters, fabrics and embroidery that seem borrowed from the time of Spanish grandees. Their two current collections combine fashion's latest chemise dresses and easy-fitting suits with traditional Spanish femininity and grace.

The clothes are shown in Trinidad de Cuba, 250 miles from Havana. In the early 1800s the city was the seat of planters' lavish palaces, but it declined and became a backwater. Recently the government made Trinidad a national monument to preserve its crumbling architectural heritage.

Photographed for LIFE by GORDON PARKS

A PLANTER'S PANAMA

Framed by leaves in the patio of a 140-year-old house is a wide-brimmed Panama, inspired by the hats worn by Cuban sugar planters. It is worn over a snood of many colored ribbons. Like all the hats on these pages, it is designed by Adolfo. In background are the ruins of town's first city hall.

FLOWING IN A BELFRY

In the belfry of the monastery of St. Francis is an evening coat of flowing taffeta, worn with a cap of white roses. The church was constructed in 1813 and now bushes sprout through cracks in the weathered stone. In the background are the Guamuhaya Mountains which encircle the town.

Fig. 3.27 "A Cuban Way with Styles," *Life*, May 5, 1968. Gordon Parks, photographer

Armstrong-Jones's working career, as it was inconceivable for someone of Beaton's generation to imagine a working photographer in the royal family. He thanked Princess Margaret for "removing my most dangerous rival." To which she replied, "What makes you think Tony is going to give up work?"[88]

Photographers everywhere took note of the impact the marriage had on the status of their profession. As an internal memo of the Magnum photo agency explained, *France Soir* recently published a cartoon: "One sees a picture editor in a magazine looking at a picture of a photographer. Finally, the picture editor says, 'These are very good pictures! But, please understand my problem: what are your nobility titles?' Conclusion: we strongly urge all Magnum photographers to title themselves to compete with Lord Snowden! How about Lord Erwitt, Baron Burton de Glinn. . . . Il faut se défendre."[89] As Beaton noted, "When I began, a photographer had no sort of social position at all; he was sort of an inferior tradesman. . . . But now photographers can go anywhere."[90]

David Bailey is a quintessential photographer of the period whose celebrity has often seemed to suggest frivolity. This image was probably not helped by the callous portrayal of the photographer in Michelangelo Antonioni's 1966 film *Blow Up,* allegedly based on Bailey. Born to working-class parents in East London, Bailey worked during his teen years at menial jobs in the Fleet Street press culture. During his stint in the Royal Air Force in Singapore he picked up a camera and subsequently never put it down.[91] Bailey's style of picture-taking reveled in the energy and youth of the fashion photography of an earlier generation, including work by Avedon, but he went even further, as did others, such as Gordon Parks, cultivating glamorous location shoots and the casual snapshot aesthetic (figs. 3.27, 3.28). He

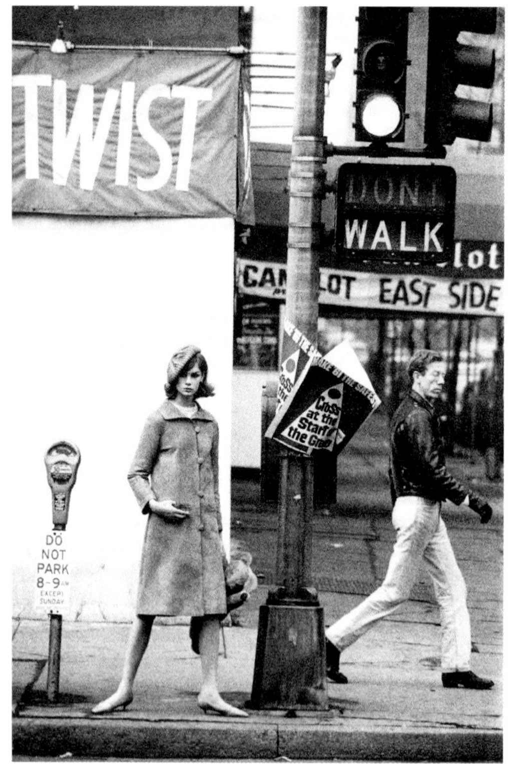

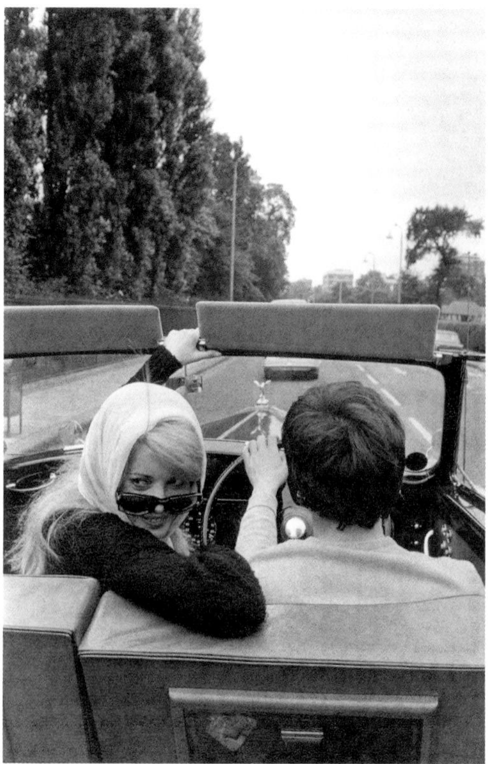

Fig. 3.28 Jean Shrimpton in New York, *British Vogue*, April 1, 1962. David Bailey, photographer

Fig. 3.29 Civil marriage of Catherine Deneuve and David Bailey, 1965. Patrice Habans, photographer

was himself an even more glamorous figure. He slept with his models, such as Jean Shrimpton, and married a movie star, Catherine Deneuve (fig. 3.29). Rock star Mick Jagger was best man at the wedding. In sum, as photographers joined the jet set, one married a princess and another a movie star. Bailey described photographers in a remarkable echo of Baudelaire's painter of modern life, now updated and transformed as a jet setter: "the first completely modern people. . . . He makes a fortune, he's always surrounded by beautiful girls, he travels a lot and he's always living off his nerves in a big-time world."[92] Bailey does not even mention the ability to take or make pictures; his social status instead entitled him to the role of picture-maker.

In 1965, Tom Wolfe wrote "Pariah Styles: Radical Chic" for the April issue of *Harper's Bazaar,* which was under the editorial direction of Avedon. The changing fortunes of photographers had become clear. The article locates a photographer's studio as the ultimate chic setting, concluding, "This after all, is the age of Pop Society, and people like photographers are *artists* today, the Braques of our era. They are no longer merely the beggar boy servants of the fashion and magazine industries, *the little box with a lens does it all, the whole thing.* What the hell kind of notion was that! Incredible."[93] Wolfe's half-ironic tone suggests he was trying to laugh off the truths of Pop Society as much as Boorstin had been startled by them. For both, magazine photography seemed to play an outsized role in what seemed new about their age, and yet photography itself had been around for more than a century.

To Boorstin, the danger of the moment he associated with the coming of the jet lay in the crossroads produced when a certain kind of image culture was crossed with this new transport experience to create what he called the "spaceless age" in a rather brilliant pun on yet another transport mode on the horizon—but one that always remained a frontier rather than a space of transport.[94] Boorstin had also invoked the mirror metaphor and fretted that "we look into a mirror instead of out of a window, and we see only ourselves." But the jet set and the picture world of which they were a part circulated so fast that they would simply be a blur on a mirror. Magazine pictures operated to capture a different kind of "flight" and motion, and in so doing reinforced the values of circulation and circulating. The impact of the jet was not simply in the expansion of travel but in the visualization of motion and the circulation of images of the jet set. Magazine photography had always been an ambulant form of picture-taking, but it comes as no surprise that the heyday of the picture magazine coincided with the jet age. Airplanes transformed magazines by allowing them to combine the values of speed with their traditional emphasis on the quality of the photographic image. At the same time, airplanes and magazines, through the promotion of constant motion and circulation, glamorized motion itself by dissolving the boundaries between the motion of traveling in a jet and the images made by and of those who did.

Disneyland may have offered everyone a chance to ride, but the construction of the jet set and the magazines of the period provided a pictorial experience of circulation and fluid motion. Rather than creating a society of narcissists, as Avedon implied and Boorstin claimed, magazines celebrated movement, allowing readers to interact with the world outside their pages as in a two-way mirror. Magazines did not simply instruct readers in "liberal humanism" or teach them to assume their dominant role in the postwar world if they were Americans. Their images offered much more than their content.[95] The photojournalists' photographs offered magazine readers images that testified to their embodied experience elsewhere. Magazines drew attention to the fact that someone had journeyed somewhere and was also looking back; this experience gripped readers as if it were their own experience. Magazines, photographers, and their images constructed a new visual culture during the jet age in which motion and circulation undercut the potential dangers of a world constituted by photography's mirror. The jet set's motion transformed photography and photographers into the modern antidote to the myth of the immobile Narcissus. Photojournalism also took new form during this period as magazines transitioned to printing mostly color photography. How color became the period's visual language for translating the experience of motion is the story we turn to next.

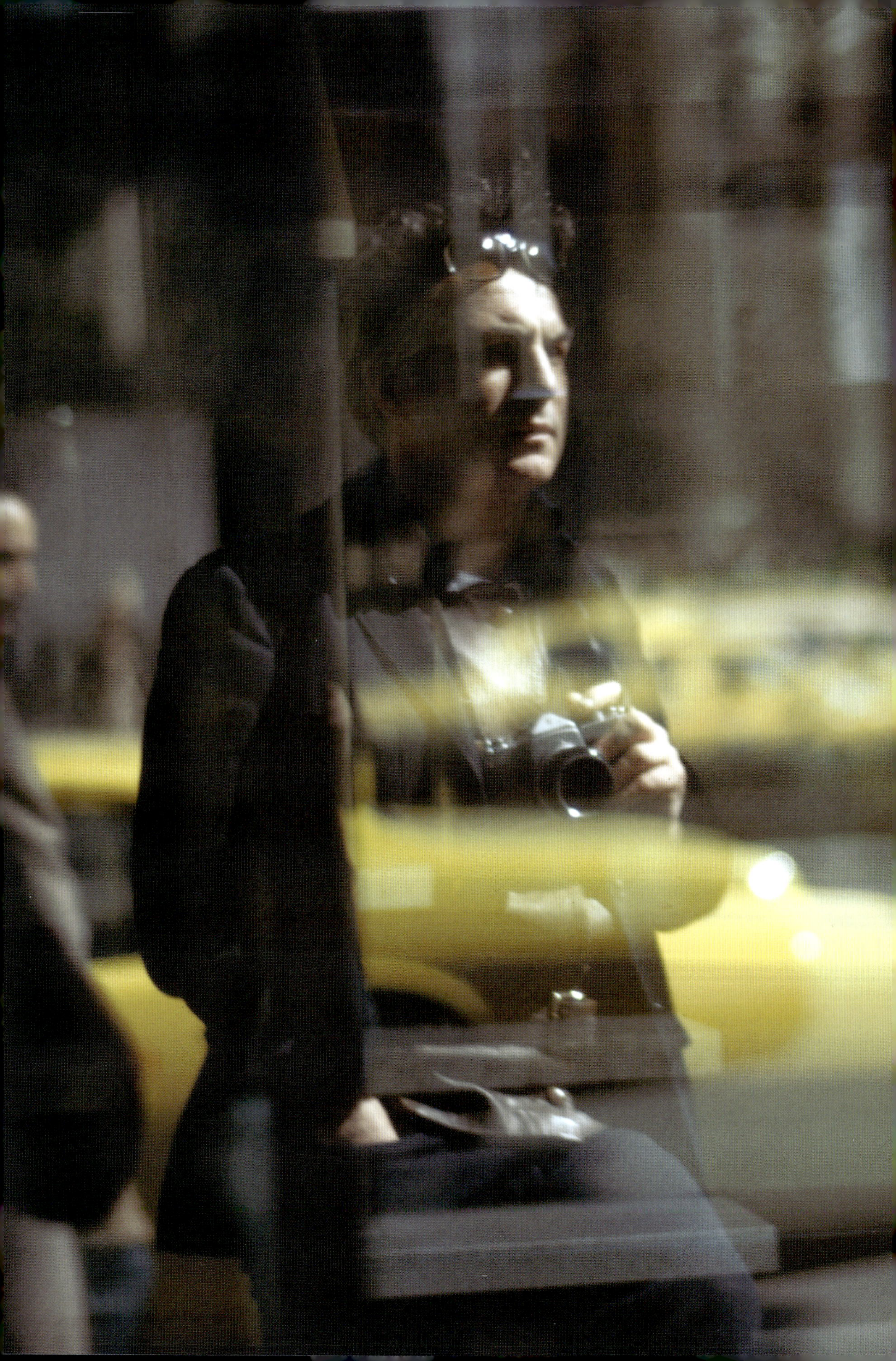

Ernst Haas and the Blurring of Color in Motion

I am overloaded. . . . There is one relief now and that is because I sit in an aeroplane flying direction west. How wonderful to seat still wyhle [sic] one is speeding around the earth. But if we would go the same speed in which the earth moves, maybe it is only an illusion that we fly, maybe we just stand still and the earth moves beyond us. But as everything is more or less an illusion, I don't care if we move or are being moved. I enjoy this activity in every direction even if it is only in a very material way of moving my body from one place to the other.

—*Letter from Ernst Haas to Robert Capa, 1954*

Daniel Boorstin had fretted about the effects of the jet, but the photographer Ernst Haas had a very different take on the effects of air travel. Although Haas also noted that flying created a lack of clarity regarding reality and illusion, he was not suspicious like Boorstin. Haas even later reflected on the fact that he considered airplanes ideal work spaces: "I feel good in airplanes. I make layouts in airplanes," explaining that he never slept on them nor did he find them boring or constraining environments.[1] Haas, like many photographers, liked to fly.

While magazine photographers had been part of the mobility of the modern world, as the last chapter suggested, the glamour associated with their peripatetic lives gave them and their work increased significance during the jet age. By 1954, even before the improvements in the quality of flight wrought by the jet, Haas had spent time in the air that provoked his reflection above on speed, pace, the perception of motion, and whether the experience of motion during flight was simply an illusion. Why would anyone who had journeyed "materially" for such long distances, as he noted, ponder such immaterial questions about human perception? The answers do not seem obvious.

Haas had been listed among the ten greatest photographers in *Popular Photography*'s survey of two hundred fifty photo professionals and was featured in the May 1958 issue of the magazine. Most of the group made their living as magazine photographers. They included luminaries such as Henri Cartier-Bresson, Ansel Adams, Philippe Halsman, Irving Penn, and Bert Stern. The two youngest and thus perhaps most of their moment were

Haas, who was thirty-six, and Richard Avedon, thirty-four. These two shared other traits as well: they worked in magazines, films, and advertising; made photobooks; and also shot photos on film sets and consulted on feature films. Avedon became one of the wealthiest and most well known of the ten on the list, and he worked well into his eighties. Haas became president of the Magnum photo agency, had a one-man show at the Museum of Modern Art in New York in 1962, and published a 1971 photobook, *The Creation,* which became one of the best-selling such books of its time. He died in 1986 at the age of sixty-five. In fact, he is the man who was the best known among those on the 1958 list in his own day and whose work is now the least well known today.

One could reevaluate and renarrate and even compare artistic careers and the merits of each photographer's contributions, as well as their artistic reputations and legacies. This would surely reveal the blind spots in what has been until now a limited art-historical perspective on the history of photography—one that has not examined the contemporary impact of the photographers. Here we return Avedon and Haas to the period context in which they became celebrated. By returning to the history of magazine photography during the jet age in order to consider the emergence of color in photographic newsmagazines, we will be unable to avoid the centrality of Haas above all, as well as of Avedon, Eliot Elisofon, Jean-Philippe Charbonnier, and others who were enmeshed in the transition to color photography as part of the glamour of media in motion.

Haas participated in, contributed to, and reflected on these changes in his time. The changes were as much about the experience and perception of new kinds of motion as they were about material developments in photographic and print culture and transport technology. In the transition to color photography, Haas drew readers' attention to the viewer's experience of time itself in a world that seemed recently set in constant motion. He exemplifies what became known as the New Journalism of the 1960s, and his work suggests that the movement was visual before it was verbal. That movement is usually attributed to such writers as Tom Wolfe and Gay Talese, who combined reporting with subjective interior literary devices. Scholars such as Fred Ritchin have identified those photojournalists who came after the 1960s, such as Raymond Depardon, as having been influenced by the New Journalism, and art photographers, such as Martha Rosler and Allan Sekula, as having blurred the borders between art and documentary photography in an art photography corollary to the New Journalism. By looking at Haas' magazine photography we can see the key role that such images played in contributing to the rise of the New Journalism in the first place.[2] By attempting to capture the subjective experience of their world and by choosing to make that subject the sensation or rather the sensationlessness of motion through color, visual journalists such as Haas translated experience in the jet age into a popular aesthetic of "color consciousness" that was at once sensual and sought to capture a world moving so fast that one did not know whether one was moving or being moved—that defines the glamour of media in motion. Ultimately, it served as an aesthetic for a moment of transition: when color in magazines was relatively new, when the jet was new, when creating consciousness through photographic technique could still convey the experience of such fluidity of motion as a novelty. Max Kozloff in 1975 called Haas the Paganini of Kodachrome. He was a critic who otherwise took a positive view of the relatively new field of color photography, and who also conceded that Haas had been a pioneer in the medium two decades earlier, observing that Haas "had taken it into his head that color photography should be about, not the sensations, but the sensationalizing of color . . . his multiple styles were all a-flutter with the meringues and frappés of a hyped-up palette."[3] But perhaps Kozloff's first impression was right—Haas's use of color in photography was about sensation and its relation to invoking the viewer's subjective experience through the photographer's lens. Haas made use of color to call forth the sensory experience of motion in his pictures, extending the photographer's eye to that of the magazine reader. Color photography did more than depict motion. It conveyed the experience of motion that underlay the photographer's reporting through its "sensationalizing." Color became a means by which photographers could convey the experience of fluid motion that characterized the world remade in the wake of the jet.

The history of color photography in mass media at mid-century remains untold and underanalyzed. Color photography in print is mostly associated with advertising images, while color in art photography emerged more or less in the 1970s, thus falsely solidifying its history into a bifurcated tale that has erased the earlier history of the photographers who worked in color, including Edward Steichen, Robert Capa, Walker Evans, Henri Cartier-Bresson, and even Ansel Adams. The story regarding color in fine art has emerged as one in which the "starburst" of William Eggleston suddenly appeared at MoMA in 1976 as the key moment in the history of color art photography.[4] Until that time, the view regarding color photography was generally negative. Representative of that view is the critic Hilton Kramer's response to one of the three inaugural exhibitions at the International Center for Photography in 1974, *Eye of the Beholder:* "These blow-ups of color photographs quickly settle—as color photographs so often do—into a series of pretty pictures. They simply cannot compete, whether as visual images or documentary reports, with the black and white masterworks to be seen in other exhibitions."[5] Evans put his critique of the medium in far more economical terms: "There are four simple words which must be whispered: color photography is vulgar."[6] This did not prevent him from photographing in color for *Fortune* magazine, among other publications, which he did with regularity.[7]

Yet if we consider the "bright modernity" that illuminated society outside the medium of photography, inaugurated by the use of aniline dyes as early as the mid-nineteenth century, color, both materially and symbolically, became associated with new regimes of bourgeois and then mass consumerism. Regina Blaszczyk has identified color's central role in the proliferation of a range of objects on a palette. Offering product choice by color, marketers could feature such things as seasonal change or could create eye-catching advertising strategies. Such palettes also offered the mass standardization of color and, through color, the mass standardization of culture. Previously, color had been derived only from materials in the natural world or through the effects of optics, since color is also produced by the separation of light. New artificial color fostered a "color revolution," but at the same time, as Laura Kalba has argued in her important study about color in the late nineteenth century, the combination of its industrialization and commercialization with opticality also allowed for more abstract ways of seeing color. Thus, it was not that painters such as the Impressionists had prepared the way for abstraction in art, but rather that they fit into a broader visual culture derived from material and scientific transformations in color theory and production.[8] It is essential to follow this notion of the opticality and the sensational quality of modern color through to the history of color photography, first as Kalba does in the history of autochromes at the turn of the century, but also as we will, by looking at mid-century color news pictures, keeping these qualities in mind.

Newsmagazines had published color photos as early as the arrival of the autochrome in 1907, but news photos in color were still rarely made. Yet by the late 1960s the major newsmagazines had essentially transitioned to all-color photography. In fact, color had become so integral to the practice of news photographers that John Morris, executive editor of Magnum, asked everyone on black-and-white assignments to also shoot in color; that way any assignment could be turned into a cover photograph, which were always in color.[9]

And yet we know relatively little about the history of color news pictures. They have been neglected because they are twice cursed, first as color and then as journalism, which is not usually studied within the history of photography, and which, in turn, is overlooked in the history of communications and journalism.[10] Of course within the beating heart of the art museum, under Steichen's legendary direction, MoMA's photography department regularly featured news, documentary, and informational photography in such exhibitions as *War Comes to the People* (1940), *Image of Freedom* (1941), *Road to Victory* (1942), *Power in the Pacific* (1945), *Memorable Life Photographs* (1951), and *The Family of Man* (1955).

Steichen did not ignore color photography, either. The blockbuster *Family of Man*, for example, ended with an eight-foot-tall color transparency of an explosion of a hydrogen bomb that had appeared in *Life* the year before (fig. 4.1). As a blown-up and backlit transparency, the image also alerts us to what may not have been as apparent to visitors at the time—the material challenges of color photography, which was hardly ever printed as positive prints by professionals. Additionally, Steichen

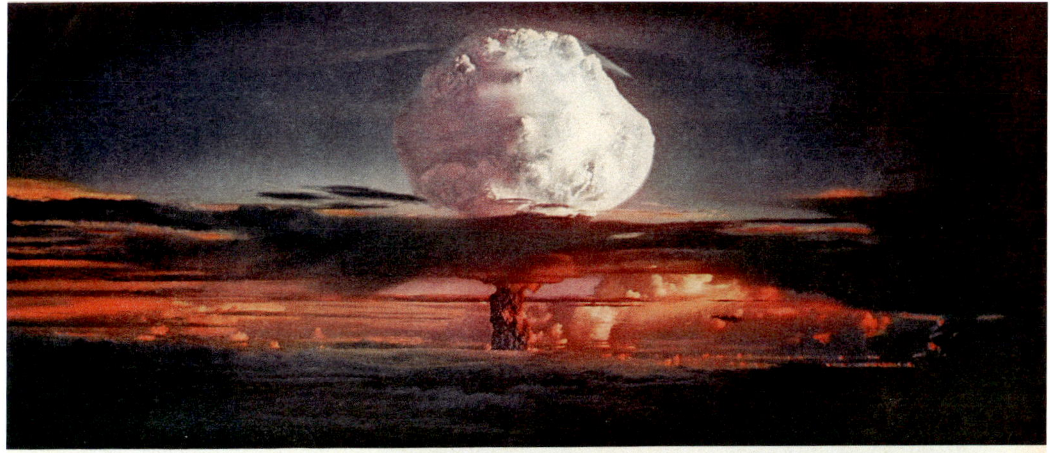

ICE CRYSTALS ENCASE MUSHROOM ABOUT SIX MILES ABOVE ATOLL

NEW 'IVY' PICTURES SHOW FIRE AND ICE

Following the color movie of the "Operation Ivy" H-bomb test (LIFE, April 19), the Civil Defense Administration last week released color still photographs of the explosion. The one at right shows the fireball passing through clouds formed by the explosion's shock wave. As it rises over the shock cloud (*above*), expanding gases from the fireball cool and freeze water vapor in the air, covering the mushroom with an icy shroud. The still turbulent stem continues to carry up debris from the atoll below.

PHOTOGRAPHED WITH DARK FILTER, FIREBALL BOILS BRIGHTLY

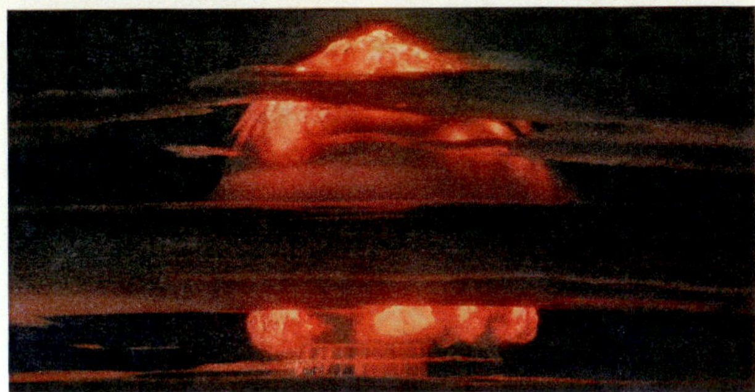

Fig. 4.1 "New 'Ivy' Pictures Show Fire and Ice," *Life*, May 3, 1954, 54–55. Federal Civil Defense Administration released photo

evidently had entertained the idea that this show, always remembered now as hundreds of large-format black-and-white images, would include many images in color. In a May 1954 letter, Inge Bondi of Magnum informed Haas that Steichen had gone to the American Society of Magazine Photographers show, featuring Haas' New York images in color, to find materials for *The Family of Man,* which she referred to as "most likely his last show." (It turned out not to be, by a good seven years.) Bondi goes on to say that Steichen then came to Magnum and looked at "your own editing of Indochina (at his request), and picked three, which he thought superb." She then asked Haas to bring more material that offered "any human situation." She said Steichen had emphasized that his show had "no axe to grind, it is just on the universality of mankind."[11]

Steichen championed color across a variety of photo genres: Eliot Porter's *Birds in Color* (1943); the *In and Out of Focus* show (1948), which featured many color photos; the 1950 *All Color Show,* dedicated to mass magazine reproductions and announced as the first in a series of color shows whose focus was primarily technological and included new color printing methods. The new methods included Aero Kodacolor, which had been used during the war for aerial reconnaissance work because these images could be developed in the field. The camera had tiny slits that opened and closed at the same speed as the plane. The *All Color Show* posed that the problem of photography's unconscious black-and-white conditioning had led, Steichen argued, to color remaining a riddle.[12] Such was Steichen's interest in both color and in Haas that he held an evening program on February 19, 1957, called "Experimental Photography in Color" at the Museum of Modern Art. Its high points, according to Morris, were Haas' work and some of Roman Vishniac's microphotographs.[13]

Steichen's exhibitions for the museum in his role as photo curator culminated in commissioning what would be the first show under the curatorial regime that followed his, that of John Szarkowski. It would be a one-man show dedicated to the work of Haas. That show, in 1962, would not be the last time Haas would be shown at MoMA, which continued to show color and news photos long before the supposed "starburst" of color in 1976. Nor was it the first time: he had had photographs hung in the museum every year since 1953. In 1965, a large exhibition called *The Photo Essay* included a rear-projection slide show of twenty stories (including four by Haas) with both color and black-and-white images organized by essay.[14]

Daily newspapers had always put a premium on speed over image quality, although there was much more color in newsprint than we have accounted for, going back as far as the *Illustrated London News*' use of color in December 22, 1855. This work merits archival recovery, from the antics of the Yellow Kid at the turn of the century, in which color played a role in the circulation wars between Pulitzer and Hearst; to the advent of ROP (run of press) color in dailies such as the *Milwaukee Journal,* beginning in 1891, and the *Chicago Tribune;* and to such odd publications as the *New York Times Midweek Pictorial,* which had a special rotogravure section in color. The history of color in newsprint is hard to trace because of the microfilming of periodicals and the pulping of hard copies.[15] But a mention in an undated letter (probably around 1955) from Morris to photographer David Seymour (also known as Chim) that the executive editor of the *Minneapolis Tribune* had been in touch about putting the agency on a retainer for a regular use of color seconds (photos already published elsewhere) because they wanted to be the "world's first newspaper to use front-page color every day" suggests there is a longer history regarding the dailies and their use of color. Charbonnier's cover image for the March 1961 issue of French magazine *Réalités,* on life in the Saint-Lazare rail station in Paris, is from this period of "color consciousness" in magazine photography, when color was becoming increasingly important on the editorial side. That color also seemed to be used here, in the center of a busy transport site, to indicate movement and life again suggests that its novelty and visual impact could convey such sensation at the time (fig. 4.2).[16]

One might imagine that the drive toward more color would fulfill the mission of newsmagazines to provide better and more complete information. As the mid-nineteenth-century lithographer Louis Prang had put it, "Color in a picture is always more satisfactory than the lack of it," because people wanted what he called "life pictures."[17] Color offered greater realism through its descriptive register. As Paul Outerbridge, a photographer

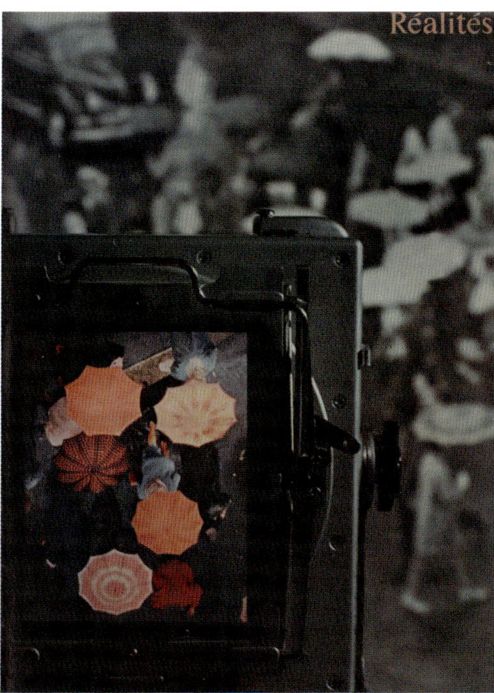

Fig. 4.2 Black and white to color: cover of *Réalités*, March 1961. Jean-Philippe Charbonnier, photographer

known for his experiments with color processes such as carbro printing, complained, "Color states rather than implies as does black and white; it is really quite a bit more difficult to handle by way of getting away from mere reporting and factual representation."[18] This would seem to make it ideally suited for documentation and news.

Yet color posed special problems for production. Robert Capa took what were among *Life*'s earliest Kodachrome news pictures in 1938, when Wilson Hicks and Edward Thompson asked him to work with the new color in Hankow during the Sino-Japanese war. The goal was to test the materials in the field because there were many unknowns, such as how the film stood up to certain weather conditions and what would happen when there was a long delay between exposure and developing.

Life published the Hankow pictures with a two-month delay. The essay drew attention to the value of using color, as was always the case when color was still rarely seen: "The spectacle of a bombed city cannot be adequately reproduced without its colors."[19] The magazine captions used color merely descriptively: red flames, black fire, blue shirt (fig. 4.3). In other words, the text conveyed that color bolstered the journalistic quality of the images as news. Twenty-five years after Hankow, photographer Larry Burrows covered the Vietnam War for *Life* and described color in a similar way: "Back came this week's pictures showing, as only color can, the blood and mud and savagery of war."[20] Although at that moment in media history television had begun to deliver the news much more quickly than magazines ever could, the idea that magazine images remained the measure of the realistic image well into the 1960s suggests that color was essential to magazines' continued

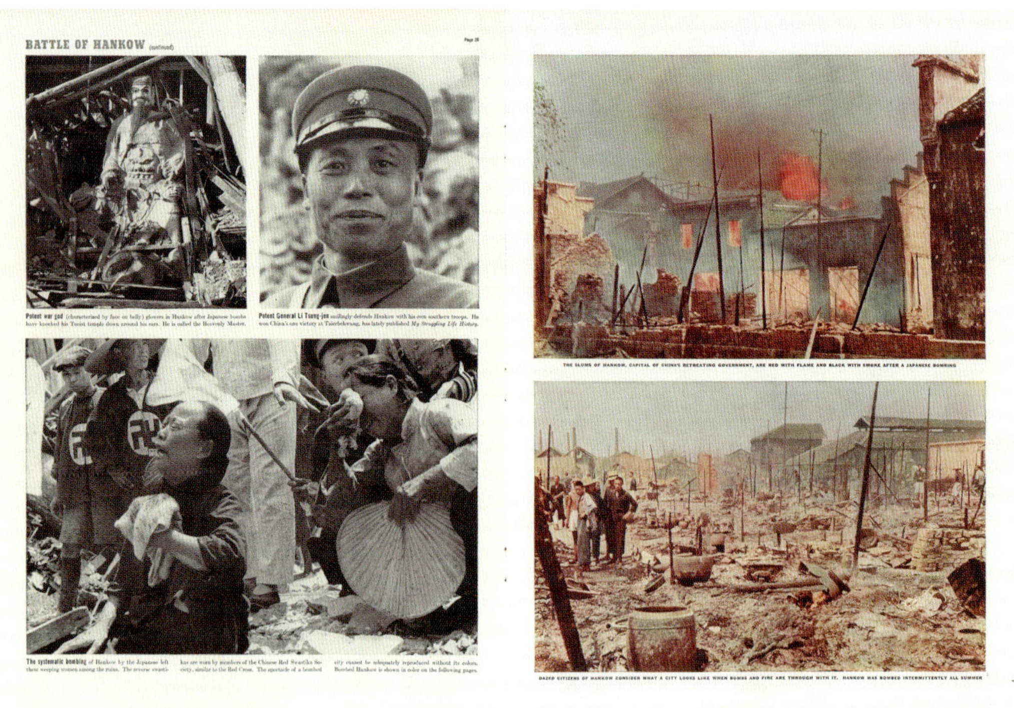

BATTLE OF HANKOW (continued)

Page 28

Potent war god (characterized by face on belly) glowers in Hankow after Japanese bombs have knocked his Taoist temple down around his ears. He is called the Heavenly Master.

Potent General Li Tsung-jen smilingly defends Hankow with his own southern troops. He won China's one victory at Taierhchwang, has lately published *My Struggling Life History*.

The systematic bombing of Hankow by the Japanese left these weeping women among the ruins. The reverse swastikas are worn by members of the Chinese Red Swastika Society, similar to the Red Cross. The spectacle of a bombed city cannot be adequately reproduced without its colors. Bombed Hankow is shown in color on the following pages.

THE SLUMS OF HANKOW, CAPITAL OF CHINA'S RETREATING GOVERNMENT, ARE RED WITH FLAME AND BLACK WITH SMOKE AFTER A JAPANESE BOMBING

DAZED CITIZENS OF HANKOW CONSIDER WHAT A CITY LOOKS LIKE WHEN BOMBS AND FIRE ARE THROUGH WITH IT. HANKOW WAS BOMBED INTERMITTENTLY ALL SUMMER

Fig. 4.3 "The Battle of Hankow in Color," *Life*, October 17, 1938, 28–29. Werner Bosshard and Robert Capa photos

informational value. Even though television offered an all-color prime-time lineup starting in the mid-1960s, it was not until 1971 that just about half of all U.S. households even had a color television set.[21]

Color photography had particular material and technical challenges, including heavier equipment and complicated lighting requirements owing to the slower film. Shooting in color also always meant carrying two cameras. As Réné Burri said, "It means always going about with a lot of cameras slung round your neck."[22] Processing took more time than black and white—from developing the transparencies and prints to the printing process itself. Magazines had to send color out to special plants where transfers for color engravings were made separately and then were printed by companies that specialized in color (fig. 4.4). In general, this is what put color news stories on a six-week turnaround, although *Life* had demonstrated a "fast color" close of two weeks during the coronation of Queen Elizabeth, as already discussed.[23] In fact, *Life* published its first "fast-closing" news color image about the far less ceremonial occasion of a ship's arrival into port in 1947 when the magazine published photos taken on October 10 in the November 3 issue.[24] In general, magazines used color reproduction for features that were not time-sensitive, such as travel stories, art features, or in issues during the holiday season.[25]

Why use color, given all the challenges? Images in color made a story appear up to date and "of the moment" in the same way that cars with fins looked aerodynamic and cutting-edge. But at the same time, as we know, color looked modern but was materially slow. *Life* magazine sought to

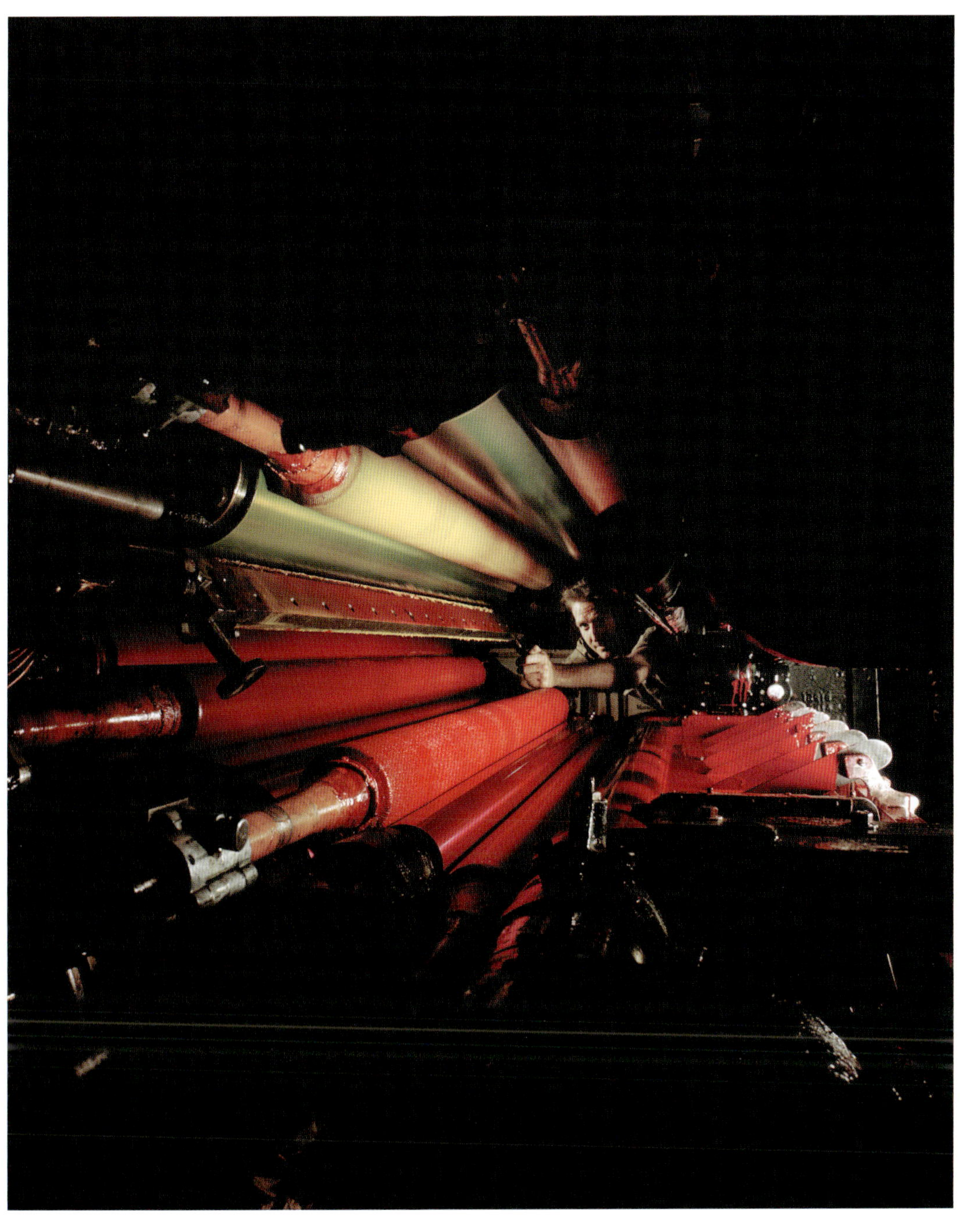

Fig. 4.4 "Davis Delaney Printing Press," *Fortune,* October 1949.
Photograph by Ezra Stoller. © Ezra Stoller/Esto

address these challenges in the period immediately after the Second World War. Use of color was still considered so experimental that *Life* described its color photo lab, established in November 1946, as "one of the few in the U.S." and noted that it was devoted to "experimentation rather than production," with the aim of shortening the production schedule and improving the quality of the reproductions. As demands for color increased, *Life* photographers started to regularly use Eastman high-speed Ektachrome film, according to staff photographer and noted color specialist Eliot Elisofon, which was faster to develop but was thought to sacrifice some image quality. In short, using color film on a story was met with many technical challenges, but the drive to use it in the postwar period led to experimentation despite the constraints.

Additional pressure to move to color in magazine photography came from competing forces in other media, such as the advent of color television, which would make magazines seem to lag behind if they did not transition to color as well. Magazines were already at a disadvantage because they could not compete with TV's fast delivery of news images. Walt Disney moved his television program from ABC to NBC in order to introduce his *Wonderful World of Color* in 1961. CBS went to all color programming in the prime-time lineup in the 1965–66 season. Feature films continued to promote the expansion begun in the 1950s of using widescreen for Technicolor movies, which also drew the public's attention and threatened to dethrone the magazine as the richest visual source of representation concerning the current world.[26]

But color photography challenged news photographers compositionally as well as in terms of speed and cost. Haas explained this problem when he wrote that "color is really basically much more difficult because it is an addition. . . . If you would have to photograph the President of the United States and next to him there would be a man in a red pullover, everybody would look at the man in the red pullover."[27] In other words, photographers are hampered by the fact that they cannot choose the interrelation of colors in the world. Advertising tableaux, on the other hand, are contrived, allowing photographers the freedom to manipulate and control color as they wish, as well as to use it for symbolic and communicative effect. And although advertising images are colorful, color is not merely a form of visual seduction and enticement. Rather, because advertising can be entirely studio produced on long production cycles and large budgets, color can be used as a design element.[28]

The cost, slow speed, and inconvenience of color production is one reason its use provoked skepticism among some of the great photo-reporters, such as Henri Cartier-Bresson. In *The Decisive Moment,* published in 1954, he argued that it was difficult to foresee how color would grow in photo-reporting because of the time differences between developing and printing in black and white and color and that, in any event, he thought them substantially different enough to require from the photographer a "different approach" altogether, based on the photographer's inability to control the interrelation of colors within the frame of a news story.[29] Of course, like everyone else, he followed the trend of working in color and produced many magazine stories in the 1950s in color, such as a *Life* spread shot in 1958 that was published in the January 5, 1959, issue, "The New China—From Inside." He later attempted to bury this work as he started to identify increasingly as a fine art photographer, which meant, he felt, perpetuating the false impression that he had worked only in black and white.

As experimentation led to implementation, editors and photographers spoke of certain stories that "demanded" color. As a 1952 Magnum photo agency report to stockholders written by Robert Capa explained, "We have to shoot far more color. . . . This again should not be indiscriminate but should focus on subjects which demand color."[30] The demand for color images was so high that Magnum could sell the British publication *Illustrated* just about anything in color, Capa reported, even as the publication was growing more picky about what Magnum provided in black and white. "While they are more difficult for black and whites they are still wide open for color. . . . Any color subject which is good enough for two pages is good enough for them and they can't get enough of it. . . . I must repeat that one of the fastest possibilities for improved earning is in shooting more color."[31] Henry Luce's Time Inc. founded *Sports Illustrated* in 1954 with the idea that it would print lots of images in color. As Norton Wood, associate editor of the new publication, explained in 1958, "On our color pages especially where the magazine makes its major visual display, we use pictures not simply to document events but for the sake of the pictures themselves."[32] In what seems an ironic reversal of contemporary ideas of what is "artistic" in photography today, in the 1950s, photographs that were "more visual" would be in color.

The changing proportion of color in relation to black and white also gave magazine people a heightened awareness of the shifting meaning of each. As Pat Hagan of Magnum noted, "The time may not be too distant when black and white will be used for dramatic impact, while most of the work . . . will be in color."[33] This is exactly what came to pass in analogue photography before digital manipulation of a variety of color palettes, including "colorization" and sepia-toning, became an everyday part of the language of photographic images.

Writing many years after the fact, Haas liked to explain his own turn to color photography as quite deliberate and not just part of a trend. He described it as a form of postwar celebration, a new practice and palette to mark the transition to a new era: "I will remember all the war years and the last five bitter post-war years—as black and white years. . . . I wanted to express that the world and life had changed. . . . As at the beginning of a new spring, I wanted to celebrate in color."[34] Haas' idea that color photography might capture a world both different and brighter than the war-torn world was obviously metaphoric—a bright new day after the darkness of war.

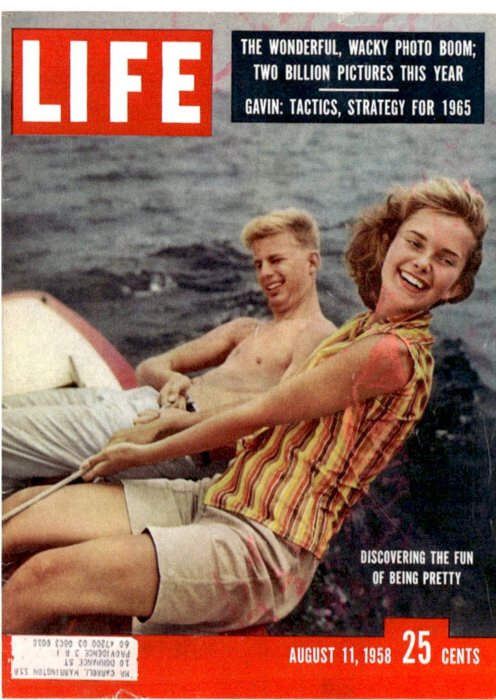

Fig. 4.5 "Discovering the Fun of Being Pretty," *Life*, August 11, 1958. Paul Schutzer, photographer

But it was more than that. Haas turned magazine photography in color into something far more resonant.[35] He used it to engage viewers in a world that was not just on the move "forward" but moving in ways that might have been imperceptible but for its sensationalizing. Through his particular use of color, Haas "reported" on the world around him, which he lived as a reporter and worked to interpret. In his photos he made color sensational in order to surmount the challenges of working in a static medium while attempting to comment on a new kind of motion, which was so fast and so smooth that it was imperceptible. He communicated this experience not by making photography "painterly" but by extending his experience—of making the pictures—to the viewer. He blurred his photos.

In midsummer 1958, Haas' work was featured in *Life* magazine, but not on its cover. Only two months before jet service across the Atlantic would become a habit, the magazine's cover featured a banner promising that in its pages readers would find information about the "wonderful, wacky photo boom; two billion pictures this year," although its cover photo seemed to suggest exactly the opposite: nothing wacky at all. Instead, a banal color photograph of two teens happily sailing on a simple boat graced the magazine's cover, with a surprising caption that read: "Discovering the fun of being pretty" (fig. 4.5).[36] Although the photo itself was hardly unusual, the text showed that a few words could shape the meaning of a picture in an unexpected way.

Playing with the impact of photography in print had been part and parcel of *Life*'s mission since 1936. Inside this issue, on the editorial page, readers learned that "the proper study of a picture magazine is photographs—and photographers." They could peruse an illustrated article about the growth of amateur photography that conceded that sometimes shutterbugs took wonderful pictures but also noted that they were marvelous photographic subjects themselves. At the same time, the publication's editors used the question of whether one could even distinguish between amateur and professional photography to introduce the first of a two-part color portfolio by Haas.

The *Life* cover served as a teasing contrast to the Haas portfolio, and the editors warned readers about it. Haas, they noted, had started making blurry images. The editors suggested that in so doing he was actually taking the medium to great new heights. Although the magazine acknowledged that its readers might themselves be expending extraordinary effort to make sharp photos of objects in motion, such as the eruption of the Old Faithful geyser, they noted that the Haas pictures showed that the "camera can produce stimulation for the mind as well as the eye." The images, they said, were "fuzzy on purpose and for a purpose."[37] Haas' blurry photos were not amateur accidents but rather proof that the camera could be deployed to create such effects when in the hands of a photographer who could draw attention to his own presence and create a personal vision. The photos in the series are the sort of visual fare that drew attention to themselves as photographs rather than merely reported events in the world outside the photographs. The blurred pictures show the photographer's hand, and in that way they are even greater expressions of the relation between photographer and viewer. But they also tempt and taunt the viewer by taking the classic "amateur mistake," the blur, and aestheticizing it.

Haas' work formed the centerpiece of the August 11, 1958, issue. It featured photographs across an eight-page spread, "The Magic of Color in Motion," that addressed both the subjectivity of vision and the seemingly difficult challenge of capturing motion in still photography by using color film and emphasizing motion through the blurring of images. The essay's captions approached the subject not as a technical matter for photo amateurs, as they might have found it described in a hobbyist publication, but instead addressed the powerful way that color photography had inspired Haas to ponder deep philosophical questions relating to time and space. Its headers and captions explained that the photographer had been troubled by the fact that life and nature "move and are seen not as fixed images but blending, blurring and flowing," and that "reality is not fixed in time." Haas, the article explained, used photography to "set out to capture a fourth dimension of time in color."[38]

In the portfolio, sailboats appear to multiply on the water; around them, the ocean reaches up, surrounding them like steel wool traces. Figures running along the beach, both human and canine, seem to be reduced to so many shadows, while water-skiers blend into the surf with only the outline of their bodies dressed in contrasting colored bathing

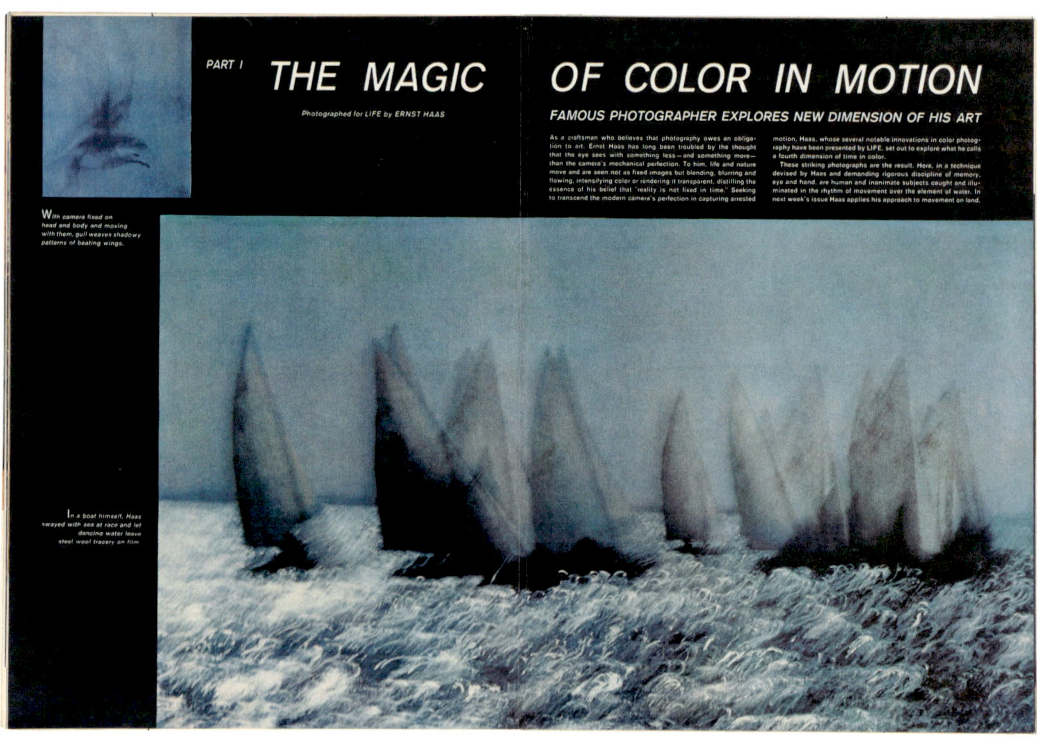

PART I THE MAGIC OF COLOR IN MOTION

Photographed for LIFE by ERNST HAAS

FAMOUS PHOTOGRAPHER EXPLORES NEW DIMENSION OF HIS ART

As a craftsman who believes that photography owes an obligation to art, Ernst Haas has long been troubled by the thought that the eye sees with something less—and something more—than the camera's mechanical perfection. To him, life and nature move and are seen not as fixed images but blending, blurring and flowing, intensifying color or rendering it transparent, distilling the essence of his belief that "reality is not fixed in time." Seeking to transcend the modern camera's perfection in capturing arrested motion, Haas, whose several notable innovations in color photography have been presented by LIFE, set out to explore what he calls a fourth dimension of time in color.

These striking photographs are the result. Here, in a technique devised by Haas and demanding rigorous discipline of memory, eye and hand, are human and inanimate subjects caught and illuminated in the rhythm of movement over the element of water. In next week's issue Haas applies his approach to movement on land.

With camera fixed on head and body and moving with them, gull weaves shadowy patterns of beating wings.

In a boat himself, Haas swayed with sea at race and let dancing water leave steel wool tracery on film.

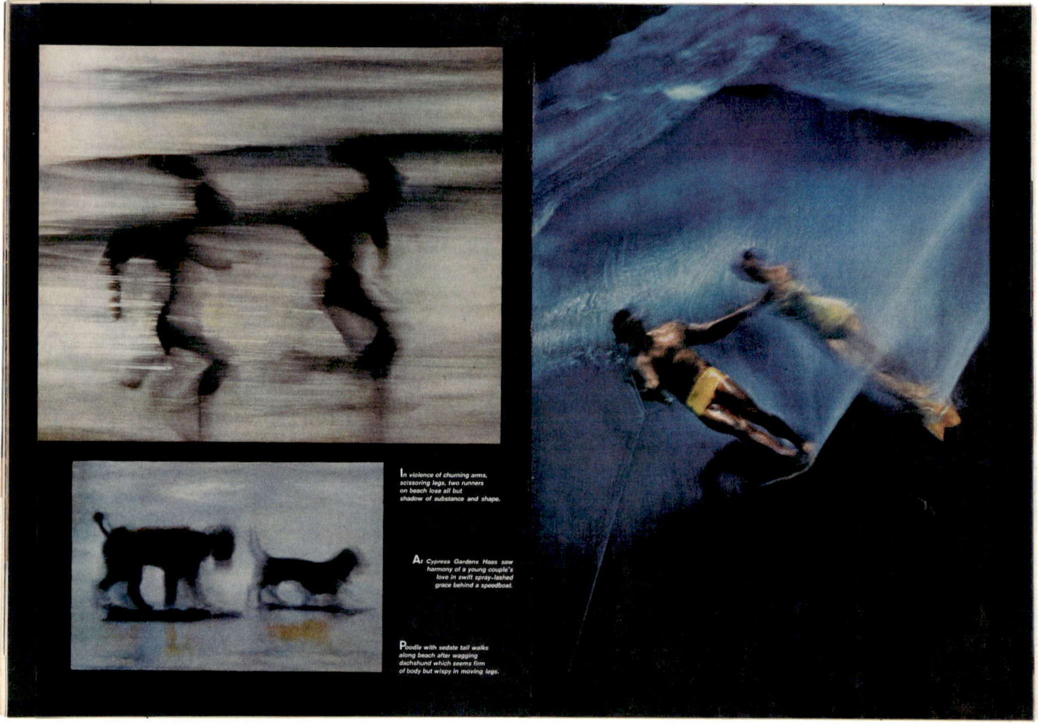

In violence of churning arms, scissoring legs, two runners on beach lose all but shadow of substance and shape.

At Cypress Gardens Haas saw harmony of a young couple's love in swift spray-lashed grace behind a speedboat.

Poodle with sedate tail walks along beach after wagging dachshund which seems firm of body but wispy in moving legs.

Figs. 4.6–4.8 "The Magic of Color in Motion," *Life*, August 11, 1958, 66–71. Ernst Haas, photographer

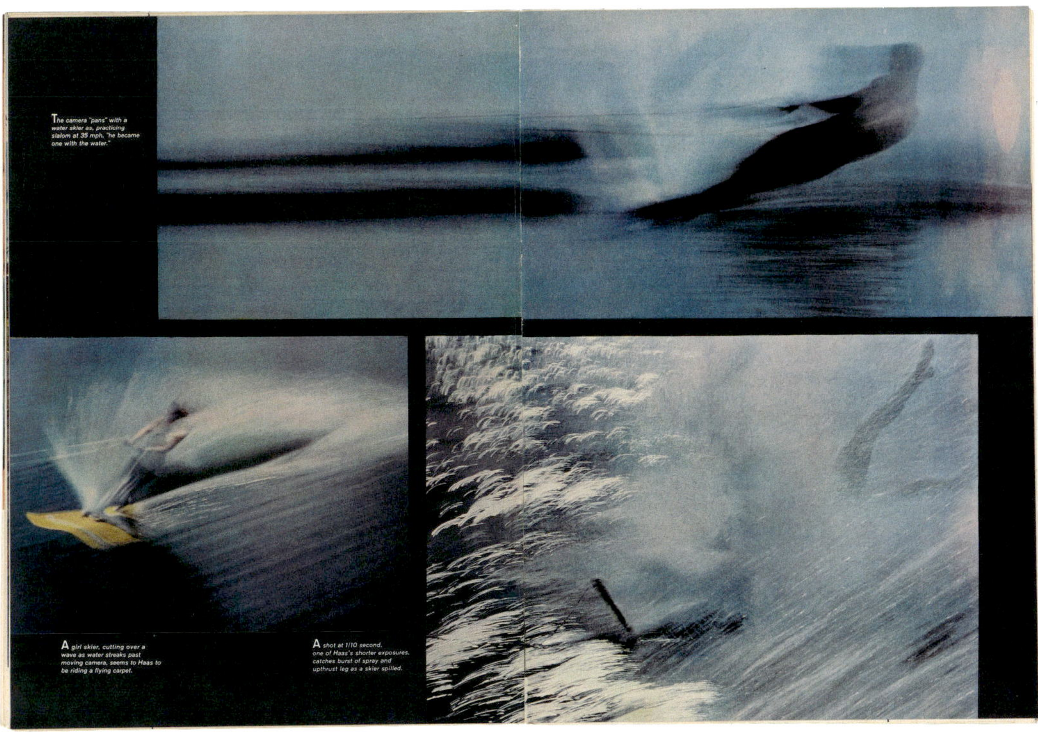

suits stand out against a dark blue mass of water. All the figures are fuzzy; their contours blend into each other, while the fact that they are in motion is captured by their blur (figs. 4.6–4.8). The following week, the magazine published the second part of the feature: "Adventure in New Camera Realm," which went from sea to land in its continuing study of color and motion. The feature's main caption promised a photographer who could "make the camera see color in motion as the eye sees it, not in fixed images but in a blended flow of color" while drawing attention to the tension "between the staccato movement of living creatures and the fluid progress of machines."[39]

To engage such problems as the fourth dimension of time and the relation of organic creatures to machines connects Haas' project to the much longer history of photography and motion studies, going all the way back to the late nineteenth-century experiments of Étienne-Jules Marey and Eadweard Muybridge, who sought to study human motion by using photography to decompose and recompose it in a series of individual moments. The Futurists had also taken up questions of technology and speed, as had Bauhaus artists, especially László Moholy-Nagy, who had urged artists to update their materials to be more in sync with their age.[40] It seems certain that Moholy-Nagy's publication *Vision in Motion* (1947) shaped Haas, as it did others of his generation. In *Vision in Motion,* Moholy-Nagy equated modern visual experience with new forms of transport, especially the car and the plane. For him, the problems of modern

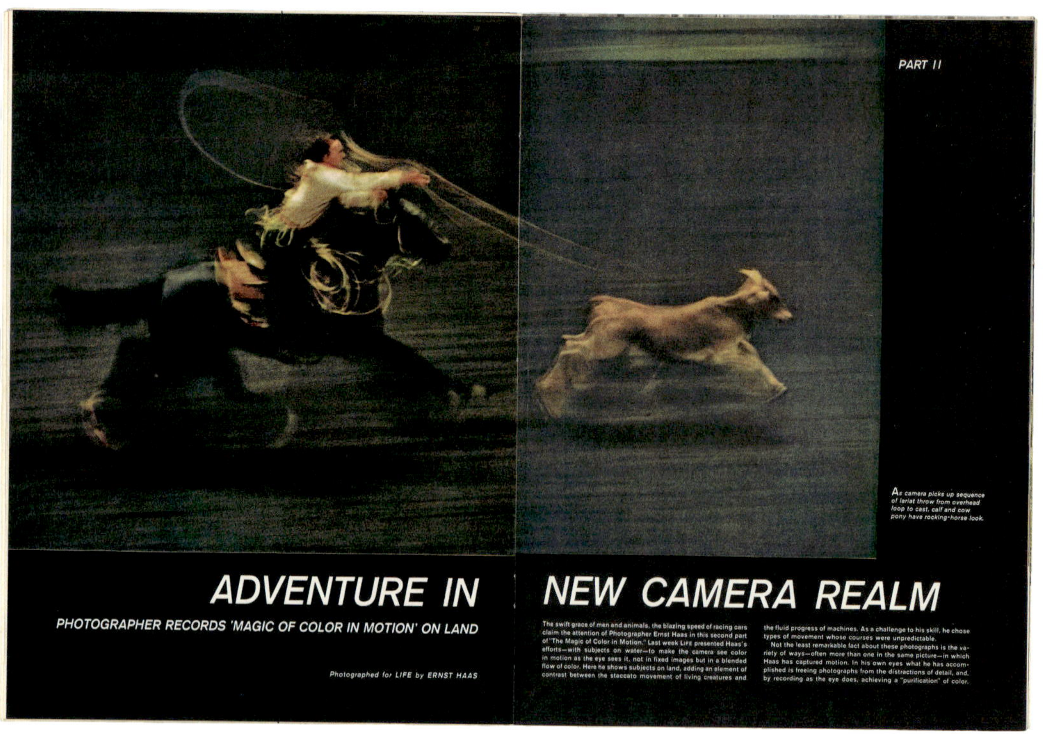

PART II

ADVENTURE IN NEW CAMERA REALM

PHOTOGRAPHER RECORDS 'MAGIC OF COLOR IN MOTION' ON LAND

Photographed for LIFE by ERNST HAAS

The swift grace of men and animals, the blazing speed of racing cars claim the attention of Photographer Ernst Haas in this second part of "The Magic of Color in Motion." Last week LIFE presented Haas's efforts—with subjects on water—to make the camera see color in motion as the eye sees it, not in fixed images but in a blended flow of color. Here he shows subjects on land, adding an element of contrast between the staccato movement of living creatures and the fluid progress of machines. As a challenge to his skill, he chose types of movement whose courses were unpredictable.

Not the least remarkable fact about these photographs is the variety of ways—often more than one in the same picture—in which Haas has captured motion. In his own eyes what he has accomplished is freeing photographs from the distractions of detail, and, by recording as the eye does, achieving a "purification" of color.

As camera picks up sequence of lariat throw from overhead loop to cast, calf and cow pony have rocking-horse look.

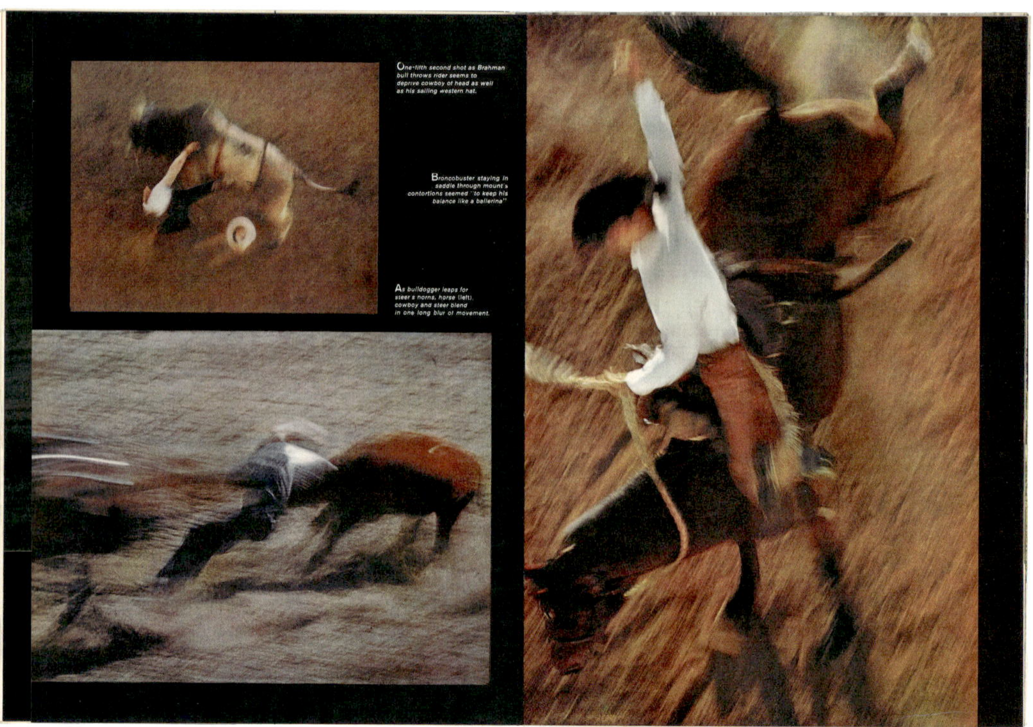

One-fifth second shot as Brahman bull throws rider seems to deprive cowboy of head as well as his sailing western hat.

Broncobuster staying in saddle through mount's contortions seemed "to keep his balance like a ballerina"

As bulldogger leaps for steer's horns, horse (left), cowboy and steer blend in one long blur of movement.

Figs. 4.9–4.11 "Adventure in New Camera Realm," *Life,* August 18, 1958, 44–40. Ernst Haas, photographer

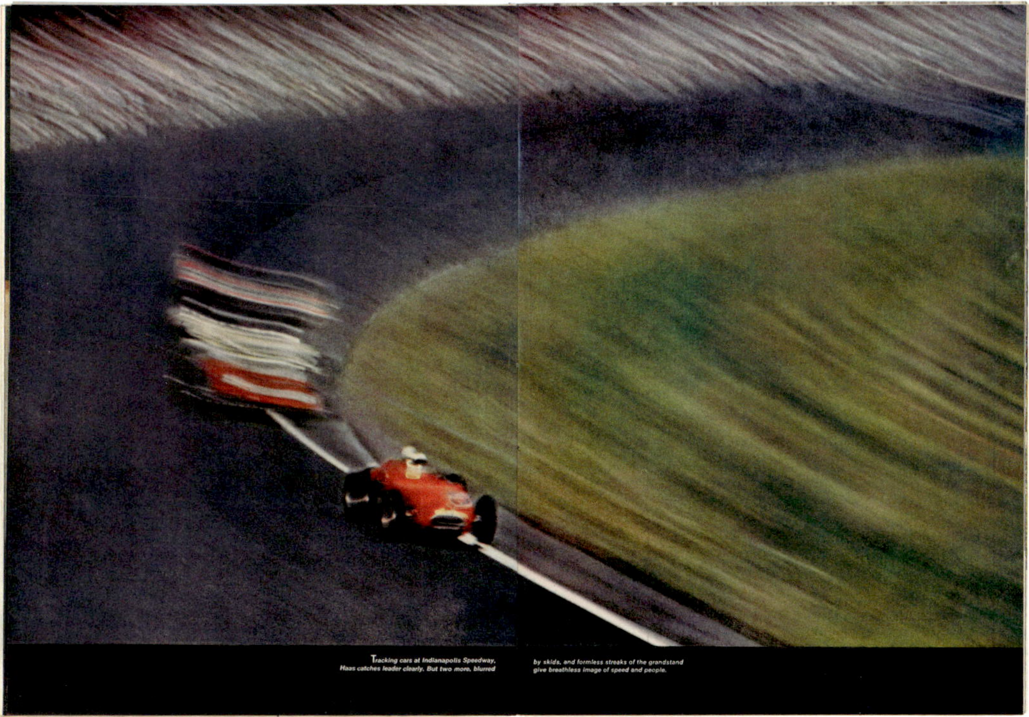

man were "seeing while moving" and the "simultaneous grasp"—which is to say considering the ways that single elements were transmuted into a coherent whole.[41] Moholy-Nagy also cared about color and argued for the importance of the modern use of light and motion in creating the effect of a "cult of color," and he considered how painters had moved toward abstraction and away from narrative in art.[42] Thus, if there were such antecedents as these to Haas' work (and surely there were), how and why the blurry color images made their way to the pages of *Life,* helping secure his reputation, requires explanation beyond the fact of such antecedents, especially as we consider the newsmagazine context.

"Adventure in New Camera Realm" engaged with what was becoming a common theme in the period regarding mobility and mechanization. Viewers were treated to a symphony of transport by land—first a series of images of man and horse (which bring to mind Muybridge's pictures of horses in motion). Haas offers an update of a "riderless horse" in the racecar, in which we can see the trace of a driver in a tiny metal bullet (figs. 4.9–4.11). He speeds so fast that it appears that the car's frame is bending around the track, leaving the vehicle distorted and blurry. In the very streaks across the printed page the viewer comes to understand that there are three men in motion: two in cars and one holding the camera. The photographer is not only obviously present but also moving and thus re-creating the experience of seeing motion. Haas helped readers manage their own experiences of a world that was going fast yet moving so smoothly that people had no idea who was moving and who was stable, an uncertainty he himself had pondered while in flight, as the epigraph of this chapter suggests.

Haas approached these issues as a photojournalist who was working as a reporter. As publications increasingly used color in news pictures, photographers such as Haas sought to create a "color consciousness" in press photography. He called for photos that were "less descriptive—more imaginative; less information—more suggestion; less prose—more poetry."[43] This moment of transition occasioned an opportunity for a photographer such as Haas to use color in a particular way. He asked viewers to look more deeply, through the reporter's eyes, rather than simply observe that he had mastered the camera's lens. As he put it in a letter to Magnum, "Don't cover, but discover. . . . Do we really want to be a catalogue of historie [*sic*]? . . . Photography is a bridge between science and art. The first bridge ever built. It enables us for the first time to transcend reality with reality in a simultaneous way of give and take."[44] Other fine artists during the period had begun to experiment with the ways that "movement and dynamic transformations are the new elements of our visual communication," as kinetic artist Yaacov Agam put it.[45] For Haas, using color photography in newsmagazines allowed him to experiment with a new language of visual communication as well. In color he could adhere to the journalist's commitment to describe the world while seizing on the chance to convey it as an experience and as a set of new sensations—of fluid motion.

Haas wanted to establish the centrality of his own vision, and he used photography to convey it but never imagined being limited by it. In a letter to John Morris of Magnum while traveling in South Africa on a *Life* assignment, Haas explained, "I am not a photographer. I am not even interested to be one. It is a pity, but for what I want to be we don't even have a name yet. Call it a subjective interpreter, call it all kinds of names and you won't find the right one."[46] Yet he was of course a news photographer, having worked in the international press since 1949, but like most photographers of the era he worked in black and white. Haas had made his reputation chronicling the return of Austrian POWs from Russian camps in the American-financed German-language publication *Heute.* That photo essay was republished in *Life,* and its most poignant image carried the heading "What's in a Picture?" (fig. 4.12).[47] As Haas explained years later, he had actually been in Vienna on an assignment for a fashion story. He abandoned it after being struck by the pathos of the women and children who waited at the train station, with photos in their hands, for their returning loved ones.[48]

At the time those photos were published, his work had garnered enough support and interest that he had been offered a position as a staff photographer at *Life* as well as received an offer from the Magnum photo agency. In reply, he wrote two letters from London. To Wilson Hicks, photo editor at the magazine, he wrote, "It is [also] the greatest wish of every young photographer to work one day for *Life.* There is no magazine with a greater understanding of the picture story." But, he explained, "there are two kinds of photographers. The ones who take pictures for magazines, and the ones who

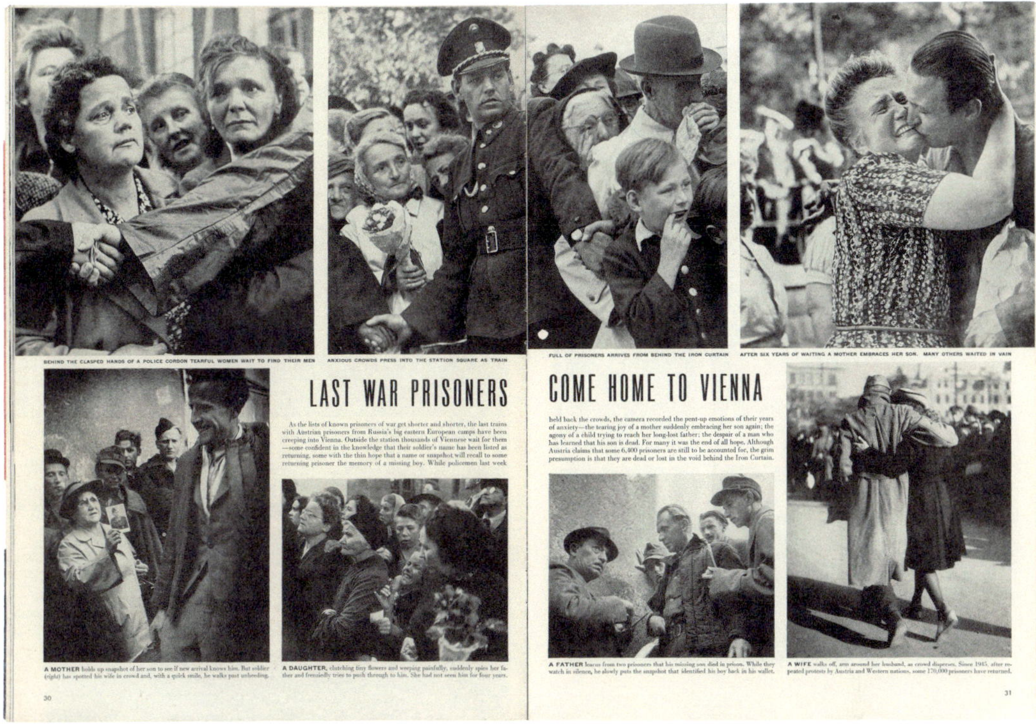

BEHIND THE CLASPED HANDS OF A POLICE CORDON TEARFUL WOMEN WAIT TO FIND THEIR MEN ANXIOUS CROWDS PRESS INTO THE STATION SQUARE AS TRAIN FULL OF PRISONERS ARRIVES FROM BEHIND THE IRON CURTAIN AFTER SIX YEARS OF WAITING A MOTHER EMBRACES HER SON. MANY OTHERS WAITED IN VAIN

LAST WAR PRISONERS COME HOME TO VIENNA

As the lists of known prisoners of war get shorter and shorter, the last trains with Austrian prisoners from Russia's big eastern European camps have been creeping into Vienna. Outside the station thousands of Viennese wait for them—some confident in the knowledge that their soldier's name has been listed as returning, some with the thin hope that a name or snapshot will recall to some returning prisoner the memory of a missing boy. While policemen last week held back the crowds, the camera recorded the pent-up emotions of their years of anxiety—the tearing joy of a mother suddenly embracing her son again; the agony of a child trying to reach her long-lost father; the despair of a man who has learned that his son is dead. For many it was the end of all hope. Although Austria claims that some 6,400 prisoners are still to be accounted for, the grim presumption is that they are dead or lost in the void behind the Iron Curtain.

A MOTHER holds up snapshot of her son to see if new arrival knows him. But soldier (*right*) has spotted his wife in crowd and, with a quick smile, he walks past unheeding.

A DAUGHTER, clutching tiny flowers and weeping painfully, suddenly spies her father and frenziedly tries to push through to him. She had not seen him for four years.

A FATHER learns from two prisoners that his missing son died in prison. While they watch in silence, he slowly puts the snapshot that identified his boy back in his wallet.

A WIFE walks off, arm around her husband, as crowd disperses. Since 1945, after repeated protests by Austria and Western nations, some 170,000 prisoners have returned.

30

31

Fig. 4.12 "Last War Prisoners Come Home to Vienna," *Life*, August 8, 1949, 30–31. Ernst Haas, photographer. "What's in a Picture" image is top row, second from right

gain something by taking pictures they are interested in. I am the second kind." He explained that he planned to travel the world for a year. And he added: "Mostly I have found that stories I did on my own ideas were published on more pages than those I did on assignment. I don't feel at all misunderstood in this world, but I also don't think there could be many editors who would be able to find quite the right stories for me."[49] He then wrote to Robert Capa, of Magnum, with whom he already had a burgeoning friendship. "I would like to work for *Life,* but only under your protection so that I do not have to accept everything and be unhappy. Please let me work in New York first and try to realize the first part of my idea."[50] After the publication of the Vienna story, Haas joined the group of ambitious photojournalists at the Magnum photo cooperative. He was not yet thirty years old.

Haas arrived in the United States by plane from Austria by way of London and Paris in May 1951, speaking (and writing) with a heavily German-inflected English.[51] Although he became an accomplished professional, his real distinction emerged after his turn to color photography. As we have seen, from the mid-1950s to the mid-1960s, magazines aggressively expanded the use of color in their pages, and editors were always on the lookout for work in color. Haas had taken his first color photographs experimentally as part of a big black-and-white shoot for an article about New Mexico for *Life.* The editors saw Haas' knack for understanding subjects that they imagined as "demanding" color, which at the time had been reserved for such events as coronations, exotic locations, fine-art reproductions, and

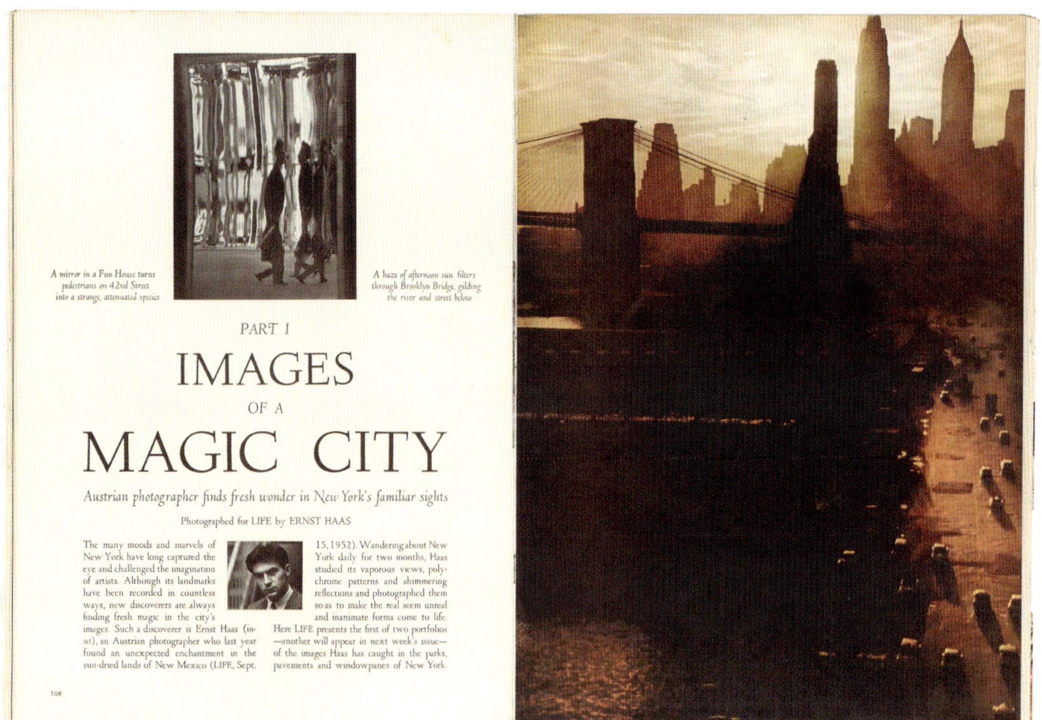

A mirror in a Fun House turns pedestrians on 42nd Street into a strange, attenuated species

A haze of afternoon sun filters through Brooklyn Bridge, gilding the river and street below

PART I

IMAGES OF A MAGIC CITY

Austrian photographer finds fresh wonder in New York's familiar sights

Photographed for LIFE by ERNST HAAS

The many moods and marvels of New York have long captured the eye and challenged the imagination of artists. Although its landmarks have been recorded in countless ways, new discoverers are always finding fresh magic in the city's images. Such a discoverer is Ernst Haas (*inset*), an Austrian photographer who last year found an unexpected enchantment in the sun-dried lands of New Mexico (LIFE, Sept. 15, 1952). Wandering about New York daily for two months, Haas studied its vaporous views, polychrome patterns and shimmering reflections and photographed them so as to make the real seem unreal and inanimate forms come to life. Here LIFE presents the first of two portfolios—another will appear in next week's issue—of the images Haas has caught in the parks, pavements and windowpanes of New York.

108

Figs. 4.13–4.15 "Images of a Magic City, Part I," *Life*, September 14, 1953, 108–17. Ernst Haas, photographer

landscapes. The New Mexico photos inspired Hicks to commission Haas, through Magnum, to do a story about New York that they would publish in an unprecedented twenty-four pages across two issues, in an article titled "Images of a Magic City" (fig. 4.13).[52]

Haas claims to have shot 150 rolls of color film on his New York assignment as if he were experimenting rather than shooting for an assignment. He culled the photos himself and made a slide presentation at the offices of *Life*, which was an unusual practice at the time. Unless they were on staff, photographers in the field generally would simply send in their undeveloped film and, sometimes, see the layout before publication. But this New York–based color story had a photographer in town and many transparencies from which to choose. It became an unprecedented occasion from which to develop a kind of working method.

The story would launch Haas as a color specialist, one who could seem to "magically" change reality into something subjective and sensational. "Images of a Magic City" is an essay made of photos rather than a text essay illustrated by photos. As Haas recalled of the assignment, "I remember when I come for the first time with my New York story to Mr. Thompson that was really an attempt to break away from the verbal, to only convince with the visual." He explained that he had had to leave the country in a hurry because his visa had run out and the magazine wanted caption material, but he frankly had no idea what he had shot where. "What one was after was the kind of essence."[53] *Life* itself clearly invested a great deal in the two-part feature, which it promoted

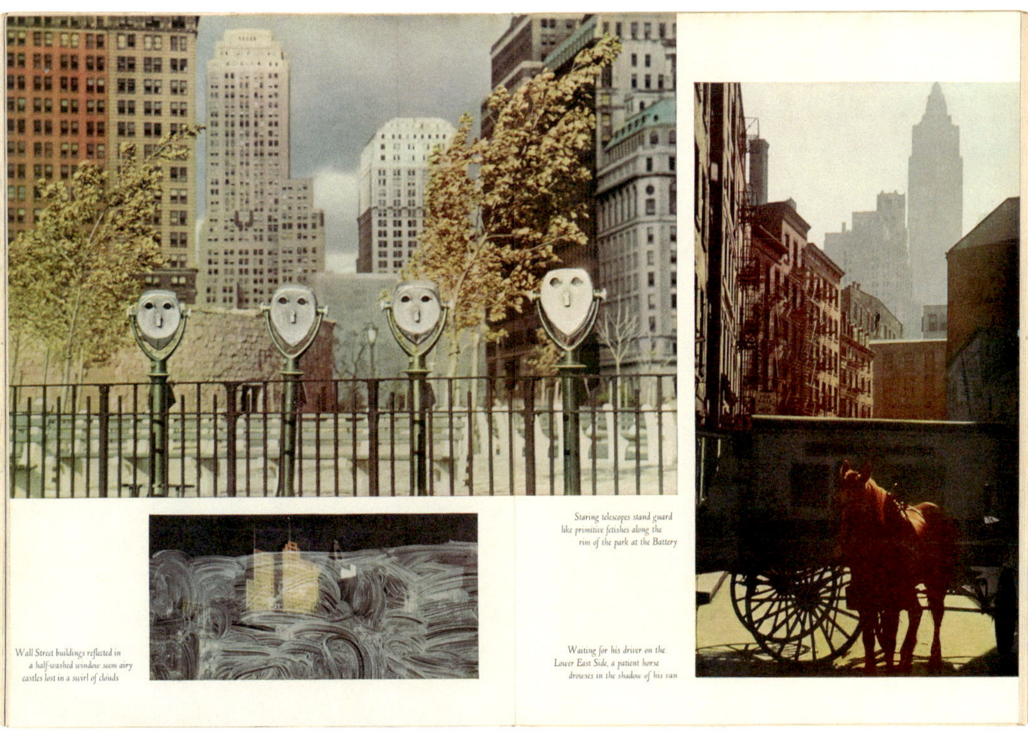

Wall Street buildings reflected in
a half-washed window seem airy
castles lost in a swirl of clouds

Staring telescopes stand guard
like primitive fetishes along the
rim of the park at the Battery

Waiting for his driver on the
Lower East Side, a patient horse
drowses in the shadow of his van

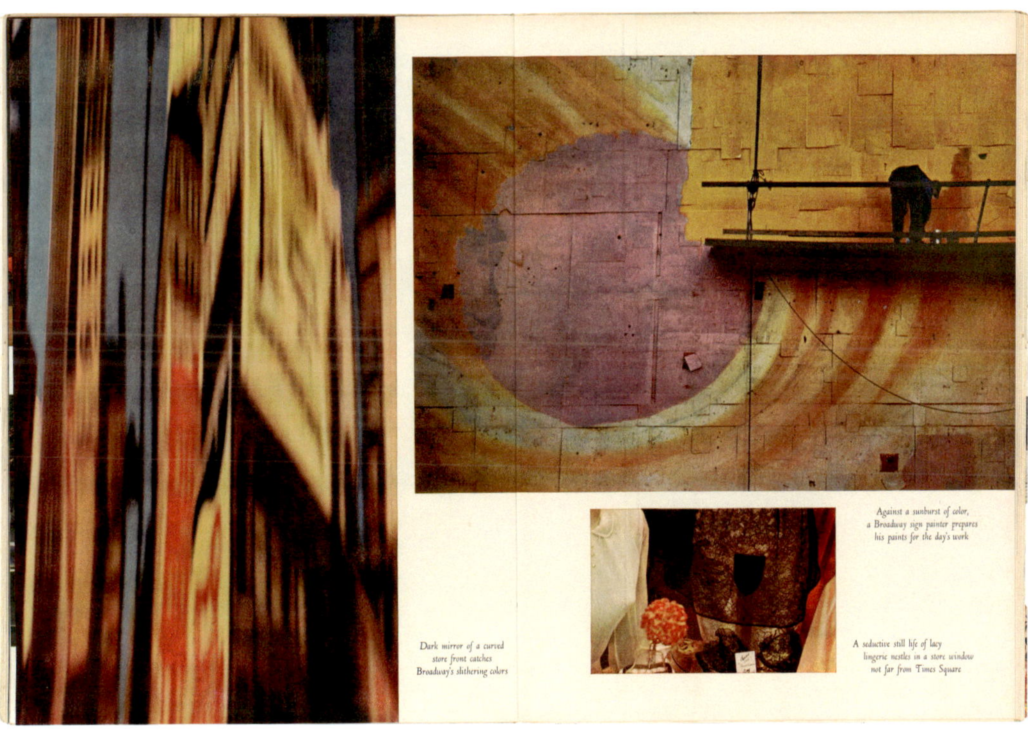

Dark mirror of a curved
store front catches
Broadway's slithering colors

Against a sunburst of color,
a Broadway sign painter prepares
his paints for the day's work

A seductive still life of lacy
lingerie nestles in a store window
not far from Times Square

with a full-page advertisement in the *New York Times,* where it was described as "two unusual portfolios of color pictures."[54] The project would lead Haas to being considered and perhaps also appreciated as a photographer who pondered the deepest philosophical problems of his age by using color to consider the experience of contemporary life.

In "Magic City," Haas first used color to render the city unfamiliar in order that it be seen with a new set of eyes (figs. 4.14, 4.15). Many of the images used reflections to encourage viewers to look beyond the subject represented (fig. 4.16, United Nations at left). Cropping and closeups produced an emphasis on a "sharp geometry of lines and shadows," as one caption, obviously written by *Life* editors, reads. The "Magic City" images used color to foreground depth, as in the balustrade image with a staircase behind on another plane (fig. 4.16, bottom right), and frequently the reader might have no idea what he or she was seeing, which includes the reflection of the Atlas sculpture at Rockefeller Center, mirrored through a shop window and overlapping with a small bit of St. Patrick's Cathedral (fig. 4.16, top right). Other images contrasted objects in ironic or playful ways. Color and the play of light and dark dominated many of the photographs in the essay: street signs, cars, painted billboards, multicolor reflections made when oil spread on water (fig. 4.17; see fig. 4.15). These images show the photographer reframing what had been seen as a problem in news reporting. Instead of regarding color as an uncontrollable element in the real world, Haas presented it as "experience." His work in color suggested that photography could make something interesting of the lack of control and inability to stage color in the world.

Haas commented on his desire to capture the fast pace of New York. "When I came to New York, I was kind of fascinated by the speed by which people were working and walking, and I tried to express the New Yorker as a robot."[55] He did this by finding such things as mechanized shapes on rooftops and in improbable places. At the same time, *Life* magazine sought to position him as a street photographer and urban ethnographer in the spirit of Alfred Kazin's 1951 book *Walker in the City,* describing Haas as a "wanderer by nature . . . with an ultra-perceptive eye alert for the obvious, yet hidden things that he might catch with his poetic camera."[56] Haas was impressed by a recent book called *Poet's Camera* that had paired poetry and photographs in the name of showing that photography could be a creative art by capturing "vivid transient perception," which is quite different from declarations of art capturing eternal truths and brings it a great deal closer to the work of journalists.[57]

The magazine's internal newsletter explained that the New York story had begun as an experiment in photographic technique and that Haas and a *Life* photo researcher, June Herman, had wandered the streets of New York for six weeks from 6 A.M. to 7 P.M. It mentions that many of the pictures were taken in the most casual of circumstances, such as the picture in Part I of the locksmith's trademark, which Haas noticed coming out of a shop

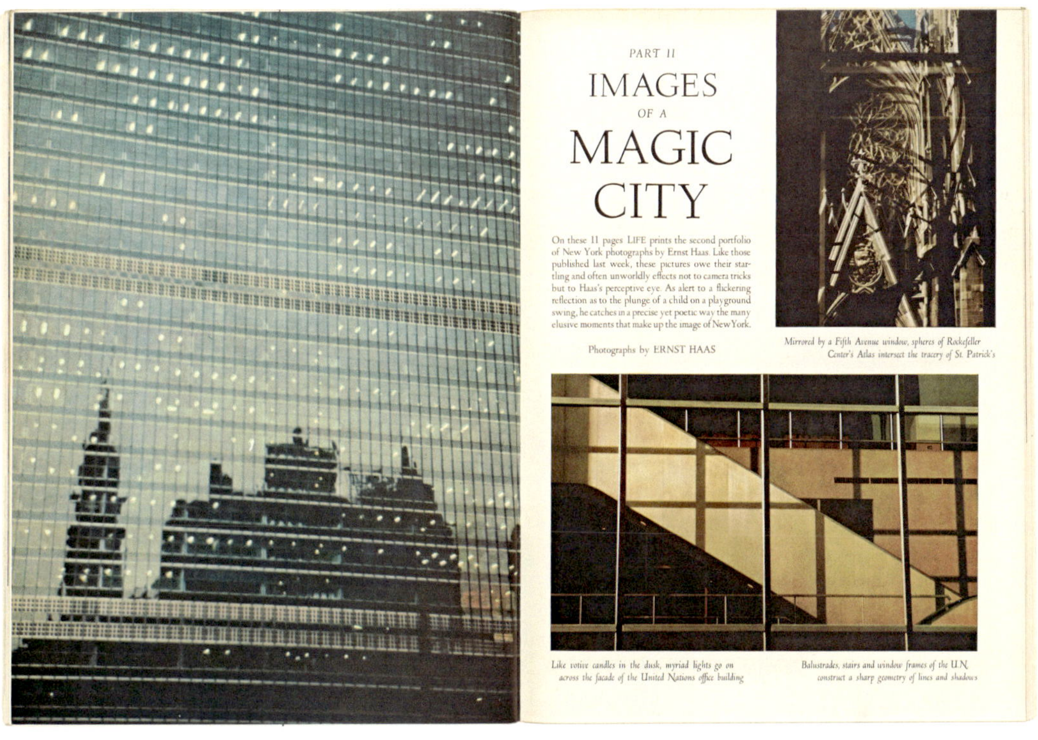

PART II

IMAGES OF A MAGIC CITY

On these 11 pages LIFE prints the second portfolio of New York photographs by Ernst Haas. Like those published last week, these pictures owe their startling and often unworldly effects not to camera tricks but to Haas's perceptive eye. As alert to a flickering reflection as to the plunge of a child on a playground swing, he catches in a precise yet poetic way the many elusive moments that make up the image of New York.

Photographs by ERNST HAAS

Mirrored by a Fifth Avenue window, spheres of Rockefeller Center's Atlas intersect the tracery of St. Patrick's

Like votive candles in the dusk, myriad lights go on across the facade of the United Nations office building

Balustrades, stairs and window frames of the U.N. construct a sharp geometry of lines and shadows

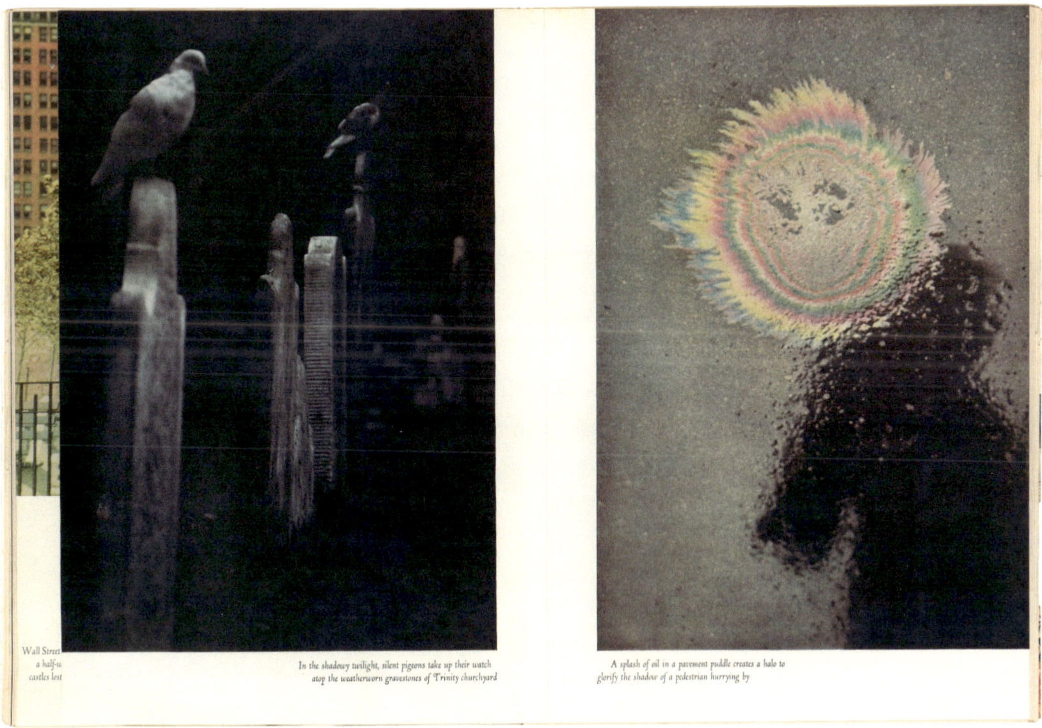

Wall Street
a half-
castles lost

In the shadowy twilight, silent pigeons take up their watch atop the weatherworn gravestones of Trinity churchyard

A splash of oil in a pavement puddle creates a halo to glorify the shadow of a pedestrian hurrying by

Figs. 4.16 and 4.17 "Images of a Magic City, Part II," *Life*, September 21, 1953, 112–17. Ernst Haas, photographer

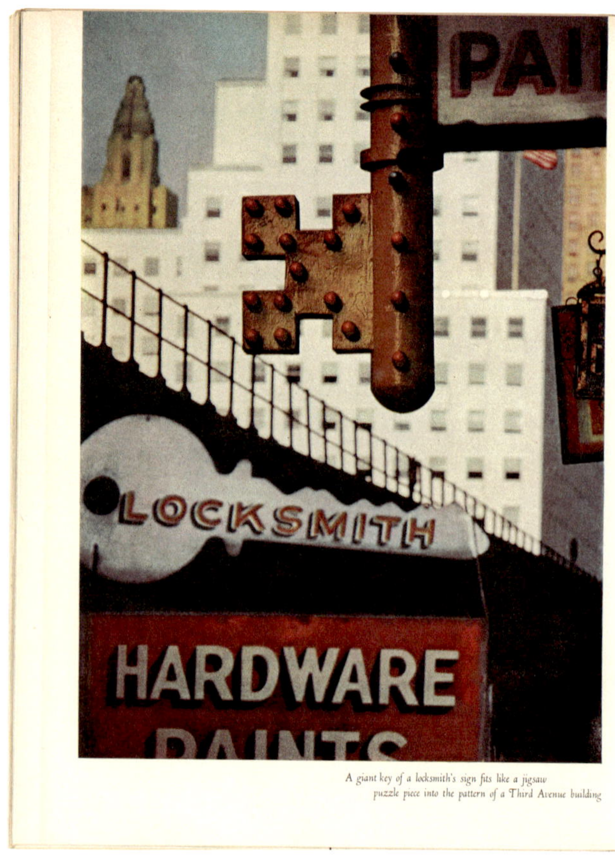

Fig. 4.18 "Images of a Magic City, Part I," *Life*, September 14, 1953, 124. Ernst Haas, photographer

where he had a duplicate key made (fig. 4.18).[58] The magazine emphasized that Haas did not use technical distortions: "Haas doesn't see anything we could not see ourselves, but in simple direct statements without tricks, he makes us look again at everyday scenes and see them this time through perceptive, sensitive eyes. . . . In stories like this, *Life* gives readers the extra pair of eyes they need to really perceive the things they look at every day." The internal newsletter goes on to describe the fact that Haas had been "trained in working in abstract art and modern design" (which was a bit of an exaggeration) and cites "his sensitivity to things [being] made more acute by study of music, poetry and philosophy" (actually true). Finally the newsletter mentions the fact that the photos are in color and that Haas never sets up any of his pictures nor crops them—as if to underscore both the strength of his eye and the magic in reality available to those who can be taught to see.[59] It was almost as if just having the photos in color allowed the magic of the real world and the perception of an original eye to take hold.

Haas followed "Magic City" with more magazine work published in Europe, in *Réalités,* and in the United States in *Holiday.* Other *Life* city features followed, on Paris and Venice (figs. 4.19–4.22). As he mentions in an undated typed note in his archive regarding a cable he sent to *Life* about his

Paris story: "This can be applied to all the city essays which were published." The cable was written from Singapore in response to *Life*'s request for caption material from his Paris photo shoot for a layout he had not seen. He explained that Capa had suggested the Paris story in the first place in order that he use his last two weeks in Paris productively before going to Indochina. Capa had nudged him, "Why don't you follow the leaves?" The cable explains that Haas shot "planless," as he put it, and "without any intention and without making any notes about where was what, either before, during, or after my search." He explains that soon he forgot the leaves and went after the light and "these moments when for the sake of compositions, forms, colors and movements relate each other in for me the most thrilling constellations." He noted that, aside from the major monuments like the Eiffel Tower, he never knew where he was, and he left before seeing the results of his work and could not go back to reshoot anything. "I feel sorry now for the people who have to search from where my pictures are shot, as they very often existed more in my photographic imagination than in reality."[60] Of course the sites were real places, but Haas makes his point clear: he intended his photos to constitute a form of subjective vision and did not feel that was foreign to the news genre.

Haas did make choices about where he went and what stories to do, and the cities were not in fact interchangeable. In an undated letter from "MHS" (probably Margot Shore) to Magnum New York to report on Haas' intentions, she explains that Haas had asked Magnum if he could go to Venice to do an autumn story: "He's chosen Venice particularly because there are no leaves—only water and boats and birds; and he doesn't want falling leaves in any more color stories for a while. This will no doubt be another Haas color triumph, he has it well in mind, and since I know both Venice and Ernst, I bet it would be a fine idea."[61] In other words, like a good journalist, he knew where to go to pick his story, and the Magnum staff had the confidence that wherever he went, he would create a "triumph" in color. In fact, Haas' reputation and success in color photo essays within the Magnum offices grew so much during that period that another memo referred to their own internal jokes about it: "One of the major jokes of the week here in New York is that the minute we sold another of Ernst Haas' color essays to *Life* he began doing water colors on the same subject in the office—and so good that I am going to determinedly suppress them!"[62] This implied that Haas was an artist who worked in color like a painter. When covering a football game whose rules he absolutely did not comprehend and asked who was playing, he simply replied, "Color against color."[63]

Haas became an evangelist for photographers as privileged "modern" imagemakers—at once capable of invoking the subjectivity of vision but able to also produce reportorial accuracy. "You really are what you see" are the final words of the television show that was authored and presented by Haas, a coproduction of PBS and the BBC. Filmed during the dead of summer in 1962 (August 15–September 1), the program offered

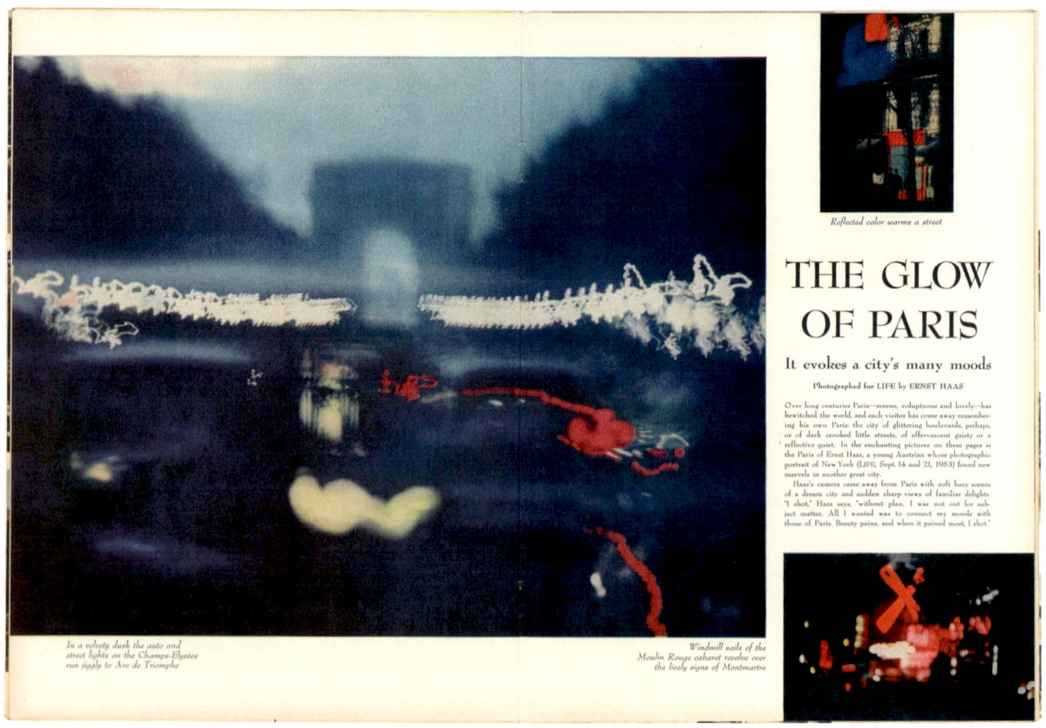

Reflected color warms a street

THE GLOW OF PARIS

It evokes a city's many moods

Photographed for LIFE by ERNST HAAS

Over long centuries Paris—serene, voluptuous and lovely—has bewitched the world, and each visitor has come away remembering his own Paris: the city of glittering boulevards, perhaps, or of dark crooked little streets, of effervescent gaiety or a reflective quiet. In the enchanting pictures on these pages is the Paris of Ernst Haas, a young Austrian whose photographic portrait of New York (LIFE, Sept. 14 and 21, 1953) found new marvels in another great city.

Haas's camera came away from Paris with soft hazy scenes of a dream city and sudden sharp views of familiar delights. "I shot," Haas says, "without plan. I was not out for subject matter. All I wanted was to connect my moods with those of Paris. Beauty pains, and when it pained most, I shot."

In a velvety dusk the auto and street lights on the Champs-Elysées run jiggly to Arc de Triomphe

Windmill sails of the Moulin Rouge cabaret revolve over the lively signs of Montmartre

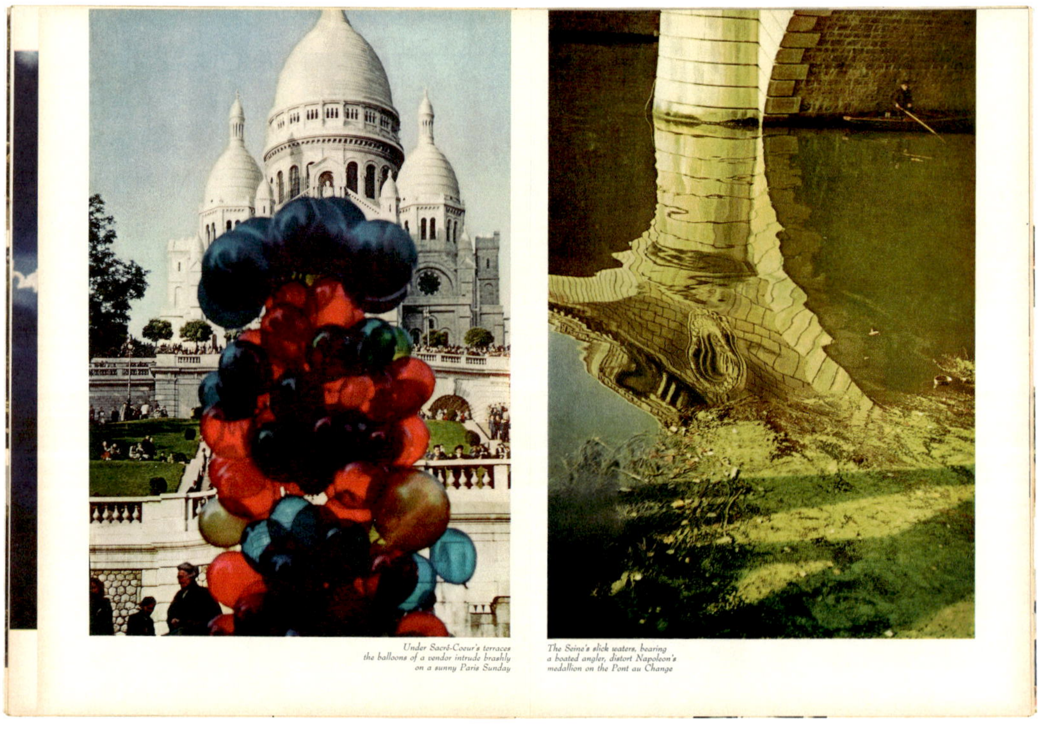

Under Sacré-Coeur's terraces the balloons of a vendor intrude brashly on a sunny Paris Sunday

The Seine's slick waters, bearing a boated angler, distort Napoleon's medallion on the Pont au Change

Figs. 4.19–4.21 "The Glow of Paris," *Life,* August 1, 1955, 56–61. Ernst Haas, photographer

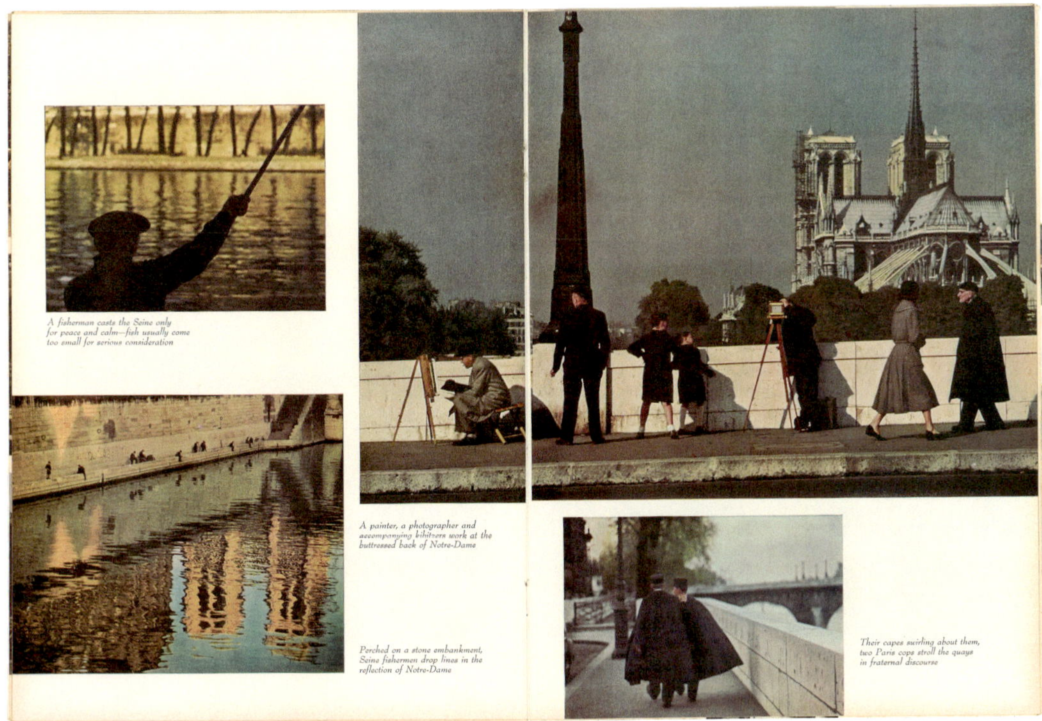
A fisherman casts the Seine only for peace and calm—fish usually come too small for serious consideration

Perched on a stone embankment, Seine fishermen drop lines in the reflection of Notre-Dame

A painter, a photographer and accompanying kibitzers work at the buttressed back of Notre-Dame

Their capes swirling about them, two Paris cops stroll the quays in fraternal discourse

an experiment in educational television. Haas celebrated the fact that the producers had chosen a photographer as host. He positioned the photographer as someone working in a new medium, and he did not acknowledge that it was more than one hundred years old. Instead, he explained that, as an artist, the photographer never uses memory but is "simultaneous" to what he is depicting. Of course he is also physically displaced by being physically present as well. The script notes, "And is it not interesting that we live in the most visual age and it is the seeing which is the least cultivated, maybe, because it is the most taken for granted sense. . . . We never really learn to see." He went on to note that photographers hold a "frame against reality: we analyze reality into values."[64]

The four half-hour presentations consisted of three- to five-minute filmed sequences of Haas walking around in the streets working as a photographer at the start, but for the most part the action took place in his photo studio, which had been transformed into a television set, and concentrated on issues of temporality and mobility and their relation to seeing. This focus no doubt came in part from the fact that the program was filmed in black and white. It may seem strange that across town, at the very same moment, the Museum of Modern Art was featuring many of Haas' color photos in a one-man show that had opened on August 21, yet the limits of filmed television's palette (a budgetary and distribution rather than a literal technological limit) shaped his television instruction and message on the four programs, which do not mention color at all.[65]

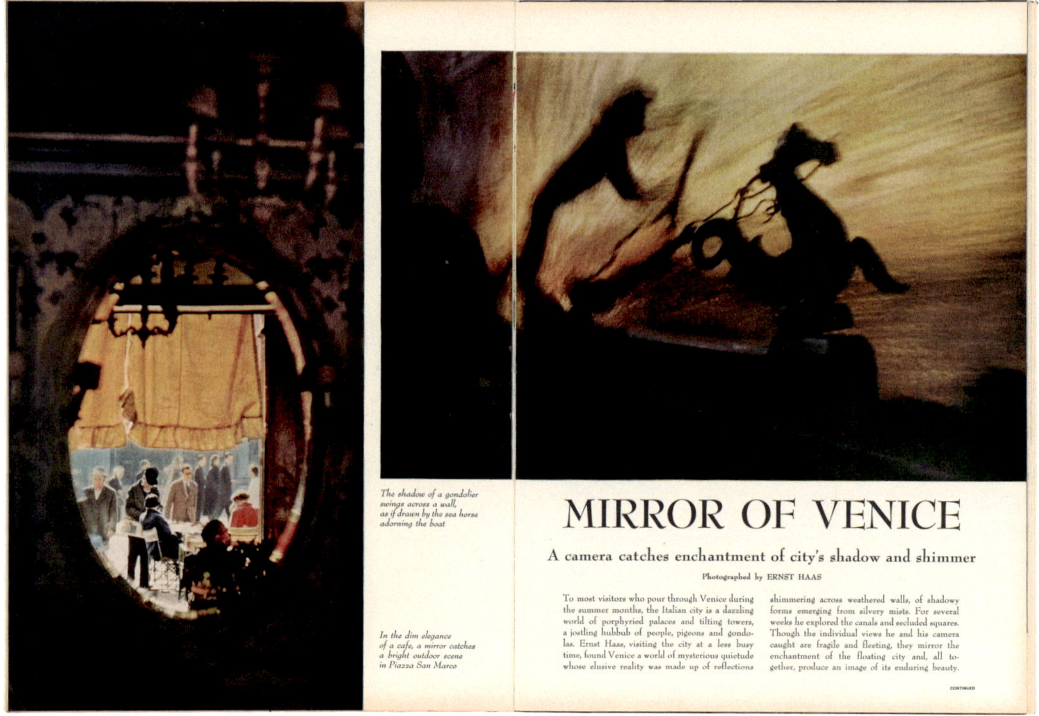

The shadow of a gondolier swings across a wall, as if drawn by the sea horse adorning the boat

In the dim elegance of a cafe, a mirror catches a bright outdoor scene in Piazza San Marco

MIRROR OF VENICE

A camera catches enchantment of city's shadow and shimmer

Photographed by ERNST HAAS

To most visitors who pour through Venice during the summer months, the Italian city is a dazzling world of porphyried palaces and tilting towers, a jostling hubbub of people, pigeons and gondolas. Ernst Haas, visiting the city at a less busy time, found Venice a world of mysterious quietude whose elusive reality was made up of reflections shimmering across weathered walls, of shadowy forms emerging from silvery mists. For several weeks he explored the canals and secluded squares. Though the individual views he and his camera caught are fragile and fleeting, they mirror the enchantment of the floating city and, all together, produce an image of its enduring beauty.

CONTINUED

Fig. 4.22 "Mirror of Venice," *Life*, June 25, 1956, 74–75. Ernst Haas, photographer

The show's most interesting content comes as Haas explicates the "decisive moment," in keeping with Cartier-Bresson's views on the subject, when he walks viewers through how contact sheets tell the story of a photographer's experience of a photo shoot, just as he must have done with Cartier-Bresson on NBC a few years earlier when the two of them appeared on the *Home* show explaining how they used contact sheets to determine the best image from a group of images.[66] He suggests that artistic composition had such moments embedded within them, from skating routines to dances. He offered the anecdote that while covering the Olympics, every photographer was led through the routine enough that they understood when it would culminate, and they would all be ready to snap a picture at the key moment. Haas explained that it is not photography per se that isolated such moments, and he showed Goya drawings of bullfights to make his point. He implied that the photographer actually seeks to reconstitute lived experience by looking at his contact sheet as though able to re-create life as though it were "choreographed"—like a skating routine (fig. 4.23–4.24).

In discussing motion Haas also introduced the question of duration. He emphasized that photography's distinction inhered in a reportorial act of presence. The photoreporter must be present at the moment in which he "put[s] together the past and the future in the present."[67] Such notions led to a discussion of the idea of stretching the moment, of representing the sensation and feeling of motion itself, and of the moments between moments, and of the simultaneity of time. He illustrated his points first by

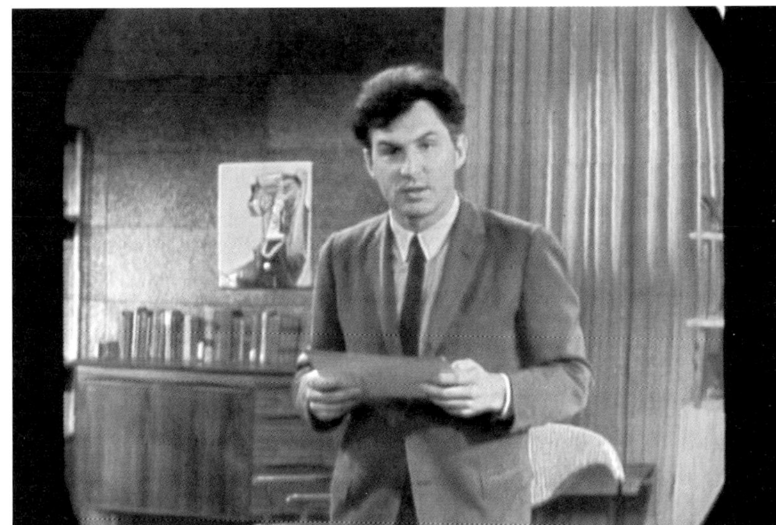

Fig. 4.23 Ernst Haas with contact sheet, *The Art of Seeing*, August 1962. New York Public Television

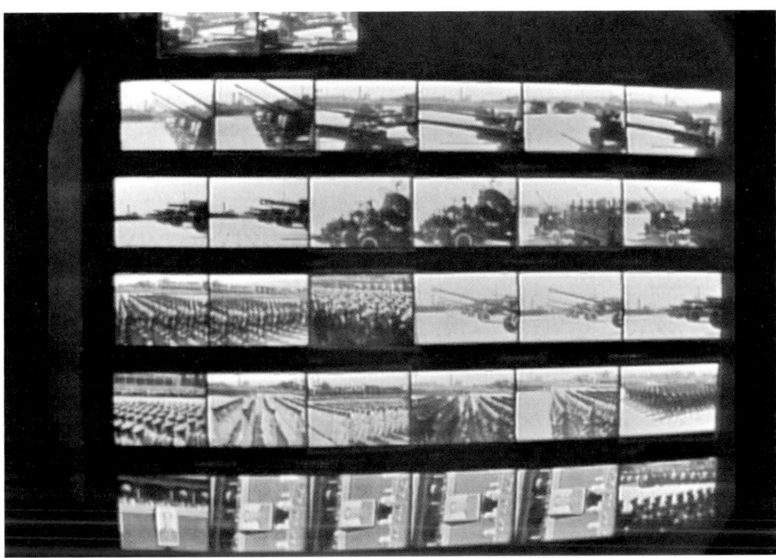

Fig. 4.24 Contact sheet, *The Art of Seeing*

turning to a discussion of the Futurists, whom he understood as having grappled with these questions earlier in the century, and then to motion photographers such as Gjon Mili whose work on stop-motion photography, which used a stroboscopic flash to keep action in sharp focus, was known as an aestheticized scientific photography.[68] Haas explicated his own motion work with images from the "Magic of Motion in Color" *Life* photos. He never mentions the importance of color to the endeavor—instead he focuses on how he used the fluidity of the water in the photos of sailboats and in his images of people running on the beach to capture and to re-create the experience of motion.

The link drawn out by Haas between the photography of motion and the moment of the 1950s and 1960s presented itself in many different kinds of magazine photography. For example, Diana Vreeland explained of Avedon: "His taste is equaled by a flamboyant sense of movement. . . . He can get more from a model than anyone I know. He's their time of day, their age and their generation. He's a super-duper craftsman."[69] Although comments about craft always seem to refer to artistic quality, Avedon's singularity as a fashion photographer also appeared to reside in his capturing his own moment through his dedication to movement. Critic Arthur Knight observed in an article published after the release of the film *Funny Face,* for which Avedon worked as a visual consultant: "The plasticity of dance, the grace of its positions—at once fixed and fluid—gave him [Avedon] an approach to photography that has since become his characteristic. Avedon's models are not posed: they are caught in mid-flight."[70] Avedon also believed that motion brought a more true-to-life dimension to his photography, despite nothing about fashion photography being remotely realistic. As he put it in *Commercial Camera* in 1949, "Real people move, they bear with them the element of time, not time in the sense of aging, but time in the sense of motion. . . . It is the fourth dimension of people that I try to capture in a photograph."[71]

Such notions permeated the Haas series. The third episode, "Stretching the Moment," begins with a tight-frame filming of the tracks from inside a railroad car, and thus is very much engaged with the mechanization of motion that Haas and contemporaries (and the Futurists before them) foregrounded in relation to questions of vision. The obvious problem with the television program having been presented in black and white is that Haas himself had explored so many of these issues with color photography. His work suggested that it was color that had changed even the most important of photojournalistic notions: "The decisive moment in black and white and color are not identical," he noted elsewhere.[72] Color leads the viewer to consider what lies between moments rather than within a moment. He said, "I am fascinated by dynamic time and the change from a three-dimensional world into a two-dimensional image with a four-dimensional awareness."[73] And so in many ways the program left him diverting some of his key issues onto other questions.

Haas explained that his experience focusing on motion began when he started to work with color because one could mix colors without losing them into a "common grey as happens in black and white photography. To follow a movement with a camera is as obvious as following a movement with one's eyes. . . . A moment does not have an absolute time length and can be stretched. The appearance of the picture will then not depend only on the shutter speed, but on the movement of the camera in relation to the movement of the subject." He describes how he moved his whole body and opened and closed his shutter manually.[74] Color offered the occasion to "see as the eye sees, not in fixed images but in a blended flow of color." In his work, Haas repeatedly referred to color as flow and a blur, eliding it with motion. He described his reporting on the Barnum Circus in 1961, explaining that, "All I saw was a blur of motion in color."[75] Haas had to use slow shutter speed to avoid underexposure, but this made it impossible to freeze the action, so he panned the camera; the blur signals action and motion. None of this technique, which had garnered him a great deal of attention, could be demonstrated on the program.

Instead, by the third episode's end, he was picking up petrified wood, stones, and red cabbages and arguing that anything that grew offered an opportunity for a motion study. Nothing, it seems, could be further from pondering the industrial mechanization of motion than these organic models. Haas himself always struggled with these "elements." In fact, his interest in structures and forms grew over time, but it is clear that the show's filming in black and white pushed him toward such a discussion. He never did another television series, and there is little archival trail regarding its success or failure, but it is instructive regarding his emphasis on subjective vision and motion because it makes evident that, absent color, Haas' unique contributions recede into generalized formalist discussions that are not that distinct from earlier twentieth-century views that combined Futurism's preoccupations with mechanization and motion with the period's interest in abstraction.

Haas experimented with color by blurring his images to capture the dynamic nature of what photography had otherwise tended to freeze and condense. He called his technique "motion photography," but he blurred only his images in color. Haas eventually turned to using the blur to depict motion itself, although here, too, he was hardly the first to apply this technique. Amateurs had been accidentally blurring their images for years, as discussed in the *Life* "Magic in Motion" article. He may well, however, have inadvertently championed or participated in a broader popular trend in blurry images. A *U.S. Camera* article suggested this trend not long after the Haas photos were published when it asked, "Are Photographers Going Blur Crazy?" That magazine, however, interpreted the blur rather differently from how Haas saw it. *U.S. Camera* saw the blur as a "lens" eye effect, explaining that the blur was proof of "images never seen in reality by the human eye. Instead they are products of the camera."[76] For scholar Kim Beil, such images also relate to the broader culture of speed associated with contemporary experiences of the open road and automobility.[77] But I would suggest that transport culture is being invoked more generally and that the jet certainly defined the "speed" of the age enough to have given it a name. But, more significantly, the point of such photography is that Haas insisted it stood as a mark of "subjective" vision rather than camera vision.

Haas' blurred motion photos were in color—which was at once the most mass cultural of modes and the most subjective of idioms; this may be one reason why it could function so effectively in *Life,* for example. The publication presented Haas as a formalist of sorts; naïve as a reporter but all the better as a knowing eye. For example, in the essay "Beauty in a Brutal Art," whose subtitle, "Great Cameraman Shows Bullfight's Perfect Flow of Motion," his incomprehension of the rules of bullfighting supposedly helped him see it better (fig. 4.25). The story, which made quite a stir upon

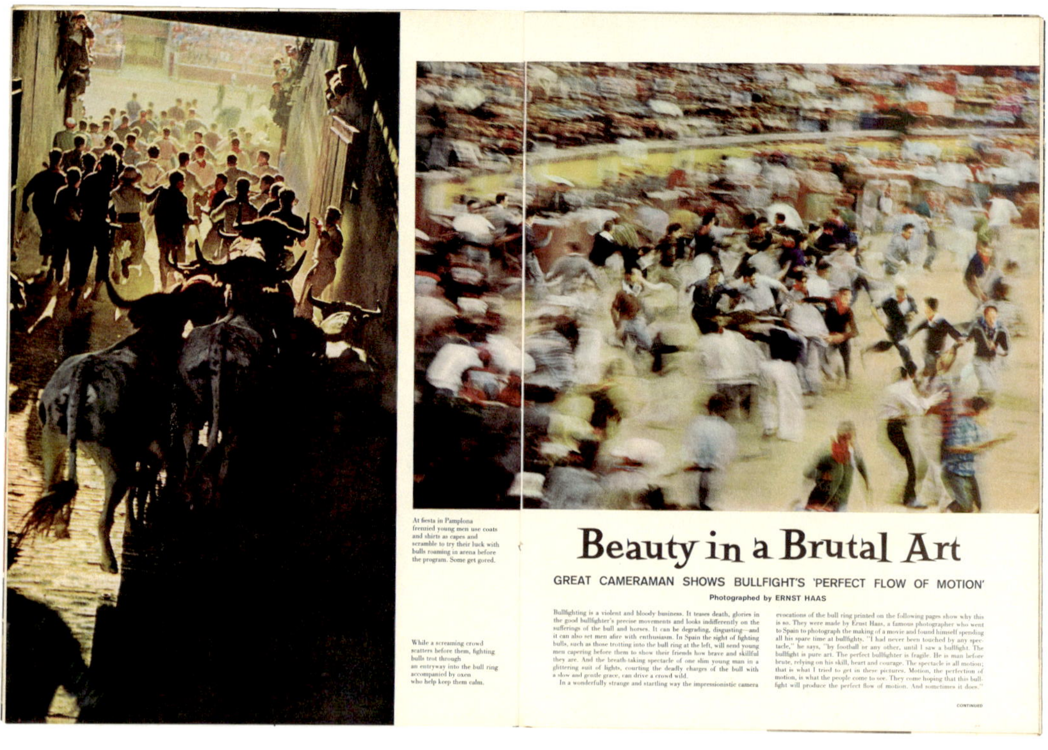

At fiesta in Pamplona frenzied young men use coats and shirts as capes and scramble to try their luck with bulls roaming in arena before the program. Some get gored.

While a screaming crowd scatters before them, fighting bulls trot through an entryway into the bull ring accompanied by oxen who help keep them calm.

Beauty in a Brutal Art

GREAT CAMERAMAN SHOWS BULLFIGHT'S 'PERFECT FLOW OF MOTION'

Photographed by ERNST HAAS

Bullfighting is a violent and bloody business. It teases death, glories in the good bullfighter's precise movements and looks indifferently on the sufferings of the bull and horses. It can be degrading, disgusting—and it can also set men afire with enthusiasm. In Spain the sight of fighting bulls, such as those trotting into the bull ring at the left, will send young men capering before them to show their friends how brave and skillful they are. And the breath-taking spectacle of one slim young man in a glittering suit of lights, courting the deadly charges of the bull with a slow and gentle grace, can drive a crowd wild.

In a wonderfully strange and startling way the impressionistic camera evocations of the bull ring printed on the following pages show why this is so. They were made by Ernst Haas, a famous photographer who went to Spain to photograph the making of a movie and found himself spending all his spare time at bullfights. "I had never been touched by any spectacle," he says, "by football or any other, until I saw a bullfight. The bullfight is pure art. The perfect bullfighter is fragile. He is man before brute, relying on his skill, heart and courage. The spectacle is all motion; that is what I tried to get in these pictures. Motion, the perfection of motion, is what the people come to see. They come hoping that this bullfight will produce the perfect flow of motion. And sometimes it does."

CONTINUED

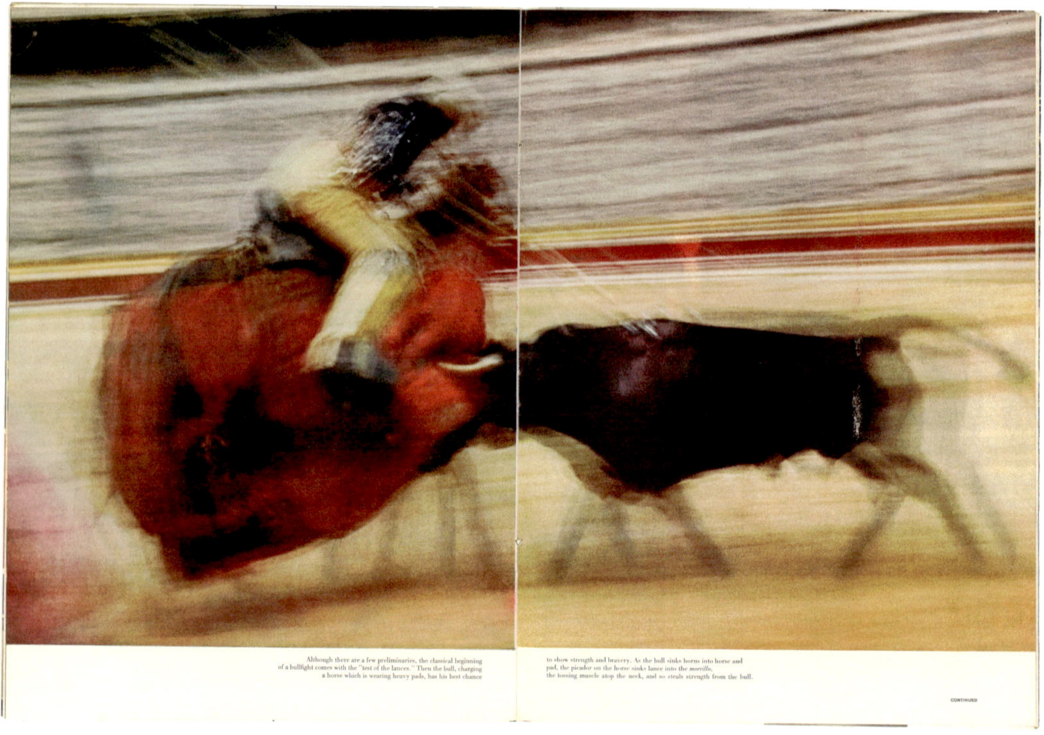

Although there are a few preliminaries, the classical beginning of a bullfight comes with the "test of the lances." Then the bull, charging a horse which is wearing heavy pads, has his best chance to show strength and bravery. As the bull sinks horns into horse and pad, the picador on the horse sinks lance into the *morrillo*, the tossing muscle atop the neck, and so steals strength from the bull.

CONTINUED

Figs. 4.25–4.27 "Beauty in a Brutal Art," *Life*, July 29, 1957, 56–65. Ernst Haas, photographer

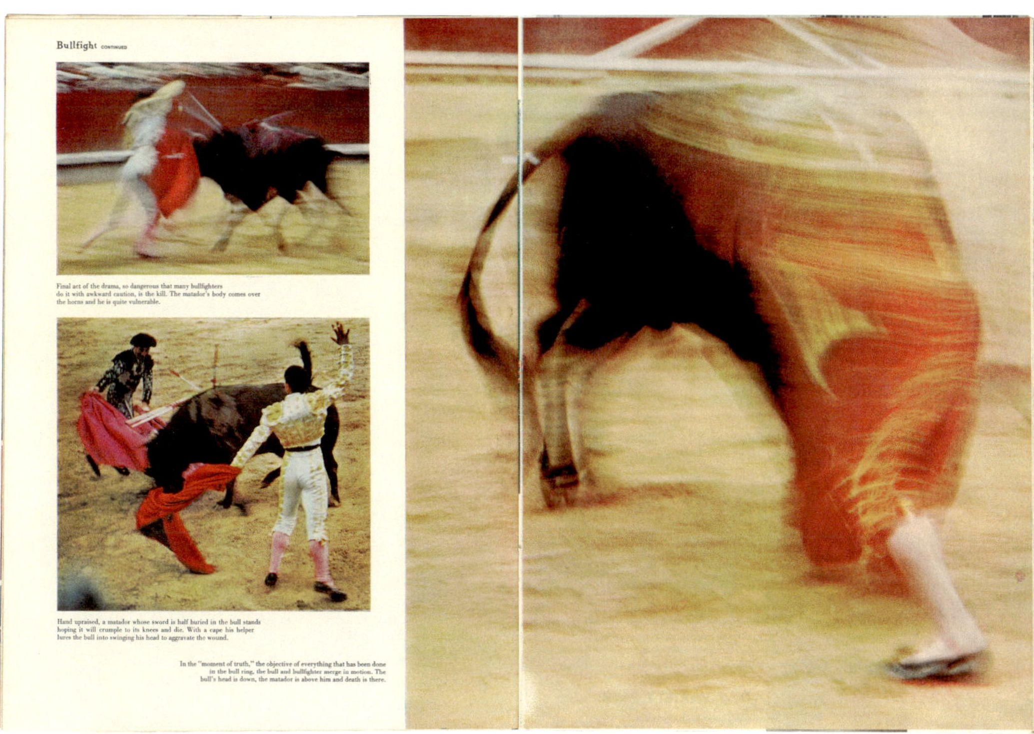
Bullfight CONTINUED

Final act of the drama, so dangerous that many bullfighters do it with awkward caution, is the kill. The matador's body comes over the horns and he is quite vulnerable.

Hand upraised, a matador whose sword is half buried in the bull stands hoping it will crumple to its knees and die. With a cape his helper lures the bull into swinging his head to aggravate the wound.

In the "moment of truth," the objective of everything that has been done in the bull ring, the bull and bullfighter merge in motion. The bull's head is down, the matador is above him and death is there.

its publication in the summer of 1957, directed readers less to the subject of bullfighting and more to how Haas had photographed it. According to Haas, "The spectacle is all motion; that is what I tried to get in these pictures. Motion, the perfection of motion, is what the people come to see. They come hoping that this bullfight will produce the perfect flow of motion. And sometimes it does."[78] The fascination with a seemingly arcane, brutal, and primitive "pre-mechanized" form of motion also emphasized the role the photographer played in negotiating for readers this transition in the history of the mechanization of motion through color photography, in which photos had a particular power to simultaneously report and interpret the experience of a fast-moving world.

Across five two-page photo spreads, including a second page centerfold of the picador astride a horse with a charging bull, the crowd in the arena behind is reduced to a blur (fig. 4.26). In the foreground the blur effect is a mere shadowy sort of double vision. The images of the matador on foot in relation to the charging bull are its most intriguing images. They capture the dance between the matador and bull as aided by his cape (fig 4.27, right). The bottom left corner image, however, offers no blur. There perhaps is the fight's decisive moment: the matador's sword is "half-buried in the bull," the caption explains. We see the two muletas stuck in the bull's back, almost like wings, knowing all these knives will eventually stop the dance of death. In letters in response to the essay, one reader noted, "Haas is a genius. No one can deny this is art. The pages seem to plunge you right into the symphony of color and motion."[79]

Letters such as this one, which comment on the quality of the image rather than on its content, underscore how Haas' work was positioned in the magazine as creating a photographic effect—color and motion.

The 1962 MoMA one-man show "*Ernst Haas: Color Photography*" also celebrated Haas for his sophisticated engagement with color photography. As the exhibition's press release explained, "The color sensation itself is the subject matter of his work. No photographer has worked so successfully to express the sheer physical joy of seeing."[80] But John Szarkowski, who inherited the show from departing photo curator Edward Steichen, could not decide whether he liked the work. In fact, years later, he critiqued Haas, saying that "he had had to sacrifice the specificity of photo (which is not abstraction) in order to make color work."[81] Preparatory notes that became wall labels included a discussion of Haas' interest in the fourth dimension, calling it, "that which lies between moments" rather than within a moment: "In music one remembers never one tone, but a melody, a theme, a movement. In dance, never a moment, but again the beauty of a movement in time and space."[82] In these color photos, Haas contemplated the questions of duration and motion that he seemed to ponder in midair, how experience was not so much broken down but put together—how it flowed.

Haas' solo show culminated more than ten years of exhibition history at the museum. He had made his MoMA debut in the *Memorable Life Photographs Show* (1951), with his Austrian returning-POW image of the small girl holding the photo and crying (see fig. 4.12). Not that long before his "Magic City" publication in 1953, in May of that year, his photos were among those in a three-hundred-photo show dedicated to European photographers that featured twenty-seven of his photos alone (more than any other photographer's); the press release for that show discussed Haas' work first. He also had five photos displayed as part of *The Family of Man* exhibition (1955). When the museum opened its photography center (named after Steichen) in 1964, Haas' color work was included in the inaugural exhibition.[83] Photographs from the "Magic of Color in Motion," from the bullfight essay, from a 1963 "Spring Comes to England" essay, and from his Austrian prisoner of war essay were all included in the 1965 exhibition *The Photo Essay,* which emphasized the photographer's subjectivity. As a wall label explained, "In the decade after World War II, the photographer became an individual observer, and emphasis shifted to the quality of his personal vision . . . not the exterior event but the photographer's reaction to it."[84] Although one might read this as a statement of transforming journalism into art by making reporters into "auteurs," it is also clear that this framing suggests a visual form of New Journalism may have coalesced in images even before it did in words.

Haas may have defined color photography as a photo whose subject "is color," but he also had a strong sense of what color could reveal: "Colors change according to the light in nature as well as to exposure. . . . The absolute color of a mountain does not exist." Such statements help us understand how Haas sought to make images drawn from the world rather

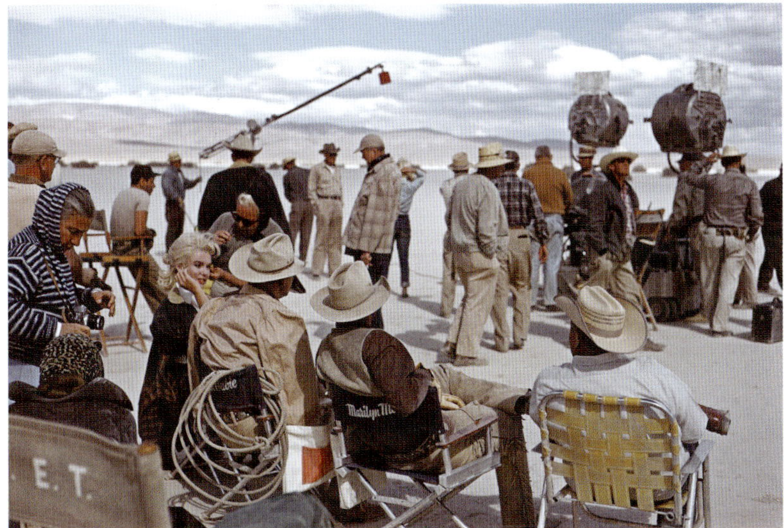

Fig. 4.28 On the set of *The Misfits*, 1960, directed by John Huston. Ernst Haas, photographer

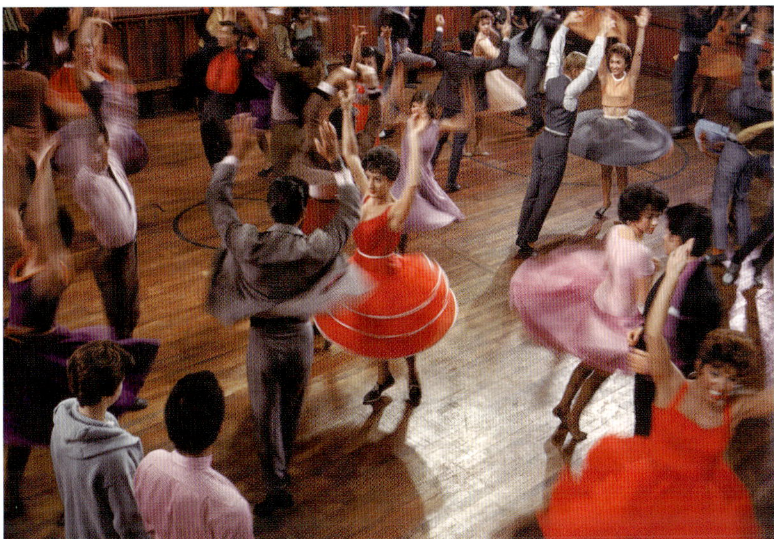

Fig. 4.29 On the set of *West Side Story*, 1960, directed by Robert Wise. Ernst Haas, photographer

than images of the world. He said that color photography worked this way: "It is the image of a fact, heightened by imagination, and not (as with a painted picture) an illusion which becomes a truth."[85] Despite later dismissal of his work for its aspiration to be painterly, Haas remained wedded to the idea that photography also could reveal fact despite his commitments to formal experimentation.

Haas braided time and space and also worked across multiple forms of media. He never committed to photography as his only medium because he was driven by his urges to visually express what could be observed regarding the major issues of the day, which he took to be mechanization more generally. As he explained at the Wilson Hicks Photojournalism Conference in Miami in 1967: "Be as flexible as possible; learn everything, go into the television field, learn the camera; learn movie making, and don't forget

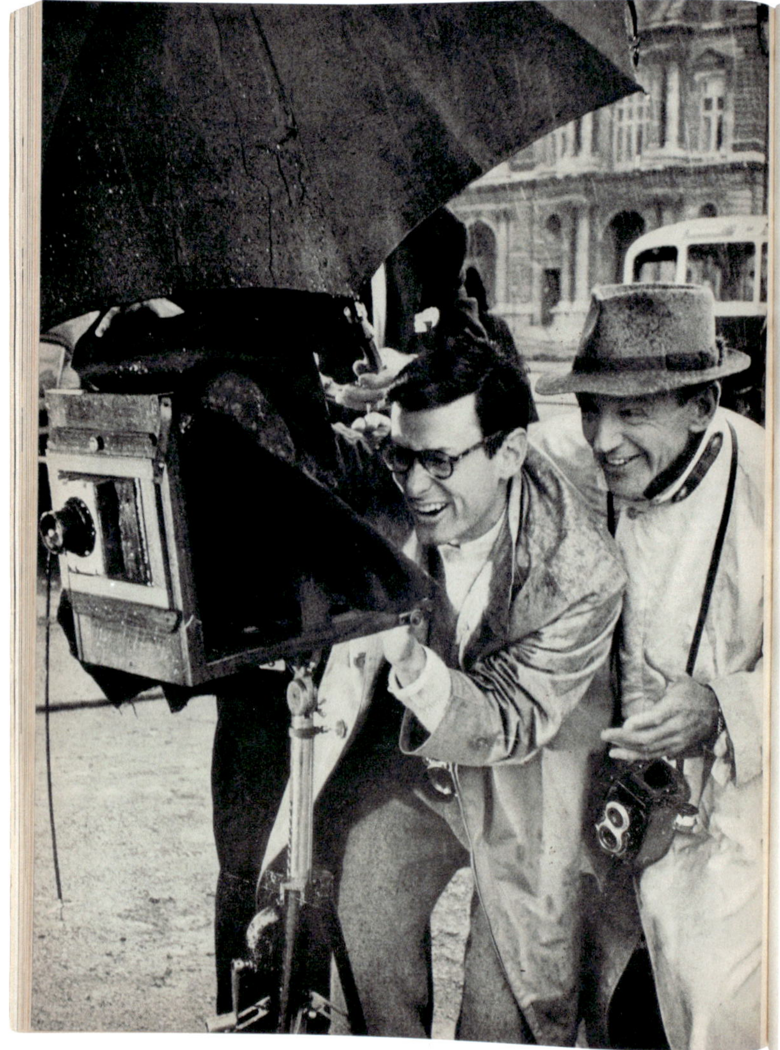

Fig. 4.30 Richard Avedon and Fred Astaire on the set of *Funny Face,* 1957, directed by Stanley Donen. Published in *Harper's Bazaar,* August 1956. David (Chim) Seymour, photographer

the hand over the finger—draw, paint, and let yourself go. Become a universal visual man."[86] This interest no doubt also derived from his work environment and the exposure he had to fields such as motion pictures.

Very few professional photographers worked only with still cameras. For example, Magnum photographers like Haas often worked on movie sets because such locations provided lucrative work for the agency. Haas photographed location shoots as well as movie sets for magazines and was one of the eight Magnum photographers to participate in an important agency contract to photograph the Reno location set of John Huston's film *The Misfits* (1960; fig. 4.28).[87] His set photographic style varied but included working in the idiom in which he took his bullfight photos, as in an image of Robert Wise's *West Side Story* (1960; fig. 4.29).[88]

Magazine photographers did more than take still photos on movie sets, and they were especially influential when it came to working with color.

Eliot Elisofon, for example, worked as a "color consultant" for the films *Moulin Rouge* (1952, dir. John Huston) and *The Greatest Story Ever Told* (1965, dir. George Stevens) (where Haas also took set photos). Avedon exercised an important visual artistic influence on the set of the Paramount musical *Funny Face,* based in no small measure on his knowledge of color. By the time of the shoot in 1956, he had become the image of the fashion photographer enough to serve as the model for the one played by Fred Astaire in the film, which opened in February 1957. And Avedon was the perfect photographer to be played by Fred Astaire. He regularly attended the theater, loved watching dance, studied dance, and was known to be an excellent dancer himself. He said, "I wanted to grow up and be Fred Astaire, that burst of energy, you're twenty-one, twenty-two. I mean I couldn't start a portrait studio. I loved to dance, to move . . . I just liked moving."[89] He also had photographed dancers early in his career and used dancers to lay out his fashion shoots before he turned to his models.

Funny Face contends with the art of capturing motion and making it into pictures via its use of color. Avedon's role extended far beyond his serving as a consultant to assure there were no errors in portraying the work and habits of photographers. This image of Avedon and Astaire on the set of *Funny Face,* published in *Harper's Bazaar,* suggests that the film did more than simply depict an Avedon-like protagonist (fig. 4.30). With the flip of a lightbox switch, and by placing a large-format negative of Audrey Hepburn's face on top, with a Rolleiflex and a set of grease pencils adorning the box to the right, Astaire sings the film's eponymous title song (fig. 4.31). The sequence plays with the art not of "taking" pictures but of making them: laying them out, working with color, and transforming the

Fig. 4.31 Title sequence, *Funny Face,* 1957, directed by Stanley Donen. Paramount Pictures. DVD screen capture

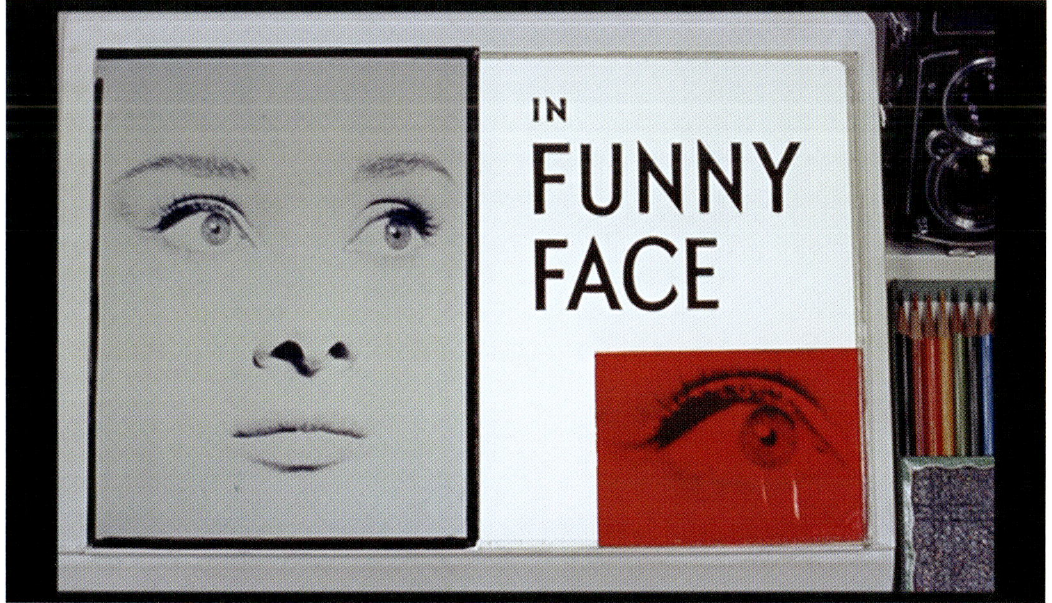

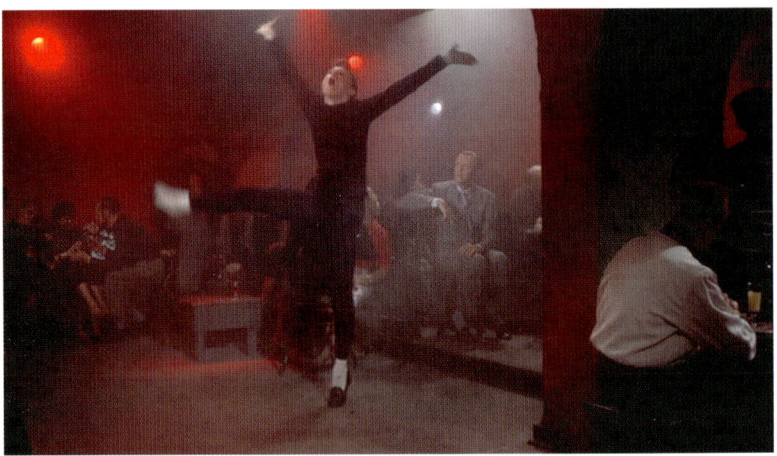

Fig. 4.32 In a dark nightclub with red lighting, from *Funny Face*. DVD screen capture

photographic image into a designed and printed object in a magazine. The film was also not a musical for nothing. It "choreographed" the photographer's actions and camera work as a form of dance—as an art in motion and color. Dance numbers highlight color photographic techniques: in Hepburn's bohemian dance, the lighting copies the use of blurred colored lights that Avedon had used in a Revlon ad campaign that also appeared on a record album (figs. 4.32—4.34); in a darkroom dance between Hepburn and Astaire under red light (not quite the appropriate darkroom lighting) the photographic process is also on display, and it ends up with Hepburn's actual face pinned against the light-table, which is then compared to the slightly overexposed portrait he had just developed. In "Think Pink," the magazine editor's song at the film's start, the VistaVision widescreen technology transforms the screen into a magazine spread—opened and laid out for a sumptuous display of commodities in the same color. For example, against a black background, big consumer objects such as shoes appear as if in an advertising campaign (fig. 4.35); in another tableau a group of three pink clad girls of successive sizes and their mother pop onto the canvas (fig. 4.36); and in yet another tableau a woman in pink chiffon slowly and luxuriously swings in and out of the frame in slow motion with the camera lingering on the fabric. The Paris location number, "Bonjour Paris," turns the screen into a color slideshow of a travel magazine such as *Holiday* (fig. 4.37).

Fashion photography mirrors filmmaking in the film, and the photographer becomes the director. The film's spectacular fashion show and its most dazzling and deliberate visual effects occur in the moment when Jo, the Hepburn character, assumes her role as a fashion model and actress to Astaire's director. She and Dick Avery go on location in the streets of Paris, and the photo shoot transforms into a film set. The photographer assumes the role of director as he establishes mock scenarios to set story, mood, and emotion, and directs her actions. In the sequence's most memorable vignette, filmed at the Louvre as Hepburn is coming down a set of stairs dressed in a red gown with *Winged Victory* behind her, Dick yells, "Stop,"

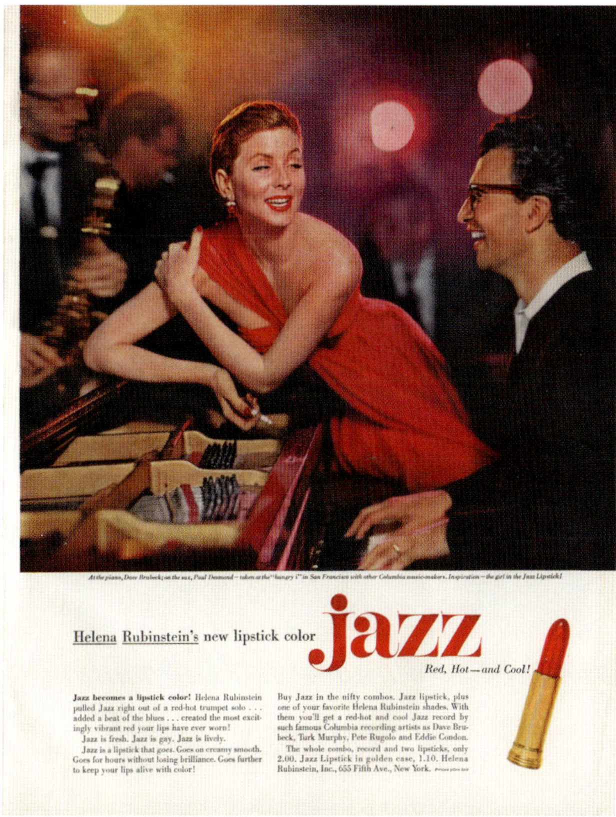

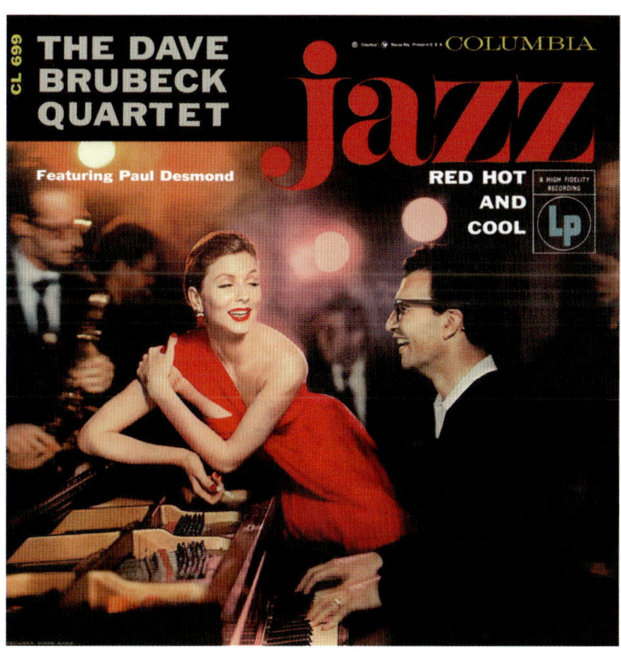

Figs. 4.33 and 4.34 Revlon advertisement, "Jazz," 1954. Album cover, "Jazz: Red Hot and Cool," Dave Brubeck Quartet, 1955. Columbia Records. Richard Avedon, photographer

Figs. 4.35 and 4.36 "Think Pink," *Funny Face*. DVD, screen captures

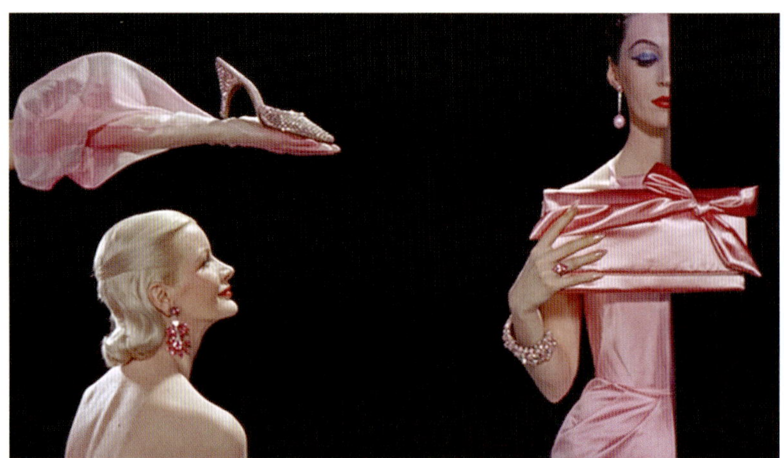

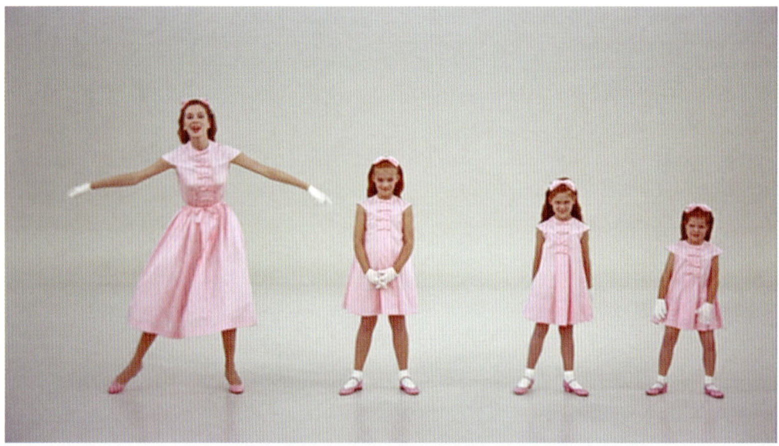

and she replies, "I don't want to stop. I like it. Take the picture. Take the picture" (fig. 4.38). In each of the Paris vignettes he freezes her motion with his shutter; the image goes from being a positive to a negative, and the image is filtered in a single color, or certain elements such as balloons or a coat are colored in and others left in black and white. The film emphasizes how color provides the visual form through which the traveling-dancing photographer-cum-film director can stop the moving subject and emphasize motion; the photograph remains stable while the colors change.

It was thus also not so unusual for Haas to get involved in a big-budget motion picture, although his arrangement was unusual. While Avedon's "camerawork" was surreptitious and advisory, Haas actually took up the moving picture camera himself and acted as what amounted to a second unit director precisely because of his photographic work in color and motion. When Dino de Lauretiis asked John Huston to direct an epic production of *The Bible,* the director turned to Haas to film the opening fifteen-minute sequence of the creation of the world. Haas went to far-off locations in Iceland with a crew of four, shooting volcanoes and waterfalls. Haas' enthusiasm

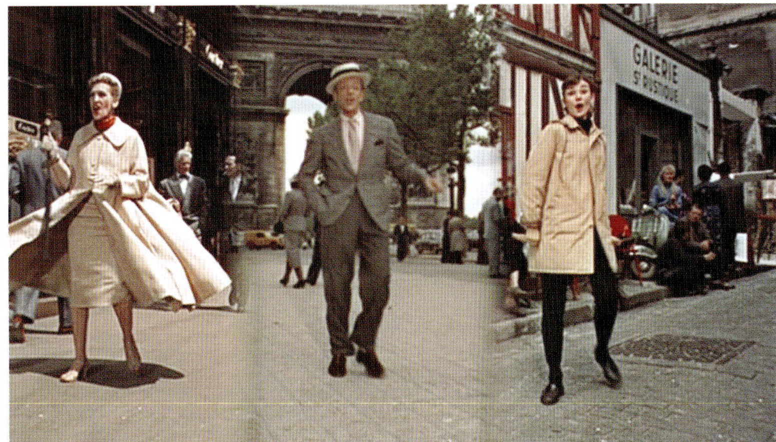

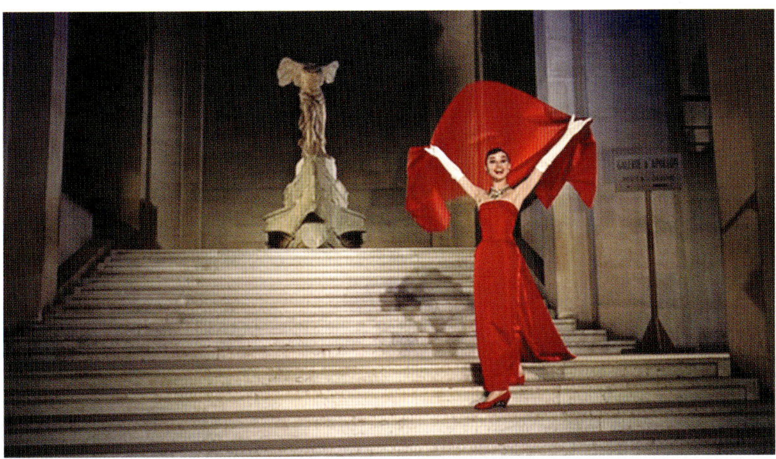

Fig. 4.37 "Bonjour Paris," *Funny Face*. DVD screen capture

Fig. 4.38 "Model in the Louvre," *Funny Face*. DVD screen capture

for handling a motion picture camera, as well as his inexperience, caused problems with Huston. In a 1964 telegraph from the director sent to Haas, who was in Ecuador, Huston complained, "Rushes of last two film shipments sadly disappointing in both conception and execution. In fact, nothing since Iceland. . . . Spoiled by amateur panning and zooming. Stop. You would agree on seeing that material falls far short of our aims and your capabilities. Stop. Sorry to Convey These Sad Tidings John Huston."[90] Perhaps the transition from still photographer to movie director was not as seamless as Haas had hoped, and although Huston may have been disappointed with Haas' work, his sequence came to define the film's visually significant contribution, which was often singled out in reviews. It appeared that Haas, finally able to film things that moved, had a free hand (fig. 4.39). The film opens with blurs of color that eventually take shape as clouds, and we see the creation of the heavens. One reviewer described the opening sequence as the film's "most imaginative and successful portion" and noted that it was shot by Haas, whom he described as the film's second unit director.[91] Images that Haas took from this project became the core for his 1971 photobook *The Creation*.

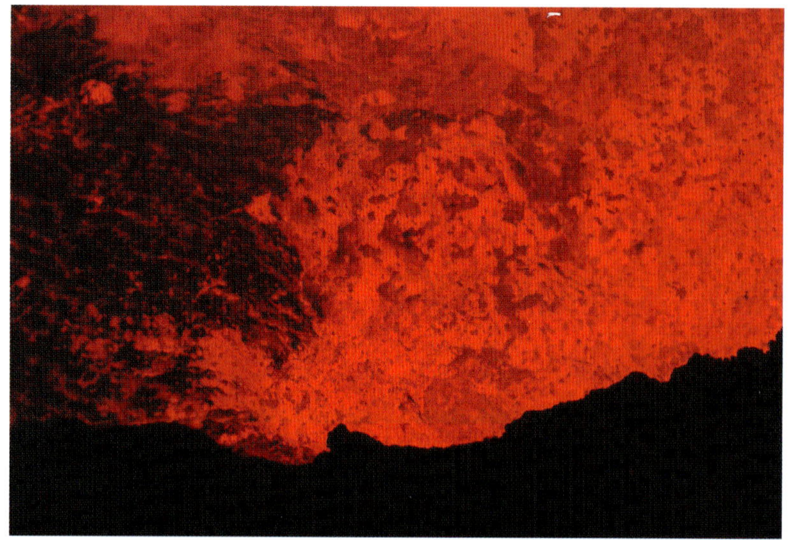

Fig. 4.39 "In the Beginning" sequence, from *The Bible,* 1964, directed by John Huston. 20th Century Fox. Ernst Haas, photographer, Getty Images

During the period under examination here, Haas exemplifies how magazines could use color in their editorial pages to capture their age. Haas' work could communicate the experience of motion while also establishing a subjective, personal, and sensational vision of it. If the jet set was proof that everyone and anyone could be in motion and the world was sent spinning and the social order reshuffled like a deck of beautiful people in pretty pictures, color photography as Haas employed it offered magazine readers the opportunity to experience the sensation of motion through the sensationalism of color. At a more mundane level, color also offered news photographers like Haas and Avedon new materials that allowed them to move between media such as widescreen Technicolor film and color television while keeping magazines visually fresh as they vied to describe the present and engage the public's attention.

Color news photographs did not simply deliver more information about the world in the 1960s, although they did offer more description, which in a journalistic setting became a pretext for using color film. For Haas, it was something different to work in color. Haas explained that "I try to find my inside image in the outside reality."[92] By considering color photography through the eyes of Ernst Haas we can understand the way that photojournalism in the jet age helped reorient the entire field of journalism toward the more subjective and expressive style of the New Journalism. Color pictures changed the written expression. It should come as no surprise that one of the classic essays of New Journalism, Tom Wolfe's famous 1963 *Esquire* essay, would be loaded with color in its title: "There Goes (Varoom! Varoom!) That Kandy Kolored (Thphhhhhh!) Tangerine-Flake Streamline Baby (Rahghhhh!) Around the Bend (Brummmmmmmmmmmmmmmmm . . .)." Perhaps these Haas images were his visual inspiration (fig. 4.40). Motion, Haas noted in his television program, was "the pulse of life itself." Color in motion, however, was not fluid or sensationless; it became sensational. Too sensational perhaps for the art critics then and ever since, but perhaps such sensation also worked to reassure those skeptics who might have doubted the promises and dreams of the jet age aesthetic that would soon, literally, come screeching to a halt.

Fig. 4.40 "Adventure in New Camera Realm," *Life*, August 18, 1958, 50–51. Ernst Haas, photographer

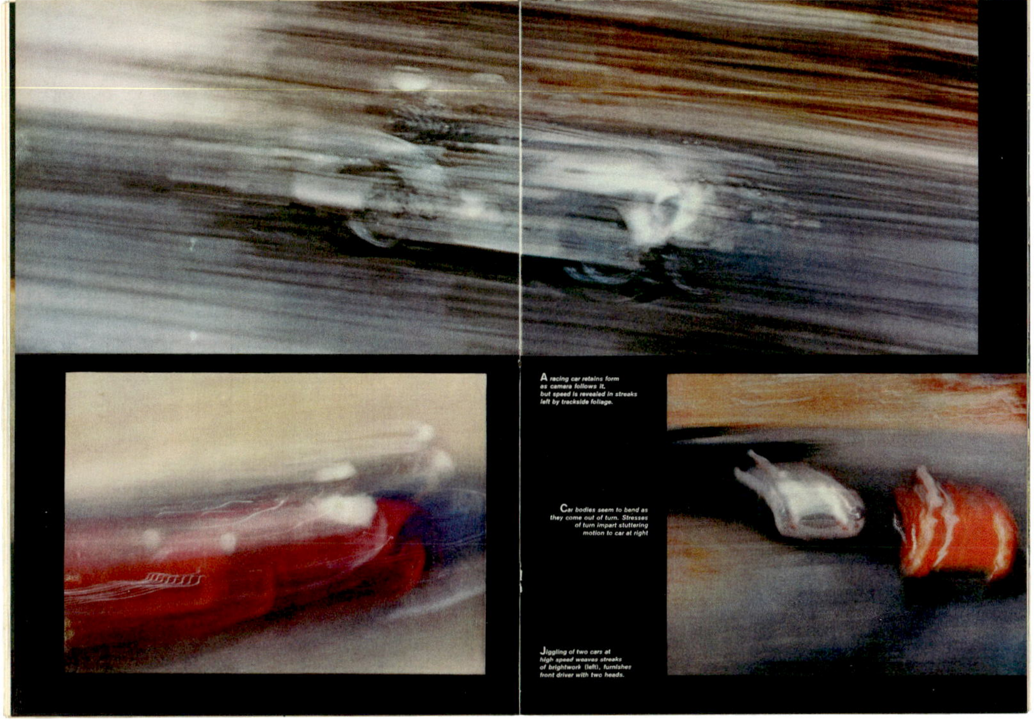

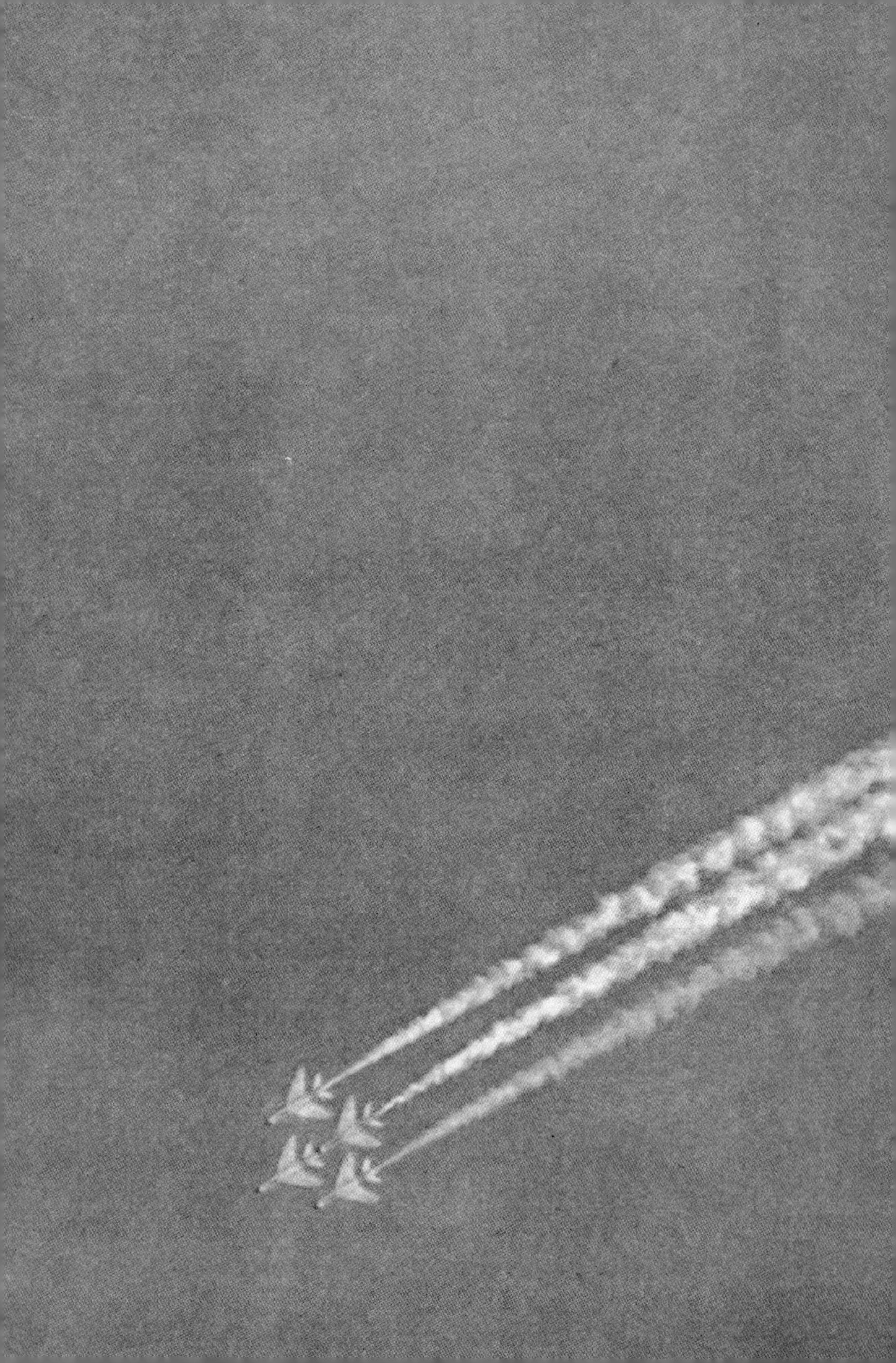

Conclusion

Writing well after the arrival of the jet, during the period when even the jumbo 747 had already become banal and the Concorde had taken flight, Andy Warhol remarked, "Airplanes and airports have my favorite kind of food service, my favorite kind of bathrooms . . . my favorite kinds of entertainment . . . my favorite conveyor belts, my favorite graphics and colors, the best security checks, the best views . . . the best optimism."[1] Warhol, the great artist of the everyday, described air travel as having a total design aesthetic, but with this book I have attempted to dig more deeply into describing why it could come to define a moment and what it really meant.

It was not a foregone conclusion that Warhol would have such a positive association with the jet or think of it as optimistic, or, for that matter, that anyone else would. We may have begun this book by observing the stuttering takeoff of the jet with BOAC's Comet, but the Boeing 707 had its challenges as well. In fact, even Warhol depicted it as a deathtrap. In 1962, Warhol began his "death and disaster series" with *129 Die in Jet!* (fig. 5.1) using the headline from the worst crash the 707 had experienced since 1958. On board Air France flight 007 was the entire board of the Atlanta Art Museum and many other cultural luminaries of that city. It was to depart Orly for the United States on June 3, 1962, after a tour of European cities. The plane crashed on takeoff, killing all on board except for two crew members. It was the first time that more than one hundred passengers had died in one crash, and it occurred in full view at the sparkling new airport. Why, despite the catastrophic deaths of these high-profile passengers, and the crash's memorialization in haunting and caustic art by the likes of Warhol, did people still fly? Is this the more "true" picture of the jet age than the optimistic visions of sailing above the weather and a life of fluid motion and constant circulation that has been depicted in this book?

Let me answer by turning to another Ernst Haas image, an ad for Delco-Remy from the 1960s (fig. 5.2). The company had little to do with the jet business. As a division of General Motors, it made alternators and motor parts (and still does). In the Haas photo, we see mostly an open blue sky, and tucked into the bottom left corner four tiny jets (not passenger 707s, but military jets) leaving beautiful smoke trails of "wake" naturalized into

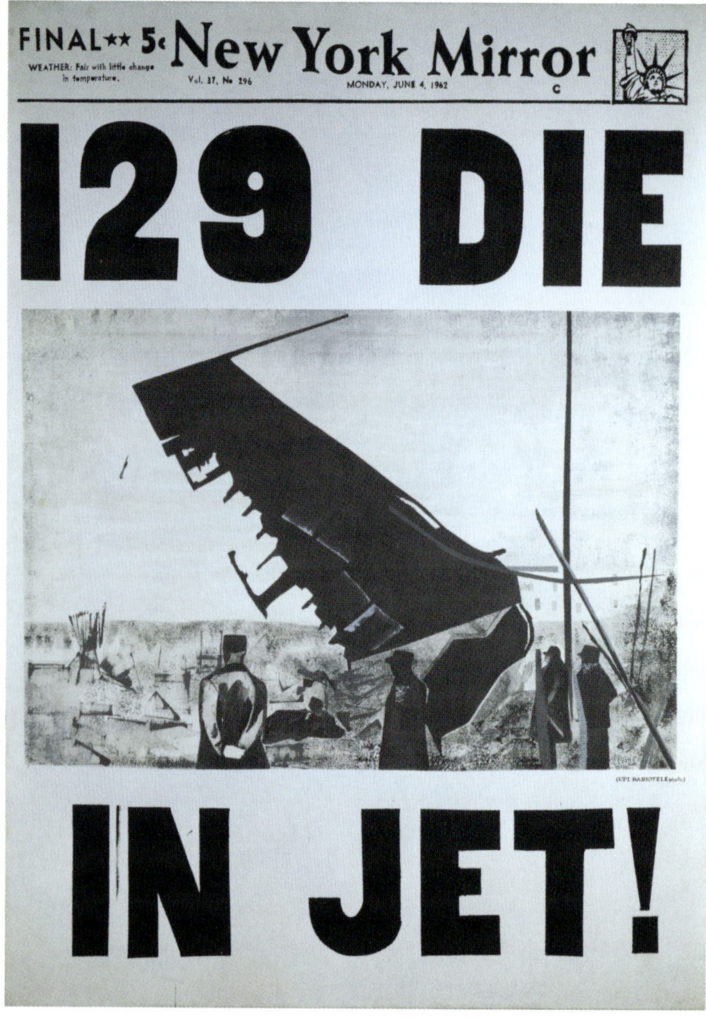

Fig. 5.1 Andy Warhol, *129 Die in Jet! (Plane Crash)*, 1962. Acrylic and pencil on linen

looking like clouds. They offer an elegant and sleek image of fluid motion, while also reminding us that the photo will record this trail of motion that will soon dissipate into the sky, leaving no trace. It is a pretty picture indeed.

The decade of the jet age came to an end, but no form of transport has outpaced the jet. Simultaneously, the jet age aesthetic changed us and helped prepare us for the world we currently inhabit. If seen as a story of optimism and excitement in a vision of air travel as pure flow, we know the jet age is long gone. In fact, one could see Arthur Hailey's best-selling novel of 1968, *Airport,* and its runaway hit film version of 1970, as signs that in only the few short years since *The VIPs* the public image of flying had changed remarkably. Rather than an assembly of elites, the people on this plane are a geriatric stowaway, a bomb-carrying maniac, and a pilot and stewardess engaging in an extramarital affair. Danger erupts in the skies. The weather—a huge snowstorm—has hobbled the airport team's ability to clear a runway of a banked plane so that a crippled 707 can land safely. Community activists, in the meantime, complaining about the "jet whine" caused by the takeoff and landing of the planes, had already forced the closure of the airport's only other runway. At the end of the day only the crazy passenger dies and the ground crew saves the day, and the film could use Frank Sinatra's song "Come Fly with Me" only as a sick joke. There did not seem to be anything glamorous or fluid about this ride.

The success of jet travel and its mass expansion presented material challenges as public expectations regarding the easy mobility of the early jet age years were dashed by airports that failed to keep up with the demands of people-moving on the ground.[2] At the same time, such freedom of movement also led to the era of skyjacking, which itself shows how symbolically meaningful such freedom was in the first place. Although the first plane was taken in 1961, the period 1967 to 1972 became the heyday of skyjackings, and terror in the sky remains one of the greatest forms of political and social violence used today. The new security-controlled airport is, without doubt, a concrete response to the limits of jet age visions of fluid motion and experiments in people-moving in real space.[3]

But to focus on airports or to say that the jet age failed or to think only about whether jet travel is still glamorous misses the larger achievement of the jet age aesthetic, which was never simply about moving people through airports. The history of this new aesthetic, wrapped in the dawn of a transport age and recounted here, shows that such transport was part of a communications network of spaces, experiences, and images. What the jet created was a kind of motion that it and other media of the period glamorized and celebrated: that you could go fast and have a sense of actually not moving at all—fluid motion. This aesthetic created "jet age people" who could better mediate between the material and image worlds, saw less antagonism between the

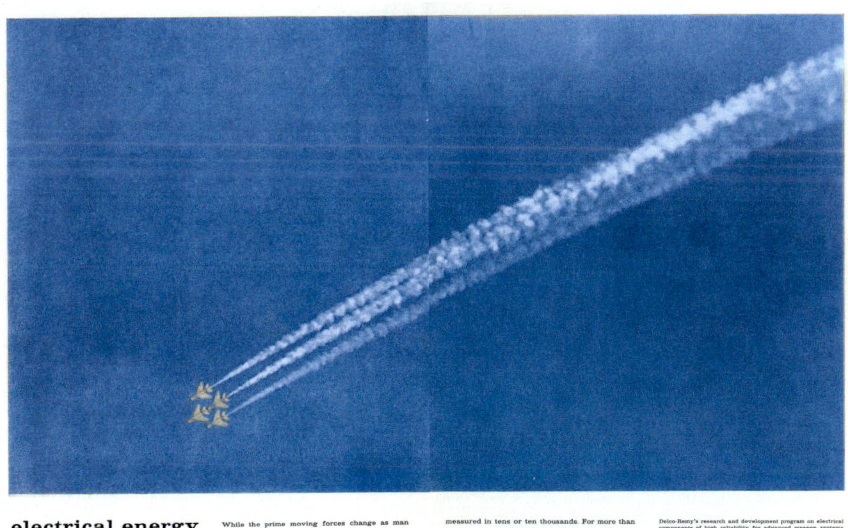

Fig. 5.2 Delco-Remy advertisement, 1960s. Ernst Haas, photographer

human and the technological spheres, and were comfortable rather than distressed at seeing themselves as spectators of their changing world. The jet age may not have invented or created these qualities, as they have also been associated with the longer history of "modern life." But the jet came to define an "age" in its own time because its impact on consciousness made a significant contribution not only through the reality of people taking to the air and traveling as never before but also by changing how people experienced life on the ground in new spaces and visual representations.

By the 1960s, the "network society" had begun to emerge as a commonplace concept or phrase among sociologists and has since been incorporated into most fields in the qualitative social sciences and the humanities. Although derived from the work of such turn-of-the-twentieth-century sociologists of modernity as Georg Simmel, more recent work by Manuel Castells has identified not just the fact of connectedness but also certain connections such as those made by technology, especially mass media and telecommunications, as the basis for contemporary social interaction and organization.[4] The concept of the network society deemphasizes the centrality of physical co-presence. In Castells' rendition, virtuality stands in for materiality. The technological mediation of form is an initial step toward the condition that media theorists describe as "intermediality" and "convergence culture"—in which content flows across media platforms.[5] This study has shown the emergence of the network society from the jet age aesthetic.

The period of the jet age also reorganized how intellectuals thought about and approached the study of technology, media, and aesthetics. In the decade before the jet, the "two cultures" debate notoriously emerged in intellectual discourse; it opposed art, on the one hand, with science and technology, on the other.[6] By the mid-1960s, astute observers such as Susan Sontag had pointed to the links between new transport technology and other media, as well as to the creation of a new sensorium. She identified the centrality of speed, giving examples about the physical speed of airplane travel and also remarking on the speed of film images and the "pan-cultural perspective on the arts that is possible through the mass reproduction of art objects," which can be thought of as a description of the globalization of culture through its reproducibility and circulation.[7] Sontag's essay "One Culture and the New Sensibility" spoke of a new unitary culture in order to dispute C. P. Snow's model on the development of two cultures, one of science and the other of the arts. She rightly grasped that an older literary culture and the cultural hierarchies it conveyed were being replaced by vibrant visual and performing arts cultures "which draw . . . on science and technology."[8] Whereas art had once served a ritual function, religious and then secular (on behalf of the state) art, Sontag included a much broader swath of culture than people such as Snow would have allowed, and it would organize a new sensory regime.[9]

Sontag was of a generation for whom questions about the role of technology and culture had become central. Slightly earlier, in the mid- to late 1950s,

Lawrence Alloway, dubbed by art critic Clement Greenberg as a "sectarian champion of most things American" and who as a young man became a key figure in the Independent Group at London's Institute of Contemporary Arts (ICA), articulated such an approach to culture before Sontag did. Alloway's intellectual agenda emerged from the technological climate of his moment, especially the advent of the jet. He refused such binary distinctions long before anyone was really talking about network theory, because his experience living as a part of jet culture changed the way he thought.[10] Alloway eradicated formal hierarchies in favor of intermedial connections and trained a keen and even favorable eye on the way technology shaped aesthetic experience.[11] In 1959, Alloway advocated that something like techno-aesthetics would be entirely salutary: "One reason for the failure of the humanists to keep their grip on public values . . . is their failure to handle technology, which is both transforming our environment and, through its product the mass media, our ideas about the world and about ourselves."[12]

The Pop critics, including Alloway and others at the think-tank-like environment at the ICA, grasped the heterogeneity of a newly abundant material culture as well as the relation between technology and culture. They were thinkers and producers young enough to enjoy the excitement of contemporary culture, which they envisioned as emphasizing novelty, disposability, movement, and America. They owed the existence of the ICA to an earlier generation of artists and critics, such as Roland Penrose and Herbert Read, who had been bathed in Surrealism, Paris, and the values of the Museum of Modern Art (MoMA). Their interest in technology, technologically mediated images, and things as well as expendability was not entirely unprecedented. The Futurists in the early decades of the twentieth century had shared such preoccupations, as had MoMA, which, influenced by the Bauhaus, held an exhibition in 1934 called "Machine Art," in dialogue with such important historical works as Lewis Mumford's *Technics and Civilization* and Read's *Art and Industry: The Principles of Industrial Design.*[13]

Unlike the earlier generation, the Pop critics wanted to know how art related to their own time rather than to all time. To legitimate such an orientation, critics such as Alloway sought to redefine culture toward an anthropological sense of the term, as a "complex of human activity." Alloway turned to the popular arts rather than to folk culture, which many anthropologists sought to describe as having timeless and eternal qualities. British intellectuals such as Richard Hoggart and the Birmingham School (founded in 1964) also had an anthropological orientation, but they fit into the nostalgic, anti–mass culture camp that fretted over the loss of traditional folk culture in the face of rapid change. The Pop critics, on the other hand, had something very different to say.

Alloway was interested in the ephemeral. "Everything that in our culture changes is the material of the popular arts," he posited, which led him to advocate for the study of such cultural forms as film not as an artform manqué but rather as a modern popular art.[14] He also embraced culture that moved fast: he saw culture as a continuum or "flat-bed visual field" and an "expendable multitude of signs."[15] Alloway believed the mass arts were one of the most remarkable and characteristic achievements of industrial society, and he celebrated their emphasis on anticlassicism.[16] Mass culture moved as fast as the jet.

If the mass arts for Alloway concerned that which changed, he also insisted in a later essay, "The Long Front of Culture," that to understand culture, the critic needed to concentrate not on production, but on reception and consumption. What was the "long front" of culture? As Jacob Bronowski put it, when he spoke at the ICA in 1951 of the relation of art and science, scholars had "come to the stage in structure where [they thought] it more interesting to look for the relations between objects than [at] the objects themselves."[17] The continuum that Alloway envisioned was a network.

Art, for Alloway, could not be separated from other visual means of communication; instead, it became part of a nonhierarchical system of public information. Although Alloway is well known to those who study the origins of Pop Art, his views are as important to twentieth-century media theories as those of the Frankfurt School, French semiotics, the Birmingham School, and American cultural studies because of his particular concerns regarding networks of media culture. His views are also of great importance in understanding the link between the origins of the network society and the jet age aesthetic.

Alloway wrote during a period of remarkable geographic mobility, due in no small measure to the expansion of air travel facilitated by the arrival of the jet. In fact, he met the dawn of the jet age by hopping a jet and visiting the United States for the first time in 1958; he would visit several times before moving there in 1961.[18] Alloway redefined culture across space, beyond national borders, and as traversing media forms because he was literally more mobile by virtue of living in the jet age. This development, I suggest, made it easier to reimagine the operations of visual media as part of a global network, and this moment has shaped not only mass media but also our study of it ever since. He envisioned a system of hubs with resonant points of connection that characterize what we think of today as global culture by embracing his experience of his visits to America not as particular and provincial but as the harbinger of a new universal—and not necessarily homogeneous—culture.

Throughout this study, jet age theorists such as Alloway and Daniel Boorstin, whose own life experiences motivated their devotion and insights into the remaking of aesthetic experience through technology, allow us to locate the emergence of a jet age aesthetic in the period under examination and, at the same time, to understand that period in genealogical relation to our own. They offer excellent theoretical guidance as we move from terrains to networks, out of national media cultures and into the circulation of a global visual and environmental culture, where connections and systems rather than national distinction and competition underlie our principal frameworks of interrogation.

This book has recovered a rich period of the history of the relation of technology to culture and experience. But it has one more ambition, which is to locate the history of the interdisciplinary field of visual studies in which the project is grounded. I suggest that the emergence of the field of visual studies hinges upon the very changes—material, technological, and intellectual—of the jet age itself, rather than the critiques of the commodity form associated with the Frankfurt School to which so many studies of mass-mediated visual culture are traced. In that way, I hope to contribute to how scholars can study not only what I have studied but why I have studied it the way I have. It offers a framework for moving beyond how theorists in the nineteenth century asked questions, defined fields of study, and chose objects deemed worthy of intellectual scrutiny.

This study is a cultural history of a moment's popular aesthetic and has continuing implications for our own present media culture and how to study it. It takes a flat-bed visual field not as a modernist picture plane but as a cultural continuum, which is what Alloway describes. It engages with a host of fields of study but does not rest comfortably in any. This approach does not "flatten," as art historians might fret, or study something "epiphenomenal" (treating culture as a reflection of something more real, like economics or politics, the way historians often treat representation), nor do I believe it approaches its objects without the skill, knowledge, or expertise to handle them, but that will have to be left to the readers to judge.

Neither the subject of motion nor the mediation of experience is unique to the jet age. These are elements of human social organization that have taken particular shape and importance in modern capitalist societies. Yet the jet named an "age" because of something much more than the increase in air travel or even the speed that made it possible to travel long distances. The jet defined its moment and ushered in our own. The jet age aesthetic created globalization at the level of subjective experience. It was only a matter of time before we could go to Disneyland on the other side of the continent or go to the other side of the world or go somewhere in our heads guided by external images without physically going anywhere at all. The jet age produced the individuals who would create the internet and immersive virtual media, not only those people who are now stuck in airports. The glamour of media in motion continues as we develop a twenty-first-century techno-aesthetics in which we seem to be extending human life on earth, while planetary changes that used to happen very slowly seem to be happening very fast. The news cycle is now constant, as are workdays and working hours, store hours and shopping hours. The jet age may have altered our sense of time for good. We are moving so fast that time may appear to have telescoped into an eternal present.[19] But it would be a shame indeed if, as a result, we have produced a world with no future. That is why I wanted to give this story a past.

Notes

ABBREVIATIONS

The following abbreviations appear throughout the Notes:

ADP: Archives of the Aéroports de Paris, Orly

DOA: Los Angeles Department of Airports

LAX: Los Angeles International Airport

NYHS: New-York Historical Society

NYPL: New York Public Library

NYWF: New York World's Fair

WDA: Walt Disney Archives

INTRODUCTION

1. William Pereira, "Airports, Planes and People," *Journal of the Air Transport Division: Proceedings of the American Society of Civil Engineers* (December 1957): Paper 1476, 2.

2. David M. Potter, *People of Plenty: Economic Abundance and the American Character* (Chicago: University of Chicago Press, 1954), 25.

3. Thomas Hine, *Populuxe: From Tailfins and TV Dinners to Barbie Dolls and Fallout Shelters* (New York: Knopf, 1986).

4. *Boys' Life*, May 1955, 59. For more on architecture and the future, see Donna Goodman, *A History of the Future* (New York: Monacelli, 2008) and Alastair Gordon, *Spaced Out: Radical Environments of the Psychedelic Sixties* (New York: Rizzoli, 2008).

5. See, for example, "Jet Propulsion Launches a New Era in Man's Locomotion," *Life*, November 27, 1944, 47–53; Rhodri Windsor-Liscombe, "Usual Culture: The Jet," *Topia* 11 (2004): 83–99.

6. *Ephémeride*, September 12, 1958. ADP. Jets travel about 505 miles per hour on average. The 707 flew on average as fast as if not faster than jets fly today because current jets carry a heavier load and are more mindful of fuel economy.

7. William D. Perreault and Anthony Vanduyk, "Did the Jet Age Come Too Soon?" *Life*, January 25, 1954, 51–52. For a general history of the rise of the jet plane, see Sam Howe Verhovek, *Jet Age: The Comet, the 707, and the Race to Shrink the World* (New York: Penguin/Avery, 2010). At the same time, behind the Iron Curtain, the Soviets flew the Tupolev Tu-104, which became the only jet to fly between 1956 and 1958, although it also had its share of accidents. Flying in the Soviet Union remained a carefully managed government program during the Cold War.

8. R. E. G. Davies, *Airlines of the Jet Age: A History* (Washington: Smithsonian, 2011), 36.

9. The history of tourism is a large field, but the definitive study of the impact of the jet remains to be written. A good place to start is Eric Zuelow, *A History of Modern Tourism* (London: Palgrave, 2016).

10. This is why, for example, Air India was one of the first all-jet carriers and why El-Al, Israel's national carrier, served an important role in national development.

11. Daniel Rust, *Flying Across America: The Airline Passenger Experience* (Norman: University of Oklahoma Press, 2009), 190–92.

12. *Le Monde Economique, Special Issue. World Air Transport in the Jet Age* (Paris, 1959), 9.

13. Verhovek, *Jet Age*, 187.

14. "12-Hour World: First American Jet Airline," *Newsweek*, March 8, 1954, 48.

15. American Airlines Brochure, "Welcome Aboard Your American Flagship" (1959), 13. San Francisco International Airport Archives.

16. *Fodor's Jet Age Guide to Europe, 1959* (The Hague: David McKay, 1959), 27.

17. Martin Caidin, *Boeing 707* (New York: Ballantine, 1959), 74.

18. The first passenger jets were the BOAC Comet, which went in and out of service beginning in 1952 due to a series of crashes, and the Tupolev TU-104, which flew within the Soviet Union exclusively between 1956 and 1958. See Davies, *Airlines of The Jet Age*.

19. Sinatra's feeling about the album cover is discussed in George Martin and Jeremy Hornsby, *All You Need Is Ears* (New York: St. Martin's, 1979), 144–5. The song was composed in 1957 by Jimmy Van Heusen with lyrics by Sammy Cahn.

20. Lawrence Azzerad, *Concorde* (Prestel, 2018). The SST flying at Mach II known as Concorde flew for twenty-six years beginning in 1976 in a very small segment of the market. Its cost and the environmental implications of the sonic boom put great limits on its routes. The spectacular July 2000 crash, which killed all 109 passengers, convinced Air France and British Airways to end the service permanently in 2003. For the more conventional histories of aviation, see Jenifer Van Vleck, *Empire of the Air: Aviation and the American Ascendancy* (Cambridge: Harvard University Press, 2013); Roger E. Bilstein, *Flight in America, 1900–1983: From the Wrights to the Astronauts* (Baltimore: Johns Hopkins University Press, 1984); Joseph J. Corn, *The Winged Gospel: America's Romance with Aviation* (Baltimore: Johns Hopkins University Press, 2002); Tom D. Crouch, *Wings: A History of Aviation from Kites to the Space Age* (Washington: Smithsonian, 2003).

21. Roland Barthes, *Mythologies*, trans. Richard Howard (New York: Hill and Wang, 2012; original French 1957), 103.

22. George Nelson, "Architecture for the New Itinerants," *Saturday Review*, April 22, 1967, 31.

23. See Jason Weems, *Barnstorming the Prairies: How Aerial Vision Shaped the Midwest* (Minneapolis: University of Minnesota Press, 2015).

24. Fortunately, that has been described. Alistair Gordon, *Naked Airport* (Chicago: University of Chicago Press, 2004); *Airworld: Design and Architecture for Air Travel* (Weil am Rhein: Vitra Design Museum, 2004); Gregory Votolato, *Transport Design: A Travel History* (London: Reaktion, 2007); Alex Taylor, "Flying Machines: Alexander Calder and the Sensations of the Jet Age" (unpublished paper); Keith Lovegrove, *Airline: Identity,*

Design and Culture (London: Laurence King, 2000); M. C. Hühne, *Airline Visual Identity, 1945–1975* (Berlin: Callisto, 2015); M. C. Hühne, *Pan Am: History, Design and Identity* (Berlin: Callisto, 2017); Roger Bezombes, "Air France: A New Series of Airline Posters," *Graphis* 37, no. 218 (March 1982): 498–501; Georg Gerster, *Swissair Posters* (Munich: Schirmer/Mosel, 2006); Pedro Gentil-Homem and Leonor Ferrão, "A Design Laboratory Above the Clouds: Black and White and Color Stories of Portugal's Airline (1945–1979)," *Design Issues* 31, no. 2 (Spring 2015): 72–87.

25. Giuliana Bruno, *Atlas of Emotion: Journeys in Art, Architecture, and Film* (London: Verso: 2002), 6. See also Pamela M. Lee, *Chronophobia: On Time in the Art of the 1960s* (Cambridge: MIT Press, 2004); Stephen Petersen, *Space-Age Aesthetics: Lucio Fontana, Yves Klein, and the Postwar European Avant-Garde* (University Park: Pennsylvania State University Press, 2009).

26. Some claim that the main distinction in the study of media and technology is between those who see the interdependence of humans and tools as a co-evolutionary scheme and those who adopt a post-humanist framework, a media studies version of Bruno Latour's actor-network theory, championed by Friedrich Kittler. Whatever one's sense of the relation between people and their tools, few doubt the central value of those technologies that have facilitated the movement of people and goods in history. See John Durham Peters, *The Marvelous Clouds: Toward a Philosophy of Elemental Media* (Chicago: University of Chicago Press, 2015).

27. See Daniel J. Czitrom, *Media and the American Mind: From Morse to McLuhan* (Chapel Hill: University of North Carolina Press, 1982), 3.

28. *Letters of Marshall McLuhan* as cited by Richard Cavell, "On the 50th Anniversary of Understanding Media," *Journal of Visual Culture* 13, no. 1 (April 2014): 33–35.

29. Marshall McLuhan, *Understanding Media: The Extensions of Man* (Cambridge, MIT Press, 1994), 213, 198.

30. See Erika Doss, *Looking at Life Magazine* (Washington: Smithsonian, 2001) for the best of the ideological readings of magazines. An alternative approach is taken in Jason E. Hill and Vanessa R. Schwartz, eds., *Getting the Picture: The Visual Culture of the News* (London: Bloomsbury, 2015).

31. Shelley Rice, "Lawrence Alloway's Spatial Utopia: Contemporary Photography as 'Horizontal Description,'" *Tate Papers*, no. 16 (Autumn 2011), https://www.tate.org.uk/research/publications/tate-papers/16/lawrence-alloway-spatial-utopia-contemporary-photography-as-horizontal-description, paragraph 12.

32. The literature on this subject is vast. Histories of global circumnavigation have considered how distance and spatial conquest stood as measures of a culture's relative power and achievement on a global scale. See, among others, Joyce E. Chaplin, *Round About the Earth: Circumnavigation from Magellan to Orbit* (New York: Simon and Schuster, 2012); Marc Desportes, *Paysages en mouvement: Transports et perception de l'espace, XVIIIe—XXe siècle* (Paris: Gallimard, 2005); Jürgen Osterhammel and Niels P. Petersson, *Globalization: A Short History* (Princeton: Princeton University Press, 2009); and Lynn Hunt, *Writing History in the Global Era* (New York: Norton, 2014); and Enda Duffy, ed., *The Speed Handbook: Velocity, Pleasure, Modernism* (Durham: Duke University Press, 2009).

33. Thomas Friedman, *The World Is Flat: A Brief History of the Twenty-First Century* (New York: Farrar, Straus and Giroux, 2005). For an interesting summary of the anti-globalization new consensus, see Nikil Saval, "Globalisation: The Rise and Fall of an Idea That Swept the World," *Guardian*, July 14, 2017; William J. Bernstein, *A Splendid Exchange: How Trade Shaped the Modern World* (New York: Atlantic Monthly Press, 2008). For limits to such paradigms, see Rogers Brubaker, *Citizenship and Nationhood in France and Germany* (Cambridge: Harvard University Press, 1994); Naomi Davidson, *Only Muslim: Embodying Islam in Twentieth-Century France* (Ithaca: Cornell University Press, 2012); and Dominic Thomas, *Africa and France: Postcolonial Cultures, Migration, and Racism* (Bloomington: Indiana University Press, 2013). On historiography, see Lynn Hunt, *Writing History in the Global Era* (New York: Norton, 2014).

34. Mobility studies, on the other hand, takes up the question of movement and circulation but can be more focused on the present or schematic in its relation to history because it is sociologically inclined. Especially important for this study has been Tim Cresswell, *On the Move: Mobility in the Modern Western World* (London: Routledge, 2006) and John Urry, *Mobilities* (Cambridge: Polity, 2007).

35. Edward Berenson, *Heroes of Empire: Five Charismatic Men and the Conquest of Africa* (Berkeley: University of California Press, 2010); Sylvain Veynayre, *La gloire de l'aventure: Genèse d'une mystique moderne, 1850–1940* (Paris: Aubier, 2002); Shelley Baranowski and Ellen Furlough, eds., *Being Elsewhere: Tourism, Consumer Culture and Identity in Modern Europe and North America* (Ann Arbor: University of Michigan Press, 2001); and Catherine Bertho-Lavenir, *La roue et le stylo: La roue et le stylo* (Paris: Odile Jacob, 1999).

36. Kay Dian Kriz, *Slavery, Sugar, and the Culture of Refinement: Picturing the British West Indies, 1700–1840* (New Haven: Yale University Press, 2008); Sharon Sliwinski, *Human Rights in Camera* (Chicago: University of Chicago Press, 2011); Megan Luke, *Kurt Schwitters: Space, Image, Exile* (Chicago: University of Chicago Press, 2014); Nancy J. Troy, *The Afterlife of Piet Mondrian* (Chicago: University of Chicago Press, 2013); and Debora L. Silverman, "Art Nouveau, Art of Darkness: African Lineages of Belgian Modernism, Part 1," *West 86th* 18, no. 2 (Fall–Winter 2011): 139–81. An exception is Daniela Bleichmar, *Visible Empire: Botanical Expeditions and Visual Culture in the Hispanic Enlightenment* (Chicago: University of Chicago Press, 2012), which is much more oriented to the visual aspect of knowledge construction.

37. Caroline A. Jones, *The Global Work of Art: World's Fairs, Biennials and the Aesthetics of Experience* (Chicago: University of Chicago Press, 2017), Winnie Wong, *Van Gogh On Demand: China and the Readymade* (Chicago: University of Chicago Press, 2014).

38. Jennifer L. Roberts, *Transporting Visions: The Movement of Images in Early America* (Berkeley: University of California Press, 2014). If Roberts' analysis assumes a "before" model, this book poses the opposite experience at a much later date. See also Daniela Bleichmar and Meredith Martin, eds., *Objects in Motion* (London: Wiley-Blackwell, 2016).

39. We need to study technology as historical phenomena and as contingent rather than as "media archaeologies" that re-essentialize form, producing a

neotechnological determinism. Erkki Huhtamo and Jussi Parikka, eds., *Media Archaeology* (Berkeley: University of California Press, 2011); See also Braxton Soderman et al., "Circulating Concepts: Networks and Media Archaeology," *Amodern* 2 (October 2013).

40. Michael B. Miller, *Europe and the Maritime World* (Cambridge: Cambridge University Press, 2012); William J. Bernstein, *A Splendid Exchange: How Trade Shaped the Modern World* (New York: Atlantic Monthly, 2008); Nathan Perl-Rosenthal, *Citizen Sailors: Becoming American in the Age of Revolution* (Cambridge: Belknap, 2016).

41. Wolfgang Schivelbusch, *The Railway Journey: The Industrialization of Time and Space in the 19th Century* (Berkeley: University of California Press, 1986).

42. Building on Schivelbusch, an entire field of "virtual and mobile spectatorship" arose, including the work of Anne Friedberg, *Window Shopping: Cinema and the Postmodern* (Berkeley: University of California Press, 1993); Giuliana Bruno, *Streetwalking on a Ruined Map: Cultural Theory and the City Films of Elvira Notari* (Princeton: Princeton University Press, 1992); and Vanessa R. Schwartz, *Spectacular Realities: Early Mass Culture in Fin-de-Siècle Paris* (Berkeley: University of California Press, 1998). See also Jeffrey Ruoff, *Virtual Voyages: Cinema and Travel* (Durham: Duke University Press, 2006). Lynne Kirby argues that the train offered a proto-cinematic experience, see Kirby, *Parallel Tracks: The Railroad and Silent Cinema* (Durham: Duke University Press, 1997). This is also noted in Stephen Groening, *Cinema Beyond Territory: Inflight Entertainment and Atmospheres of Globalisation* (London: British Film Institute, 2014), 45.

43. See Matthieu Flonneau, *Les Cultures du volant: Essais sur les mondes de l'automobilisme* (Paris: Autrement, 2008) for how independent control of a speedy vehicle changed subjectivity; Mitchell Schwarzer, *Zoomscape: Architecture in Motion and Media* (New York: Princeton Architectural Press, 2004); and John Urry, *Mobilities* (London: Polity, 2007); Adnan Morshed, *Impossible Heights: Skyscrapers, Flight, and the Master Builder* (Minneapolis: University of Minnesota Press, 2015). For a local culture version of transport aesthetics, see Jason Weems, *Barnstorming the Prairies: How Aerial Vision Shaped the Midwest* (Minneapolis: University of Minnesota Press, 2015).

44. An excellent overview of Paul Virilio's early work is John Armitage, "Paul Virilio: An Introduction," *Theory, Culture and Society* 16, no. 5–6 (December 1999): 1–23. His books *Speed and Politics* (Cambridge: MIT, 2006), first published in France in 1977, and *War and Cinema: The Logics of Perception* (London: Verso, 1984), are the most germane here.

45. Aviation is divided into three major periods: the rise of aviation, the post–World War II rise of the jet, and the deregulation era. The field is divided among archival histories of planning and architecture, sociologically oriented works in the field of "mobility studies," and the recent "boom" in ethnographically oriented studies of "airportness." For the latter, see especially the three descriptive books of Christopher Schaberg, starting with *The Textual Life of Airports* (London: Bloomsbury, 2011). On jet lag, see Till Roenneberg, *Internal Time: Chronotypes, Social Jet Lag, and Why You're So Tired* (Cambridge: Harvard University Press, 2012) and Christopher J. Lee, *Jet Lag* (New York: Bloomsbury, 2017); Robert Wohl, *A Passion for Wings: Aviation and the Western Imagination, 1908–1918* (New Haven: Yale University Press, 1996); Robert Wohl, *The Spectacle of Flight: Aviation and the Western Imagination, 1920–1950* (New Haven: Yale University Press, 2007). See esp. Nathalie Roseau and Marie Thébaud-Sorger, eds., *L'Emprise du vol de l'invention à la massification: Histoire d'une culture moderne* (Geneva: Métis, 2013) for a volume that has largely influenced my own work and in which I have an essay, "Optimisme technologique et pensée de l'obsolescence," 165–80. On *Earthrise*, see https://www.nytimes.com/2018/10/02/opinion/earthrise-moon-space-nasa.html. Also see Fred Turner, *From Counterculture to Cyberculture: Stewart Brand, the Whole Earth Network and the Rise of Digital Utopianism* (Chicago: University of Chicago Press, 2006).

46. See also Karen Caplan, *Aerial Aftermaths: Wartime from Above* (Chapel Hill: Duke University Press, 2018).

47. See esp. Roseau and Thébaud-Sorger, *L'Emprise du vol de l'invention à la massification;* Mark Dorrian and Frédéric Pousin, *Seeing from Above: The Aerial View in Visual Culture* (London: Tauris, 2013); Weems, *Brainstorming the Prairies.*

48. François Lugassy, "Les attitudes vis-à-vis du voyage aérien et de l'aéroport," *Phase B* (September–May 1966): 15. ADP.

49. *FYI*, July 16, 1948. Box 530, Time Inc. Archive, NYHS.

50. This ad predates the actual "jet age," but many of these artifacts are anticipatory in meaningful ways.

51. Emanuele Coccia, *Sensible Life: A Micro-Ontology of the Image*, trans. Scott Alan Stuart (New York: Fordham University Press, 2016), 17.

52. *Mad Men*, "The Wheel." Season 1, episode 13, originally aired October 18, 2007.

CHAPTER ONE
FLUID MOTION ON THE GROUND

1. Ben Mutzabaugh, "Exclusive First Look: Inching Closer to Launch, TWA Hotel Unveils Room Design," *USA Today*, April 16, 2018.

2. Chandra Mukerji, *Territorial Ambitions and the Gardens of Versailles* (Cambridge: Cambridge University Press, 1997); Chandra Mukerji, *Impossible Engineering: Technology and Territoriality on the Canal du Midi* (Princeton: Princeton University Press, 2009); and Daniel Headrick, *The Tools of Empire: Technology and European Imperialism in the Nineteenth Century* (Oxford: Oxford University Press, 1981). Bringing the United States into the narrative is Michael Adas, *Dominance by Design* (Cambridge: Belknap, Harvard University Press, 2009).

3. Pan Am built its airline by flying to Cuba. While European powers initially used air power for mail and for shuttling diplomats, by the mid-1930s British Imperial Airways had over fifty-nine thousand miles of interconnecting airways and five hundred stops around the world. See Alistair Gordon, *Naked Airport: A Cultural History of the World's Most Revolutionary Structure* (New York: Metropolitan, 2004), 76.

4. An additional way to consider airport "symbolics" is to study airport art programs. See Alex J. Taylor, "Flying Machines: Calder and the Sensation of the Jet Age" (unpublished manuscript). Gordon's *Naked Airport* offers a history of airport design and is a general cultural history of the airport. Gordon argues, however, that the airport supplied a "sense of movement, transition, and

excitement that flight itself no longer provided" (177).

5. Thomas S. Hines, *Architecture of the Sun: Los Angeles Modernism, 1900–1970* (New York: Rizzoli, 2010); Deyan Sudjic, *Norman Foster: A Life in Architecture* (London: Weidenfeld and Nicolson, 2010); Eeva-Liisa Pelkonen and Donald Albrecht, *Eero Saarinen: Shaping the Future* (New Haven: Yale University Press, 2006); Brian Edwards, *The Modern Airport Terminal: New Approaches to Airport Architecture* (London: Taylor and Francis, 2005). Sammy Goldenberg wrote an undergraduate honors thesis in the History Department at USC, "Rejecting Futurama: Los Angeles International Airport and the American Turn Against Growth" (2010). See also Vanessa R. Schwartz, "LAX: Designing for the Jet Age," in *Overdrive: Architecture in Los Angeles*, ed. Wim DeWit and Christopher Alexander (Los Angeles: Getty Publications, 2013), 163–83.

6. "Airport Cities: Gateways to the Jet Age," *Time*, August 15, 1960, 68.

7. "Allocution Inaugurale de Charles de Gaulle," February 24, 1961. Box 37, doc. 19993055, ADP. Also published in Charles de Gaulle, *Discours et messages: Avec le renouveau, 1958–1962* (Paris: Plon, 1979), 283–84.

8. George Nelson, "Architecture for the New Itinerants," *Saturday Review*, April 22, 1967, 30–31.

9. See Vanessa R. Schwartz, *It's So French! Hollywood, Paris, and the Making of Cosmopolitan Film Culture* (Chicago: University of Chicago Press, 2007), 192–98, and Mark Dierikx, *Clipping the Clouds: How Air Travel Changed the World* (Westport: Praeger, 2008), 71.

10. Richard Witkin, "U.S. Jet Starting Daily Ocean Runs," *New York Times*, October 26, 1958.

11. Robert Buron, Ministère des Travaux Publics and Transports, Inauguration of Orly, February 24, 1961, Orly Inauguration, ADP.

12. Andrew M. Shanken, *194X: Architecture, Planning, and Consumer Culture on the American Home Front* (Minneapolis: University of Minnesota Press, 2009); Amy F. Ogata, *Designing the Creative Child: Playthings and Places in Midcentury America* (Minneapolis: University Of Minnesota Press, 2013).

13. Robert Venturi, Denise Scott Brown, and Steven Izenour, *Learning From Las Vegas* (Cambridge: MIT Press, 1972); Larry Busbea, *Topologies: The Urban Utopia in France, 1960–1970* (Cambridge: MIT Press, 2007); Reyner Banham, "The Obsolescent Airport," *Architectural Review* 132, no. 790 (October 1962): 252–53.

14. Banham, "Obsolescent Airport," 252.

15. For excellent work on the Independent Group, see Anne Massey, *The Independent Group: Modernism and Mass Culture in Britain, 1945–59* (Manchester: Manchester University Press, 1995); Lucy Bradnock, Courtney J. Martin, and Rebecca Peabody, eds., *Lawrence Alloway: Critic and Curator* (Los Angeles: Getty Research Institute, 2015); and Daniel Horowitz, *Consuming Pleasures: Intellectuals and Popular Culture in the Postwar World* (Philadelphia: University of Pennsylvania Press, 2012).

16. Lionel Brett, "Arrival and Departure," *Architectural Review* 118, no. 703 (July 1955): 7–8.

17. Jacques Block, "Planning Airports System in Paris Area," *Transportation Engineering Journal* (May 1969): 253. 016 A.69.3.6, ADP.

18. Banham, "Obsolescent Airport," 253.

19. Lockheed Aircraft Service, *Proposal for Los Angeles International Airport Intra-Terminal Transportation System*, 1960, 11. Flight Path Learning Center, LAX.

20. William Pereira, *Journey to the Airport* (Pereira Associates, 1967), 13. Box 107, William Pereira Archives, USC Special Collections.

21. American Airlines brochure, "Welcome Aboard Your American Flagship" (1959), 13. San Francisco International Airport Archives.

22. "The Expanding Airport" (1958). Eames Papers, Box 201, Folder 16, Library of Congress.

23. François Lugassy, "Les attitudes vis-à-vis du voyage aérien et de l'aéroport," *Phase B* (September–May 1966): 89, 126.

24. Lugassy, "Les attitudes," 8, 11–18, and "Voyageur aérien, vu par le personnel travaillant en aéroport" (December 1965): 53. ADP.

25. Interview with Paul Andreu, "La ville aéroport," in *La vitesse* (Paris: Cartier/Flammarion, 1991), 116.

26. Allan Temko, "An Interview with Eero Saarinen," *Horizons* 2, no. 6 (July 1960): 123.

27. Pelkonen and Albrecht, *Eero Saarinen: Shaping the Future*, esp. Susanna Santala, "Airports: Building for the Jet Age," 300–307; see also Alice T. Friedman, *American Glamour and the Evolution of Modern Architecture* (New Haven: Yale University Press, 2010).

28. "Expanding Airport."

29. Temko, "Interview with Eero Saarinen," 123.

30. John Harwood, *The Interface: IBM and the Transformation of Corporate Design, 1945–1976* (Minneapolis: University of Minnesota Press, 2011), 96. Harwood's reading of ergonomics is as a posthumanist construction, which is interesting, but I question whether designers and architects such as Saarinen really imagined it that way.

31. Antonio Roman, *Eero Saarinen: An Architecture of Simplicity* (New York: Princeton Architectural, 2003), 43, 60.

32. Aline Saarinen, ed., *Eero Saarinen on His Work* (New Haven: Yale University Press, 1962), 60; see also Nathalie Roseau, "The Obsolescence of the Monument, the Future of the Airport Icon," in *The Challenge of Change: Dealing with the Legacy of the Modern Movement*, ed. D. Van den Heuvel, M. Mesman, W. Quist, and B. Lemmens (Amsterdam: IOS, 2008), 87–92.

33. This connection appears important to me even though Kevin Roche implies that it isn't possible. He said in an August 2, 2007, interview with Kornel Ringli, "As far as the concept of the building is concerned, TWA as a company has no input at all." Ringli, *Designing TWA: Eero Saarinen's Airport Terminal in New York* (Zurich: Park, 2015), 155.

34. Ringli, *Designing TWA*, 58, 126.

35. Dedication Program, Dulles International Airport, November 17–18, 1962. Eero Saarinen Papers, Group 593, Box 54, Series III, Folder 101, Manuscripts and Archives, Yale University. Letter from Aline Saarinen to Sigrid Asmus, December 21, 1961. Eero Saarinen Papers, Group 595, Box 462, Series IV, Folder 1305, Manuscripts and Archives, Yale University.

36. Saarinen as cited in Allan Temko, *Eero Saarinen* (New York: G. Braziller, 1962), 115.

37. Joseph A. Loftus, "At Dulles Airport, Traffic Is Light Year After Opening—Buses into Washington a Problem," *New Times*, November 17, 1963.

38. "Dulles International Airport," FAA Brochure (circa 1962). Flight Path Learning Center, LAX.

39. "Mobile Lounge, Dulles Airport," FAA Brochure (circa 1961). Eero Saarinen Papers, Group 593, Box 54, Series III, Folder 101, Manuscripts and Archives, Yale University.

40. Allan Temko, "An Interview with Eero Saarinen" *Horizons* 2, no. 6 (July 1960): 123.

41. Report, E. W. Fuller, "A Proposed Mobile Gate House," September 26, 1952. Eames Papers, Box 201, Folder 14, Library of Congress.

42. Letter from Eero Saarinen to Robert McDonnell, July 25, 1958. Eero Saarinen Papers, Group 593, Box 462, Series Iv, Folder 1304, Manuscripts and Archives, Yale University. See also Alexandra Lange, "This Year's Model: Representing Modernism to the Post-War American Corporation," *Journal of Design History* 19, no. 3 (Autumn 2006): 233–48. The idea has been credited to Saarinen, which is not quite right, since it also adapted the common practice already used in smaller European airports and an earlier proposed by an FAA report.

43. "The Eames Design," Public Broadcast Laboratory, interview with Edward P. Morgan, April 6, 1969, in Daniel Ostroff, ed., *An Eames Anthology: Articles, Film Scripts, Interviews, Letters, Notes, Speeches* (New Haven: Yale University Press, 2015), 269.

44. Letter from Aline Saarinen to Judy and Walter McQuade of *Fortune* magazine, January 8, 1962. Eero Saarinen Papers, Group 593, Box 463, Series IV, Folder 1310, Manuscripts and Archives, Yale University.

45. *The Expanding Airport: A Study of Service and Convenience for Washington International,* directed by Charles and Ray Eames, 1958.

46. Amid Amidi, *Cartoon Modern: Style and Design in 1950s Animation* (San Francisco: Chronicle, 2006).

47. Archival materials suggest they had written to NASA in search of prototype drawings for the vertical launch planes (rockets) that they imagined would soon be part of everyday travel, which did not turn out to be the case. Eames Papers, Box 201, Folder 14, Library of Congress.

48. DOA, *1960 Annual Report.* Flight Path Learning Center, LAX.

49. Charles Luckman, *Twice in a Lifetime: From Soap to Skyscrapers* (New York: Norton, 1988), 299.

50. Marvin Miles, "LAX," *New Frontiers* (Spring 1955): 5.

51. Eero Saarinen, "Dry Run Presentation," July 1, 1958, 6. Eames Papers, Box 201, Folder 16, Library of Congress.

52. A new wing was added to the TWA terminal in 1969 to facilitate the introduction of jumbo jets. The building was landmarked in 1994 to prevent its destruction and overhaul, showing that it had outlived its use. In 2008, Jet Blue Airlines renovated the interior and reopened it as one the first new terminals built after September 11, 2001. The airline initially envisioned using the original TWA terminal as a ceremonial lobby but ended up bypassing it entirely to use the 1969 expansion. The airline announced in October 2015 that it would build a hotel there, which did not materialize. The "TWA Hotel" opened in May 2019.

53. Victor Cusack, *A Symbol of Los Angeles: The History of the Theme Building at the Los Angeles International Airport, 1952–1961* (Virginia Beach: Donning, 2005), 21.

54. Michael Brawne, "Airport Passenger Buildings," *Architectural Review,* November 1962, 341–48. For the branding by virtue of the unit terminal system, see Thomas Leslie, "The Pan Am Terminal at Idlewild/Kennedy Airport and the Transition from the Jet Age to the Space Age," *Design Issues* 21, no. 1 (Winter 2005): 63–80.

55. Charles Luckman talk at the Seagram Sales Meeting, July 1954. Charles Luckman Papers, Series 3, Box 3, Loyola Marymount University.

56. Paul Friedman interview with Grant Anderson, March 28, 1997, Flight Path Learning Center, LAX; DOA, 1957 Master Plan, 18 and 20, Flight Path Learning Center, LAX.

57. "Facts About Interior Treatment of New Terminal Area Buildings, 1961," DOA, PR Files, Flight Path Learning Center, LAX.

58. Master Plan Development for LAX, 1966–67, 61, William Pereira Archives, USC. According to Thomas S. Hines, *Architecture of the Sun,* 690. Eero Saarinen had consulted the Pereira & Luckman LAX Master Plan as he designed Dulles. I have not found evidence of that in the Saarinen papers at Yale.

59. Pereira, *Journey to the Airport,* 27–28.

60. DOA, 1958 Annual Report, Flight Path Learning Center, LAX.

61. DOA, 1962 Annual Report, 22, Flight Path Learning Center, LAX. Admission to the deck initially cost 10 cents.

62. Thomas S. Hines, *Architecture of the Sun* (New York: Rizzoli, 2010) and Philip J. Ethington, "Los Angeles and the Problem of Urban Historical Knowledge," a multimedia essay to accompany the December 2000 issue of the *American Historical Review.* See the web essay at http://lapuhk.usc.edu/. By the time the Theme Building was being constructed, Pereira was already off the project, having split with Luckman, who took over the LAX project in the split.

63. For more on the specifics, see Chapter Two.

64. Gladwin Hills, "A Disneyland for Adults," *New York Times,* May 28, 1961.

65. Speech by Najeeb Halaby at Airport Dedication, June 25, 1961, DOA, PR Files, Flight Path Learning Center, LAX.

66. Chris Nichols and Charlene Nichols, *Walt Disney's Disneyland* (Cologne: Taschen, 2018), 63.

67. Karal Ann Marling, "Imagineering the Disney Theme Parks," in *Designing Disney's, Theme Parks: The Architecture of Reassurance,* ed. Marling (Paris: Flammarion, 1998), 58.

68. Donald W. Ballard, *Disneyland Hotel: The Early Years, 1954–1988* (Riverside: Ape Pen, 2005).

69. "Special Issue: The Call of California, Its Splendor Its Excitement," *Life,* October 19, 1962, 17.

70. Memo from Peggy Hereford, PR director, to Erwin Baker, editorial department, *LA Examiner,* September 25, 1961. Flight Path Learning Center, LAX.

71. For more on visits to other airports, see Nathalie Roseau, *Aerocity: Quand l'avion fait la ville* (Marseille: Parenthèses, 2012), 181–89, and Nicholas Dagen Bloom, *The Metropolitan Airport: JFK International and Modern New York* (Philadelphia: University of Pennsylvania Press, 2015), 70.

72. Conseil d'administration, "Rapport. Débats. Orientations générales de l'Aéroport de Paris," August 1966, 4. ADP. In the U.S., service was distributed across many more airports, which therefore had proportionally less service by jet.

73. "Vous entrez à l'aéroport de Paris" (January 1967): 11. 016.A69.3.6., ADP.

74. *Installations Terminales Orly*, April 1960. Air France Archives.

75. Lugassy, "Les attitudes," 37.

76. Pierre Boursicot, Inaugural Speech, February 24, 1961. Box 37, Inauguration, ADP.

77. *Interavia. Revue Internationale de l'aviation* 4 (1961).

78. John D. Kasarda and Greg Lindsay, *Aerotropolis: The Way We'll Live Next* (New York: Farrar, Straus and Giroux, 2011). See also Roseau, *Aerocity*.

79. *La Nation*, June 8, 1963. Hilton, ADP.

80. K. L. H. Wells, *Weaving Modernism: Postwar Tapestry Between Paris and New York* (New Haven: Yale University Press, 2019).

81. "Inauguration du super-marché de l'aérogare d'Orly, 17 Septembre 1962." Dossier de Presse, Felix Potin, ADP.

82. Internal memo, dated Noël 1962. "Quinzaine commerciale Nocturne de l'Aérogare d'Orly," 016.A.69.37, ADP.

83. Visits to the airport were common in the early era of the jet, and most airports created viewing platforms and restaurants that overlooked the arrivals area. See also, Schwartz, "LAX: Designing for the Jet Age," 163–83.

84. Commentaire, "Film-Orly-Terminal" script. Recorded November 13, 1961, 1, 141, A.61.3.1. "L'anticipation, ce n'est plus de la littérature. Aujourd'hui, c'est la démarche au rendez-vous du progrès," ADP.

85. *La Jetée*, directed by Chris Marker, Argos Films, black and white, 28 mins., 1962.

86. "Evolution de l'activité 'Visites'" de 1951 à 1957, Memo, Secrétariat général, service commercial; "Comptes des résultats des visites," Secrétariat général, service économique, service commercial, January 1962; Letter from Pierre Cot to Maurice Kungler, French representative to the IATA in Montréal, February 15, 1966, ADP; Rapport du Secrétaire général, "Réajustement des tarifs des visites pour la saison 1961," 016 A.69.3.6, ADP; Cot, *Interveravia* 4 (1961), 016 a.69.3.7, ADP.

87. Letter from Pierre Cot to Maurice Kungler, French representative to the IATA in Montreal, February 15, 1966. ADP.

88. *Orly-Sur-Seine*, directed by Pierre Zimmer and Jean-Marc Pipert, Les films du Chapiteau, black and white, 19 mins., 1962. Viewed at the Forum des Images, Paris.

89. "Réajustement du droit d'accès à l'aérogare sud d'Orly," April 8, 1968. 001 AH 055, ADP.

90. Roland Merlin, "Orly, Pôle Touristique, Concurrence la Tour Eiffel" (August 17, 1965). 001 AH 055, ADP.

91. Letter from Jacques Meuley to ADP, October 3, 1966, and response from R. Layet, chef du service économique, October 12, 1966. 001 AH 055, ADP.

92. Lugassy, "Les attitudes," 43. ADP.

CHAPTER TWO DISNEYLAND AND THE ART OF PEOPLE-MOVING

Epigraphs: Walt Disney, Speech, "New Traffic Signals for the Entertainment Industry," 1959, and *The EPCOT Film*, Walt Disney Productions, 25 minutes, color, 1966. Script by Marty Sklar, draft September 8, 1966, p. 20. WDA.

1. Van Arsdale France and Dick Nunis, *Window on Main Street: 35 Years of Creating Happiness at Disneyland Park* (Orlando: Theme Park Press, 2015), 187.

2. Kelly Comras, *Ruth Shellhorn* (Athens: University of Georgia Press, 2016); and Stephen M. Fjellman, *Vinyl Leaves: Walt Disney World and America* (Boulder: Westview, 1992).

3. *EPCOT Film*.

4. For more on mid-century ideas of happiness, see Justus Nieland, "Making Happy, Happy-Making: The Eamses and Communication by Design," in *Modernism and Affect*, ed. Julie Taylor (Edinburgh: Edinburgh University Press, 2015), 203–25.

5. This definition comes from a letter from Harrison Price to Dick Irvine, October 5, 1960. WDA.

6. The press coverage makes for a valuable historical source but is notably different from what one might call the critical and analytical reception of Disney animation or "Disney Studies." Disney had been hailed as an artistic genius very early in his career and received a great deal of attention from intellectuals. As early as 1942 one could find books such as Robert Field, *The Art of Walt Disney* (New York: Macmillan, 1942). Walter Benjamin and Erwin Panofsky wrote about Disney in the 1930s and 1940s. By the 1970s intellectuals had adopted a more negative stance, and the Marxist critique by such scholars as Ariel Dorfman and Armand Mattelart in *How to Read Donald Duck* (New York: International General, 1975) became more dominant, making such phrases such as "Mickey Mouse history" common parlance. This change is not my subject, however. Writing about Disneyland constitutes a separate, less well-developed, and even less-appreciated subject. For a Disney bibliography, see John A. Lent, *Comic Art of the United States Through 2000, Animation and Cartoons: An International Bibliography* (Westport, Conn.: Praeger, 2005), and Lynn Gartley and Elizabeth Leebron, *Walt Disney: A Guide to References and Resources* (Boston: G. K. Hall, 1979). The best newer volume about the parks is Kathy Merlock Jackson and Mark I. West, eds., *Disneyland and Culture: Essays on the Parks and Their Influence* (Jefferson, N.C.: McFarland, 2011).

7. Louis Marin, "Disneyland: A Degenerate Utopia," *Glyph* 1 (1977): 50–66; Jean Baudrillard, "Simulacra and Simulations," in *Selected Writings*, ed. Mark Poster (Stanford: Stanford University Press, 2001), 169–87; and Umberto Eco, "Travels in Hyperreality," in *Travels in Hyperreality* (San Diego: Harcourt Brace, 1986), 1–58.

8. Baudrillard, "Simulacra and Simulations," 175.

9. Eco, "Travels in Hyperreality."

10. "Disneyland Paris," Wikipedia, accessed August 20, 2017. https://en.wikipedia.org/wiki/Disneyland_Paris

11. See, for example, Roberta Panzanelli, ed., *Ephemeral Bodies: Wax Sculpture and the Human Figure* (Los Angeles: Getty Research Institute, 2008); Barbara Maria Stafford and Frances Terpak, *Devices of Wonder: From the World in a Box to Images on a Screen* (Los Angeles: Getty Publications, 2001); Adelheid Voskuhl, *Androids in the Enlightenment: Mechanics, Artisans, and Cultures of the Self* (Chicago: University of Chicago Press, 2015); Schwartz, *Spectacular Realities*. Still regarded as one of the great studies about America is Neil Harris, *Humbug: The Art of P. T. Barnum* (Chicago: University of Chicago Press, 1981).

12. Richard Schickel, *The Disney Version: The Life, Times, Art and Commerce of Walt Disney* (New York: Simon and Schuster, 1968).

13. Schickel, *Disney Version*, 318.

14. The corporate archives of The Walt Disney Company, Walt Disney Imagineering, and the Walt Disney Animation Research Library are generally closed to the public. I was fortunate to gain limited access to the Disney archives, but, like many corporate archives, they are incomplete. Although Walt Disney's correspondence is ample (although not accessible), it is unclear whether the materials of the Park Operations Committee and other key Disneyland entities exist. I am especially grateful for the access I received, and for the generous research support provided by archive director Becky Cline, as well as Kevin Kern.

15. Elizabeth Bell et al., *From Mouse to Mermaid: The Politics of Film, Gender and Culture* (Bloomington: Indiana University Press, 1995); Project on Disney, *Inside the Mouse: Work and Play at Disney World* (Durham: Duke University Press, 1995). For a more nuanced collection, see Eric Smoodin, ed., *Disney Discourse: Producing the Magic Kingdom* (New York: Routledge, 1994).

16. This literature is vast. A good place to start is Janet Wasko, *Understanding Disney: The Manufacture of Fantasy* (London: Polity, 2001).

17. The best publication about Disneyland that also is based on remarkable use of the Walt Disney Imagineering archives was written for an unprecedented exhibition. See Marling, *Designing Disney's Theme Parks.* See also John M. Findlay, *Magic Lands: Western Cityscapes and American Culture After 1940* (Berkeley: University of California Press, 1992), and Eric Avila, *Popular Culture in the Age of White Flight: Fear and Fantasy in Suburban Los Angeles* (Berkeley: University of California Press, 2006).

18. Scott A. Lukas, *Theme Park* (London: Reaktion, 2008), 77. Two lavishly illustrated and well-researched books published with support from Disney are Chris Nichols, *Walt Disney's Disneyland* (Cologne: Taschen, 2018), and Don Hahn, *Yesterday's Tomorrow: Disney's Magical Mid-Century* (Los Angeles: Disney Editions, 2017).

19. "Marc Davis and the Haunted Mansion," *"E" Ticket* 16 (Summer 1993): 27.

20. Scott A. Lukas, ed., *A Reader in Themed and Immersive Spaces* (Pittsburgh: Carnegie Mellon–ETC, 2016).

21. For Michael Sorkin, the ride is reduced to free-market capitalist circulation: "If culture is being Disneyfied . . . the royal road there is precisely that: going for a ride!" Sorkin, "See You in Disneyland," in *Variations on a Theme Park: The New American City and the End of Public Space,* ed. Michael Sorkin (New York: Hill and Wang, 1992), 216. Although this is not my interpretation, his observations about the operations of the park are astute.

22. "Walt Profile Press release," circa 1955, 16. WDA.

23. Walt Disney, "People and Places," May 21, 1953. WDA.

24. Disneyland Inc., "Report on Amusement Parks," June 1954, 5. WDA.

25. TWA Press Release, "Disneyland New West Coast Magnet," n.d. (circa 1954–55), 1.

26. Didier Ghez, "The Reluctant Dragon," in *The Walt Disney Film Archives: The Animated Movies, 1921–1968,* ed. Daniel Kothenschulte (New York: Taschen, 2016), 184–93. The departments were actually re-created on soundstages.

27. As Disney alumnus Jimmy Johnson explained, "What began as an impromptu art form was transformed into an efficient business." This was a typical expression about the early company. See Johnson, *Inside the Whimsy Works: My Life with Walt Disney Productions,* ed. Greg Ehrbar and Didier Ghez (Jackson: University of Mississippi Press, 2014), 20.

28. Karal Ann Marling, "Disneyland, 1955: Just Take the Santa Ana Freeway to the American Dream," *American Art* 5 (Winter/Spring 1991): 189.

29. Peter Westwick, ed., *Blue Sky Metropolis: The Aerospace Century in Southern California* (Berkeley: University of California Press, 2012).

30. Marling, "Disneyland, 1955," 179–80.

31. This connection is made convincingly by Marling, "Disneyland, 1955," 180–84

32. Schivelbusch, *Railway Journey;* Jeffrey Ruoff, ed., *Virtual Voyages: Cinema and Travel* (Durham: Duke University Press, 2006); and Teresa Castro, *La pensée cartographique des images* (Paris: Aléas, 2011). Earlier and fundamental studies of such mobilized spectatorship include Friedberg, *Window Shopping;* Giuliana Bruno, *Street-Walking on a Ruined Map: Cultural Theory and the City Films of Elvira Notari* (Princeton: Princeton University Press, 1993); and Schwartz, *Spectacular Realities.*

33. Neal Gabler, *Walt Disney: The Triumph of the American Imagination* (New York: Knopf, 2006), 508.

34. Wasko, *Understanding Disney,* 21; also see Gabler, *Walt Disney.*

35. *"Walt Disney's 'Disneyland,'"* Episode 1, October 27, 1954.

36. Marling, "Imagineering the Disney Theme Parks," 74–75.

37. John Hench and Peggy Van Pelt, *Designing Disney: Imagineering and the Art of the Show* (New York: Disney Editions, 2003), 67.

38. France and Nunis, *Window on Main Street,* 187.

39. For the best account of the early history of Disneyland, see Todd James Pierce, *Three Years in Wonderland: The Disney Brothers, C. V. Wood, and the Making of the Great American Theme Park* (Jackson: University of Mississippi Press, 2016).

40. Marling, "Imagineering the Disney Theme Parks," 58.

41. Letter from William Pereira to Walt Disney, April 10, 1952. WDA. Pierce, *Three Years in Wonderland,* 37.

42. Harrison Price, *Walt's Revolution! By the Numbers* (Orlando: Ripley, 2004), esp. 28–32.

43. Donald W. Ballard, *The Disneyland Hotel: The Early Years, 1954–1988* (Riverside: Ape Pen, 2005).

44. Price, *Walt's Revolution,* and James Skee, "By the Numbers: Confidence, Consultants, and the Construction of Mass Leisure, 1953–1975" (PhD diss., University of California, Berkeley, 2016).

45. Skee, "By the Numbers." Disney sold his interest in WED Enterprises in February 1965, and although it was renamed Walt Disney Imagineering in 1986, the creative and other ties during Disney's lifetime were profound. Dave Smith, *Disney A to Z,* 5th ed. (Glendale: Disney Enterprises, 2016), 813.

46. "Interview with John Hench and Marty Sklar by Richard Hubler," May 14, 1968, 26. WDA.

47. Hench and Van Pelt, *Designing Disney,* 30.

48. Dreyfuss as cited in John Harwood, *The Interface: IBM and the Transformation of Corporate Design, 1945–1976* (Minneapolis: University of Minnesota Press, 2011), 96. Harwood's reading of ergonomics is as a posthumanist construction, which I am not sure is useful.

49. *EPCOT Film;* Walt Disney, "Disneyland Dedication Speech," July 17, 1955.

50. WED Monorail Script, "revised" September 27, 1966, 7. WDA.

51. "Interview with Dick Irvine by Bob Thomas," April 24, 1973, 20. WDA.

52. See Leslie, "Pan Am Terminal at Idlewild/Kennedy Airport."

53. "Interview with Bruce Bushman," no date and no interviewer. WDA.

54. WED Press Release, Summer 1967. WDA. See also Hench quoted in *"E" Ticket* 17 (Winter 1993–94): 9. WDA.

55. "Peoplemover and Omnimover," *News From WED,* n.d. (circa early 1967), 1. Anaheim Public Library.

56. For the evolution of the attraction, see http://samlanddisney.blogspot.com/2011/03/wedway-peoplemover.html

57. Peter Blake, "Lessons of the Park," in *The Art of Walt Disney: From Mickey Mouse to the Magic Kingdom,* ed. Christopher Finch (New York: Abrams, 1975), 430–31.

58. "Disneyland Data 1961," A6. Box 96, NYPL, NYWF.

59. Paul F. Anderson, "Disney and the World's Fair," *Persistence of Vision* 6/7 (1995): 69.

60. Michael A. Crawford, "New Heights: Walt and the Winter Olympics," Walt Disney Family Museum. http://www.waltdisney.com/blog/new-heights-walt-and-winter-olympics.

61. Memo from Robert Moses to Martin Stone, June 4, 1962. Box 60, NYPL, NYWF. There had been a monorail at the Seattle World's Fair in 1962, but Disney's was considered to be superior.

62. WED Press Release, Summer 1967, 3. Anaheim Public Library.

63. Jack Sayers, Memo, October 1960. WDA.

64. WED Press Release, December 26, 1963, 8 A5. Folder A 1169, NYPL, NYWF. During the World's Fair, WED used stationery listing addresses in Glendale and Forest Hills, Queens.

65. Letter from Harrison Price to Dick Irvine, October 5, 1960. WDA.

66. Memo from Marty Sklar to Card Walker, July 31, 1963. WDA.

67. Letter to Jack Sayers, August 1, 1962. Box 28, AO3, Folder 636, NYPL, NYWF.

68. Report on the World's Fair by Jack Sayers, November 8, 1960. WDA.

69. Memo from WED to Mr. Mott Heath at Ford, May 24, 1961. WDA.

70. Letter from Martin Stone to Robert Moses, February 13, 1963. Box 28, Folder P1. 42, NYPL, NYWF.

71. Anderson, "Disney and the World's Fair," 37.

72. Letter from Martin Stone to Robert Moses, February 13, 1963. Box 28, Folder P1.42, NYPL, NYWF.

73. The exhibit's end was absolutely reminiscent of Norman Bel Geddes' work for Chrysler in Futurama at the 1939 Fair. "Ford Meets Disney at the Magic Skyway," Henry Ford Museum, May 9, 2014. https://www.thehenryford.org/explore/blog/ford-meets-disney-at-the-magic-skyway.

74. "Ford Pavilion Booklet," April 14, 1964, n.p.

75. 1964 WED Brochure. Anaheim Public Library.

76. John Canemaker, *Magic Color Flair: The World of Mary Blair* (San Francisco: Walt Disney Family Foundation, 2014), 34.

77. Canemaker, *Magic Color Flair,* 34.

78. WED Profile, *It's a Small World,* 1964. I want to thank Suzanne Hudson for her astute analysis.

79. Letter, Robert Moses to Martin Stone, February 13, 1963. Box 28, Folder P1.42, NYPL, NYWF.

80. WED Profile, *It's a Small World,* 1964. Anaheim Public Library.

81. Rolly Crump as told to Jeff Heimbuch, *It's Kind of a Cute Story* (Baltimore: Bamboo Forest, 2012), chapter 9, location 1370. See also "Sheet Metal Contractor Builds the World's Largest Mobile," *American Artisan* (April 1964): 54–58.

82. Press Release, 1964 World's Fair. WDA.

83. "Disney's Edison Square," *"E" Ticket* 22 (Winter 1995): 7–11.

84. The carousel is a powerful 1960s metaphor: a wheel, as ancient as time, that is updated by becoming automatic. The 1960s also saw the introduction of the circular slide holder, also called a carousel. While Kodak introduced various round tray-holder formats in 1961, the technology evolved until 1966; in 1965 the device design made "automatic" shows possible, and one can't help but wonder whether there is a connection between the Kodak carousel and the GE Carousel of Progress of 1964.

85. Memo from Robert Moses to Stuart Constable, February 28, 1961. Box 97, A6, NYPL, NYWF.

86. WED Presentation for World's Fair, "One Nation Under God," n.d. (likely 1961), 2. Box 97, A6, P.6, NYPL, NYWF.

87. WED Presentation for World's Fair, "One Nation Under God," 2.

88. "Disneyland's Great Moments with Mr. Lincoln," in *News From Disneyland* 1, n.d. Anaheim Public Library. Such innovative uses of sound built on Disney's earlier installation of Fantasound for "Fantasia" and anticipates multichannel processes such as Dolby.

89. Interview with Jim Algar by Bob Thomas, n.d., 23. WDA.

90. Ford, "Survey," "World's Fair Business Survey," December 30 to January 30, 1965. WDA.

91. Paul Anderson, "Disney and 1964," *Persistence of Vision* 6/7 (1995): 124.

92. Anderson, "Disney and 1964," 30.

93. "Interview with Donn Tatum by Bob Thomas," May 24, 1973, 27. WDA.

94. *EPCOT Film.*

95. *EPCOT Film.*

96. Sam Gennawey, *Walt Disney and the Promise of Progress City* (Orlando: Theme Park Press, 2014), 136.

97. Neal Gabler, *Walt Disney: The Triumph of the American Imagination* (New York: Knopf, 2006), 610.

98. *EPCOT Film.*

99. *EPCOT Film.*

100. *EPCOT Film.*

101. The Walt Disney Company Annual Report, 1966, 23. Anaheim Public Library.

102. "Peoplemover and Omnimover," *News from WED,* n.d. (circa early 1967), 5. Anaheim Public Library.

103. Walt Disney, "Disneyland Dedication Speech," July 17, 1955.

CHAPTER THREE
ARRIVALS AND DEPARTURES

Epigraphs: The Wilson Hicks quotation is from Otha Spencer, "Twenty Years of *Life:* A Study of Time Inc.'s Picture Magazine and Its Contribution to Photojournalism" (Ph.D. diss., University of Missouri, 1958), 412. Abbott is cited by Susan Sontag in *On Photography* (New York: Picador, 1977), 67.

1. Lanfranco Rasponi, *The International Nomads* (New York: Putnam, 1966), 11.

2. For more on Arnold Newman and environmental portraiture, see Arnold Newman, *Artists: Portraits from Four*

Decades (London: Weidenfeld and Nicolson, 1980); Roger Clark, "Arnold Newman," *British Journal of Photography* 128, no. 6332 (1981); Véronique Vienne, "Arnold Newman: Historical View," *Graphis*, no. 328 (2000): 102–11; Arnold Newman, *Arnold Newman* (Cologne: Taschen, 2000); and William A. Ewing, *Masterclass: Arnold Newman* (London: Thames and Hudson, 2012), 1268–71, 1282.

3. See William Stadiem, *Jet Set: The People, the Planes, the Glamour, and the Romance in Aviation's Glory Years* (New York: Ballantine, 2014), for a very good descriptive portrait of the social group.

4. For the phrase Nowism, see Richard Meyer, *What Was Contemporary Art?* (Cambridge: MIT Press, 2014).

5. C. Wright Mills, *The Power Elite* (New York: Oxford University Press, 1956), 73, 93.

6. See Ryan Linkof, *Public Images: Celebrity, Photojournalism and the Making of the Tabloid Press* (London: Bloomsbury, 2018). There is a long history of the press and access. See Schwartz, *Spectacular Realities*, 22–44, on the history of the interview; Thierry Gervais, "Interview of Chevreul, France, 1886," in *Getting the Picture: The Visual Culture of the News*, ed. Jason E. Hill and Vanessa R. Schwartz (London: Bloomsbury, 2015), 35–37; Charles L. Ponce de Leon, *Self-Exposure: Human-Interest Journalism and the Emergence of Celebrity in America, 1890–1940* (Chapel Hill: University of North Carolina Press, 2002); and Kate Flint, *Flash! Photography, Writing, and Surprising Illumination* (Oxford: Oxford University Press, 2017).

7. It is noted that 1962 is in fact a key year in Peter Simonson et al., "The History of Communication History," in *The Handbook of Communication History*, ed. Simonson et al. (New York: Routledge, 2013), 30.

8. Lawrence Alloway, "The Long Front of Culture," in *Imagining the Present: Context, Content, and the Role of the Critic*, ed. Richard Kalina (London: Routledge, 2006), 61; Ben Highmore, "Brutalist Wallpaper and the Independent Group," *Journal of Visual Culture* 12, no. 2 (August 2013): 211.

9. Daniel J. Boorstin, *The Image: A Guide to Pseudo-Events in America* (New York: Harper and Row, 1961), 13.

10. See Neil Harris, "Iconography and Intellectual History: The Halftone Effect" (1979), in Neil Harris, *Cultural Excursions: Marketing Appetites and Cultural Tastes in Modern America* (Chicago: University of Chicago Press, 1990), 304–317; Thierry Gervais and Gaëlle Morel, *The Making of Visual News: A History of Photography in the Press* (London: Bloomsbury, 2017).

11. Boorstin, *Image*, 240.

12. Boorstin, *Image*, 10.

13. Boorstin, *Image*, 257.

14. Wilson Hicks, *Words and Pictures: An Introduction to Photojournalism* (New York: Harper Brothers, 1952), xv.

15. See Peter Parshall, "The Education of a Curator: William Mills Ivins Jr. at the Met," in Freyda Spira and Peter Parshall, *The Power of Prints: The Legacy of William M. Ivins and A. Hyatt Mayor* (New York and New Haven: Metropolitan Museum of Art and Yale University Press, 2016), 13–25.

16. The literature on the subject is vast. Additionally, the link between photography and tourism has its own history. Art photographers who portrayed transport are Robert Frank and Garry Winogrand. See Lee Friedlander and Alex Harris, eds., *Arrivals and Departures: The Airport Pictures of Garry Winogrand* (New York: Steidl, DAP, 2004).

17. Boorstin, *Image*, 94.

18. Stephen Groening, "Aerial Screens," *History and Technology* 29, no. 3 (September 2013): 281–300.

19. Boorstin, *Image*, 115, 117.

20. Vance Packard, *The Hidden Persuaders* (New York: D. McKay, 1957).

21. I. Willis Russell, "Among the New Words," *American Speech* 41, no. 2 (May 1966): 139–40.

22. Peter Mass, "Boswell of the Jet Set," *Saturday Evening Post*, January 19, 1963, 33.

23. Arthur Herzog, "It's the Innest, It's the Jet Set," *New York Times*, October 28, 1962.

24. Mills, *Power Elite*, 92.

25. Herzog, "It's the Innest."

26. Stephen Gundle, *Glamour: A History* (New York: Oxford University Press, 2008), 286. Gundle argues that glamour itself, which he takes to be a modern concept, always involves people who make "entrances and exits," which I think is an important observation.

27. On the mishaps of Cassini, see Stadiem, *Jet Set*.

28. Rasponi, *International Nomads*, 44–45.

29. Tony Judt, *Postwar: A History of Europe Since 1945* (New York: Penguin, 2005), 337.

30. Julie Kavanaugh, *Nureyev: The Life* (New York: Pantheon, 2007).

31. Andy Warhol, *The Philosophy of Andy Warhol (From A to B and Back Again)* (New York: Harcourt, 1975), 160.

32. Kavanaugh, *Nureyev*, 352.

33. Nicholas Coleridge and Stephen Quinn, eds., *The Sixties in Queen* (London: Ebury, 1987), 142–43.

34. Marylin Bender, *The Beautiful People* (New York: Coward-McCann, 1967), 190.

35. Natasha Fraser-Cavassoni, *Vogue on Yves Saint Laurent* (New York: Abrams Image, 2015), 18.

36. Bender, *Beautiful People*, 301.

37. Herzog, "It's the Innest."

38. Bender, *Beautiful People*, 24, 77.

39. Rasponi, *International Nomads*, 30.

40. Mary Quant, *Quant by Quant: The Autobiography of Mary Quant* (London: V and A, 2012), 106.

41. Gillian L'Eplattenier [Jill Kellogg], "Jill Kellogg and the Beatles: Recap of Beatles Trip to US on PAA Flight 101, London–New York, February 7, 1964," Pan Am Historical Foundation, last modified January 2019, https://panam.org/the-jet-age/367-jll-kellogg-the-beatles-2. Newsreels estimate that three thousand people came to the airport; see https://www.youtube.com/watch?v=YxgEwZ1qw5I.

42. Memo from Peggy Hereford, PR director, to Don Dwiggins, September 28, 1964, 1. Flight Path Learning Center, LAX, Ethel Pattison personal files.

43. Mary Panzer, "State of Emergency," in *Avedon: Murals and Portraits*, ed. Panzer et al. (New York: Abrams, 2012), 13.

44. See the work of Nadya Bair, *The Decisive Network: Magnum Photos and the Postwar Image Market* (Berkeley: University of California Press, 2020); Nadya Bair, "The Decisive Network: Producing Henri Cartier-Bresson at Mid-Century," *History of Photography* 40, no. 2 (June 2016): 146–66; and Nadya Bair, "Their Daily Bread: American Sponsorship and Magnum Photos' Global Network," *American Art* 31, no. 2 (Summer 2017): 109–17. Also, the recent acquisition of the Time-Life Inc. Archive at the New-York Historical Society is making important new archives available.

45. Robert E. Park, "News as a Form of

Knowledge: A Chapter on the Sociology of Knowledge," *American Journal of Sociology* 45, no. 5 (March 1940): 685.

46. Ludwig Wittgenstein, *Tractatus Logico-Philosophicus,* trans. C. K. Ogden (London: Routledge, 1974), 2, 1511, 1512.

47. This text also appears in Lynn Hunt and Vanessa R. Schwartz, "Introduction—Capturing the Moment: Images and Eyewitnessing in History," in *Journal of Visual Culture* 9, no. 3 (December 2010): 259–71. I am indebted to Hunt for her insights into Wittgenstein as a way of thinking about embodied vision.

48. See Jason E. Hill, "On the Efficacy of Artifice: PM, Radiophoto, and the Journalistic Discourse of Photographic Objectivity," *Études Photographiques* 26 (November 2010): 51–85; Zeynep Devrim Gürsel, "A Short History of Wire Service Photography," in Hill and Schwartz, *Getting the Picture,* 206–11; Zeynep Devrim Gürsel, *Image Brokers: Visualizing World News in the Age of Digital Circulation* (Berkeley: University of California Press, 2016); and Jonathan Dentler, "Wiring the World Picture: Wire Photography as an Interwar Global Information Technology," in *Transbordeur—Photographie, histoire, société,* no. 3 (2019).

49. Charles Baudelaire, "The Painter of Modern Life," in *The Painter of Modern Life and Other Essays,* trans. than Mayne (London: Phaidon, 1995), 9.

50. This phrase is widely attributed to Robert Capa and yet no one has been able to trace its origin.

51. John Morris, *Get the Picture: A Personal History of Photojournalism* (Chicago: University of Chicago Press, 2002), 9.

52. Clément Chéroux, *Henri Cartier-Bresson: Here and Now* (New York: Thames and Hudson, 2014), 95.

53. Douglas Collins, *The Story of Kodak* (New York: Abrams, 1990).

54. Jordan Bear, "Magnum Orbis: Photographs from the End(s) of the Earth," *Journal of Visual Studies* 25, no. 2 (September 2010): 113.

55. Regarding vehicles: on Weegee, see Christopher Bonanos, *Flash: The Making of Weegee, The Famous* (New York: Holt, 2018); on paparazzi, see Kim McNamara, *Paparazzi: Media Practices and Celebrity Culture* (Cambridge: Malden, 2016); on Ron Gallela, see the film *Smash His Camera,* directed by Leon Gast (Magnolia, 2010).

56. Joanna Zylinska, *Nonhuman Photography* (Cambridge: MIT Press, 2017).

57. A. J. Ezickson, *Get That Picture! The Story of the News Cameraman* (New York: National Library, 1938), 34–35. For more on the speed of the image, see also Jason Hill, "Snap-Shot: After Bullet Hit Gaynor" in Hill and Schwartz, *Getting the Picture,* 190–97.

58. Ezickson, *Get That Picture!* 33.

59. Ezickson, *Get That Picture!* 34.

60. *FYI,* June 10, 1949. Box 531, Time-Life Inc. Archive, NYHS.

61. Margot Shore to Ernst Haas, December 21, 1953. Ernst Haas Archive, Getty Images, London.

62. Memo from temporary Paris bureau chief to John Morris, April 17, 1955. Magnum Memos, Archives of John G. Morris. As one memo noted, Magnum added an account with Pan Am to their Air France account in 1955 for a daily flight between Paris and New York because one left two hours later than the other, giving them additional flexibility.

63. See Dentler, "Wiring the World Picture," and Gürsel, "Short History of Wire Service Photography," 206–11.

64. Trudy Feliu, 1956 Magnum European Distribution Report. Archives of John G. Morris.

65. John Loengard, *Life Photographers: What They Saw* (Boston: Bulfinch, 1998), 8.

66. Gundle, *Glamour: A History,* 207. The event was also filmed in color and played as *A Queen Is Crowned* in theaters for more than a year.

67. See Hill and Schwartz, *Getting the Picture.* For the way publications engaged readers in matters of visual literacy in particular, see Jason E. Hill, *Artist as Reporter: Weegee, Ad Reinhardt, and the PM News Picture* (Oakland: University of California Press, 2018).

68. "In Next Week's *Life,*" *Life,* June 8, 1953, 118.

69. Both letters from *Life,* July 6, 1953, 4.

70. "Dangerous Living by Editors and Climbers," *Life,* June 15, 1953, 25.

71. Horace Sutton, "From Motion to Mobilism," *Saturday Review,* April 22, 1967, 27.

72. See Richard K. Popp, *The Holiday Makers: Magazines, Advertising, and Mass Tourism in Postwar America* (Baton Rouge: Louisiana State University Press, 2012), and Bair, *Decisive Network.*

73. Mary Panzer, "On Holiday," *Aperture* 198 (Spring 2010): 50. *Holiday* was founded on a large budget by Curtis Publications of Philadelphia, the publisher of *Ladies' Home Journal* and the *Saturday Evening Post.*

74. See Bair, *Decisive Network.*

75. For an excellent explanation of such media transformations, see Fred Turner, *The Democratic Surround: Multimedia and American Liberalism from World War II to the Psychedelic Sixties* (Chicago: University of Chicago Press, 2013).

76. Alberto Oliva and Norberto Angeletti, *In Vogue: An Illustrated History of the World's Most Famous Fashion Magazine* (New York: Rizzoli, 2012), 19.

77. Nast was among the first American publishers to create foreign editions with *British Vogue* (1912) and *Spanish Vogue* (1918–23, a failure), *French Vogue* (1920), and *German Vogue* (1928–29). See Angeletti and Oliva, *In Vogue,* 26–27.

78. I took these issues up in *Spectacular Realities,* where I also linked the issue to the rise of cinema. Schwartz, *Spectacular Realities.* See also Gervais and Morel, *Making of Visual News.* Linkof, *Public Images,* rightly argues that the pictorial news itself appeared in the dailies long before the magazine format.

79. Justine de Young, "Not Just a Pretty Picture," in Hill and Schwartz, *Getting the Picture,* 109–15.

80. Caroline Evans, *The Mechanical Smile: Modernism and the First Fashion Shows in France and America, 1900–1929* (New Haven: Yale University Press, 2013), 243.

81. See Mark Haworth-Booth, *The Art of Lee Miller* (New Haven: Yale University Press, 2007); and Becky Conekin, *Lee Miller in Fashion* (New York: Monacelli, 2013).

82. The other photographers were: Richard Avedon, Irving Penn, Gjon Mili, Ernst Haas, Henri Cartier-Bresson, W. Eugene Smith, and Alfred Eisenstadt. "The World's Best Photographers," *Popular Photography* (March 1958): 63–85, 140.

83. "Photography in Fashion, Fashion in Photography," *Portfolio* 1, no. 1 (Winter 1950).

84. Panzer, "On Holiday," 52.

85. Ray Mackland, 1957, 8–9. Box 11, Wilson Hicks Conference Tapes and Transcripts Collection, 1957–73, Special Collections of the University of Miami Libraries.

86. Frank Zachary, 1964, 18. Box 11, Wil-

son Hicks Conference Tapes and Transcripts Collection, 1957–73, Special Collections of the University of Miami Libraries.

87. Eliot Elisofon, 1957, 2. Box 11, Wilson Hicks Conference Tapes and Transcripts Collection, 1957–73, Special Collections of the University of Miami Libraries.

88. Anne De Courcy, *Snowdon: The Biography* (London: Phoenix, 2008), 101.

89. Magnum Photos Internal memos and logs, Magnum Photo Collection, 1959–90, AG104: 2/1, February 1962, Center for Creative Photography, University of Arizona, Tucson.

90. David Bailey and Martin Harrison, *Black and White Memories: Photographs, 1948–1969* (London: Dent, 1983), 25.

91. Bailey and Harrison, *Black and White Memories*, 27.

92. Bailey and Harrison, *Black and White Memories*, 27.

93. Tom Wolfe, "Pariah Styles: Radical Chic," *Harper's Bazaar*, April 1965, 235.

94. Boorstin, *Image*, 115.

95. Erika Doss, ed., *Looking at Life Magazine* (Washington: Smithsonian, 2001); Blake Stimson, *The Pivot of the World: Photography and Its Nation* (Cambridge: MIT Press, 2006); Liam Kennedy, *Afterimages: Photography and U.S. Foreign Policy* (Chicago: University of Chicago Press, 2016).

CHAPTER FOUR
ERNST HAAS AND THE BLURRING OF COLOR IN MOTION

Epigraph: Letter from Ernst Haas to Robert Capa, n.d., 1954. Notebooks of Ernst Haas, Ernst Haas Archives, Getty Images, London.

1. "In and Out of Focus," December 15, 1978, CAC 79:055. Casey Allen Collection, Center for Creative Photography, University of Arizona, Tucson.

2. Fred Ritchin, *Bending the Frame: Photojournalism, Documentary, and Citizen* (New York: Aperture, 2013), 31–32.

3. Max Kozloff, "Photography: The Coming to Age of Color," *Artforum* 13, no. 5 (January 1975): 33.

4. Kevin Moore et al., eds., *Starburst: Color Photography in America, 1970–1980* (Ostfildern: Hatje Cantz, 2010) summarizes the "art perspective" of such work as Sally Euclaire, ed., *New Color/New Work: 18 Photographic Essays* (New York: Abbeville, 1984). Recent "revisionist" work, of which this chapter is a part, either acknowledges an earlier art photography trajectory in color and/or does not see the sharp distinctions between art photography and press photography in color. This includes Nathalie Boulouche, *Le ciel est bleu: Une histoire de la photographie couleur* (Paris: Textuel, 2011); Lisa Hostetler and Katherine A. Bussard, *Color Rush: American Color Photography from Stieglitz to Sherman* (New York: Aperture, 2013); Cynthia Young, *Capa in Color* (New York: International Center of Photography, 2014); Kim Timby, "Look at Those Lollipops! Integrating Color into News Pictures," in *Getting the Picture: The Visual Culture of the News*, ed. Jason E. Hill and Vanessa R. Schwartz (London: Bloomsbury, 2015), 236–43; Patricia A. Johnston, *Real Fantasies: Edward Steichen's Advertising Photography* (Berkeley: University of California Press, 2000); and Sally Stein, "The Rhetoric of the Colorful and the Colorless: The American Photography and Material Culture Between the Wars," vols. 1 and 2 (Ph.D. diss., Yale University, 1991), Sally Stein, "FSA Color: The Forgotten Document," *Modern Photography* (January 1979): 90–99, 162–64, 166, and Sally Stein, "Toward a Full-Color Turn in the Optics of Modern History," *American Art* 29, no. 1 (2015): 15–21.

5. Hilton Kramer, *New York Times*, November 23, 1974, 33. Folio 10, box 94, Beaumont and Nancy Newhall Papers, 1929–1993 (bulk 1929–93), Getty Research Institute, Research Library, Accession no. 920060.

6. Mary Panzer, "Introduction," in Inge Morath, *First Color* (Göttingen: Steidl, 2009), 10.

7. David Campany, *Walker Evans: The Magazine Work* (Göttingen: Steidl, 2014).

8. Laura Kalba, *Color in the Age of Impressionism: Commerce, Technology and Art* (University Park: Pennsylvania State University Press, 2017), 6; Regina Lee Blaszczyk and Uwe Spiekermann, eds., *Bright Modernity: Color, Commerce, and Consumer Culture* (Cham: Palgrave Macmillan, 2017); and Regina Lee Blaszczyk, *The Color Revolution* (Cambridge: MIT Press, 2012).

9. Memo from John Morris, July–August 1962. Magnum Photos Collection, 1950–90, AG104, Center for Creative Photography, University of Arizona, Tucson. There had been experimental early forms such as the Hillotype and the autochrome in the twentieth century, but the explosion of color photography really came with Kodachrome, made first in 1935 for 16mm movie cameras, then for still cameras in 1936, and eventually and importantly for professionals in 1938 in different medium-sized formats. Kodak remained the only processor. Although color film was more expensive (initially three times the cost of black and white), by 1964 more pictures were taken in color than black and white. Color film was made of transparencies, which is to say slides, rather than positive prints. Not until 1941 were there even marketable color prints or color negatives. See Alexander Liberman, *The Art and Technique of Color Photography* (New York: Simon and Schuster, 1951), 144, and *Color* (Alexandria: Time-Life, 1978), 68.

10. See Hill and Schwartz, *Getting the Picture*, Introduction. The exception especially has been the important work by Barbie Zelizer, Robert Hariman, and John Lucaites: Barbie Zelizer, *About to Die: How News Images Move the Public* (New York: Oxford University Press, 2010); Robert Hariman and John L. Lucaites, *No Caption Needed: Iconic Photographs, Public Culture, and Liberal Democracy* (Chicago: University of Chicago Press, 2011); Robert Hariman and John L. Lucaites, *The Public Image: Photography and Civic Spectatorship* (Chicago: University of Chicago Press, 2016).

11. Letter from Inge Bondi to Ernst Haas, May 18, 1954. Ernst Haas Archive, Getty Images, London.

12. Edward Steichen, introductory label, *All Color Show*, 1950, Museum of Modern Art, New York.

13. Magnum Paris bureau chief to John Morris, March 3, 1957. Archive of John G. Morris. The memo also explains that the following morning Steichen's wife, Dana Desboro Clover, died.

14. In the 1965 show Haas had work from four of his essays, three in color. See Master Checklist, "The Photo Essay," MoMA. https://www.moma.org/documents/moma_master-checklist_326377.pdf.

15. Robert H. Dumke," The Development of Color Photography in Newspapers," *Image* 6, no. 7 (1957): 161; "Newspaper in Color," *Fortune*, July 1931, 32–39, 120–26.

Simultaneously, magazines promoted their image production values, so they are easier to assess in this first research phase.

16. It is important to note how much this image resembles the opening credits of the film *Les parapluies de Cherbourg* (The umbrellas of Cherbourg, 1964). The filmmaker, Jacques Demy, was married to Agnès Varda, whose photography was also featured in the issue.

17. Neil Harris, *Cultural Excursions: Marketing Appetites and Cultural Tastes in Modern America* (Chicago: University of Chicago Press, 1990), 320.

18. Paul Outerbridge, *US Camera*, "About Color" column 34, December 18, 1956. ox 3, folder 4, Paul Outerbridge papers, 1915–79 (bulk 1915–58), Getty Research Institute, Research Library, Accession no. 870520.

19. "War in China Gambles Asia's Future," *Life*, October 17, 1938, 28.

20. Susan D. Moeller, *Shooting War: Photography and the American Experience of Combat* (New York: Basic, 1989), 390.

21. "Color It Color," *Broadcasting*, July 26, 1971, 7. See also Susan Murray, *Bright Signals: A History of Color Television* (Durham: Duke University Press, 2018).

22. Réné Burri. Magnum Photos Collection, 1950–90, AG104, Center for Creative Photography, University of Arizona, Tucson.

23. This is noted in a memo prepared by John Morris, *Magnum and Its Markets*, June 21, 1954 (New York, 12 pages). Magnum Photos Collection, 1950–90, AG104, 3, Center for Creative Photography, University of Arizona, Tucson.

24. *FYI*, November 3, 1947. Box 530, Time-Life Inc. Archive, NYHS.

25. Melissa Renn, "Life in Color: *Life* Magazine and the Color Reproduction of Works of Art," in *Bright Modernity: Color, Commerce, and Consumer Culture*, ed. Regina Lee Blaszczyk and Uwe Spiekermann (Cham: Palgrave Macmillan, 2017), 167–88.

26. Timby, "Look at Those Lollipops!" 236–43.

27. "Lecture at Rochester Institute of Technology in April 1986" as cited in Philip Prodger, "Another History of Color," in William Ewing, ed., *Ernst Haas: Color Correction* (Göttingen: Steidl, 2011).

28. Sally Stein, *Harry Callahan: Photographs in Color/The Years 1946–1978* (Tucson: Center for Creative Photography, University of Arizona, 1980), 19.

29. Henri Cartier-Bresson, *The Decisive Moment* (New York: Simon and Schuster, 1952), 48–52.

30. *Magnum Stockholder Report*, February 15, 1952, prepared by Robert Capa. Magnum Photos Collection, 1950–90, AG104, 3, Center for Creative Photography, University of Arizona, Tucson.

31. *Magnum Stockholder Report*.

32. Norton Wood, "Color in Sports Illustrated," 1958, 3. Box 11, Wilson Hicks Conference Tapes and Transcripts Collection, 1957–73, Special Collections of the University of Miami Libraries.

33. Pat Hagan to All Magnum Shareholders, "U.S. Editorial Progress and Plans," May 29, 1952. Archive of John G. Morris. I am grateful for Nadya Bair for sharing this source.

34. Bryan Campbell and Ernst Haas, *Ernst Haas* (London: Collins, 1983), 4; Ewing, *Ernst Haas*, n.p.

35. Lynda Nead, *The Tiger in the Smoke: Art and Culture in Postwar Britain* (London: Yale University Press, 2017), devotes a section of her book to untangling the complexity of color in local and historically specific and in more metaphoric terms.

36. *Life*, August 11, 1958.

37. *Life*, August 11, 1958, 2.

38. *Life*, August 11, 1958, 2.

39. *Life*, August 18, 1958, 45.

40. For general time and motion, see Marta Braun, *Picturing Time: The Work of Etienne-Jules Marey* (Chicago: University of Chicago Press, 1994); Mary Ann Doane, *The Emergence of Cinematic Time: Modernity, Contingency, the Archive* (Cambridge: Harvard University Press, 2002); Stephen Petersen, *Space-Age Aesthetics: Lucio Fontana, Yves Klein, and the Postwar European Avant-Garde* (University Park: Pennsylvania State University Press, 2009); Jeffrey Schnapp, ed., *Speed Limits* (Milan: Skira, 2009); Linda Henderson, *The Fourth Dimension and Non-Euclidean Geometry in Modern Art* (Cambridge: MIT Press, 2013).

41. László Moholy-Nagy, *Vision in Motion* (Chicago: P. Theobald, 1947), 10; Oliver Botar, *Sensing the Future: Moholy-Nagy, Media and the Arts* (Baden: L. Müller, 2014); Achim Borchardt-Hume, ed., *Albers and Moholy-Nagy: From the Bauhaus to the New World* (New Haven: Yale University Press, 2006).

42. László Moholy-Nagy et al., *László Moholy-Nagy: Color in Transparency. Photographic Experiments in Color, 1934–1946* (Göttingen: Steidl, 2006), 39.

43. Ernst Haas, "Haas on Color Photography," *Popular Photography, Color Annual*, 1957, 30.

44. "Letter to Magnum, 1960." Notebooks of Ernst Haas 54, Ernst Haas Archive, Getty Images, London.

45. Yaacov Agam, "Syllabus of the Carpenter Center Course," Harvard University, 1968. Centre Pompidou Library.

46. "Letter to John Morris During South Africa Trip 1958, Magnum Letters—Early." Notebooks of Ernst Haas, 48, Ernst Haas Archive, Getty Images, London.

47. Haas's essay was published in *Life* on August 8, 1949, 30–31, and May 28, 1951, 124.

48. "In and Out of Focus," January 6, 1972, CAC 79:005. Casey Allen Collection, Center for Creative Photography, University of Arizona, Tucson.

49. Letter from Ernst Haas to Wilson Hicks, November 30, 1949. Ernst Haas Archive, Getty Images, London.

50. Letter from Ernst Haas to Robert Capa, November 30, 1949. Ernst Haas Archive, Getty Images, London.

51. Haas' lack of mastery of English is revealed in the archival materials consulted here.

52. Ernst Haas, "Color vs. Black and White: The Reading of a Photograph," panel, 1968, 3–4. Box 11, Wilson Hicks, University of Miami Libraries.

53. Ernst Haas, "What I've Been Up to Lately," 1967, 9. Box 11, Wilson Hicks, University of Miami Libraries.

54. *New York Times*, September 14, 1953.

55. Quoted from the script for "Sight and Insight," *Ernst Haas: The Art of Seeing*, Part 1 (PBS in cooperation with the BBC, 1962), 5. Ernst Haas Archive, Getty Images, London.

56. "Poet of the Streets," *FYI*, September 18, 1953. Box 338, Folder 3, Time-Life Inc., NYHS.

57. Bryan Holme and Thomas Forman, eds., *Poet's Camera* (New York: American Studio, 1946), preface.

58. "Poet of the Streets," *FYI*, September 18, 1953. Box 338, Folder 3, Time-Life Inc., NYHS.

59. *FYI*, September 1953, "Images of a Magic City," Part II. Box 532, Time-Life Inc., NYHS.

60. Ernst Haas, cable to *Life* New York concerning Paris story, n.d. (probably 1955). Notebooks of Ernst Haas, 25, Ernst Haas Archive, Getty Images, London.

61. Undated letter from MHS (probably Margot Shore) to Magnum NY office, signed "Miss Busyfingers," circa 1955. Magnum box, Ernst Haas Archive, Getty Images, London.

62. Magnum Paris bureau chief to John Morris, memo, April 19, 1957. Archive of John G. Morris.

63. Magnum Newsletter (draft), December 7, 1955. Archive of John G. Morris.

64. Script, "Sight and Insight," Part 1, 2, 4. Ernst Haas Archive, Getty Images, London. The four episodes were titled "Sight and Insight," "The Decisive Moment," "Stretching the Moment," and "Beyond Reality."

65. It was precisely the exploitation of color television that led the BBC to sign Kenneth Clark to narrate and write what become a game-changing series, *Civilisation,* for the BBC in 1969. In two later episodes of "In and Out of Focus," a WNYC show, both broadcast in the 1970s in color, Haas is introduced as "the world's greatest color photographer," CAC 79:055. Casey Allen Collection, Center for Creative Photography, University of Arizona, Tucson.

66. Bair, *Decisive Network.*

67. Script, "The Decisive Moment," Part 2, *Ernst Haas: The Art of Seeing* (PBS in cooperation with the BBC, 1962), 7. Ernst Haas Archive, Getty Images, London. For more on the relation between the artist and the reporter, see Hill, *Artist as Reporter.*

68. Kate Flint, *Flash! Photography, Writing, and Surprising Illumination* (Oxford: Oxford University Press, 2017). See also Jason E. Hill, "Sight After Sight: *Life's* Time," unpublished paper.

69. Phyllis Lee Levin, "Fantasy Marks the Work of Fashion Photography," *New York Times,* April 5, 1957.

70. Arthur Knight, "Choreography for Camera," *Dance Magazine* 22, no. 6 (June 1970): 21.

71. Richard Avedon, "Time for Motion . . . the Fourth Dimension," *Commercial Camera* 2, no. 2 (1949): 9.

72. Campbell and Haas, *Ernst Haas,* 4.

73. Ruth A. Peltason, ed., *Ernst Haas Color Photography* (New York: Abrams, 1989), 13.

74. "Motion." Notebooks of Ernst Haas, Ernst Haas Archive, Getty Images, London.

75. "Story from Magnum: Ernst Haas at Barnum Circus," October 6, 1961. Job Books, Ernst Haas Archive, Getty Images, London.

76. *U.S. Camera* 28, no. 12 (December 1961): 50.

77. Kim Beil, "Vision Control: The Inversion of Motion Blur and the Thrills of Speed on the Page," unpublished manuscript, to appear in a forthcoming book with Stanford University Press. I would like to thank the author for sharing her work with me.

78. *Life,* July 29, 1957, 57.

79. *Life,* August 19, 1957, 12.

80. MoMA Press Release, "Ernst Haas—Color Photography," August 4, 1962. https://www.moma.org/documents/moma_press-release_326283.pdf.

81. As cited in Inge Bondi, critique of Haas to Fritz Semak, unpublished manuscript on Ernst Haas, 228. Thanks to Bondi for sharing her unpublished work with me.

82. Peltason, *Ernst Haas Color Photography,* 13–14.

83. MoMA Press Release, "Art in a Changing World," May 27, 1964. https://www.moma.org/calendar/exhibitions/3448?locale=en.

84. MoMA Press Release, "The Photo Essay" March 16, 1965. https://www.moma.org/documents/moma_press-release_326378.pdf.

85. Ernst Haas, "Ernst Haas on Color Photography," *Popular Photography, Color Annual* (1957): 30.

86. Ernst Haas, "What I've Been Up to Lately," 1967, 29, 9. Box 11, Wilson Hicks Conference Tapes and Transcripts Collection, 1957–1973, Special Collections of the University of Miami Libraries.

87. Alain Bergala and Magnum Photos Inc., *Magnum Cinema: Photographs from 50 Years of Movie-Making* (London: Phaidon, 1995).

88. For more on Haas movie set photographs, see Walter Moser, *Ernst Haas Cinéma,* ed. John P. Jacob (Göttingen: Steidl, 2014).

89. Marianne Le Gaillard, "Jacques Henri Lartigue dans l'air du temps (1966–1967). Entre la naissance et la consecration veritable de sa photographie," *Etudes photographiques* (Spring 2015): 64–84.

90. Telegram from John Huston to Ernst Haas, July 14, 1964. Ernst Haas Archive, Getty Images, London.

91. Henry Hart, "The Bible," *Films in Review* 17, no. 8 (October 1966): 518.

92. Notebooks of Ernst Haas, 15. Ernst Haas Archive, Getty Images, London.

CONCLUSION

1. Andy Warhol, *The Philosophy of Andy Warhol: (From A to B and Back Again)* (New York: Harcourt, 1975), 160.

2. Vanessa R. Schwartz, "LAX: Designing for the Jet Age," in *Overdrive: Architecture in Los Angeles,* ed. Wim DeWit and Christopher Alexander (Los Angeles: Getty Publications, 2013).

3. Brendan I. Koerner, *The Skies Belong to Us: Love and Terror in the Golden Age of Hijacking* (New York: Crown, 2013).

4. The body of Simmel's writing is relevant, but see especially "The Metropolis and Mental Life," in *The Sociology of Georg Simmel,* ed. Kurt H. Wolff (Glencoe, Ill.: Free Press, 1950), 409–24; Howard S. Becker, *Art Worlds* (Berkeley: University of California Press, 1982); Manuel Castells, *The Rise of the Network Society* (1996; 2nd ed., Cambridge: Blackwell, 2010).

5. Henry Jenkins, *Convergence Culture: Where Old and New Media Collide* (New York: New York University Press, 2006).

6. This refers to C. P. Snow, *The Two Cultures and the Scientific Revolution* (Oxford: Oxford University Press, 1959).

7. Susan Sontag, "One Culture and the New Sensibility," in *Against Interpretation and Other Essays* (New York: Farrar, Straus and Giroux, 1966), 296.

8. Sontag, "One Culture," 299.

9. An article by Justus Nieland, "Midcentury Futurism: Expanded Cinema, Design and the Modernist Sensorium," *Affirmations of the Modern* 2, no. 1 (December 2014): 46–84, draws very well on this essay.

10. Clement Greenberg, "How Art Writing Earns Its Bad Name" (1962), in *Clement Greenberg: The Collected Essays and Criticism, Volume 4: Modernism with a Vengeance, 1957—1969,* ed. John O'Brian (Chicago: University of Chicago Press, 1993), 137.

11. Anne Massey, *The Independent Group: Modernism and Mass Culture in Britain, 1945–59* (Manchester: Manchester Uni-

versity Press, 1995); Lucy Bradnock, Courtney J. Martin, and Rebecca Peabody, eds., *Lawrence Alloway: Critic and Curator* (Los Angeles: Getty Research Institute, 2015); Horowitz, *Consuming Pleasures*. See also Lawrence Alloway, "Network: The Art World Described as a System," in *Network: Art and the Complex Present* (Ann Arbor: UMI Research Press, 1984), 3–15.

12. Lawrence Alloway, "The Long Front of Culture," *Cambridge Opinion* 17 (1959): 25; reprinted in Lawrence Alloway et al., eds., *Modern Dreams: The Rise and Fall of Pop* (Cambridge: MIT Press, 1988), 32–33.

13. See Massey, *Independent Group;* Nigel Whiteley, *Reyner Banham: Historian of the Immediate Future* (Cambridge: MIT Press, 2002); and Sidney Lawrence, "Declaration of Function: Documents from the Museum of Modern Art's Design Crusade, 1933–1950," *Design Issues* 2, no. 1 (Spring 1985): 65–77.

14. Massey, *Independent Group*, 78.

15. Quoted in Ben Highmore, "Brutalist Wallpaper and the Independent Group," *Journal of Visual Culture* 12 (August 2013): 205–21. See also Highmore, *The Art of Brutalism: Rescuing Hope from Catastrophe in 1950s Britain* (New Haven: Yale University Press, 2017).

16. Lawrence Alloway, "The Arts and Mass Media," *Architectural Design and Construction* (February 1958).

17. Ben Cranfield, "'Not Another Museum': The Search for Contemporary Connection," *Journal of Visual Culture* 12 (August 2013): 327.

18. Bradnock et al., *Lawrence Alloway*.

19. For more on time and the image, see Daniela Bleichmar and Vanessa R. Schwartz, "Visual History: The Past in Pictures" *Representations* 145 (March 2019): 1–31.

Selected Bibliography

ARCHIVES AND SPECIAL COLLECTIONS

Archives of the Aéroports de Paris, Orly (ADP)
Air France Archives
San Francisco Airport Museum
Flight Path Learning Center, LAX
Air and Space Museum, Smithsonian
Pan Am Collection, University of Miami Library
Wilson Hicks Conference Tapes and Transcripts Collection, University of Miami Library, Special Collections (Wilson Hicks, University of Miami)
Yaacov Agam Files, Kandinsky Library, Centre Pompidou, Paris.
Magnum Photo Collection, Center for Creative Photography
Reyner Banham Papers, Getty Research Institute Library
Lawrence Alloway Papers, Getty Research Institute Library
Beaumont Newhall Papers, Getty Research Institute Library
Anaheim Heritage Center, Anaheim Public Library
The Walt Disney Studios Archive
Walt Disney Imagineering Archive
Walt Disney Photo Archive
Ernst Haas Archive, Getty Images, London
R. R. Donnelley and Sons Company Archive, University of Chicago Library, Special Collections
Time-Life Archive, New-York Historical Society (NYHS)
Eero Saarinen Papers, Yale University
Eames Collection, Library of Congress
William Pereira Archives, Special Collections, USC Library
Papers of the 1964–65 New York World's Fair, New York Public Library (NYPL)
Center for Creative Photography, University of Arizona, Tucson (CCP)

GENERAL READINGS

Aerial History and Culture

Asendorf, Christoph. *Super Constellation. L'influence de l'aéronautique sur les arts et la culture.* Foreword by Angela Lampe. Trans. (from German) Didier Renault and Augustine Terence. Paris: Macula, 2013.

Bilstein, Roger E. *Flight in America, 1900–1983: From the Wrights to the Astronauts.* Baltimore: Johns Hopkins University Press, 1984.

Corn, Joseph J. *The Winged Gospel: America's Romance with Aviation.* Baltimore: Johns Hopkins University Press, 2002.

Crouch, Tom D. *Wings: A History of Aviation from Kites to the Space Age.* Washington: Smithsonian National Air and Space Museum, 2003.

Davies, R. E. G. *Airlines of the Jet Age: A History.* Washington: Smithsonian National Air and Space Museum, 2011.

Dorrian, Mark, and Frédéric Pousin. *Seeing from Above: The Aerial View in Visual Culture.* London: I. B. Tauris, 2013.

Morshed, Adnan. *Impossible Heights: Skyscrapers, Flight, and the Master Builder.* Minneapolis: University of Minnesota Press, 2015.

Rust, Daniel. *Flying Across America: The Airline Passenger Experience.* Norman: University of Oklahoma Press, 2009.

Roseau, Nathalie, and Marie Thébaud-Sorger, eds. *L'Emprise du vol: De l'invention à la massification. Histoire d'une culture moderne.* Geneva: Métis, 2013.

Van Vleck, Jenifer. *Empire of the Air: Aviation and the American Ascendancy.* Cambridge: Harvard University Press, 2013.

Weems, Jason. *Barnstorming the Prairies: How Aerial Vision Shaped the Midwest.* Minneapolis: University of Minnesota Press, 2015.

Networks, Mobility, and the Image

Alloway, Lawrence. "Network: The Art Described as a System." In *Network: Art and the Complex Present,* 3–15. Ann Arbor: UMI Research Press, 1984.

Alloway, Lawrence, et al., eds. *Modern Dreams: The Rise and Fall of Pop.* Cambridge: MIT Press, 1988.

Baranowski, Shelly, and Ellen Furlough, eds. *Being Elsewhere: Tourism, Consumer Culture and Identity in Modern Europe and North America.* Ann Arbor: University of Michigan Press, 2001.

Bruno, Giuliana. *Atlas of Emotion: Journeys in Art, Architecture and Film.* London: Verso 2002.

Castells, Manuel. *The Rise of the Network Society.* Cambridge: Blackwell, 2010.

Cresswell, Tim. *On the Move: Mobility in the Modern Western World.* London: Routledge, 2006.

Desportes, Marc. *Paysages en Mouvement: Transports et Perception de l'Espace, XVIIIe–XXe siècle.* Paris: Gallimard, 2005.

Giedion, Sigfried. *Mechanization Takes Command: A Contribution to Anonymous History* (1948). Minneapolis: University of Minnesota Press, 2013.

Hariman, Robert, and John L. Lucaites. *The Public Image: Photography and Civic Spectatorship.* Chicago: University of Chicago Press, 2016.

Hill, Jason E., and Vanessa R. Schwartz, eds. *Getting the Picture: The Visual Culture of the News.* London: Bloomsbury, 2015.

Hine, Thomas. *Populuxe: From Tailfins and TV Dinners to Barbie Dolls and Fallout Shelters.* New York: Knopf, 1986.

Horowitz, Daniel. *Consuming Pleasures: Intellectuals and Popular Culture in the Postwar World.* Philadelphia: University of Philadelphia Press, 2012.

Hunt, Lynn. *Writing History in the Global Era.* New York: Norton, 2014.

Lee, Pamela M. *Chronophobia: On Time in the Art of the 1960s.* Cambridge: MIT Press, 2004.

Massey, Anne. *The Independent Group: Modernism and Mass Culture in Britain, 1945–59.* Manchester: Manchester University Press, 1995.

McLuhan, Marshall. *Understanding Media: The Extensions of Man.* Cambridge: MIT Press, 1994.

Peters, John Durham. *The Marvelous Clouds: Toward a Philosophy of Elemental Media.* Chicago: University of Chicago Press, 2015.

Petersen, Stephen. *Space-Age Aesthetics: Lucio Fontana, Yves Klein, and the Postwar European Avant-Garde.* University

Park: Pennsylvania State University Press, 2009.
Roberts, Jennifer L. *Transporting Visions: The Movement of Images in Early America*. Berkeley: University of California Press, 2014.
Schivelbusch, Wolfgang. *The Railway Journey: The Industrialization of Time and Space in the 19th Century*. Berkeley: University of California Press, 1986.
Schwartz, Vanessa R. *Spectacular Realities: Early Mass Culture in Fin-de-Siècle Paris*. Berkeley: University of California Press, 1998.
Turner, Fred. *From Counterculture to Cyberculture: Stewart Brand, the Whole Earth Network and the Rise of Digital Utopianism*. Chicago: University of Chicago Press, 2006.
Urry, John. *Mobilities*. Cambridge: Polity Press, 2007.
Whiteley, Nigel. *Reyner Banham: Historian of the Immediate Future*. Cambridge: MIT Press, 2002.
Zelizer, Barbie. *About to Die: How News Images Move the Public*. New York: Oxford University Press, 2010.

CHAPTER 1

Bezombes, Roger. "Air France: A New Series of Airline Posters." *Graphis* 37, no. 218 (March 1982).
Bloom, Nicholas Dagen. *The Metropolitan Airport: JFK International and Modern New York*. Philadelphia: University of Philadelphia Press, 2015.
Dierikx, Mark. *Clipping the Clouds: How Air Travel Changed the World*. Westport: Praeger, 2008.
Friedman, Alice T. *American Glamour and the Evolution of Modern Architecture*. New Haven: Yale University Press, 2010.
Gordon, Alistair. *Naked Airport*. Chicago: University of Chicago Press, 2004.
Gerster, Georg. *Swissair Posters*. Munich: Schirmer/Mosel, 2006.
Harwood, John. *The Interface: IBM and the Transformation of Corporate Design, 1945–1976*. Minneapolis: University of Minnesota Press, 2011.
Hühne, M. C. *Airline Visual Identity, 1945–1975*. Berlin: Callisto, 2015.
Hühne, M. C. *Pan Am: History, Design and Identity*. Berlin: Callisto, 2017.
Kasarda, John D., and Greg Lindsay. *Aerotropolis: The Way We'll Live Next*. New York: Farrar, Straus and Giroux, 2011.
Lovegrove, Keith. *Airline: Identity, Design and Culture*. London: Laurence King, 2000.
Pelkonen, Eeva-Liisa, and Donald Albrecht. *Eero Saarinen: Shaping the Future*. New Haven: Yale University Press, 2006.
Ringli, Kornel. *Designing TWA: Eero Saarinen's Airport Terminal in New York*. Zurich: Park, 2015.
Roseau, Nathalie. *Aerocity: Quand l'avion fait la ville*. Marseille: Parenthèses, 2012.
Schwartz, Vanessa R. "LAX: Designing for the Jet Age." In *Overdrive: L.A. Constructs the Future, 1940–1990*, ed. Wim DeWit and Christopher Alexander, 163–83. Los Angeles: Getty Publications, 2013.

CHAPTER 2

Ballard, Donald W. *The Disneyland Hotel: The Early Years, 1954–1988*. Riverside: Ape Pen, 2005.
Canemaker, John. *Magic Color Flair: The World of Mary Blair*. San Francisco: The Walt Disney Family Foundation Press, 2014.
Comras, Kelly. *Ruth Shellhorn*. Athens: University of Georgia Press, 2016.
Findlay, John M. *Magic Lands: Western Cityscapes and American Culture After 1940*. Berkeley: University of California Press, 1992.
Gabler, Neal. *Walt Disney: The Triumph of the American Imagination*. New York: Knopf, 2006.
Gennawey, Sam. *Walt Disney and the Promise of Progress City*. Orlando: Theme Park Press, 2014.
Hahn, Don. *Yesterday's Tomorrow: Disney's Magical Mid-Century*. Los Angeles: Disney Editions, 2017.
Hench, John, and Peggy Van Pelt. *Designing Disney: Imagineering and the Art of the Show*. New York: Disney Editions, 2003.
Kothenschulte, Daniel, ed. *The Walt Disney Film Archives: The Animated Movies, 1921–1968*. New York: Taschen, 2016.
Jackson, Kathy Merlock, and Mark I. West, eds. *Disneyland and Culture: Essays on the Parks and Their Influence*. Jefferson: McFarland, 2011.
Lukas, Scott A. *Theme Park*. London: Reaktion, 2008.
Marling, Karal Ann, ed. *Designing Disney's Theme Parks: The Architecture of Reassurance*. Paris: CCA/Flammarion, 1997.
Nichols, Chris, and Charlene Nichols. *Walt Disney's Disneyland*. Cologne: Taschen, 2018.
Nieland, Justus. "Making Happy, Happy-Making: The Eamses and Communication by Design." In *Modernism and Affect*, ed. Julie Taylor, 203–25. Edinburgh: Edinburgh University Press, 2015.
Pierce, Todd James. *Three Years in Wonderland: The Disney Brothers, C. V. Wood, and the Making of the Great American Theme Park*. Jackson: University of Mississippi Press, 2016.
Price, Harrison. *Walt's Revolution! By the Numbers*. Orlando: Ripley, 2004.
Schickel, Richard. *The Disney Version: The Life, Times, Art and Commerce of Walt Disney*. New York: Simon and Schuster, 1968.
Smoodin, Eric, ed. *Disney Discourse: Producing the Magic Kingdom*. New York: Routledge, 1994.
Sorkin, Michael, ed. *Variations on a Theme Park: The New American City and the End of Public Space*. New York: Hill and Wang, 1992.
Wasko, Janet. *Understanding Disney: The Manufacture of Fantasy*. London: Polity, 2001.

CHAPTER 3

Bair, Nadya. *The Decisive Network: Magnum Photos and the Postwar Image Market*. Berkeley: University of California Press, 2020.
Bear, Jordan. "Magnum Orbis: Photographs from the End(s) of the Earth." *Journal of Visual Studies* 25, no. 2 (September 2010): 113.
Bender, Marylin. *The Beautiful People*. New York: Coward-McCann, 1967.
Boorstin, Daniel J. *The Image: A Guide to Pseudo-Events in America*. New York: Harper and Row, 1961.
Clark, Catherine. *Paris and the Cliché of History: The City and Photographs, 1860–1970*. New York: Oxford University Press, 2018.
Conekin, Becky E. *Lee Miller in Fashion*. New York: Monacelli, 2013.
Evans, Caroline. *The Mechanical Smile: Modernism and the First Fashion Shows in France and America, 1900–1929*. New Haven: Yale University Press, 2013.
Flint, Kate. *Flash! Photography, Writing, and Surprising Illumination*. Oxford: Oxford University Press, 2017.
Fox-Amato, Matthew. *Exposing Slavery: Photography, Human Bondage and the Birth of Modern Visual Politics in America*. New York: Oxford University Press, 2019.

Fraser-Cavassoni, Natasha. *Vogue on Yves Saint Laurent.* New York: Abrams Image, 2015.

Gervais, Thierry, and Gaëlle Morel. *The Making of Visual News: A History of Photography in the Press.* London: Bloomsbury, 2017.

Gundle, Stephen. *Glamour: A History.* New York: Oxford University Press, 2008.

Hicks, Wilson. *Words and Pictures: An Introduction to Photojournalism.* New York: Harper Brothers, 1952.

Hill, Jason E. *Artist as Reporter: Weegee, Ad Reinhardt, and the PM News Picture.* Oakland: University of California Press, 2018.

Kennedy, Liam. *Afterimages: Photography and U.S. Foreign Policy.* Chicago: University of Chicago Press, 2016.

Linkof, Ryan. *Public Images: Celebrity, Photojournalism and the Making of the Tabloid Press.* London: Bloomsbury Academic, 2018.

Ponce de Leon, Charles L. *Self-Exposure: Human-Interest Journalism and the Emergence of Celebrity in America, 1890–1940.* Chapel Hill: University of North Carolina Press, 2002.

Popp, Richard K. *The Holiday Makers: Magazines, Advertising, and Mass Tourism in Postwar America.* Baton Rouge: Louisiana State University Press, 2012.

Stadiem, William. *Jet Set: The People, the Planes, the Glamour, and the Romance in Aviation's Glory Years.* New York: Ballantine, 2014.

Stimson, Blake. *The Pivot of the World: Photography and Its Nation.* Cambridge: MIT Press, 2006.

Zylinkska, Joanna. *Nonhuman Photography.* Cambridge: MIT Press, 2017.

CHAPTER 4

Blaszcyk, Regina Lee. *The Color Revolution.* Cambridge: MIT Press, 2012.

Blaszcyk, Regina Lee, and Uwe Spiekermann, eds. *Bright Modernity: Color, Commerce, and Consumer Culture.* Cham: Palgrave Macmillan, 2017.

Botar, Oliver. *Sensing the Future: Moholy-Nagy, Media and the Arts.* Baden: L. Müller, 2014.

Campbell, Bryan, and Ernst Haas. *Ernst Haas.* London: Collins, 1983.

Ewing, William, ed. *Ernst Haas: Color Correction.* Göttingen: Steidl, 2011.

Hariman, Robert, and John L. Lucaites. *No Caption Needed: Iconic Photographs, Public Culture, and Liberal Democracy.* Chicago: University of Chicago Press, 2011.

Henderson, Linda. *The Fourth Dimension and Non-Euclidean Geometry in Modern Art.* Cambridge: MIT Press, 2013.

Hostetler, Lisa, and Katherine A. Bussard. *Color Rush: American Color Photography from Stieglitz to Sherman.* New York: Aperture, 2013.

Johnston, Patricia A. *Real Fantasies: Edward Steichen's Advertising Photography.* Berkeley: University of California Press, 2000.

Kalba, Laura. *Color in the Age of Impressionism: Commerce, Technology and Art.* University Park: Pennsylvania State University Press, 2017.

Le Gaillard, Marianne. "Jacques Henri Lartigue dans l'air du temps (1966–1967): Entre la naissance et la consecration veritable de sa photographie." *Études Photographiques* (Spring 2015): 64–84.

Moholy-Nagy, László et al. *László Moholy-Nagy: Color in Transparency. Photographic Experiments in Color, 1934–1946.* Göttingen: Steidl, 2006.

Moholy-Nagy, László. *Vision in Motion.* Chicago: P. Theobald, 1947.

Moore, Kevin, et al., eds. *Starburst: Color Photography in America, 1970–1980.* Ostfildern: Hatje Cantz, 2010.

Moser, Walter. *Ernst Haas Cinéma.* Ed. John P. Jacob. Göttingen: Steidl, 2014.

Nead, Lynda. *The Tiger in the Smoke: Art and Culture in Postwar Britain.* New Haven: Yale University Press, 2017.

Peltason, Ruth A., ed. *Ernst Haas Color Photography.* New York: Abrams, 1989.

Ritchin, Fred. *Bending the Frame: Photojournalism, Documentary, and Citizen.* New York: Aperture, 2013.

Stein, Sally. "The Rhetoric of the Colorful and the Colorless: The American Photography and Material Culture Between the Wars." Ph.D. diss., Yale University, 1991.

Stein, Sally. *Harry Callahan: Photographs in Color/The Years 1946–1978.* Tucson: Center for Creative Photography, University of Arizona, 1980.

Young, Cynthia. *Capa in Color.* New York: International Center of Photography, 2014.

Index

Page numbers with *italics* indicate illustrations.

Illustration Credits

The photographers and the sources of visual material other than the owners indicated in the captions are as follows. Every effort has been made to supply complete and correct credits; if there are errors or omissions, please contact Yale University Press so that corrections can be made in any subsequent edition.

Author's collection: 0.1, 0.2, 0.7, 1.11–1.18, 1.32, 3.1, 3.2, 3.4–3.8, 3.22–3.24, 4.2, 4.23, 4.24, 4.31–4.39
Boeing Collection: 0.5
Los Angeles Public Library, Herald Examiner Collection: fig. 0.3
University of Miami, Special Collections: 0.4
Time, Inc./NYHS: 0.8
Lockheed Aircraft Service: 1.3
Aéroports de Paris: 1.4, 1.28–1.31, 1.33–1.35
Photograph by Balthazar Korab. Library of Congress, Prints & Photographs Division, Balthazar Korab Archive at the Library of Congress: 1.5, 1.8
Photograph by Robert C. Lautman: 1.9
LAX Flight Path Learning Center: 1.21–1.26
Courtesy of Don Ballard: 1.27, 2.10
Dick Whittington Studio photographs, Special Collections, USC Libraries, University of Southern California: 2.8
Photograph by Bill Briner. © 1960. All rights reserved. Used by permission: 2.26
From the Collections of The Henry Ford Museum: 2.27, 2.29–2.32
Courtesy of Bill Cotter of worldsfairphotos.com: 2.28
©Arnold Newman Properties/Getty Images: 3.3
© Patrick Lichfield/Condé Nast via Getty Images: 3.9
© Pierre Bergé: 3.11
© Roland Briens/Téléphotos/Air France: 3.12
© Air France Collection/Air France Museum: 3.13, 3.14
© Patrice Habans/Paris Match via Getty Images: 3.15, 3.29
Currier & Ives, Library of Congress, Prints & Photographs Division: 3.16
Roger Fenton, Library of Congress, Prints & Photographs Division, Fenton Crimean War Photographs: 3.17
Robert Capa © International Center of Photography/Magnum Photos: 3.18
International Center of Photography, Bequest of Wilma Wilcox, 3.19
© Archivio Franco Pinna, Rome: 3.20
Time, Inc. Getty Research Institute, Los Angeles: 3.21, 3.25, 3.27, 4.1, 4.3, 4.5–4.22, 4.25–4.27, 4.40
© Lee Miller Archives, England 2019. All rights reserved. Leemiller.co.uk: 3.26
David Bailey/Vogue © The Condé Nast Publications Ltd.: 3.28
Ernst Haas/Getty Images/ © Ernst Haas Estate: 4.28, 4.29
© 2019 The Andy Warhol Foundation for the Visual Arts, Inc./Licensed by Artists Rights Society (ARS), New York: 5.1
Ernst Haas Archive, Getty Images: 5.2